HISTORY OF THE INTERNATIONAL

HISTORY OF THE INTERNATIONAL

Volume 1: 1864 – 1914

Julius Braunthal

Translated by Henry Collins and Kenneth Mitchell

FREDERICK A. PRAEGER, *Publishers*
New York · Washington

BOOKS THAT MATTER

Published in the United States of America in 1967
by Frederick A. Praeger, Inc., Publishers
111 Fourth Avenue, New York, N.Y. 10003

First published in Germany in 1961 by Verlag J. H. W. Dietz Nachf, GmbH under the title *Geschichte der Internationale*, Volume 1

Library of Congress Catalog Card Number *67–17667*

Printed in Great Britain

Dedicated to the memory of my friend
FRIEDRICH ADLER

Contents

Plates

Preface

This study is an attempt at a comprehensive history of the International. No historian will fail to acknowledge the idea of Socialism and its movement as one of the great intellectual, moral and social forces of society. But, surprisingly enough, while books on the history of Socialist ideas and Socialist movements constitute a rich and ever-expanding library, up to now there has appeared no universal history of the International as the organized expression and moral leadership of the world Socialist movement. There are valuable studies of particular periods. There is, above all, G. D. H. Cole's monumental five-volume *History of Socialist Thought*, containing a history of the First and Second Internationals, presented against a general background of the development of Socialist ideas and movements. However, even in this comprehensive history of Socialism the International can be traced as only one among a larger number of its aspects.

This is the first of three volumes devoted to the narration of the story of the International from its very inception up to the centenary of the founding of the First International. Two of these volumes have already been written and published in Germany and the English versions of the two books present a revised edition of their German original; the third volume, destined to conclude the story, is in preparation.

In an attempt to ascertain the origin of the International I went further back in tracing its root than the prevailing view of some historians would allow. Communist historians, in particular, insist that the historic International, known as the First, had only a single forerunner —the Communist League with which Karl Marx was associated. But in fact there were, as the investigations clearly show, a number of working-class associations, aiming at an international brotherhood of the dispossessed, which came into being before the Communist League emerged in the late 1840s and after its demise in the beginnings of the 1850s. They were imbued, like the Communist League, with Socialist ideas which emanated ultimately from the humanitarian ideals of the French Revolution of 1789. The Communist League indeed, before Marx joined it in 1847, scarcely differed in its ideology and social composition from its predecessors and successors among the forerunners of the International. It assumed its historical significance as the first distinctly proletarian forerunner of the historic International only by the programme drafted by Marx in his *Communist Manifesto*. But although the other forerunners lacked such a concrete Socialist programme, they were guided by precisely the same aim as the Communist League—the establishment of a fraternity of the workers in all countries in their struggle for a Socialist society.

Thus Part One of the present volume, starting with an examination of the significance of the ideas of the French Revolution of 1789, is devoted to the forerunners of the International, their characteristics, beliefs and traditions which became embodied in the historic International. Part Two covers the history of the First International up to the Hague Congress of 1872, and Part Three the history of the Second International up to its collapse at the outbreak of the First World War.

The second volume, starting with an investigation of the deeper reasons of the crisis of the International, narrates the history both of the Socialist and Communist Internationals up to their dissolution during the Second World War. During this period the history of the Labour movement was dominated by the conflict between Bolshevism and Social Democracy. It was over this fundamental difference of ideology that the International split. Each of the two Internationals, formed in the process of this bifurcation, has of course its own history. But the history of the one as well as of the other becomes comprehensible only out of the history of the cleavage of the original International and their struggle as rivals for the leadership of the European working class. In that volume the attempt has been made to present the history of both Internationals in the entanglement of their struggles against and in the reciprocal effects of their actions upon each other.

It is intended that the third volume of this work should cover the period from the end of the Second World War to the completion of the International's first century in 1964.

In the appendices of the present volume I have reproduced two documents of considerable importance. The first is the 'General Rules of the International Working Men's Association', as finalized at the London Conference in 1871, reflecting the spirit of the organization and providing a rough outline of its conception and aims. The second—the Resolution of the Stuttgart Congress in 1907 on the attitude of the Socialist parties towards war—is essential for the understanding of the internal conflicts on which the Second International foundered. I have further added to these documents a Table of the Congresses and Conferences of the International 1864–1914, and of the officers and members of the Provisional General Council of the First International.

An indispensable source for the history of the First International are the Minutes of the General Council, which may be found in the International Institute of Social History in Amsterdam. A perusal of these volumes has served to dissipate a good many myths which had accumulated about the history of the International.

My thanks are due to the many colleagues and friends who have read over my manuscript, corrected errors and enriched it greatly by suggestions. I should mention, in particular, Leo Valiani of Milan, author of *L'Epoca della Prima Internazionale* and *Della Prima alla Seconda Internazionale*, and my late friend, Werner Blumenberg, Head of the German Department of the Amsterdam Institute, both of whom read the entire manuscript. In addition, several chapters on the First International were read by Friedrich Adler. The chapter on evolutionary and revolutionary Socialism was read by Dr Carl Landauer, a professor at California University and author of the two-volume *European Socialism*, and by Dr R. P. Morgan, a lecturer at the University of Sussex and author of *The German Social Democrats and the First International, 1864–72*, as well as by the biographer of Karl and Jenny Marx, the late Boris Nikolaevsky, in New York. I also owe a debt of gratitude to the late Professor A. J. C. Rüter, Director of the Amsterdam Institute, and to Miss Marie Hunink, the Librarian, for their generosity and help in enabling me to make use of the rich resources of that library, as well as to my wife Tini, who read the entire manuscript and the proofs of the book with painstaking devotion.

This work is dedicated, in deepest gratitude, to the memory of Friedrich Adler, one of the great figures of the International and also my teacher and friend.

J. B.

PART ONE

The Forerunners

1 · The Birth of the Idea

The Socialist International was born on 28 September 1864. But the International Working Men's Association, the name by which it was first known, had predecessors whose ideas and traditions it embodied and carried farther. For a clear grasp of the spirit and history of the Socialist International we must take the story back to the first of those predecessors. We can find the origins of the First International in the great movement for freedom and democracy, comprising many peoples, inspired by the French Revolution in 1789. This movement was decidedly international in its character and was imbued with a feeling of international solidarity among the oppressed. It also brought about the first independent political movement of the working class in England and Scotland, while in France it gave rise to the first organization of militant Socialists.

The ideas which kindled the Revolution in France and, through its rays, lit up a movement for freedom in many lands, had developed much earlier in England where the middle classes had secured a measure of civic rights and political freedom. There, feudalism had disintegrated many centuries earlier. The rights of the people and their equality before the law were guaranteed by long-standing custom and by a constitutional enactment—the *Habeas Corpus* Act of 1679. Absolutism could not therefore develop as strongly as in France, Spain, the Habsburg Empire and the German Principalities. Finally, and most undramatically, the Glorious Revolution of 1688 had abolished absolutism in all its forms and divided power between king and Parliament.

At the time of the French Revolution, however, the power of the king was still very apparent, while Parliament was dominated by the aristocracy. England was an oligarchy, and democracy still an unrealized ideal, while the contrasts between wealth and poverty were sharper than ever. The French Revolution stimulated the aristocracy to challenge the predominance of the king, the middle classes to claim a share of parliamentary power and the workers to resist the terrible forms of wage-slavery arising out of the Industrial Revolution.

For the peoples of the Continent, however, the ideas of the French Revolution had a different and deeper significance. They were still subjected to a system of domination which rested on a complete denial of the principles of freedom and equality. In these countries the principle that all authority stems from Divine Right was still undisputed. According to this theory, the king had been called to his throne by the grace of God, and all power therefore resided in the Crown; the nobility and the bishops, through ancient custom, were entitled to share the wealth of the nation with the king; the common people in town and country were his subjects. And as all rights came from the king, every right enjoyed by the people of town and country was a gift of royal grace. The idea that men had rights by virtue of their humanity was utterly alien to the way of thought of a feudal society.[1]

The Declaration of the Rights of Man by the French Constituent Assembly therefore challenged in all these countries the moral, ideological and legal bases on which depended the social status, political power and economic position of king, aristocracy and church. It overthrew the principle of Divine Right, replacing it with the idea of a 'natural right' inherent in human nature and revealed by eternal reason. It proclaimed the 'sacred rights of men'. It declared, 'Men are born, and always continue, free and equal. . . .' It challenged the claim that kings derived their sovereignty from the grace of God and declared the people

1. The idea of Divine Right was most explicitly defined by James I in a speech to the English Parliament in 1609. 'Kings are justly called gods,' he told the assembled Parliament, 'for they exercise a manner of resemblance of divine power upon earth. For if you will consider the attributes of God, you shall see how they agree in the person of a king. God hath power to create or destroy, make or unmake at His pleasure, to give life or send death, to judge all and to be accountable to none. And the like power have kings. They make and unmake their subjects; they have power of raising up and casting down; of life and death; judges over all their subjects and in all cases, yet accountable to none but God'—G. P. Gooch, *Political Thought in England from Bacon to Halifax* (London, 1914), pp. 14–15. Frederick William IV of Prussia had the same idea a good half-century after the French National Assembly had proclaimed the sovereignty of the people in 1789. In a letter to Von Schön, President of East Prussia, he said in 1841: 'I feel myself entirely a creature of God's grace. . . . Believe me on my word as a king: while I reign, no prince or farmhand, parliament or Jewish school will take over anything which belongs—rightly or wrongly—to the Crown, without my assent. . . . A German prince should rule his regiment of subjects like a father, and since it is my birthright to reign over my father's domain . . . I fully intend to guide my immature children, chastise the backsliders but let the good and worthy take part in administering my estate'—H. von Treitschke, *Deutsche Geschichte im 19. Jahrhundert* (Leipzig, 1879–94), vol. IV, p. 57.

collectively to be sovereign—the source of all power in state and society.[1] It proclaimed the commonwealth, founded on the people's will, to be the natural constitution for society in France as well as in the rest of the world.

These ideas were not new. They were developed by philosophers and glorified by poets during the period of the Enlightenment. But now for the first time in the history of Europe they were proclaimed in the basic constitutional document of a state—a state, moreover, in the foremost position which France occupied among the great powers at the time. To thinkers and poets it seemed that a wonderful dream was about to come true, that the reign of reason was just beginning and that the Revolution had opened the doors of a new era, an era in which states and societies would be moulded in the spirit of the Enlightenment, an era in which men would live in brotherhood and perpetual peace. All who wanted an end to repression—political, social and intellectual—identified themselves fully with the Revolution. Kant, Fichte, Hegel, Schiller, Herder, Wieland and Hölderlin in Germany, Blake, Burns, Coleridge, Southey and Wordsworth in England, greeted the Revolution with exuberance as a triumph of reason, justice and social equality, as a creative force raising a world of freedom and equality out of the chaos of tyranny and superstition.

> My brethren, these are truths, and mighty ones:
> Ye are all equal; nature made ye so.
> Equality is your birthright,

cried Southey,[2] and Klopstock wished he had a hundred voices to proclaim the birth of liberty. Many years later, Hegel described how deeply the Revolution had moved him as a young man. 'It was a brilliant sunrise. Every thinking being celebrated the event. It was a time for noble endeavour. The world was full of spiritual joy, as if the spirit of God had now become a reality in the world.' And even Goethe, although he viewed with tranquil scepticism the processes of the Revolution, avowed, deeply moved:

> Who will dare to deny that his heart was exalted within him,
> And that his spirit, enfranchised, throbbed with a purer devotion
> When he beheld the first and the radiant glory of morning,
> Heard of the rights of man to be shared in common with all men.
> Learned of fair liberty, learned of equality, greatest of values.[3]

But the message of Liberty and Equality, the freshly awakened hope

1. 'Sovereignty resides in the people. It is indivisible, illimitable and unchangeable'—Article 25 of the Constitution of 1793.
2. Robert Southey, *Wat Tyler*, Act III.
3. Goethe, *Hermann und Dorothea* (Klio, Das Zeitalter).

among the oppressed that a new era was approaching, naturally appeared to the ruling class as the grossest possible provocation. Driven by its own inner logic, the Revolution had gradually embodied its original principles in the enactments of the French constitution. It had abolished all privileges of birth and status, destroyed the nobility and the secular power of the church, deprived the king of his power, and finally overthrown the monarchy. This upheaval took place in the country with the oldest dynasty, a great power at that time foremost among the European states. The example France gave in raising the banner of popular sovereignty threatened every European dynasty, the entire European aristocracy and the power of the Church.

The Revolution was the common enemy of princes, nobility and clergy, and they decided to stamp it out by force. Pope Pius IV had, in the spring of 1791, formally condemned the principles of the Revolution, opposing the doctrines of the Church of Rome to the Declaration of the Rights of Man and Citizen. The *émigrés* publicly, and Louis XVI secretly, implored the crowned heads of Europe to defend their own cause. Armed intervention was considered in the Cabinets of Vienna, St Petersburg and Berlin, and after Louis XVI, having failed to escape, had been removed from the throne, they were implemented. In the summer of 1792, the coalition armies of Austria, Prussia and the German princes, to which corps of fleeing French aristocrats and officers had attached themselves, approached the borders of France. With a manifesto in the name of the Emperor of Germany and the King of Prussia, the Duke of Brunswick, commander of the allied armies, demanded the immediate restoration of the old régime. If Paris refused and resisted, he threatened her with 'a vengeance which would never be forgotten'; she would be razed to the ground.

Through the war of the allied princes of Europe against revolutionary France, the Revolution became the concern of all those, in many countries, who felt themselves victims of absolute governments. In its victory they saw the triumph of freedom in their own lands, in its defeat the dreaded end of their hopes. Thus in a good many countries the French Revolution split the nation sharply in two.

The international action of kings and princes, the war of the European coalition against France—blessed by the church and supported by the conservative wing of the middle class—brought into being a democratic International. A section of the middle class, a few aristocrats, but a large number of workers and artisans in a variety of organizations corresponded with fraternal organizations across national boundaries and with the revolutionary clubs in France. They saw Paris, the heart of the Revolution, as the centre of an international society fighting for freedom.

> During those strenuous days, were not the eyes of all nations
> Turned to the spot that so long had been the world's capital city,
> Now, more than ever before, deserving that glorious title?
> Did not mankind wax strong in courage, in spirit, in utterance?
> Were not the names of those men who first spread abroad the good tidings
> Equal in fame to the loftiest heroes among the mortals?

Thus Goethe, and his lines reflected the prevailing atmosphere of the time. And even in 1799, when in France itself reaction had already set in and the revolutionary wars of liberation had degenerated into imperialist wars of conquest, Fichte still saw France as 'the fatherland of the upright man', since, he declared, 'the most precious aspirations of mankind' were bound up with her fate.

In France itself, Girondists as well as Jacobins were genuinely convinced that they were the pioneers of freedom not only for the people of France but for the whole of mankind. When the Constituent Assembly debated the draft Declaration of the Rights of Man, speaker after speaker referred to the universal character of the rights and claimed that they were valid for the peoples of all countries.[1]

They felt themselves linked, in common struggle, with the oppressed of all nations. They spoke of the brotherhood of peoples and demonstrated, symbolically, the idea of international solidarity. Thus Lafayette handed the key of the Bastille—symbol of the vanquished despotism—to Thomas Paine, hero of the American War of Independence, and the French National Assembly ordered mourning on the death of Benjamin Franklin. In this spirit the National Assembly conferred French citizenship on men of eminence in many a country—Washington, Wilberforce, Schiller, Klopstock, Pestalozzi and Paine among others—'because they paved the way for the liberation of mankind'. It was explained, in the decree granting citizenship, that although the French National Assembly could not hope to see as yet 'men establish by law what exists in nature, a single family, a single society, nevertheless the friends of freedom must be dear to a nation which has renounced all conquests and proclaimed its desire for the brotherhood of nations'. This was especially true at a time 'when a National Convention decides the fate of France and perhaps prepares the future for mankind'.[2]

The princes had joined forces in a war against revolutionary France; the French National Convention called on the peoples to join the revolution against princes. In the Convention, Robespierre moved that the constitutional law then under debate should declare France's complete solidarity with the revolutionaries of all lands. It should state,

1. Eric Thompson, *Popular Sovereignty and the French Constituent Assembly, 1789–91* (Manchester, 1952), p. 135.

2. A. Aulard, *Politische Geschichte der Französischen Revolution* (Munich/Leipzig, 1924), vol. I, p. 207.

he proposed, that 'the men of all countries are brothers, and the various peoples should help each other, according to their strength, as citizens of one and the same country. The oppressor of one single nation declares himself the enemy of all nations.' A more moderate version of Robespierre's idea was adopted by the Convention in the Constitution of 1793, Article 118, which said that 'the French people is the friend and the natural ally of all free peoples'.

In the life-and-death struggle in which France was engaged, she decided to carry the Revolution into the enemy camp. Soon after the outbreak of the war against the coalition, the Council of Paris—the real leadership of the Revolution—decided to ask the National Assembly to declare: 'The nation renounces all plans of conquest, but it does not renounce the help of neighbouring states which wish to extricate themselves from slavery.'[1] When a year later the French revolutionary armies invaded the territory of the coalition powers, Danton proposed to the Convention that the armed forces of France be appointed instruments of the Revolution. 'For as long as we are surrounded by tyrants,' he said, 'their coalition can endanger our own freedom.' He further asserted that: 'In sending us here the French nation has at the same time created a grand council to head the uprising of the peoples against all the kings of the world.'[2]

The idea of France's armed solidarity with revolutionaries abroad was later embodied in the following decree by the Convention on 19 November 1793: 'In the name of the French nation, the National Convention declares that it will grant fraternal protection to all peoples trying to win back their freedom. It gives authority to issue to the generals the necessary orders instructing them to help those peoples and to protect those citizens who are, or are likely to be, oppressed because of their love of freedom.' Cambon, the Convention's Finance Minister, and one of the Girondist leaders, was asked to submit a draft of the procedure laid down for generals in the occupied territories.

The decree, put before the Convention by Cambon and adopted on 15 December 1793, said basically that the aim of the revolutionary war was the abolition of privilege. 'All privilege and all tyranny must be regarded as our enemy.' In the occupied territories, where the people did not themselves overthrow the feudal system, France must declare herself a revolutionary power and destroy the old régime. The French generals were instructed to abolish immediately tithes and all other forms of feudal dues as well as every kind of manorial right. All the old authorities were to be dissolved and replaced by elected provisional administrations, but only those citizens were to vote who undertook to

1. Aulard, op. cit., vol. I, p. 396.
2. Albert Mathiez, *Die französische Revolution* (Zurich, 1950), vol. I, p. 386.

maintain freedom and equality and forfeit all privileges. The generals were also to abolish the existing system of taxes and confiscate as security for the *assignats* all the property of the Exchequer, the princes and of secular and religious institutions. Should the elected administration be forced to levy taxes, it must take care that the burden did not fall on the working class.[1]

Many political refugees from abroad found asylum in revolutionary France. The clubs opened their doors to them, they secured posts in the National Guard and in the central and local administrations and were even elected as representatives of the people: Thomas Paine and the Prussian revolutionary, Anarcharsis Cloots, were members of the Convention. After the declaration of war they formed the Foreign Legion, which was given the task, after the war, of freeing their countries from feudalism and despotism. There was a Belgian legion in the northern army, a legion from Liège in the army of the centre, a legion of Allobrogen, made up of men from Savoy, Geneva, Neuenburg and Waadtländ, and a Batavian and a German legion under the command of Colonel Dambach, who had served under Frederick II. The foreign legion played a major part in the decisive victory at Valmy in September 1792, which forced the Duke of Brunswick to retreat, and in the victory at Jemappes a month later, which destroyed the power of Austria over Belgium.

In some countries, the French revolutionary armies were received as liberators. 'The advance of my army [in Savoy],' reported General Montesquiou to the Convention, 'is a triumphal procession. In country and town, people rush to welcome us; everywhere they are wearing the tri-coloured cockades.' The country was full of revolutionary clubs, inspired, as they stated in their resolutions, to 'throw themselves into the arms of the French Republic and form, with it, a single nation of brothers'. A National Assembly of Allobrogen, with members sent from all the municipalities, deposed the King of Sardinia, overthrew the aristocracy and the rule of the landlords, confiscated the property of the clergy and declared its wish to be united with France.

Not everywhere in Europe did the population respond so vigorously to the Revolution. But in several towns in the German states, in Switzerland, northern Italy and even in Hungary, friends of the Revolution formed themselves into secret societies, clubs and study circles, into 'nests of democracy' as they were described in the German counter-revolutionary press. Speeches by the leaders of the French Revolution, reports of the Convention's activity, revolutionary periodicals, almanacs, proclamations and songs of freedom were distributed, despite a strict censorship and threats of severe punishment. The Decree on Riots of the government of Saxony in 1791 threatened 'leaders and ringleaders . . .

1. Mathiez, op. cit., vol. I, p. 396.

who incite others to form an association . . . and who produce or distribute seditious literature' with death by the sword and, when circumstances aggravated the crime, on the wheel.[1]

In some districts invaded by French troops, the tree of liberty, symbol of the Revolution, was widely planted, and the old régime was overthrown in Belgium, the principality of Lüttich, the diocese of Basle, Worms, and also in Mainz, which declared itself a republic. In some secular and clerical estates on the left bank of the Rhine, the peasants refused to pay tithes, contribute forced labour or recognize other feudal rights.[2] In Saxony the peasants rose in 1790, in Silesia they rose, together with the weavers and artisans, in 1792 and 1793, while in Breslau there was a rising of merchants and handicraftsmen in April 1794. The revolutionary ferment, which had begun in France, spread over the whole of western and central Europe. But this ferment was unable to crystallize into mass revolutionary movements in countries still industrially undeveloped, because the social forces capable of bringing about a revolution in society were still in their infancy.

The French Revolution was the work of a strong, self-conscious *bourgeoisie* which was no longer prepared to tolerate its position as the Third Estate and which claimed to be the most important class in state and society. It was also in revolt against the aristocratic structure of society, which had become a fetter on economic development; and it found support from a massive industrial proletariat in the suburbs of Paris, Lyon and Marseille which looked to the Revolution for the fulfilment of its hopes and endeavours.[3]

Among France's neighbours, however, there was, except in Belgium, no strong industrial and commercial middle class and no industrial proletariat. Italy and Spain were impoverished and exhausted. The German states, at the time of the French Revolution, were still agrarian with a few industrial enclaves, such as the weaving districts of Silesia and the medieval homesteads of the handicraft cutlers of Remscheid and Söllingen. Only a few German towns had recovered from the devastation and depopulation of the Thirty Years War. At the end of the eighteenth century, the population of Paris alone was greater than the total population of all the German free cities, including the university towns. The French Revolution, as we have seen, produced a powerful echo in Germany. But the social forces which could have transformed the radical, democratic and cosmopolitan tendencies of the intellectuals and artisans into a revolutionary political movement were absent.

1. Hedwig Voegt, *Die deutsche jakobinische Literatur und Publizistik*, *1789–1800* (Berlin, 1955), p. 134.
2. See Georges Lefebvre, *The French Revolution*, vol. I (London, 1962), pp. 184–5.
3. Lefebvre, op. cit., pp. 108, 118–20.

2 · Thomas Paine, Internationalist

England provided fertile, if uneven, soil for the seeds of the French Revolution. There, some decades earlier, the Industrial Revolution had started, destined to transform the country into the 'workshop of the world'. The process of industrialization inevitably strengthened the middle class in numbers, giving rise at the same time to an industrial proletariat.

The ideas of the French Revolution had already been familiar there for a hundred and fifty years. In the middle of the seventeenth century England had risen against, and destroyed, the idea of the Divine Right of Kings. For ten years, from 1649 to 1659, under the Commonwealth of Cromwell, England had been a republic. In that period, Milton had produced his brilliant defence of free thought and a free press.[1] By the turn of the century, the philosopher John Locke, in his treatise *On Civil Government*, had already deduced the existence of individual and civic rights from the prevailing theories of natural law. These ideas provided America with moral justification for her break with England, and inspired the Declaration of Independence in 1776, which was the prototype of the Declaration of the Rights of Man proclaimed by the French National Assembly in 1789.

Locke's ideas formed part of the intellectual climate shared by educated, liberal-minded men in England and Scotland. Such men greeted the French Revolution as a triumph of these ideas. Significant of the mood of the times was the enthusiastic reception given to a sermon by the highly respected scholar Dr Richard Price, in London, on 4 November 1789, six months after the Revolution.

I deem myself happy [he said] to be able to witness such great times . . . when the Rights of Man are better understood than ever before, when nations thirst for freedom . . . when freedom's flames spread everywhere and the rule of kings gives place to the rule of law. . . . See the lands which, taught by you, have woken from their slumbers, broken their chains and now demand justice

1. John Milton, *Areopagitica* (London, 1644).

from their oppressors! See the light you have kindled; it has freed America, its light has spread to France where it has kindled new flames, reducing despotism to ashes while it warms and illuminates Europe.[1]

The speech was received by the meeting with wild applause. The Society of the Revolution (of 1688) decided to send a message of greetings to the French National Assembly; it celebrated 14 July 1790, and set up contact with clubs in France. Price's sermon was so warmly received throughout the whole country that in a very short time twelve editions were printed. Burke's book, *Reflections on the French Revolution*, was an attempt to refute Dr Price. In its turn it provoked Thomas Paine into writing what came to be a classic of English working-class literature, *The Rights of Man*.[2]

Edmund Burke, a Member of Parliament with great gifts as a writer and speaker, began as a radical exponent of Locke's theory of natural law. In his essay, *A Vindication of Natural Society*, he developed from the theory of natural law a charming, socialistic critique of the existing social order. Consistently with this idea he warmly defended the legal rights of the American colonists against the home country. But as he grew older he became reactionary.

In his attack on Dr Price, Burke no longer spoke of the 'inalienable rights of man' based on natural law. European civilization, he declared, derived its strength from tradition, whose guardians were the aristocracy and the Church. He argued that it was the aristocracy and the Church which held society together. Without them it would dissolve into anarchy. A stable society, he maintained, could not be built on an inadequate, fallible human judgement based on abstract philosophical theories. It must develop organically out of custom and tradition, passed down from one generation to another. The French Revolution, in overthrowing the aristocracy, abolishing the power of the Church and destroying the heritage of tradition, had erected in their place the power of human judgement. In doing so, it had opened the gates to chaos. Burke expounded these ideas in powerful prose. His book was without doubt the most outstanding piece of anti-revolutionary propaganda of its day. It was translated into German by Friedrich Gentz, adviser to Metternich, as 'the most impressive refutation of the revolutionary idea'. It became, and has remained, the gospel of counter-revolution. The year 1790, the year in which Burke's book appeared, also saw the arrival in England, via France, of Thomas Paine, already a citizen of three countries.

1. Max Beer, *Geschichte des Sozialismus in England* (Stuttgart, 1913), pp. 51–2.
2. A character-sketch of Paine and an assessment of his ideas can be found in H. N. Brailsford's brilliant work, *Shelley, Godwin and their Circle* (London, 1913).

Thomas Paine (1737–1809) proved to be one of the great figures of the English working-class movement, its revered teacher for half a century and remembered down to our own time as a pioneer. He was born in 1737 in Thetford, Norfolk, the son of a poor stay-maker and smallholder. Paine first learned his father's trade. Then, studying on his own, he gained a considerable knowledge of philosophy, politics, political economy and even mathematics. Through the writings of Locke and the works on rationalism and natural law published by his English radical contemporaries, he became a fervent revolutionary. His ideas were to develop a good deal further in America.

Paine arrived in America in 1774 with a letter of introduction from Benjamin Franklin, whom he had met in London. From the outset he had every intention of helping the settlers in their struggle for freedom. He arrived in Philadelphia and at once threw himself, as a journalist, behind the colonists' demand for some control over their own taxation, in essence a fight of republicanism against monarchy and of democracy against oligarchy.

When the settlers finally rose against the mother country, Paine wrote early in 1776 an inspiring pamphlet, *Common Sense*. It was circulated on a huge scale and fanned the spark of revolution, which was already flickering, into a gigantic flame. When the pamphlet appeared, Americans were still wavering. Paine supplied them with arguments for the Declaration of Independence, which was duly proclaimed five months after the appearance of his pamphlet.[1]

The style of Paine's work—its fire, pathos and revolutionary spirit—made him famous at once throughout America. Meanwhile, he enlisted as a private in Washington's army. He soon became Adjutant to General Green, then Foreign Minister to the American Congress and finally Secretary of the National Assembly in Pennsylvania. In 1781 he was sent by the American government on a diplomatic mission to Paris, where he befriended such men as Lafayette, Brissot, Condorcet and others who were later to be leaders in the Revolution. When he returned to England in 1790 he was already a figure of European renown. Burke's attack on the French Revolution has already been mentioned. Paine at once undertook its defence in his work, *The Rights of Man*.

In this book Paine did not develop any original ideas. To Burke's view of the state and society Paine counterposed the ideas of the natural law and rationalist school of thought. But these had previously been written in academic language. Paine wrote in a simple, clear style which could be understood by any working man. The philosophers of the

1. Vernon Louis Parrington, *Main Currents in American Thought* (New York, 1927–30), vol. I, pp. 327–41.

Enlightenment had expressed their ideas in terms of cold logic. In Paine's writing they glowed with a revolutionary fire and passion.

Burke had denied the right of the people to make a revolution on the grounds that each generation was bound by the traditions of its predecessors. Paine denied the right of any generation to govern beyond the grave. 'Every age and generation,' he declared, 'must be free to act for itself in all cases as the ages and generations which preceded it. The vanity and presumption of governing beyond the grave is the most ridiculous and insolent of all tyrannies. . . . Every generation is, and must be, competent to all the purposes which its occasions require. It is the living,' he insisted, 'and not the dead, that are to be accommodated.'[1] To justify authority on the grounds of inherited right was 'a fraud against humanity'. The people as a whole were the source of all power in state and society. There could be neither freedom nor social justice in the world until the people changed their constitution for one based on the principles of the rights of man, as had happened in France and America. Only when royal absolutism—the enemy of mankind and the source of all misery—had been abolished, and the 'natural sovereignty of the people' reinstated, would an age of perpetual peace begin.

Thomas Paine's *The Rights of Man* was the first political work in England to state the case of working people in their own terms and with concepts drawn from their own world of experience. It was also the first to express a programme of social reform which had wide popular appeal.

The first volume of Paine's book appeared in 1791, the second a year later. It had a tremendous effect. In the course of a few months, edition after edition appeared. Before the government suppressed it as subversive, it had sold 200,000 copies and earned its author £1,000. He gave the money to the Corresponding Society, a working-class organization. Even after its prohibition, however, it continued to be produced and sold, though to do so involved the risk of a heavy prison sentence and transportation to the Australian penal settlement of Botany Bay.

A warrant was issued for Paine's arrest. Warned in time by the poet William Blake, he fled to France, wherc he had meanwhile been elected to the National Assembly as representative of the people of Calais. He was convicted in his absence of high treason, declared an outlaw and his book burned by the hangman. The Tories, whom Paine had escaped, found consolation in the genial device of 'TP nails' fixed in the heels of their boots to witness how they trampled on his base principles and the hated name.

But neither the hangman, nor the abuse which aristocrats, bishops

1. Thomas Paine, *The Rights of Man*, Part I, p. 4.

and respectable citizens showered on Paine, could lessen the popularity of his book. It served two generations of English and Scottish workers as their Bible. In it they found, as can be seen from their manifestoes right up to the end of Chartism in the 1850s, the justification in natural law of their demands for political equality and social justice. The book does not belong to the history of Socialist thought. But it belongs to the history of the International, because it implanted the idea of international solidarity for the oppressed deep in the minds and hearts of English workers. This can be seen in the Chartist paper, the *Northern Star*, in the speeches and writings of the Chartist leaders, Julian Harney and Ernest Jones, and in the programme of the Society of Fraternal Democrats, founded in 1845, the real prototype of the International.

3 · The Corresponding Society

Out of the ferments which spread from France to the intellectuals and ordinary citizens of England, there sprang the first independent political working-class movement in history. Its founder was Thomas Hardy (1752–1832), a Scottish shoemaker of strong character, thoughtful and well read. In 1773 he had left his Scottish home in Stirlingshire for London, where he opened a small workshop in Piccadilly. In 1792, when he was forty years old, he called a meeting in a public house with eight of his friends and fellow artisans. He suggested to them that they establish a society to agitate for parliamentary representation. It was to be called the London Corresponding Society. Since national political organizations were prohibited, local societies would co-ordinate their activities through correspondence, in the form of letters, circulars and delegate conferences. The membership fee was fixed at one penny, and all present immediately contributed. The society, therefore, started life with a capital of 9*d*. Hardy remained its secretary until his arrest in 1794.[1]

Hardy's idea evoked an unexpectedly strong response among educated workers, artisans and small shopkeepers. English branches were established in Sheffield, Coventry, Leeds, Nottingham and Norwich; Scottish ones in Glasgow and Dundee. Soon after, branches appeared in the great industrial centres of Lancashire and Yorkshire. By the end of 1792 the societies had 20,000 members; in 1795 they had 80,000. In October 1795 an open-air demonstration attracted 150,000 people. Justifying the suspension of *Habeas Corpus* in May 1795, Pitt, the Prime Minister, told Parliament that 'the London Corresponding Society has reached the height of audacity. It is a Jacobin body, and aims at destroying the rich.'

1. The best account of the history of the London Corresponding Society in German can be found in Max Beer, *Geschichte des Sozialismus in England*, ch. 4 (see p. 71, n.1, for details of English edition). A detailed description in English can be found in Anthony Brown, *The French Revolution in English History* (London, 1918).

It was indeed Jacobin, and like the Jacobins of France it hoped to replace oligarchy with a democratic form of society. The Corresponding Society did not aim at a social upheaval directed against property. Socialism was no part of its programme. It fought for political equality and universal parliamentary suffrage. It wanted to end government by a rich minority and transfer political power to the poor. It stood simply for democracy. But Pitt knew only too well that if democracy meant power in the hands of the poor, it would not be long before they used that power to threaten the property and privileges of the rich.

The prevailing system of oligarchy did not only deny power to the mass of working people. The bulk of the middle class was equally excluded, and it supported the cause of parliamentary reform principally to transfer power to itself. Consequently the Corresponding Society found itself linked with the liberal-minded section of the middle class in a common struggle for democracy.

But above all, its members identified themselves with the French Revolution. Thomas Paine's *The Rights of Man* was printed by the Corresponding Society and distributed free, in great numbers, to working people. After the first victory of the French revolutionary armies in September 1792, the society sent a message of congratulation to the Assembly. It spoke of the hopes of working people, the fulfilment of which was to be expected from the victory of the French Revolution.

> You are already free [it said], and we now prepare ourselves for the victory of freedom in our country. . . . Whilst you enjoy the enviable honour of being the pioneers of freedom, we, in our own minds, think of the blessings which are imminent for mankind. If you, as is our dearest wish, are finally victorious, there will then be a Triple Alliance, not of the Crowns but of the people. Americans, Frenchmen and citizens of Great Britain will then bring freedom to the people of Europe and peace to the whole world.

The Assembly replied with a spirited message of thanks. In Britain, members of the societies, after the fashion of the French Revolution, took to calling each other 'citizen' instead of 'Mr' and referred to their conferences as 'conventions'. And many societies also corresponded directly with the revolutionary clubs in France.

The government was dismayed. As early as May 1792 a royal proclamation warned the country against such 'revolutionary writings' as Thomas Paine's *The Rights of Man*. In December, the government reported to Parliament that British subjects were working together with foreigners to destroy the constitution and overthrow the government. Vigorous counter-measures were threatened.

Three months later, war broke out between Britain and France, a war which Edmund Burke, in the House of Commons, demanded should become a crusade against the ideas of the French Revolution. The war should have as its aim 'the complete destruction of the frenzied hordes' who were 'responsible for these ideas'. The government intensified the persecution of the Corresponding Society, which Burke described as the 'mother of all evil'. The authorities began to infiltrate the working-class movement with spies and *agents provocateurs* in an attempt to bring its leaders to heel.

The first victim was in Scotland. There the society was known as the Friends of the People. At a meeting of weavers, Thomas Muir, a young and talented pioneer of the movement, had demanded the right of the workers to be represented in Parliament. He was charged with preparing for high treason and sentenced to fourteen years' banishment in the penal settlement of Botany Bay. He managed to escape on a pirate ship which some American sympathizers had sent to rescue him. He was received with honour in France, but soon died from exhaustion, the effect of his imprisonment.

The entire movement now decided to call a convention in Edinburgh, with representatives of all the branches in Britain, to protest against the savage sentence. At an open-air meeting in a working-class district of London, attended by 30,000 men and women, M. Margarot and J. Gerrald were elected delegates of the London Corresponding Society.

The convention met at the end of November. The government ordered it to dissolve. When it refused to do so it was dispersed by armed force. A number of delegates were arrested, including Margarot and Gerrald. After being found guilty of 'conspiring to overthrow the constitution', all the accused were sentenced to fourteen years in Botany Bay. Only one of them survived the fever and hardship. In both England and Scotland, and for a good many years, the workers kept alive their memory as honoured martyrs. In 1843 a monument was erected to them in Edinburgh.

The Corresponding Society refused to be intimidated. On 20 January, only a few weeks after the verdict, they issued a manifesto protesting against the imprisonment of their delegates and also against the war. They called on all workers and citizens throughout the country to support them in their fight for freedom. 'We must now choose,' the manifesto declared, 'between freedom and slavery. . . . Shall we wait until barracks are built in every village and the Hessians and Hanoverians are on our backs?' The manifesto made it clear that if foreign troops were brought into the country, *Habeas Corpus* repealed, martial law enforced or the right of assembly destroyed, a convention would be called in London. This was a thinly disguised threat of revolution. At the same time, a large number of meetings were quickly called in London and the provinces against the war—the 'conspiracy of kings against freedom'.

Pitt now decided to attack the leaders of the working-class organizations. In the early hours of 12 May 1794 Thomas Hardy and eleven other leading members of the society were arrested, taken to the Tower and charged with high treason. They were accused of having 'maliciously and treacherously, alone and together with others, waged war against the King'—a crime which, in the gruesome conditions of English law at the time, carried the most cruel death sentence.

Four days later, Pitt, on the authority of the king, asked the Commons to suspend *Habeas Corpus* until 1802, so that political suspects could be kept in custody without trial. The country, he declared, in justifying the emergency legislation, was in the grip of a dangerous conspiracy, whose aim it was to overthrow the constitution and replace it with the Rights of Man. Government, law, property and religion, so dear to the English people, were in danger of being swept away as in France. Pitt accused the London Corresponding Society of being the most dangerous element in the conspiracy.

Parliament endorsed Pitt's move, and *Habeas Corpus* was suspended. The working-class leaders were brought before the Assizes on 20 October 1794. The proceedings lasted for five days, but they did not go according to the government's wishes. The public prosecutor failed to prove that the accused had sworn to wage 'war against the King' by force of arms. But he claimed to have proof that ideas of the kind propagated by the Corresponding Society had led in France to the overthrow of the monarchy and the execution of the king. As the society had quite openly proclaimed its sympathy with the French Revolution and with Paine's *The Rights of Man*, he argued, it had declared by implication its intention to overthrow the monarchy in England, on the model of France.

The proceedings were followed with intense emotion. London had been radical since the days of Cromwell, and a London jury was not to be intimidated. The court-room was crowded every day, and in towns and villages people gathered in the streets waiting for the stage-coach to bring news of the trial. On 5 November, the day of the verdict, a dense crowd filled the roads round the court-house from early morning. When it was announced that the accused had been acquitted, the crowd broke into cries of joy and did not disperse until Thomas Hardy had been carried home in triumph.

The government had not yet broken the back of the working-class movement. The poverty resulting from the war had led to hunger riots. When George III drove to the House of Lords for the opening of Parliament in October 1795, the royal procession was greeted with hisses and wild shouts of 'Down with the war! Down with Pitt!' On the king's return to St James's Palace, soldiers of his bodyguard who were escorting the procession were pelted with stones and mud.

In 1797 the disturbances reached a climax. Leaders of the United Irishmen had planned an invasion of Ireland with the help of the French government. A small detachment of French troops had actually landed.

There was violent resistance to the new militia law in the eastern counties of Scotland. Still more serious was the naval mutiny, provoked by the harsh conditions of life on board, which broke out at Spithead and spread as far as Duncan's squadron in Yarmouth. The mutineers blocked the mouth of the Thames and appealed to the people for support. The uprising was finally crushed.

In effect, nearly all traces of freedom in Britain had now been wiped out. Soon after the public demonstrations against the king, a new and stronger law against high treason was passed, together with another law forbidding meetings not authorized by the authorities. No further meetings, in fact, took place. In 1798 the government ordered the arrest of the entire executive committee of the London Corresponding Society, and held them in prison for three years without trial. A law passed in 1799 prohibited debating societies and forbade political societies to make contact with each other, either verbally or in writing. Finally, in 1800 and 1801, the workers were denied the right of trade-union organization. The law remained in force until 1825.

The first political working-class association in history was destroyed by force. The industrial proletariat was still in process of developing into a modern, self-confident working class. It was not yet mature enough, either morally or intellectually, to defy the supreme power of the state or bring off a successful revolution. Moreover, the peasants had been effectively crushed for some time by a series of Enclosure Acts. And the liberal-minded middle class, who had greeted the French Revolution with such joy and sympathized with the Corresponding Society, were by no means revolutionary. Their aims were limited to political reform. Also, among the intellectuals, many of the earliest friends of democracy, such as Coleridge, Southey and Wordsworth, were disillusioned with the French Revolution when, at home, internecine struggles became continually more grim, while, abroad, what had begun as a war of liberation against despotism, degenerated into a war of conquest. Such men became terrified of the Revolution. Francis Place, a faithful friend of Hardy who later continued his work, testified of the repressive laws that 'infamous as these laws were, they were popular measures'.[1] As the main conditions for revolution were absent, the fate

1. Graham Wallas, *The Life of Francis Place, 1771–1854* (London, 1937), pp. 14–15.

of the first attempt at a working-class political society was sealed.

Its story forms, nevertheless, an important chapter in the history of both the English Labour movement and the International, because it was infused with the conviction that the fate of the working people of all countries was linked together in a common destiny. In this way, it established the tradition of international solidarity in the English Labour movement.

4 · The Conspiracy of the Equals

1

The French Revolution of 1789, the beginning of a social ferment which spread over half of Europe, started as a revolt of the wealthier section of the middle class against absolutism. Nothing was further from their thoughts than the overthrow of the monarchy. They intended only to establish a constitutional monarchy on the English model, with a sharing of power between king and Parliament. Their ultimate object, if only vaguely conceived, was the transformation of the existing aristocratic system into a middle-class capitalist society.

The absolute monarchy of Louis XVI was justified in terms of Divine Right, which was based in its turn on a transcendental, mystical interpretation of the Bible. According to this doctrine all authority is divine in origin and therefore eternal and irrevocable, unaffected either by human rights or human desires. The theory was revived in the Middle Ages in the course of the struggle between pope and emperor as to which Divine Right, the spiritual or the temporal, had precedence over the other. However, the idea of the Divine Right of kings was not, as such, brought into question during the course of the dispute. It was accepted as dogma by the great mass of people and was not questioned, even by scholars, until the middle of the seventeenth century.

The French *bourgeoisie*, in its struggle to curb the absolute power of the king, to challenge the theory of Divine Right and to divide power between king and people, required a legal doctrine. In the theory of the social contract they found a rational basis for opposing the absolutist doctrine of Divine Right.

Justification for this new view was found in the Old Testament, which said that King David made a treaty with his people and that his power had accordingly been based, as it were, on a social contract. The Middle Ages was a deeply religious period in which every word of both Old and New Testaments was taken to be divinely inspired. It was the task of the theologians to reconcile these two conflicting doctrines. This was undertaken by Thomas Aquinas (1225–74). In his treatise, *De Regimine Principum*, he distinguished three elements in secular power: its essential substance, bestowed by God; its constitutional form (which could be monarchical, aristocratic or democratic); and the form in which the ruling power was exercised—the two latter being bestowed on government by the people. It followed that if a government misused the power entrusted to it by the people and degenerated into a form of slavery, the people were entitled to revoke the power they had granted. This doctrine contained the nucleus of both the social contract and the sovereignty of the people. It was the prevailing view in the Middle Ages among both theologians and lawyers.[1]

Philosophers in seventeenth-century England and eighteenth-century France combined these theological teachings with the theories of natural law, also derived from the thinking of the ancient world. According to this view, people are free and equal in natural law and actually enjoyed freedom and equality while living in natural conditions. When, however, they began to establish a social order, they installed a government and made a treaty by which they assigned to it their sovereignty in return for an undertaking to protect their rights and freedom.

From this premiss, one school of thought concluded that the social contract was indissoluble and irrevocable, and therefore that sovereignty and royal power were absolute and indivisible. Another school came to the opposite conclusion that, since the sovereignty of the people was inalienable and irrevocable, the people retained the right to alter the contract with the king, or to revoke it and take back the power vested in him. Since the people were the source of all power, the sovereignty enjoyed by the king was delegated to him only by the people.

The execution of Charles I in 1649 and the deposition of James II in 1688 brought to an end in England the controversy about Divine Right and popular sovereignty. The people, represented by Parliament, took back power into their own hands and beheaded Charles I for resisting by force the sovereignty of the people. They dethroned James II for abusing the power with which he had been entrusted by the people and so, as the Convention of 1688 stated in its proclamation, of 'having endeavoured to subvert the constitution of the Kingdom by breaking the original contract between king and people'. The theoretical justification for this act of popular sovereignty was provided by John Locke in 1690. His work *On Civil Government* was epoch-making. Based on the theory of natural law, Locke's clear and logical demonstration that power in state and society resided in the people contributed powerfully

1. The theory of the Social Contract was actually developed by the Greek Sophists, discussed by Plato in the *Republic*, Book 2, and in the *Gorgias*.

to the American Revolution of 1776 and the French Revolution of 1789. In France, the theory of popular sovereignty found its classical expression in Rousseau's *Du Contrat Social*, which appeared in 1762.

Contemporary religious and metaphysical views of regal harmony as the embodiment of divine grace had already been destroyed, at a philosophical level, by such writers as Helvétius, Holbach, Diderot and Voltaire. But Rousseau's idea that, since the sovereignty of the people derived from men's 'natural rights', every individual in consequence participated in sovereignty through his own 'natural right' was circulated far and wide in thousands of vehement pamphlets, reaching far beyond a limited circle of intellectuals to the broad mass of the people.[1] It became a popular myth, a source of political enthusiasm, a symbol of salvation. When Louis XVI summoned the States General in May 1789 and instructed the electors of the Third Estate—the tax-paying male population—to submit a list of their grievances and demands, it was the spirit of Rousseau which permeated the *cahiers*. They demanded equality of rights, equal justice, free speech, the abolition of feudal dues and, above all, a responsible executive and an elected Assembly.[2]

Inspired by such ideas, the majority of the electorate called for a 'solemn declaration of the natural, inalienable and sacred Rights of Man', since, as was subsequently stated when the Constitution of 1791 drew up its preamble to the 'Declaration of the Rights of Man and of the Citizen', 'the ignorance, neglect or disregard of the Rights of Man is the sole source of public misfortune and the corruption of governments'.

2

But how were the 'natural, inalienable and sacred Rights of Man', proclaimed by the French National Assembly in August 1789, to be reconciled with the economic and social requirements of a middle-class, capitalist society? The Declaration opened boldly with the statement: 'Men are born and remain free and equal.' But the recognition of freedom and equality as the basic natural rights of men was not necessarily compatible with a society based on economic and social inequality, a society in which the propertied and propertyless classes were sharply divided.

1. An excellent appreciation of the importance of Rousseau's *Du Contrat Social* can be found in G. D. H. Cole's introduction to the English edition of 1913, published in Everyman's Library. See also the edition published in 1946 by the Oxford University Press, containing in addition Locke's treatise, with an introduction by Ernest Barker, an essay on the place of these writings in the history of European political thought.

2. Thompson, op. cit., p. 25; Kingsley Martin, *French Liberal Thought in the Eighteenth Century* (London, 1929), p. 75.

The National Assembly at first tried to solve this conflict of principles and class interests by dividing the people into 'active' and 'passive' citizens—into tax-payers, the 'true shareholders in the great social enterprise', according to the constitution drafted by Sièyes, and those whose incomes were too low to be taxed.[1] The latter were deprived, on Sièyes's proposal, of 'the right to participate actively in public life'. They were denied the right to vote. Even the active citizens were divided into two electoral groups so as to guarantee the predominance of the larger 'shareholders'. Finally, the right to be elected was restricted to such a high income level that, as Camille Desmoulins pointed out in the debate on the electoral laws, Rousseau, Corneille and Mably among others would not have been eligible for election. In this way, the propertied middle class secured an electoral system which guaranteed it political power. It could now establish itself as a new privileged class. Eventually it secured for itself complete control over the state. As Aulard remarked, they 'acted on the not very fraternal view that the middle class alone constitutes the nation'.[2] The aristocracy of birth gave way to an aristocracy of money.

The middle class used its power chiefly to establish security for private property. The Declaration of the Rights of Man had already proclaimed this to be a 'natural and immutable right . . . inviolable and sacred'. When hunger provoked popular uprisings this right seemed to be threatened. Danton demanded in the Convention that 'all personal property in land and industry should be, for all time, protected by the nations'. The Convention accordingly, on 18 May 1793, passed a unanimous decree that made even propaganda against the existing property laws punishable by death. This was applied to 'anyone who proposes agrarian or other subversive legislation concerning landed,

1. The debates in the French National Assembly in 1791 on the right of the poor to vote had their precedents in the famous Putney debates of 1647. There the delegates of Cromwell's revolutionary army (both privates and officers) had met to discuss the Agreement of the People, which was to lay the foundation for popular rights. The representatives of the units demanded as an 'absolute natural right' an equal vote for all subjects. General Ireton denied the existence of any such 'absolute natural right'. People who had nothing to lose had no right to elect the law-makers. Mr Rich, another representative of the propertied class, argued that those without property would naturally elect non-propertied people to represent them. 'It could then happen,' he went on, 'that the majority would abolish property and decree equal possessions for all.' For the Minutes of these discussions, see W. Clarke, *The Clarke Papers, 1847–9*, ed. C. H. Firth (London, 1891), vol. I, pp. 299–307, 315. In fact, more than two thousand years ago, the concept of *demokratia* (literally, 'rule of the people') was interpreted by the political theorists of democracy's birthplace, Plato and Aristotle, as 'government by the poor'. See H. D. F. Kitto, *The Greeks* (Harmondsworth, 1951), p. 125.

2. Aulard, *Politische Geschichte der Französischen Revolution*, vol. I, p. 44. 'The Legislative Assembly . . ., master of the state . . ., was the French *bourgeoisie*'—Lefebvre, op. cit., vol. I, p. 153.

commercial or industrial property'.[1] Even earlier, the Convention had issued a decree on 14 June 1793, dissolving all trade unions and journeymen's associations as a 'threat to freedom' and incompatible with 'the Declaration of the Rights of Man', forbidding them to be reconstituted, under threat of punishment, while at the same time instructing the authorities to suppress by force all associations of artisans, labourers and journeymen formed for the purpose of bargaining on wage questions.[2] Isaac Le Chapelier, supporting this in the Convention, did not deny that the low level of wages made for a condition of dependence 'little better than slavery'.[3] But property had to be protected against the threat of an organized proletariat. Indeed, it is fair to say that perhaps nowhere, at no time, and in no country, has the right of private property been more firmly claimed and more firmly guaranteed than by the French Revolution.

Workers employed in factories and small workshops looked to the Revolution for an improvement in their conditions. They hoped for better pay, the legal control of food prices and an easing in their constant struggle for economic independence. As artisans and journeymen who hoped one day to set up as masters on their own on a small scale, they had no intention of questioning the institution of private property. All they sought was security for the small property-owner. They were against the large estates. They wanted a maximum size of property to be laid down for private ownership, so that 'one and the same citizen may possess only one shop and one workshop' and that 'no one may hold more land in tenure than is required for a stipulated number of ploughs'.[4] But such strivings were irreconcilably opposed to the built-in drive of a capitalist economy towards the concentrated ownership of capital and industry.

In the period of the French Revolution, the workers did not yet constitute a class. Whereas the middle class had their own political organization in the Jacobin clubs, there was no independent party to represent the workers. Though they provided the vanguard in all the popular uprisings, they were content to follow the intellectual leadership of the middle class. The frequently occurring strike movements were only undercurrents in the social development of the Revolution. Indeed, the workers did not produce a single important figure in the course of the revolutionary struggles. Even at the height of the ferment, in 1793

1. Aulard, op. cit., vol. I, p. 366.
2. For the text of these decrees, see Heinrich Cunow's documented study, *Die Parteien der Grossen Französischen Revolution und ihre Presse* (Berlin, 1912), p. 145.
3. Cunow, op. cit., p. 301.
4. Albert Soboul, 'Klassen und Klassenkämpfe in der Französischen Revolution', in the symposium *Jakobiner und Sansculotten*, edited by Walter Markov (Berlin, 1956), p. 67.

and 1794, members of the *petite bourgeoisie*, journalists, lawyers, priests and tradesmen, functioned as spokesmen for the proletariat. Such men inevitably reflected the outlook and interests of the middle rather than the working class.[1]

Workers and other humble folk—the *sansculottes*—had defended the Revolution with their blood. It was they who stormed the Bastille and they who, at Marsfeld, engaged the royal forces whom the Court had ordered on 14 July 1789 to suppress the Revolution. They had fought for the Revolution on numerous battlefields. And all the time they saw the rich grow richer, their wealth swollen by the sale of the lands which the state had confiscated from the nobility and the church, their pockets lined with the proceeds of army contracts, financial speculation and juggling with food supplies. Meanwhile, the poor grew poorer. The peasants at least had been freed from their feudal overlords and become owners of the land they tilled. But the workers had gained nothing. The Rights of Man and the gospel of Liberty, Equality and Fraternity had left them destitute.

The disinherited were well aware of the marked contrast between the principles of the Revolution and those of a social order based on middle-class property. As Jacques Roux complained to the Convention, 'Liberty is only an empty illusion if one class of people can with impunity starve another. Equality is only an empty illusion while the rich retain their monopoly, which gives them power of life and death over their fellow creatures.'[2] This precisely expressed the feelings of the wage-earners, artisans and urban poor. Their revolt brought Marat and Robespierre to power.

Some decades earlier, Morelly and Mably, in their philosophical writings, had projected a utopian version of Socialism. But to Jacques Roux, on the extreme left of the Convention, and to the Jacobin leaders, Marat and Robespierre, this did not seem a realistic solution to the conflict. They were merely against the abuses of wealth. They believed in a maximum size for property holdings. They wanted to lessen the contrasts between rich and poor.[3] Their ideal was that portrayed by Rousseau in his *Du Contrat Social*, in which 'all have something and none too much'. They hoped to create a republic of small farmers and handicraftsmen. They did not consider the destruction of the existing basis of property, the replacement of private by common ownership, to be a matter for serious consideration.

1. cf. Cunow, op. cit., p. 355. 2. Cunow, op. cit., p. 357.

3. 'There was in the minds of the Jacobins no definitive resolution to impair individual property and to proceed to a reorganization of society along new lines. The expressed beliefs of all the Jacobins and the decrees of the National Convention are unanimous in their respect for property'—André Lichtenberger, *Le Socialisme et la révolution française* (Paris, 1899), p. 128.

The struggle to solve the insoluble conflict between the Rights of Man, based on a concept of 'natural' freedom and equality, and the interests of middle-class property-owners, determined the internal development of the Revolution from its inception. It was fought out in the Convention between the Gironde, the party of the propertied middle class and the substantial citizens, and the Jacobins, who represented the *petite bourgeoisie*, artisans, wage-earners and peasants. In May 1793 the Gironde was overthrown. The Jacobins became heirs to the Revolution, but it was an inheritance fraught with danger. France was at war, surrounded by powerful enemies who had invaded her from north and east. At the same time, in the west and south, in the Vendée, Lyon, Marseille, Bordeaux and Toulon, an armed counter-revolution had broken out against Paris. A rapid currency depreciation had forced food prices to fantastic heights. It seemed as though the Revolution would succumb to its enemies at home and abroad. To avert the danger, the Jacobins established a revolutionary dictatorship and a reign of terror. With their arrival in power there began a second revolution, a revolution of the broad urban masses.

But this revolution too was doomed to fail, since it could not aim at the destruction of the capitalist order. What distinguished the second revolution from the first was only its more pronounced democratic tendency and more advanced social aims. It abolished the tax qualification for the right to vote. It proclaimed, in the Constitution of 1793, that the aim of society was the 'general welfare'. Apart from that, however, property was still listed in the Constitution as one of the natural and inalienable rights, with every citizen having the right to 'enjoy his property and his earnings . . . and to dispose of them at his own discretion'.

Such encroachments on private property as were made by the Committee of Public Safety—the organ of the revolutionary dictatorship—were war measures, taken to deal with a national emergency. The Committee issued decrees to prohibit speculation in foodstuffs and other vital necessities. It controlled the price of food, but at the same time put a ceiling on wages. While it confiscated the property of 'enemies of the Republic' and allocated the proceeds for the relief of destitution, it also made it clear that 'the property of patriots is sacred and inviolable'.[1]

To the cry of 'Down with the tyrant Robespierre! Freedom!', the wealthier section of the middle class brought about the downfall of

1. As to the confiscation of property of the rich, Lichtenberger observes: 'The property of the rich is not attacked because it is unjust in itself, but because the owners are counter-revolutionary; and the poor are benefited, not only because they have a right to subsistence, but because they are patriots'—Lichtenberger, op. cit., p. 270.

the Jacobin dictatorship and its reign of terror on 9 Thermidor—27 July 1794. But in fact this marked the beginning of the 'period of the demolition of freedom', as F. A. Mignet, historian of the French Revolution, called it. The general franchise was abolished, and replaced by the two-tier electoral law. The Press was once more in shackles, and finally, by the end of the Consulate, its freedom was completely destroyed. One after another the clubs were closed down, and every movement of the lower middle class and of the workers was crushed by a régime of terror. The revolutionary wars of 1792, 1793 and 1794, which had been conducted as a struggle for liberating enslaved peoples, degenerated into imperialist wars of conquest. And a few weeks after 18 Brumaire—9 November 1799—the Constitution of 1799 placed the entire power of government in the hands of the First Consul, Napoleon Bonaparte. William Hazlitt had cause to complain that 'the sun of freedom was swallowed up by the night of despotism'. With the fall of the Jacobins, the Revolution was left drained of its power. Tired of the struggle, the workers subsided into apathy. Disillusioned by the Revolution, they surrendered in defeat.

3

But some embers were still glowing beneath the ashes of the Revolution. Before the 'night of despotism' fell over France, they broke just once again into towering flames. This outbreak, Babeuf's Conspiracy of the Equals in 1796, is an important event in the history of Socialism and the International.

François-Noël Babeuf (1760–97) was twenty-nine at the beginning of the Revolution. His father had served for a time as a major in the army of Maria Theresa. On returning to France he had fallen into deep poverty, supporting his family first as a wage-earner, later as a junior official employed in collecting the salt tax. The young Babeuf began work as a personal servant. After teaching himself law, he became surveyor and archivist in a land-records office in Picardy. There, he later wrote, 'in the dusty archives of the feudal aristocracy', he discovered 'the appalling secrets of illegal appropriation by the caste of noblemen'. When in 1789 the peasants of Picardy rose in revolt, Babeuf burned the documents and title deeds of the feudal aristocracy in the market-square of Rouen.

From then on he felt himself to be in the service of the Revolution. He steeped himself in the writings of Diderot, Rousseau, Brissot and, particularly, Mably and Morelly, the first exponents of utopian Socialism in French literature. He organized a movement of peasants in Picardy against the taxes on salt and drink, the poll tax and the tithe, and for the restoration and redistribution of the confiscated lands. In October 1790 he founded a paper, *Le Correspondent Picard*, in which he untiringly pointed out the discrepancy between the Declaration of the Rights of Man, with its promise of equality, and the actual inequality prevailing in economic, political and social life. In September 1792 he was elected district administrator in the Department of the Somme, but at the beginning of 1793, with a prosecution pending against him, he fled to Paris. There he found a position in the city supply department.

Babeuf played no part in the momentous and fateful struggles of the time, which culminated in the overthrow of the Gironde. The rule of the guillotine, inaugurated by the Jacobins, aroused his strong abhorrance. He had been an unhappy eye-witness of the terrible cruelties to which the turbulent masses of Paris had succumbed after the storming of the Bastille on 14 July 1789. He wrote at the time to his wife: 'How terribly have the practices of torture, the wheel, the stake and the gallows which the hangmen are operating all round us debased our standards! Instead of civilizing us, the masters are turning us into barbarians.'[1] With his hatred of cruelty, Babeuf detested the 'vile tyrant Robespierre', and welcomed his fall as the re-birth of freedom.

But he soon realized that 'tyranny has passed only from one hand to another'. Soon after 9 Thermidor, Babeuf had founded another paper, *Tribune du peuple*. In it he admitted that his earlier assessment of Robespierre and the Jacobin dictatorship had been a mistaken one; 9 Thermidor represented the peak of revolutionary achievement. Up to that date the Revolution had advanced over all obstacles. Since then it had been in steady retreat.

The victors of 9 Thermidor had sent the Jacobin leaders to the scaffold and closed down their clubs. After a time, however, a number of Jacobin members of the Convention and of the club sections tried to collect their scattered supporters together and to rebuild their organization. They called the new body the Club of the Panthéon. It had no special programme, but it kept alive the Jacobin tradition of democratic republicanism as the champion of the artisans and the lower middle classes.

The formation of the club in November 1795 coincided with a desperate economic crisis and widespread impoverishment. The government of the wealthy *bourgeoisie* had abandoned a number of Jacobin policies, including maximum food prices and the requisitioning of supplies, the distribution of food to the needy and the laws against speculation. At the same time, as inflation proceeded, the depreciation of the currency sent the price of food soaring. Wages failed to keep pace with prices and the

1. Mathiez, op. cit., vol. I, p. 68.

workers grew desperate. Deaths from malnutrition were widespread.[1] While Babeuf was in prison at Arras he lost a seven-year-old daughter, who died from exhaustion. There were hunger riots in Paris.[2] The members of the Panthéon called for the relief of suffering, whereupon the government ordered Bonaparte, at that time in command of the army of the interior, to suppress the club at the end of February 1796.

Babeuf, who assumed the name Gracchus in honour of the popular tribune, Gaius Gracchus, in ancient Rome, was especially concerned with the interests of the impoverished working people. He had joined the Panthéon Club on its formation, and organized within it a small group of like-minded people, a secret society which called itself the Society of the Equals.

Babeuf's society was organized as a conspiracy. It aimed at the forcible overthrow of the Directorate—the government of the day—the seizure of the state, and the establishment of a dictatorship which would over a period construct a democratic society on a Socialist basis. Its story was told thirty years later by his faithful friend and spiritual heir, Philippe-Michel Buonarroti, in a documented history. In it, the author described the main ideas of Babeuf, his plan of conspiratorial organization, the technique of propaganda which he developed and, finally, the course of the trial following the arrest of the conspirators.[3]

Babeuf's consistent aim since 1789 had been to resolve the discrepancy between the natural right to equality, which the Revolution nominally upheld, and the intolerable social and economic inequality which actually existed. The Constitution of 1793 had proclaimed the principle of political equality. But it did nothing to abolish the glaring inequality, both social and economic, between rich and poor.

He saw, in Socialism, the logical outcome of man's struggle to realize his natural equality. 'Nature gave everyone an equal right to the enjoyment of all goods,' ran a sentence at the head of the manifesto which Babeuf pinned on the walls of Paris, containing a brief summary of his ideas. 'We must have this equality,' the *Manifeste des Égaux* announced, 'not merely transcribed in the Declaration of the Rights of Man and of the Citizen: we must have it in our midst, under the roof of our houses. . . .' 'In a true society,' it went on, 'there is no room for either rich or poor.' But in order to achieve a true society, it would be

1. Mathiez, op. cit., vol. III, pp. 37–8. Mathiez's early death prevented him from completing the work. The third volume, cited here, was edited by G. Lefebvre.

2. The hunger riots in Paris in October 1795 were the last mass risings of the suburban poor during the French Revolution. For a detailed description, see E. V. Tarle, *Germinal und Prairial* (Berlin, 1953).

3. See also Victoire Advielle, *Histoire de Gracchus Babeuf et du babouvism* (Paris, 1884). For an examination of Babeuf's ideas, see G. D. H. Cole, *A History of Socialist Thought*, vol. I (London, 1953), pp. 11–22.

necessary to make a further revolution. The French Revolution, as it had developed so far, must, he said, be 'only a prelude to another revolution which, with loftier aims and more far-reaching effects, would be the final revolution . . . doing away with private property in land . . . and with the terrible contrasts between rich and poor, masters and servants! The time has come to set up the republic of equals, whose welcoming doors will be open to all mankind.'

Babeuf's Socialism had all the characteristics of its day. A majority of the population consisted of peasants, tenant farmers and farm labourers working for private landowners. The Communism of Morelly and Mably, from which Babeuf drew his inspiration, had been for the most part agrarian, impelled rather by the unequal distribution of land than by the contrasts stemming from industrial development. Manufactures were still mainly the products of artisans in small workshops, of workers in small factories and, to a certain extent, even of farmers' households. The idea of socializing industry, an idea which presupposes its concentration in very large units, was still unknown.

His objective was the common ownership of property. Land was to be redistributed to the cultivators, farmers and farm workers, who lacked it. But the ownership of land would be transferred not to the farmers but to the nation as a whole, as its inalienable property. Working farmers would enjoy only the right of use, without being able to transmit land to their heirs. The produce would be delivered to public storehouses. To prevent the accumulation of wealth in private hands, there was to be no right of inheritance, and productive capital would on the death of its owner become public property. In this way individual wealth would gradually accrue to the nation, to be administered by elected officials under public control. Everyone would be liable to labour service, and the livelihood of all would be guaranteed by the state. The nation would ensure the just distribution of the wealth produced by society. Equality of education was a major item in Babeuf's programme, designed to secure to everyone an equal opportunity of rising in the world.

Though working in secret and under constant threat from the authorities, the Society of the Equals won a considerable following. By May 1796, according to Paul Louis, it had about 17,000 supporters in Paris alone, together with a number of branches in the provinces.[1] It was joined by a good many of the earlier Jacobins, democratic republicans and officers, released by the Directorate, when their own Panthéon Club was suppressed by the police. Aulard, though he gives no figures, confirms on the basis of contemporary documents, including

1. Paul Louis, *Histoire du socialisme en France* (Paris, 1936), p. 56.

police files, that Babeuf's propaganda reached the mass of the people in Paris, that they knew of his doctrines and 'took them seriously'.[1]

The society was organized on conspiratorial lines, with its full Socialist aims known only to a small circle of initiates. At the head was a central body calling itself the Secret Committee of Public Safety, with Babeuf, Antonelle, Sylvian Maréchal and Buonarroti as members. Subordinate to it were twelve deputies, one for each district of Paris, charged with preparing mass insurrections in the districts, through a network of underground propaganda cells. Neither the deputies, nor the agents through whom they kept contact with the central committee, were known to each other. Besides Babeuf's *Tribune du peuple* and *L'Éclair du peuple*, edited by Simon Duplay, propaganda was carried on by means of leaflets, posters, revolutionary songs in the coffee-houses, mass demonstrations in the streets and underground meetings. Members of the cells were also instructed to keep the central committee informed, through the deputies, about the state of public feeling.

A 'military commission' was attached to the central committee, with the task of recruiting support for the conspiracy inside the army and police force. It was also to keep the central committee informed about the morale of the forces and supply it with details about arsenals and ammunition depots.

The society's propaganda seems to have been particularly intensive in one particular police unit. The government grew suspicious and ordered its posting to the front. The unit mutinied and two days later, on 30 April 1796, it was disbanded.

In the view of the central committee, this incident showed that the time was ripe for an uprising. It set up an 'insurrection committee' consisting of Babeuf, Darthé, a former member of the Convention, Buonarroti and Félix Le Peletier. It established contact with a group of Jacobins who had been members of the Convention until they were deprived of their mandate after 9 Thermidor, and had then devoted themselves to overthrowing the government.

The two groups agreed on the measures to be taken after a successful uprising. Those citizens of Paris who had given armed support to the insurrection were to gather on the Square of the Revolution and install the insurrection committee as a provisional government, by acclamation. Next, the Convention would meet, consisting only of those members whose mandates had been withdrawn by the Directorate. The places of the excluded deputies were to be filled by eighty staunch democratic republicans, on a list compiled by Buonarroti. The Convention would then repeal all laws passed since 9 Thermidor and re-establish the Constitution of 1793.

1. Aulard, op. cit., vol. II, p. 524.

The rising was prepared down to the smallest detail. Under cover of night, the armed conspirators would converge on the centre of the town and then occupy the headquarters of the Directorate and the Town Hall. Posters were printed, ready for sticking on the walls during the night. They carried the rallying-cry of the insurrection: 'The Constitution of 1793! Liberty! Equality!' The date and the exact hour of the rising were fixed.

But a few days before the rising was due to begin, a member of the military committee, Captain Georges Grisel, betrayed the plans to the government. On 10 May 1796 a large number of the leaders were arrested. They included Babeuf, Darthé, Buonarroti and Jean-Baptiste Drouet, the famous postmaster from Saint-Menehould, who had discovered Louis XVI on his flight to Varennes. Another 245 warrants for arrest were issued. In Babeuf's home the police found all the plans of the conspiracy. The government at once issued a proclamation to the people and called up 10,000 men. About three months later, on the night of 26 August, the accused were brought in cages to Vendôme, where the Supreme Court assembled. But another six months were to elapse before the trial opened.

Meanwhile, Babeuf's followers attempted a desperate *coup*. During the night of 9 September six or seven hundred armed conspirators made their way, with the help of supporters in the army, into the military camp at Grenelle. They called on the soldiers to join them in overthrowing the government. The commander of the garrison ordered his men to attack, and in the ensuing battle the conspirators were put to flight. Some lost their lives, a number were arrested. Thirty-one of the prisoners, including three former members of the Convention, were sentenced to death by a military tribunal. Of the remainder, thirty were deported and twenty-four imprisoned.

4

The trial of Babeuf and his associates began at the end of February 1797 and lasted about three months. Of the sixty-four conspirators, forty-six were in the dock; eighteen were tried in their absence, as was Drouet, who had escaped from prison.

The indictment made no mention of the Socialist aims of the conspiracy. It confined itself to the charge that the accused had tried to dissolve the legislature by force and restore the Constitution of 1793. A government decree of the previous year (passed on 16 April 1796) made propaganda for the restoration of this Constitution a capital offence. On the strength of this, the public prosecutor demanded the death sentence. The jury found Babeuf and Darthé guilty; and Buonarroti and a number of the others guilty with mitigating circumstances. Fifty-five of the accused were acquitted.

In a dignified and moving speech, lasting over six court sessions, Babeuf defended himself. He described the outcome of the Revolution, contrasting the noble principles it had proclaimed with the bitter reality of its degeneration.

'The Revolution [he declared] cannot be a deed without issue. It would be intolerable if the sacrifice of so much blood ended merely in a worsening of conditions for the people. . . . The Revolution aims at happiness for the majority. Until this aim is reached, the Revolution has not ended. . . . If this were really the end of the Revolution, it would be nothing but the terrible sequel of a crime.'

Babeuf went on to explain the outcome of the Revolution for which he and his followers had been striving.

'There are epochs in history [he explained] when the hard and inflexible laws of development have concentrated all the wealth of a people in the hands of a tiny minority. . . . The mass of the people is appropriated by others; they are confronted with a caste which has grabbed everything for itself and hangs on to it pitilessly. Such conditions determine the moment at which a mighty revolution breaks out. They precipitate one of those notable epochs, foreseen by the prophets of ancient times, in which a general upheaval in property relations becomes inevitable, and in which the revolutionary uprising of the poor against the rich becomes a historical necessity.'

That moment, said Babeuf, had arrived.

Almost all the accused remained steadfast.

They none of them belied themselves [said Mignet], they spoke as men who feared neither to avow their object, nor to die for their cause. At the beginning and the end of each sitting, they sang the *Marseillaise*. This old song of victory, and their firm demeanour, struck the public mind with astonishment, and seemed to render them still more formidable.[1]

Babeuf and Darthé were condemned to the guillotine. When sentence was pronounced they tried to kill themselves with a dagger which Babeuf's son had smuggled into the prison cell. Covered in blood, they were taken back to their cell, and they were still covered in blood when next day they were dragged to the guillotine. They died on 28 May 1797. The others who had been found guilty, including Buonarroti, were sentenced to terms of imprisonment and deportation. Embracing Babeuf for the last time, Buonarroti promised to write the story of his life, his ideas, the history of the conspiracy and of the trial.

Babeuf's execution was received by the Parisian workers and *petite bourgeoisie* with the same indifference that they had shown when the

1. F. A. Mignet, *History of the French Revolution* (London, 1846), p. 325.

conspiracy was discovered. Only one paper, the democratic *Journal des hommes libres*, honoured Babeuf and Darthé as 'martyrs of liberty'. Though Babeuf's name was well known to the inhabitants of the Paris suburbs, he never enjoyed the popularity of Marat.[1] His Socialist message was unable to reawaken the revolutionary spirit of the masses, which had subsided since 9 Thermidor. Only a very few people shared his ideas.

And, indeed, in the prevailing social and economic conditions, Babeuf's ideas were utopian. Even had the conspiracy succeeded, the policy of restricting property rights to the use of land, without the possibility of transmitting such property to their heirs, would have provoked a successful peasant uprising. And the attempt to abolish the inheritance of artisan property would have shared a similar fate. Even had they captured power, the Babeuvists would at the most have been able to continue the Jacobin tradition. And they would then have been overthrown by an alliance of the *bourgeoisie*, the peasants and the army, because of their threat to the security of private property.

Nevertheless, the Conspiracy of the Equals was a significant episode in the history of Socialism and the International. With this conspiracy, the idea of Socialism made its first appearance on the stage of world history. No previous social movement had aimed at the abolition of the social system based on private property. Such movements as the agrarian agitation led by Gaius Gracchus in the second century B.C., or the Levellers in the seventeenth century A.D., had striven merely for a fair distribution of the land, or—as in the German Peasant War of the sixteenth century—for the ending of intolerable conditions of economic and social oppression. Babeuf's conspiracy, however, had as its object the complete overthrow of the system of property: the abolition of private ownership and the establishment of a social order based on common property.

The Socialist vision which inspired the Conspiracy of the Equals was not in itself new. It had been painted in vivid colours by Mably in mid-eighteenth-century France, by Campanella in Italy at the beginning of the seventeenth century, by Thomas More in England in the sixteenth century, and long before that, by Plato in Greece in the fourth century B.C. But the society described by these earlier thinkers was a fantasy, an expression of moral values and in no way seen as the achievable programme of a social movement.

What was new in Babeuf's conception was the idea of a Socialism which would not be, as with Plato, the tool of a philosopher king nor, as with Mably, a product of 'the advancement of knowledge', but the outcome of a class struggle—in Babeuf's terms, 'the war of plebeian

1. Aulard, op. cit., vol. II, p. 325.

1 François-Noël Babeuf

2 Louis-Auguste Blanqui

against patrician, of poor against rich', a struggle to win control of the state and use it as an instrument for the overthrow of private property. He saw clearly that the state served as a tool in the interests of the classes which controlled it: the *grande bourgeoisie*, the 'golden millions', as he called it, under the Girondins, and the 'plebs'—farmers, artisans and workers—when the Jacobins were in power. State power, he concluded, could be used as an instrument of social revolution. In this idea we find the origin of the theory, which Marx later developed, of state power as a lever in the process of Socialist revolution.

It was also Babeuf who introduced the concept of proletarian dictatorship into the body of Socialist theory. His ultimate aim was without doubt a democracy, finding its fulfilment in a universal, economic, social and political equality. But from the tragic outcome of the French Revolution he concluded that, since the mass of the people had formed their ideas and habits of thought under an aristocratic régime, based on class divisions, they had become in a sense 'corrupted'. In the first period of proletarian revolution, such a people would not be able to summon up the necessary sacrifice and self-denial. A transitional stage would be needed.

The idea of a minority dictatorship in the interests of the majority was by no means new. It had been one element in the French revolutionary tradition. It had originated in Rousseau's *Du Contrat Social*, which justified the 'despotism of freedom over tyranny'. Marat had called for the establishment of a people's dictatorship and Robespierre had, up to a point, achieved it. What was new in Babeuf's conception was the idea of a dictatorship as a transitional political stage in the process of social revolution. This contained the origin of the theory of proletarian dictatorship as it later evolved in the ideologies of Blanqui, Marx and Lenin.

Babeuf's Conspiracy of the Equals also originated the theory of an armed seizure of power by a disciplined vanguard through a *coup d'état*, later developed by Blanqui and employed with world-shaking consequences by Lenin. Babeuf's organization supplied a model of the structure, technique and propaganda methods of all the conspiratorial secret societies in the subsequent history of the Socialist movement—the Blanquists, the Russian Social Revolutionaries and the Bolsheviks.

It was Buonarroti's book, *Babeuf and the Conspiracy for Equality*,[1] which conveyed to posterity the ideas and methods of the Babeuvists. It appeared in Brussels in 1828 and two years later in Paris. In 1838 the Chartist leader, Bronterre O'Brian, published an English translation.

1. The full title of the German edition, appearing in Stuttgart in 1909, was: *Babeuf und die Verschwörung für die Gleichheit mit dem durch sie veranlassten Prozess und den Belegstücken.*

Marx read the book in 1844 and, together with Engels, considered arranging for a German edition, to be translated by Moses Hess.[1]

The impact of this book on Socialist thought and activity has earned it a lasting place among the classics of Socialist literature. Babeuf's ideas as expounded in this book exercised until the middle of the nineteenth century a dominating influence on the Communist secret societies in France[2] and on the left wing of the Chartist movement, led by George Julian Harney and Ernest Jones. Through the League of the Just, which was founded in 1838, they were transmitted to the Communist League, a forerunner of the International. It was this organization which embodied the ideas of Babeuf and preserved them for posterity in the famous *Communist Manifesto*.

1. See Arthur Lehning, 'Buonarroti's Ideas on Communism and Dictatorship' in *International Review of Social History*, vol. II (1957), p. 282.
2. For the survival of Babeuf's ideas in the Communist secret societies in France, see Georges Sengier, *Babeuvisme après Babeuf. Sociétés secrètes et conspirations communistes, 1830–48* (Paris, 1912).

5 · The Counter-Revolutionary International

On 9 Thermidor the rule of the common people in France had been overthrown. The Conspiracy of the Equals was a desperate and unsuccessful attempt to restore it. After the brief transitional period of the Directorate, the *bourgeois* capitalist state was consolidated under the dictatorship of Napoleon. But if Bonapartism marked the end of the French Revolution, it still embodied in relation to feudal-absolutist Europe the ideas of that revolution. True, there was no longer under the French Empire any question of sovereignty of the people. But the main achievements of the *bourgeois* revolution were preserved. The domination by the aristocracy and Church had been abolished; the property of the peasants freed from feudal obligations; trial by jury and the equality of all citizens before the law were maintained. And wherever the popular armies of France, themselves the products of revolution, overran foreign territories, feudalism was destroyed and the *bourgeois* legal system of the *Code Napoléon* replaced the old laws of feudal absolutism.

While in France itself every trace of democracy had already been eradicated, the movement towards democracy received a new and powerful impetus in the countries subjugated by French imperialism. With the entry of French troops and prefects there also entered the spirit of the French Revolution and the springs of revolt against native absolutism. French rule in its turn stimulated the spirit of nationalism. But nationalism was at its inception a revolutionary idea, with its concept of national unity and democratic rule.

In 1792 the conservative powers had formed an alliance to destroy the French Revolution. Yet on the morrow of their victory over Napoleon in 1814 they still felt themselves threatened by revolution. They had indeed overthrown Napoleon, the heir of the Revolution.

But in the meantime, the germs of the Revolution had spread to their own countries.

The princes of Europe, assembling at the Congress of Vienna after the fall of Napoleon, were determined to restore once again the old 'legitimate' order as it had existed before the Revolution of 1789.

On the face of it, the Congress of Vienna was able to restore the old 'legitimate' dynastic order and to reinstate the royal families which had succumbed to the Revolution or, later, to Napoleon. It was not so easy, however, to restore absolutism, after the idea of democracy had spread outwards from France and engulfed half of Europe. As early as 1812 a parliament had met in the Spanish city of Cádiz and established a democratic constitution with a constitutional monarchy. Giving way before the democratic movements in the German states, their princes responded to the threat from Napoleon by pledging themselves to institute, after the war, constitutions based on popular representation. Louis XVIII, who returned to Paris with the victors' baggage in 1814, had also, under the pressure of public opinion in France, undertaken in the Declaration of Cambrai to rule on the basis of a parliamentary constitution. In the northern Italian states, which, after the collapse of the French Empire, were given back once more to the hated rule of the Habsburgs, and in Poland, which had been placed once again under the dreaded rule of the Tsar, a passionate feeling of nationalism had developed.

Metternich, by far the cleverest of the statesmen assembled in Vienna, recognized with perfect clarity that even the most modest advance of democracy must develop through its own inherent laws into a deadly threat to the existing political and social system and, in particular, to the newly restored dynasties. Once the principle of popular sovereignty had been acknowledged, democracy would make continuing encroachments until the rule of the propertyless majority finally threatened the existing distribution of property and state power. In nationally divided countries such as Italy, he explained, democracy would overthrow the newly restored rule of the Habsburgs and Bourbons and create a united Italian republic. The German princes faced the same threat, as Metternich made very clear to Frederick William IV of Prussia when the latter was considering whether or not to keep his promise and grant a constitution. The introduction of a parliamentary system based on popular representation, Metternich insisted, would mean the end of Prussia and the triumph of the 'revolution'.[1]

The Congress of Vienna had based the political systems of Europe on a 'counter-revolutionary principle', as Metternich expressed it.

1. *Aus Metternichs nachgelassenen Papieren*, edited by Richard Metternich-Winneburg and Alfons von Klinkowström (Vienna, 1880–9), vol. III, pp. 171–81.

The revolutionary principle of democracy, the concept of popular sovereignty, was the threat, and it was in the common interests of all conservative powers to repel the danger. But this would only be possible if they all acted together. It was not enough for governments to repress liberal and democratic movements and resist all democratic reforms in their own countries alone. They must, as Tsar Nicholas suggested, guarantee each others' sovereignty and pledge themselves to forcible action against states in which absolute sovereigns felt themselves threatened by 'revolutionary inroads'. The Congress of Vienna, in fact, saw the establishment of a counter-revolutionary International, committed to the task of 'saving Europe from democracy'.[1]

The three feudal powers of Russia, Austria and Prussia linked themselves together in the Holy Alliance, which served as the executive power of the counter-revolutionary International. Metternich was at once its architect and general secretary. Its object was to secure joint action by the conservative powers in the fight against democracy. Its method was to intervene by diplomatic pressure or by armed force against European states whose governments introduced, voluntarily or under popular pressure, democratic institutions. Whenever the danger threatened, the leading powers of Europe assembled in conference and discussed ways and means of intervening in the interests of counter-revolution.

From 1815 to 1849 the history of Europe records the triumph of the Holy Alliance in its fight against democracy. The German princes who had solemnly undertaken, in Article 13 of the Act which constituted their Confederation in 1815, to grant their peoples democratic constitutions, were prevented from doing so by diplomatic pressure. The Holy Alliance compelled the German Bundestag in September 1819 to pass the Karlsbad Act, denounced as a disgrace by Wilhelm von Humboldt, which suppressed throughout the states of Germany all freedom of thought, publication and teaching. It secured the addition of further decrees to the Karlsbad Act, pledging the German princes to maintain absolutist forms of government. The Federal authority was empowered to intervene forcibly against any German states which might nevertheless institute popular representation.

Additional decrees were embodied in the Karlsbad Act, making explicit the principle of armed intervention in the interests of the counter-revolution. It was put into practice for the first time in the Kingdom of Naples and Sicily. A rising of the Carbonari, a revolutionary

1. cf. the remarks of the Russian Ambassador to Vienna, in Alfred Stern, *Geschichte Europas von 1815–71* (Stuttgart, 1894–1925), vol. I, p. 460, and Castlereagh's Cabinet papers in *Memoirs and Correspondence* (London, 1848–53), vol. III, p. 62.

democratic secret society, had compelled Ferdinand IV to carry out his pledge and grant a constitution. He duly promulgated one at the opening session of Parliament. At the same time he wrote to Metternich, asking him to restore him 'once again to absolute power with the help of the Austrian army'. The members of the Holy Alliance consequently met in conference at Troppau in October 1820 and authorized Austria to intervene. The Austrian army entered Naples, annihilated the revolutionary forces in the battle of Rieti on 7 March 1821, and restored the absolute monarchy once more.

The revolution in Naples touched off an uprising in Piedmont. There also a constitution was proclaimed by the Prince Regent, and cancelled five days later, in March 1821. Once again Austria was authorized at a conference of the Holy Alliance in Laibach in May 1821 to intervene, this time in Piedmont. At the same time, Russia was asked to have ready an army of 100,000, to march into the states of Germany in the event of a revolutionary uprising.

The classic case of armed counter-revolutionary intervention was in Spain. That country had had a constitution since 1812. When Ferdinand VII returned to Spain in the band-wagon of the allies—like his cousin Louis XVIII somewhat earlier—he declared the constitution 'null and void'. A nation-wide movement, however, forced him to recognize it again. Then he begged the members of the Holy Alliance to send forces against his own people. At a conference in Verona in August 1822, the governments of Russia, France, Austria and Prussia met to organize a crusade against democracy in Spain. Tsar Alexander offered to march into the country with an army of 150,000. As, however, he was already holding an army of 100,000 in readiness against a possible revolution in Germany, whilst Austria was still occupied in suppressing the revolution in Naples and Piedmont, France was instructed to intervene in Spain. The four powers signed a joint ultimatum in January 1823, demanding that the Spanish government should abolish the Constitution of 1812.

A few days later, Louis XVIII announced in a speech from the throne the impending invasion of Spain by an army of 100,000. The constitutional government of Spain was overthrown by the French troops and the old, undiluted absolutism reinstated. It behaved with a cruelty born of terror. Even Louis XVIII was moved to request that by joint diplomatic actions his Austrian, Russian and Prussian associates should stop the barbaric slaughter of the constitutionalists. But the three powers of the Holy Alliance refused. On the contrary, they urged Ferdinand to wipe out every trace of democracy in his country with fire and sword.

Acting entirely in the spirit of the Holy Alliance, with its dedication to the cause of counter-revolution, Metternich supported the Sultan of Turkey against the efforts of the Greeks to free themselves from his despotic rule between 1821 and 1827. The Sultan had his Christian subjects murdered in tens of thousands. Nevertheless, he was undoubtedly the legitimate sovereign, while his Greek subjects were revolutionaries. Like all revolutions, this one had to be quelled. About the extermination of Greeks by the Sultan, Metternich casually remarked that it was of no great significance if, over the eastern border, 300,000 or 400,000 people were being hanged, slaughtered or cut to pieces. He rejected protests from the British government against his pro-Turkish policy on the grounds that 'His Royal Majesty regards it as not only his right, but his duty, to give what help he can to every legitimate authority under attack by the common enemy'. And in the Treaty of Berlin in 1833 the members of the Holy Alliance pledged themselves yet again to recognize 'the right of every independent sovereign to summon to his assistance, whether in the internal or external difficulties of his country, any other independent sovereign whom he shall deem best able to assist him'.[1]

The Holy Alliance, however, found itself unable to intervene against the revolution in Paris of July 1830, when the rule of the Bourbons collapsed like a house of cards. Armed intervention in the internal affairs of a major power such as France would have unleashed a European war. The full power of the Alliance was nevertheless employed to suppress the revolution of 1848. When news of the February uprising in Paris reached St Petersburg, Tsar Nicholas sent a note to the other powers on 5 March asking them to resist by force 'the spread of anarchy which threatens the whole of Europe', and to have ready for this purpose strong military forces which could be employed wherever they were required. When, a few days later, revolutions broke out in Italy, Austria, Hungary and Germany, he concentrated a strong force on the German frontier and told Count Thun, the Austrian Emperor's special emissary in St Petersburg, that the granting of constitutions to Galicia and Hungary would be intolerable for Russia. 'I could not allow a centre of insurrection on my doorstep, so close to my Polish "friends". If constitutions are granted in those areas, or if revolution begins in Galicia and is not vigorously suppressed, I shall be forced against my will to intervene. In that event I should not hesitate for a moment to cross the Austrian frontier and restore order in the name of the Emperor Ferdinand.'[2]

In the event the absolute monarchy in Austria proved capable of suppressing the revolution first in Lombardy and Venetia, then in

1. Metternich, op. cit., vol. III, p. 483, quoted in A. F. Pollard, 'The German Federation', in *Cambridge Modern History*, vol. X, p. 376.

2. Vicomte de Guichen, *Les Grandes Questions européennes et la diplomatie des puissances sous la Seconde République* (Paris, 1925). Quoted in L. B. Namier, *1848: The Revolution of the Intellectuals* (London, 1946), p. 94.

Prague and Vienna, without help from the Tsar. But resistance in Hungary was prolonged, and it was then the counter-revolutionary International went into action. In June 1849 a Russian army of 140,000, at whose disposal the Prussian government had very readily placed the railway network of Posen and Silesia, entered Hungary and put down the revolution. At the same time a French army attacked and destroyed the Roman republic, which was being defended by Garibaldi.

Conservative Britain was not a member of the Holy Alliance. No British government, however reactionary, could openly approve the 'anti-revolutionary principles' of legitimacy on which the Holy Alliance was founded and from which it derived its right of armed intervention against democratic movements and governments. As Castlereagh, English Foreign Minister and himself a deadly enemy of democracy, explained: 'If the King were to sanction them he would be on the road to his own abdication. . . . The House of Hanover cannot recognize principles contrary to those in the name of which the House of Stuart forfeited its throne.'[1] And in a memorandum to the European powers on 5 May 1820, he declared that 'no country with a representative system of government could act on the principle of intervention by one state in the internal affairs of another'.

In spite of this, the counter-revolutionary International enjoyed the full moral support of Castlereagh, as well as of most British Conservatives, including 'the Tory ministers of Great Britain, who even secretly encouraged attacks on the constitutions which had been set up with the direct connivance of British representatives'. Whilst Castlereagh protested officially against the Karlsbad Act as an infringement of the Acts of Federation, also guaranteed by Britain, he congratulated Metternich on his success. 'The monster [i.e. the democratic revolution] is still alive, and shows itself in a new form,' he wrote in a confidential letter to Metternich, 'but we do not despair; we shall be able to destroy it with patience.' Castlereagh 'showed complete indifference to the brutality and deceit of the Kings of Spain and Naples, when they suppressed those movements for freedom in their countries which it was in English interests to strengthen. Indeed, he stands convicted of a conspiracy with Metternich.'[2]

Even when, under Castlereagh's successor Canning, British foreign policy embarked on a more liberal course, it was thwarted by the intrigues of George IV and his advisers. England's most powerful figure, the Duke of Wellington, officially protested against Louis XVIII's

1. Quoted in C. K. Webster, *The Foreign Policy of Castlereagh, 1815–22* (London, 1925), pp. 301–2

2. C. K. Webster, *The Congress of Vienna* (London, 1923), p. 147; Castlereagh, correspondence, op. cit., vol. xII, p. 259; R. S. Seton-Watson, *Britain in Europe, 1789–1914* (Cambridge, 1937), pp. 49–50.

openly expressed intention of armed intervention in Spain; but privately he urged the Bourbons to set their armies in motion. With Metternich, and with the great majority of British Conservatives, Wellington was convinced that any concession to democracy 'would lead sooner or later to anarchy, and that it was necessary for some kind of despotism to restore order'. For this reason he opposed every democratic reform not only in England but anywhere in the world. Like Metternich he supported the Sultan in the Greek War of Independence. He protested against the recognition of the South American republics, which had freed themselves from Spanish rule. He pressed the Tsar to intervene against the Hungarian revolution. 'March! But with sufficient power,' he told the Russian ambassador, Baron Brumov. Even Palmerston, who encouraged liberal movements in Europe, refused to recognize the revolutionary government of Hungary and allowed without protest Russia's military intervention against the Hungarians, which energetic action from England could probably have prevented.[1]

The counter-revolutionary International was a tremendous power. Its nucleus consisted of the feudal monarchies of Russia, Austria and Prussia. Around this core were grouped the feudal dynasties of Germany, Italy and Spain, with powerful allies in all European countries, above all the Catholic Church, the conservative, property-owning *bourgeoisie* of England and the financial aristocracy which had come to power in France after the July revolution of 1830.

The counter revolutionary International was based on the solidarity of the various ruling classes in defence of the existing political and social system. It took the form of internationally co-ordinated actions by conservative governments against movements for democracy and national independence wherever they appeared. From these experiences the subject classes and nations drew some weighty conclusions. They must confront the counter-revolutionary International with one of their own, in which they would co-operate to secure the defeat of reaction and the furtherance of revolution. This feeling gave rise to the international revolutionary organizations which developed in France, England, Italy and Germany after the overthrow of the Bourbons in July 1830. This feeling of revolutionary solidarity inspired the heroic rising of the Viennese workers in October 1848 against the dispatch of the forces which would crush the Hungarian revolution. The same feeling of international solidarity was behind the revolt of the Paris workers in May of the same year, when they stormed the Chamber of Deputies to demand war against Russia in support of the Polish revolution. The counter-revolutionary International had stimulated the birth of a revolutionary International.

1. Kingsley Martin, *The Triumph of Lord Palmerston* (London, 1924), p. 51.

6 · The Communist League

1

The revolution of July 1830 witnessed the first success for revolution and for the principles of popular sovereignty since the formation of the Holy Alliance fifteen years earlier. It gave rise to extravagant hopes among the mass of the people that at last an era of liberty and social justice had begun.

But the promise of the 'honeymoon period' was soon betrayed. As in July 1789, so in July 1830, the workers and lower middle classes of the Paris suburbs served only as assault troops for a revolution of the *haute bourgeoisie*. This time, too, they were robbed of the fruits of their struggle. Instigated by the liberal middle class, they had risen and expelled the hated Bourbons who had been imposed on them by the united monarchs of Europe in 1814. They hoped to set up a democratic republic. But when they met outside the Town Hall in Paris they found themselves confronted by a *fait accompli*. Louis-Philippe, Duke of Orléans, and confidant of Thiers and Lafayette, had been proclaimed king.

The *bourgeoisie*, who had begun the revolution, had limited aims. Regal despotism; ruling 'by God's grace'; Catholic clericalism, the political power of which had increased to a frightening extent under Charles X; most of all, the rule of large landed property—these were the principal targets for attack. They were to be ended, but only to give place to the power of the *bourgeoisie* itself. Protected by a constitutional monarchy, it intended to keep power in its own hands. It had no wish for a democratic republic in which power would have to be shared with the *petite bourgeoisie*, workers and peasants.

This aim had now been achieved. The revolution of 1830 marked the completion of the *bourgeois* revolution which had begun in 1789. Tocqueville, the shrewd and penetrating observer of the period, wrote in his memoirs: 'In 1830 the triumph of the middle class had been definite and so thorough that all political power, every franchise, every prerogative, and the whole government was confined and, as it were, heaped up within the narrow limits of this one class, to the statutory exclusion of all beneath them and the actual exclusion of all above.'[1]

The middle class, now in complete possession of state power, was determined to assert its 'rights' against 'everything beneath it'. Through an electoral system based on property qualification, they precluded the *petite bourgeoisie* and working class from all influence over law-making. Because of the prohibition of trade unions and political associations, the workers were without the legal means of combining. Critics of the régime were effectively muzzled by Press restrictions. And when in November 1831, less than a year and a half after the July Revolution, the weavers of Lyon were driven by hunger to revolt—they earned about 90 centimes in wages for an eighteen-hour day worked in their homes—the government raised an army under the command of Marshal Soult to suppress them. Since every legal means of resistance had been taken away, opposition to the régime took the form of secret societies, of which a number soon appeared in Paris.

2

One of the secret organizations was the Society of the Outlaws, formed in Paris in 1834 by a group of German intellectuals and artisans. Two years later, a section under the leadership of Herman Ewerbeck and German Mäurer broke away and founded the Society of the Just, a forerunner of the International. The aim of the society was defined in Article 2 of its Statutes as 'the liberation of Germany from the yoke of an infamous oppression and the establishment of conditions which will, as far as humanly possible, prevent the return of misery and slavery'. Admission to the society was conditional on a solemn pledge that

> we workers are at last tired of working for the idle, of suffering privations whilst others regale themselves in abundance. We want no further burdens placed on us by the self-seeking. We will no longer recognize laws which keep the most numerous and useful classes in conditions of humiliation, contempt and insecurity, so as to provide a few with the means of lording it over the working masses. We intend to become free and we wish for all men on earth the opportunity of living as freely as ourselves. No man will be deemed better or worse than his neighbour, but all will share equally in burdens, troubles, pleasures and enjoyment. This is what it means to live in a true community.

The Society of the Just had close links with the French revolutionary

1. Alexis de Tocqueville, *Recollections* (London, 1948), pp. 2–3.

secret organization, the Society of the Seasons, led by Louis-Auguste Blanqui, Armand Barbès and Martin Bernard.[1]

Louis-Auguste Blanqui, who lived from 1805 to 1881, and who founded the Society of the Seasons, was one of the great revolutionary figures of working-class Socialism. He devoted his life selflessly to the cause, which he served without fear or compunction. He controlled his followers by his example, his intellectual gifts and his rigorous moral standards.[2] His father had been a Girondist member of the Convention and later, under Napoleon, a *sous-préfet* in Puget-Theniers, a small town at the foot of the Alps. At the age of seventeen, Blanqui underwent an experience decisive for his later career. While still a pupil at the Charles the Great High School, in La Rochelle, he witnessed the execution of four non-commissioned officers sentenced to death for their membership of the Carbonari. Blanqui swore to avenge the martyrs. He joined the Carbonari and fought on the barricades during the July Revolution, for which he was decorated by the government of Louis-Philippe. Strongly influenced by Buonarroti's history of the Conspiracy of the Equals, he developed the technique of the revolutionary *coup d'état* as a military art. This was the method by which, in Blanqui's theory, power would be captured and the 'dictatorship of the proletariat' established. Under the name of 'Blanquism' this theory became part of the history of Socialist thought.[3]

Blanqui was the inspiration of all uprisings in Paris from 1839 to the Commune in 1871. Sentenced to death after his first attempt at an armed *coup*; his sentence commuted to life imprisonment; freed by the revolution; soon afterwards sentenced to ten years' solitary confinement, and hardly free again; finally, a victim of his own fight for social justice—this was the rhythm of his life. Altogether he was inside prison walls for nearly thirty-seven years. He became a legendary figure to the workers of Paris, who called him *l'enfermé*—'the incarcerated'. Tocqueville, a member of the Constituent Assembly, saw him when on 15 May 1848 he stormed into the assembly hall of the Chamber at

1. cf. Paul Louis, 'Blanqui und der Blanquismus', *Die Neue Zeit* (1900–1), vol. II, p. 76.

2. For the story of Blanqui's life, see Neil Stewart, *Blanqui* (London, 1939); Gustave Geffroy, *L'Enfermé—Auguste Blanqui* (Paris, 1897); for a brief account of his ideas, see Paul Louis, op. cit., vol. II; for a comprehensive examination, see Alan B. Spitzer, *The Revolutionary Theories of Louis-Auguste Blanqui* (New York, 1957).

3. Marx defined the characteristics of Blanqui's version of Socialism as follows: 'This Socialism means a commitment to permanent revolution, to revolutionary class dictatorship, to the class dictatorship of the proletariat as a milestone on the way to the abolition of all class distinctions and the mode of production on which these distinctions are based, and of the ideas which follow from these social relationships'—Karl Marx, *Die Klassenkämpfe in Frankreich* (Berlin, 1951), p. 130.

the head of a large crowd, to demand the government's intervention against Tsarist Russia on behalf of the Polish revolution. At the time Blanqui had been out of prison for hardly three months. 'He had wan, emaciated cheeks, white lips . . . a dirty pallor, the appearance of a mouldy corpse; he wore no visible linen; an old black frock-coat tightly covered his lean, withered limbs'—so Tocqueville described his impressions of the man.[1] George Sand described him as the 'Marat of our time', while to Marx he was 'the head and heart of the proletarian party in France'. Two hundred thousand Paris workers followed his coffin, among them Clemenceau and Louis Blanc. At his graveside, representatives of every Socialist and Anarchist trend in France spoke in his honour. Prominent among them was Édouard Vaillant, at one time a member of the General Council of the International, and later one of the founders of the United Socialist party of France.

The first uprising instigated and led by Blanqui was that of the Conspiracy of the Seasons. It was also the last to take place until the end of the July Monarchy. On 12 May 1839, several hundred of Blanqui's followers took over the arsenals in the suburbs of Saint-Denis and Saint-Martin and threw up barricades. But the uprising was overwhelmed on the same evening. Blanqui and other leaders were arrested.

3

The League of the Just had taken part in the conspiracy. Its sections had marched with the others and were involved in the general defeat. Two leaders of the League, Karl Schapper, a printer, and Heinrich Bauer, a shoemaker, were also arrested and eventually, together with Joseph Moll, expelled from France.[2] They went at once to London.

Soon after their arrival they formed a new organization. Since there was complete freedom of association and assembly in England, they decided on a public body—the German Workers' Educational Society—as a propaganda front for their secret organization. The society, which began in February 1840, lived on through many historic upheavals. It was dissolved only at the end of 1917, during the First World War, when the British government interned German citizens.[3]

1. Tocqueville, op. cit., p. 138.
2. Weitling, who was an eye-witness of the barricade fighting, mentions another German worker who participated: 'The last barricade was stormed. Barbès himself sank wounded to the ground. . . . One man remained standing by his side though wounded, a German shoemaker, Austen, from Danzig'—*Garantien der Gerechtigkeit und Freiheit* (Hamburg, 1849), p. 14.
3. See B. Nikolaevsky, 'Towards a History of the Communist League, 1847–50', *International Review of Social History*, vol. I (1956), p. 236.

The Workers' Educational Society and, with it, the League, soon assumed an international character. It was joined by Scandinavians, Dutchmen, Hungarians, Czechs and south Slavs, together with a handful of Russians and Alsatians. As it propagated the idea of Communism, it changed its name to the Communist Workers' Educational Society. Its membership card carried in twelve languages the slogan: 'All men are brothers'. In 1845, five years after it was founded, the society had more than 500 members. It met in a public house in Soho, a working-class district in the centre of London inhabited by colonies of exiles, where later Marx was to live for a number of years. According to the *Northern Star*, the walls of the big, lofty meeting-hall carried portraits of Shakespeare, Schiller, Mozart and Dürer, surrounded by flowers. There was a life-sized statue of a woman in a red Jacobin cap, bearing the symbols of liberty and equality. On either side of the speaker's rostrum stood a statue of freedom and justice, and above the chairman's seat was a painting representing the brotherhood of the working class. An enormous frieze along the four walls, surrounded by golden wreaths on a red background, bore in twelve languages the same sentence: 'All men are brothers'.[1] Although the main work of the Society was in London, its central direction remained for a time in Paris. It was transferred to London only in the autumn of 1846, when Schapper and Moll were entrusted with the leadership.

Besides a strong branch in London, in close contact with French refugees, the society also had groups in Paris, a number of sections organized by Wilhelm Weitling and Philipp Becker in the Swiss cantons of Geneva, Zurich, Berne, Waadt, Neuenburg and Aarau, and a number of small groups in Germany. But, if one can believe the reports of Metternich's police, its sphere of activity extended far beyond its own branches. 'In all workers' associations in Germany, France, England, Holland and Switzerland they are firmly entrenched and almost the dominant influence,' states one of these police reports from Zurich (15 June 1845), 'and all parts of the network keep in constant touch through correspondence, provide each other with mutual encouragement, inform each other of their plans and resolutions and warn each other if they are kept, more or less, under police observation.'[2]

Friedrich Engels arrived in London in November 1842, visited the Workers' Educational Society and met its leading members, Schapper,

1. John Saville, *Ernest Jones, Chartist* (London, 1952), p. 92. For the history of the Communist Workers' Educational Society, see W. Brettschneider, *Entwicklung und Bedeutung des deutschen Frühsozialismus* (Königsberg, 1936), and Friedrich Lessner, 'Vor und nach 1848, Erinnerungen eines alten Kommunisten', *Deutsche Worte* (1898).

2. Quoted in Ludwig Brügel, *Geschichte der österreichischen Sozialdemokratie* (Vienna, 1922), vol. I, p. 43.

Bauer and Moll. They left on him, as he recounted more than forty years later, a 'deep impression'. This was especially true of Schapper (1813–70), who had taken part, as a student of forestry, in Georg Büchner's agitation among the peasants of Hesse. A year later, with a group of fellow conspirators, he broke into the police guard-room in Frankfurt, and then fled the country. In 1834 he joined Mazzini's campaign in Savoy for the liberation of Italy from Austrian rule. In 1836 he founded the League of the Just. Together with Blanqui, he attempted the *coup d'état* of May 1839. Engels described him as 'of gigantic stature, resolute and energetic, always ready to jeopardize his means of livelihood and life itself. In the 1830s he fulfilled the role of professional revolutionary, of which he was a superb example.'[1]

When Marx, who was still living in Brussels in the summer of 1845, paid his first visit to England in the company of Engels, his friend introduced him to the Workers' Educational Society. Marx was most impressed by the spirit of the society and the theoretical interests of its leaders. Up to that time, he had held aloof from secret societies and refused to take them seriously. He was repelled by their atmosphere of romantic conspiracy and their confused utopian ideas. His own outlook was quite free of romanticism. He saw in the working class the force which would overturn capitalism. The Blanquist conception of social revolution proceeding from an armed *coup d'état* was completely alien to him. In English Chartism he saw a hopeful example of an independent, class-conscious workers' movement. What they still lacked, as did the budding Labour movement in other countries, was a clear recognition of their historic aims.

4

When Marx visited the league in London, the members were engrossed in a discussion with Weitling, lasting over many weeks, about the essence and prospects of Communism.

Wilhelm Weitling (1808–71) was born in Magdeburg, the illegitimate son of a French officer and a German seamstress. After a childhood of poverty and privation, he had learned the tailoring trade. His great abilities as writer and speaker, his idealism and his manifest integrity won him an enthusiastic following among the German workers. 'He is a fanatic,' remarked Wilhelm Marr, who had long watched his development with interest, adding that 'his enthusiasm for the cause has almost

1. Friedrich Engels, introduction to the third edition of Karl Marx's *Enthüllungen über den Kommunistenprozess zu Köln* (1885); Engels's summary of the history of the Communist League was supplemented by a number of important documents in Franz Mehring's introduction to the fourth edition of the book (1914).

the character of a religious mania'.[1] He was, as Marx said, an 'athletic figure', one of the outstanding personalities of early German Socialism. His brooding mind, nourished by the Bible as well as by the French Socialist writings of Fourier, Cabet and Lamennais, fashioned for itself a curious vision of a Christian Communist Utopia.

As a wandering handicraftsman, Weitling arrived in Paris in 1837, and soon joined the League of the Just. He apparently expounded his version of Communism with great effectiveness, since he was commissioned by the central committee to 'put into writing his demonstration of the possibility of Communism'.[2] It appeared in 1838 under the title, *Die Menscheit, wie sie ist und wie sie sein sollte.* Four years later in Switzerland, to where he had moved in 1841, he published his main work entitled *Garantien der Harmonie und Freiheit.* Marx rated it the 'brilliant début of the German worker'. The book obtained a surprisingly large circulation, not only in Switzerland, but also in Germany and Austria, where despite a close police watch and under threat of heavy gaol sentences (in Austria there was even the danger of the death penalty), it was smuggled across the borders by travelling artisans. The first edition of 2,000 in 1842 was followed by a second, printed in Hamburg in 1844, and a third in 1849. The book was also translated into French, English and Norwegian.[3]

Weitling's career in Switzerland, as organizer, propagandist and writer, came to an abrupt end in 1843. He had written a new book, *Das Evangelium eines armen Sünders,* and had publicly invited subscriptions. In his advertisement he claimed to have proof 'in over a hundred places in the Bible' that Christ was a prophet of freedom and a forerunner of Communism. This, in the view of the sanctimonious ecclesiastical court at Zurich, was veritable blasphemy, and the public prosecutor was asked to institute criminal proceedings. The book was confiscated and its author arrested. He spent ten months in prison on remand and was then sentenced to six months in gaol and life-long banishment from Switzerland. After that, gagged and handcuffed, he was taken to the German border and handed over to the police in Baden. They passed him on to the Prussians. Weitling, after a good deal of moving from placc to place, arrived in London in September 1844.

In London he was received with great honour. The Workers'

1. W. Marr, *Das junge Deutschland in der Schweiz* (Leipzig, 1846), p. 45. See also Otto Brugger, *Die Wirksamkeit Weitlings 1841–3* (Berne, 1932), and Robert Grimm, *Geschichte der sozialistischen Ideen in der Schweiz* (Zurich, 1931).

2. Max Nettlau, 'Londoner deutsche Kommunistische Diskussionen, 1845', in *Archiv für die Geschichte des Sozialismus und der Arbeiterbewegung*, vol. x, p. 363.

3. Emil Kaler, *Wilhelm Weitling* (Hottingen, Zurich, 1887), p. 38; see also Otto Brugger, *Geschichte der deutschen Handwerkervereine in ber Schweiz* (Berne, 1932), and Carl Wittke, *The Utopian Communist, Wilhelm Weitling* (Louisiana, 1950).

3 *Karl Marx*

4 Friedrich Engels

Educational Society arranged an international banquet, at which English and French as well as German speakers paid tribute to him as a 'martyr in the cause of Communism'. This was the first international Socialist demonstration; as such, it was a factor in the formation of the Society of the Democratic Friends of All Nations, whose importance for the history of the International will be considered later.

Inevitably, Weitling was invited to attend the weekly discussions of the Workers' Educational Society, to explain in more detail his ideas on Communism. The minutes of these discussions, mainly between Weitling and Schapper, were published in 1922 by Max Nettlau. They provide us with a great deal of insight into the world of ideas of early German Socialism.[1] From them it is clear that Schapper and his friends did not accept Weitling's version of Socialism. Despite the veneration with which he was received in London, his intellectual leadership was rejected.

5

Marx's first visit to England coincided with the Weitling debate, and he must have been kept fully informed. He saw the value of the league, both as a means of theoretical development and as an instrument of Communist propaganda. But he also saw that this propaganda must have a clear basis in theory, and that the theory should derive, not from abstract ideas or chains of deductive reasoning, but from existing social and economic conditions.

The Socialist ideas from which the members of the Communist League derived their inspiration were many and varied. Saint-Simon, Cabet, Fourier, Proudhon, Blanqui, Louis Blanc, Robert Owen and Wilhelm Weitling were among the main contributors. Marx found value in many of their ideas, while rejecting the methods and body of such thinking as utopian. After returning to Brussels it seemed very necessary to him, as we find from the outlines and plans which he projected at the time, to develop some clarity on the main question of Socialist theory. This called for sustained discussion and the detailed elaboration of a programme. His first idea, after returning to Brussels, was to found an international journal which would serve as a forum for discussing all trends in the Socialist movement. When this plan misfired, he formed together with Engels in 1846 a 'Communist correspondence committee', which was intended to develop and inspire the various sections of the league through letters and circulars.

The league's central committee in London also came to the conclusion that the movement required a programme. In the autumn of

1. Nettlau, op. cit., pp. 362–91.

1846 they called for the following year a congress in London which would represent every section of the league and would have the task of preparing a common programme. At the same time, they decided to invite Marx and Engels to draft the programme.

Marx, though still only twenty-eight, was already known as the leading representative of democracy and Socialism in Germany. His critical writings in the *Rheinische Zeitung*, which he had edited when barely twenty-four, had established his reputation as one of the foremost political and philosophical writers of the time. 'Think of Rousseau, Holbach, Lessing, Heine and Hegel combined in one person—I say combined and not thrown together—and you have Dr Marx,' declared Moses Hess in a letter (2 September 1841) to Berthold Auerbach.[1] The line of the paper was much too advanced for the Prussian government to tolerate, and it was soon suppressed. In Paris, to which he had moved later in 1843, Marx wrote his *Kritik der Hegelschen Rechtsphilosophie* in 1844, and in Brussels, where he first settled after being expelled from France in 1845, he wrote *Die Heilige Familie*, a criticism of the contemporary philosophical schools. All the leading ideas, which were later to comprise what became known as Marxism, were contained in embryo in that book. Meanwhile Engels, two years younger than Marx, had made a reputation for himself through a book appearing in 1845, entitled *The Condition of the Working Class in England*, and through his contributions to the Chartist *Northern Star*. The central committee of the league was most anxious to secure the collaboration of Marx and Engels in formulating the party programme. On behalf of the central committee, Joseph Moll visited Brussels at the beginning of 1847 to invite both of them to the congress. According to Engels, Moll said that the league 'was convinced of the general correctness of our conception as well as of the necessity to free the league from all conspiratorial traditions and forms of organization'. The Congress of the League would give Engels and Marx the opportunity of 'developing their critical Communism in a manifesto, which would then be published as the Manifesto of the League'. Marx and Engels accepted the invitation.

The Congress of the League met in London on 1 June 1847. Engels attended as the representative of the Parisian branch of the Communist Correspondence Committee, while Wilhelm Wolff represented its Brussels branch. Marx was unable to attend, owing to lack of money.

The congress decided to transform the league into a propaganda organization, to reorganize it along democratic lines, with an elected executive committee which would be subject to replacement, and to get

1. *Moses Hess Briefwechsel*, edited by Edmund Silberner (The Hague, 1959) p. 80.

rid of the 'old mystic name, a hangover from the period of conspiracy', as Engels termed it. It called itself from then on the Communist League. The first article of the draft statutes declared the aim of the league to be 'the downfall of the *bourgeoisie*, the rule of the proletariat, the overthrow of the old society of the middle class, based on class distinction, and the establishment of a new society without classes and without private property'. It was agreed to submit the draft statutes to the branches for discussion, and to meet again in the late autumn for a final decision. It was also agreed to consider, at the second congress, the draft of a programme for the league and to publish in the meantime a monthly journal. The first and only issue of the journal, known as the *Kommunistische Zeitschrift* and edited by Schapper, appeared in September. Above the title, the journal carried the slogan, 'Proletarians of all lands, unite!'

The second congress met in London with Schapper as chairman on 30 November 1847. There were delegates of branches from England, France, Belgium and Germany, and this time Marx himself was able to come. Between the first and second congresses, Marx had founded, together with Wilhelm Wolff, Joseph Weydemeyer, and Edgar von Westphalen, one of Marx's brothers-in-law, the Brussels section of the German Workers' Educational Society. According to Marx's report to the second congress, its membership was already 105.[1]

The first item at the congress was the final form of the statutes which were to define the new structure of the League. It was to consist of local circles, leading circles, a central governing body and a congress. The congress, as the highest authority, was to meet annually in August, and the central governing body, elected by congress and responsible to it, was to act as the executive. Since there was at the time hardly a country outside England where a workers' organization could openly propagate Communist views, workers' educational societies were to be established and directed by secret organization. But the main point on the agenda was the party programme, the leading ideas of which had been debated during the ten days of the congress. Marx and Engels were instructed to draft it. The decision was of historical importance, because it gave rise to a document which was to prove almost without rival in its power to affect the entire future course of social thinking.

The *Communist Manifesto*,[2] which supplied the Communist League

1. Max Nettlau, 'Marxanalekten', *Archiv für die Geschichte des Sozialismus und der Arbeiterbewegung*, vol. III, p. 397.

2. In his Introduction to the German edition of the *Communist Manifesto* of 1890, Engels explained why at the time of its drafting in 1847 it could not be called Socialist. 'Socialist' was at that time applied to the representatives of Utopian ideas who stood outside the working class and directed their appeal to the 'educated' classes. 'Communists' was the term applied to those who stood for a 'thorough reconstruc-

with its programme, is notable for the bold, messianic sweep of its ideas. The triumph of Socialism is presented as the outcome of an iron historical necessity; the development of the productive forces and the class struggles which stem from it must inevitably give rise to 'a revolutionary change in the whole of society'. 'In place of the old *bourgeois* society, with its classes and class differences,' said the *Manifesto*, 'appears an association in which the free development of each is the condition for the free development of all.'

Embodied in the *Manifesto* is another messianic theme: the idea that the working class cannot free itself from the exploitation and oppression under which it suffers without at the same time liberating the whole of society. Consequently, the emancipation of the working class would emancipate the whole human race from all traces of social injustice. This idea infused the struggle of the workers for their own interests with a moral as well as a historical significance. It supplied the class struggle with a double objective: the moral notion of freedom and equality for all human beings, together with the prediction that the transformation of capitalism into Socialism is inherent in the social process.[1]

6

While the *Manifesto* was being written, Europe was poised on the threshold of revolution. The feeling that a great social convulsion was pending runs through a good many passages in the document. When the congress met in London at the end of November, news came through that the Swiss government, defying the threats from Russia, Austria, Prussia and France, had overthrown the reactionary Catholic separatist party. In January 1848, with Marx still at work on the *Manifesto*, revolts broke out in Lombardy and Sicily, and revolutions in Naples, Turin and Florence. Marx predicted that the revolution would spread to France and Germany. The *Manifesto* pointed to the imminence of a social upheaval.

The *Manifesto* appeared in London in the German language in the beginning of February 1848. About a fortnight later, revolution broke

tion of society', and who appealed to the working class. 'Socialism,' explained Engels, 'referred to a *bourgeois* movement; Communism, to a working-class movement.'

1. For a historical appreciation of the *Communist Manifesto*, republished at its centenary by the British Labour party in acknowledging 'its indebtedness to Marx and Engels as two of the men who have been the inspiration of the whole working-class movement', see Harold J. Laski, *Communist Manifesto. Socialist Landmark* (London, 1948); for a comprehensive analysis of the Manifesto, see Cole, op. cit., vol. I, pp. 247–62.

out in France. A peaceful demonstration demanding electoral reform was fired on by soldiers in the streets of Paris on 23 February. Next day the lower orders had, in Tocqueville's words, 'suddenly become masters of Paris'. Having made a thorough study of the Revolution of 1789 and personally witnessed the revolutions of 1830 and 1848, Tocqueville was at once aware of the presence of a new social element in the latest outbreak. For the first time in history, he wrote, it was a revolution 'made entirely outside the *bourgeoisie* and against it. . . . This time it was not only the question of a party; the aim was to establish a social science, a philosophy, I might almost say a religion . . . this was the really new portion of the old picture.'[1]

When news of the outbreak of revolution in France reached London, the league's central committee decided to transfer its powers to the Brussels district committee; this in turn authorized Marx to set up a new central committee in Paris. Schapper, Moll and Heinrich Bauer from London, Marx, Engels and Wolff from Brussels, moved to Paris at the beginning of March.

But before Marx could get the new central committee going, he was forced to take on his own responsibility a political decision which was to cause a good deal of discord among the German *émigrés* in Paris. There were then in the city thousands of refugees from Belgium, Italy, Poland and Germany. They naturally gave a rapturous welcome to the new French revolution. Inevitably too there was a revival of the earlier tradition of revolutionary legions of foreign refugees who had fought beside the French revolutionary armies in 1792 and 1793 for the liberation of their fatherland. The Society of German Democrats, which had just been established under the leadership of the poet Georg Herwegh, decided to form a German Revolutionary Legion.

The meeting which took this decision was held on 6 March, the day after Marx's arrival in Paris. Marx attended the meeting and spoke against the idea. He insisted that revolution could not be carried at the point of a bayonet from a foreign country into one's native land. An armed invasion from outside would serve only to strengthen local absolutism, since it would be able to appeal to the patriotic feelings of the masses and rouse them in defence of their national independence. Marx advised the workers to return singly to Germany and work for revolution on their home ground.

The new central committee of the league, which was set up soon afterwards with Marx as president and Schapper as secretary, agreed entirely with Marx. It drew up for the impending German revolution a list of 'Demands of the Communist Party of Germany'. The first of the seventeen points read: 'The whole of Germany will be declared a single,

1. Tocqueville, op. cit., pp. 78–9.

indivisible republic.' The central committee went on to form a German Communist club, which organized the return of hundreds of refugees to Germany. And when revolution broke out on 13 March in Vienna and on 18 March in Berlin—as Marx had foreseen, the 'crow of the Gallic cock' had given the signal—most of the league's members hurried back and were soon at the head of the working-class movement. Marx and Engels went to Cologne and founded the *Neue Rheinische Zeitung*, which became the leading organ of the revolution. Its first number appeared on 1 June 1848.

Marx and Engels now thought that the league had become superfluous. Marx told a meeting of its leading members in Cologne, soon after his arrival, that it was 'not a conspiratorial but a propagandist' organization. 'Under existing conditions, they could make propaganda openly, and there was no need for secrecy, as they enjoyed freedom of the press and of assembly.' He proposed the dissolution of the league, and when Schapper and Moll protested, Marx used the authority delegated to him in Paris to dissolve it himself.[1]

After the defeat of the European revolution, the league was revived in London in the late autumn of 1849. After his expulsion from Cologne in May and from Paris in August 1849, Marx had moved to London, as had the members of the old central committee. Only Moll was missing; he had fallen in the fighting at Baden.

7

The league anticipated an early resumption of revolution, 'called forth by an independent uprising of the French proletariat or through the intervention of the Holy Alliance against the revolutionary Babel', according to the *First Address of the Central Committee to the League*, edited by Marx in March 1850. The *Address* gave clear directions for the conduct of the working class in the next revolution, and ended with the battle-cry, 'the revolution in permanence'. In June 1850 Marx still believed, as he stated in his second *Address*, 'that the early outbreak of a new revolution could not be far away'.[2]

Soon both Engels and Marx began to have their doubts. In a joint investigation into the revival of world trade, they had acknowledged it

1. On the dissolution of the Communist League in 1848, see the very informative statement of Peter Gerhardt Röser, chief among the accused at the Communist trial. It has been taken from the files in the Berlin police headquarters and published as an appendix in Otto Mänchen-Helfen and Boris Nikolaevsky, *Karl und Jenny Marx* (Berlin, 1933), p. 152.

2. The full text of both *Addresses* is published as an appendix to Marx, *Enthüllungen über den Kommunistenprozess zu Köln*.

to be the main reason for the triumph of counter-revolution. The economic crisis of 1847—the 'mother of the revolution'—had been surmounted in 1849. A period of prosperity had begun. This prosperity was, they declared, 'the mother of counter-revolution'. These studies led them to the conclusion that the period of revolutions was temporarily at an end. 'With this general prosperity,' wrote Marx, 'there can be no question of a real revolution. . . . A new revolution is only possible as the result of a new crisis.'[1]

The question of the possibility of an early revolution gave rise to a conflict in the league which culminated in a split at the meeting of the central committee on 15 September 1850.[2] A group led by Schapper and Willich expected a new revolution in the very near future, and demanded that the league should frame its policy accordingly.[3] In the spirit of the Blanquist doctrine of the revolution in permanence—this was the slogan with which the *Address* of March 1850 concluded—they saw in the revolution merely a problem of military strategy and will-power on the part of the resolute leadership. They believed that the working class could win power in the next revolution and could secure its permanent supremacy, providing that the right 'measures' were taken.

This was the lesson they had deduced from the history of the revolutions in 1789, 1830 and 1848. The course of events between 1789 and 1793 had proved that the working people could win if they were united, took up arms, and fought courageously on the streets for political power. July 1830 and February 1848 in Paris, March 1848 in Vienna and Berlin had seemed to confirm the lesson even more strongly. What had happened yesterday could happen again tomorrow. If the proletarian revolution had so far failed, they explained, this was due solely to the 'mistakes' of the leadership.

Schapper and Willich had lived through the battles, the triumphs and the failures of 1848. August Willich, a former Prussian officer, now a fervent revolutionary Socialist, had fought together with Engels in a guerrilla detachment during the Baden-Pfalz campaign. Foremost in his

1. *Neue Rheinische Zeitung. Politisch-ökonomische Revue*, nos. 5 and 6 (1850).

2. For the Minutes of the last meeting of the central committee, see Nikolaevsky, op. cit., pp. 248–52.

3. In a circular to the members of the Communist League, Schapper and Willich gave their own version of the reasons for the split as follows: 'The only difference of principle between us and them [Marx and his comrades], while we were still united, was that they told the people that we should have to be in opposition for at least fifty years, which would mean acting purely as critics. We thought and still think that, given the right organization, our party will be able to put through such measures in the next revolution as to lay the foundation for a workers' society.' The circular, under the title, *Ansprache der Partei Willich für das erste Quartal 1851*, can be found in Appendix XVI to the collection of documents, *Die Kommunistischen Verschwörungen des neunzehnten Jahrhunderts*, vol. I (Berlin, 1853), p. 276, published by the Royal Prussian Directorate of Police, Dr Wermuth and Dr Stieber.

mind was the need for a military dictatorship to be established on the day of revolution. Schapper had explained to Weitling the need for the workers to be 'ready' for revolution. From the events of 1848, however, he had concluded that the intellectual and moral maturity of the leadership was above all the decisive factor.

Schapper and Willich were not the only ones to expect an early recurrence of the revolution. The colonies of French, Italian, Polish, Hungarian and German refugees in London resounded with vehement discussions on the same theme. They drafted revolutionary programmes and debated the composition of revolutionary governments. The poet Gottfried Kinkel, a modest man who nevertheless carried the romantic halo of revolutionary heroism, had the idea of raising a loan in America and England for financing a revolution in Germany. This was enthusiastically supported by the German refugees, and particularly by Schapper, Willich and Weitling.

Marx disdainfully rejected what he considered to be 'playing with revolution'. He did not believe that a revolution could be unleashed simply by the power of a dedicated leadership. It sprang, in his view, from a complex of particular political, economic and social conditions. Nor did he believe that society could leap over the phase of *bourgeois* revolution. 'There can be, for the time being, no talk of achieving Communism; the *bourgeoisie* must first take the rudder,' he declared, in the course of a vehement discussion with Weitling.[1] Marx repeated the same idea in the *Manifesto*. But as early as 1846 he had rejected Weitling's 'playing with revolution' with the remark: 'To arouse fantastic hopes can never relieve the conditions of the suffering; it can lead only to their ruin.'[2]

Marx had been confirmed in these ideas through the experience of revolution and counter-revolution in 1848. 'Louis Blanc had provided the best example,' he told Schapper, 'of the result of coming to power too soon.' His attempt to achieve the 'right to work' through the experiment with 'national workshops' had culminated in the massacre of the Paris workers on 24 June 1848. Marx went on to explain that 'whilst we say to the workers: you have to undergo fifteen, twenty, fifty years of civil war and national wars in order to change the condi-

1. See Weitling's letter to Moses Hess of 31 March 1846 concerning his argument with Marx in *Moses Hess Briefwechsel*, p. 151. The argument took place at a meeting of the Communist Correspondence Committee on 30 March 1846 in Brussels. Those present were Marx, Engels, the Belgian Philippe Gigot and the Germans Louis Heilberg, Sebastian Seiler, Edgar von Westphalen, Wilhelm Weitling and Joseph Weydemeyer. The Russian liberal writer, P. W. Annenkov, attended as a guest.

2. See Annenkov's account of the meeting in Mänchen in Nikolaevsky, op. cit., p. 104.

tions, and to qualify yourselves for governing, they were told instead: we must either come to power at once or retire to our beds'.

The discussion ended with the decision that the two sections of the Communist League should part company. This was the last meeting of the central committee. It was formally transferred to Cologne. Schapper and Willich, supported by a majority of the London members, formed a separate organization.

8

The Communist League had never been a mass organization. Its members, grouped together in small local sections, and committed by their rules to 'revolutionary zeal and vigorous propaganda', had acted as seed-carriers of Socialism in workers' educational, athletic and choral societies. In Schleswig-Holstein and Mecklenburg they had also been active in unions of peasants and wage-earners.

The German governments became alarmed at the extent of Communist propaganda, which they assumed to be centred in London, under the leadership of Marx. In the spring of 1851 the Prussian government considered proposing, jointly with Austria and Russia, that the British government should 'render the chief revolutionaries, whose names are known, ineffective as declared enemies of the European political and social order . . . by deporting them to the colonies'.[1] King Frederick William IV favoured a more realistic, if in his own words less 'above-board', approach. In a letter which he personally wrote to his prime minister, Freiherr von Manteuffel, he ordered 'the public exposure of this network of subversive conspiracy, so that the people of Prussia may derive full value from the spectacle of a plot discovered and, in particular, its perpetrators amply punished'. The king recommended the Prussian chief of police, Wilhelm Stieber, as the man for this somewhat unsavoury task.[2]

1. *Aus den Akten des Deutschen Zentralarchivs II*, in Karl Obermann, *Zur Geschichte des Bundes der Kommunisten 1849 bis 1852* (Berlin, 1955), pp. 66–7. See also the letter from the Austrian Ambassador in London, B. Koller, to his prime minister, Prince Schwarzenberg, on 8 June 1850, about his conversation with the British Home Secretary, Sir George Grey. He had informed the minister that the members of the Communist League, whose leaders were Marx, Engels, Bauer and Willich, 'even discussed regicide', and he suggested that they be prosecuted. According to Koller, Grey replied that 'under our laws, mere discussion of regicide, so long as it does not concern the Queen of England and so long as there is no definite plan, does not constitute sufficient grounds for the arrest of the conspirators'. From the 'Österreichischen Haus-, Hof- und Staatsarchiv', quoted in Ludwig Brügel, *Aus den Londoner Flüchtlingstagen von Karl Marx*, in *Der Kampf*, XVII (1924), p. 237.

2. For the letter, in the king's handwriting, see Mehring, op. cit., p. 165. Frederick Wilhelm really believed that the League was plotting against his own life, as he wrote, in 1849, to Bettina von Arnim. See *Bettina von Arnim und Friedrich*

Stieber was duly given the assignment. An unexpected stroke of luck put him on the trail of eleven members of thc League. They were arrested in May 1851 and brought to trial on 4 October 1852 after a year and a half in prison. As the coach surrounded by dragoons arrived with the prisoners in front of the court-house, they were greeted, according to an eye-witness, with 'a loud, resounding "*Hoch*" from a large crowd of people with bared heads'.[1] The prosecution charged the prisoners with 'having plotted to overthrow the constitution, to arm the citizens and inhabitants for a civil war against the throne and against each other'. In the indictment the state attorney added, as an aggravating factor, the charge that the party of the accused 'went so far . . . as to aim at the suppression of all feelings for God and man'.[2]

As the king had anticipated, the trial lasting five weeks was 'a prolonged spectacle', which revealed, in fact, extraordinarily little. In searching the houses of the accused, the police had found a number of publications, including the *Manifesto* and the Statutes of the Communist League, together with several circulars from the central committee. But none of these documents contained evidence of a 'plot' to foment civil war. Nor could they have done. The League was indeed a secret organization, since after the revolution had been suppressed in Germany no public propaganda for the ideas of Communism was possible. The League was a secret, but in no way conspiratorial, organization. Since the state attorney had no genuine documents with which to establish a plot to overthrow the government, Stieber undertook, most probably on the wishes of the king, to provide the incriminating documents himself. The grotesque story of the forgeries was described by Marx in his *Enthüllungen über den Kommunistenprozess zu Köln*.

On the jury benches sat six aristocrats, four members of the financial aristocracy and two state officials. The forgeries were exposed in the course of the trial. But the jury could not oppose the desire of the king to use the trial as a public demonstration of the retribution in store for plotters, even though no plot had been discovered. Six of the accused were given prison sentences of three to six years, with the loss of civil rights and subsequent police supervision. The others were acquitted. 'A degrading and completely unjust sentence,' wrote Varnhagen von Ense, who could hardly be suspected of treasonable sentiments, in his diary.

Wilhelm VI. Ungedrückte Briefe und Aktenstücke, edited by Ludwig Geiger (Frankfurt am Main, 1902).

1. See the letter from Bermbach to Marx in Mehring, op. cit., p. 165. A. Bermbach was a Cologne notary, a democrat, elected a deputy of the first Prussian House of Representatives in 1849.

2. *Der Kommunistenprozess zu Köln 1852 im Spiegel der zeitgenössischen Presse*, edited by Karl Bittel (Berlin, 1955), pp. 48–50.

The government prepared everything with detestable thoroughness, kept the accused in custody for eighteen months, nominated its own jury and instigated every kind of knavery. . . . Everyone here with any legal knowledge was convinced that the accused could not have been sentenced under existing laws. But what have Prussian judges and Prussian jurymen allowed themselves to become? It causes me a good deal of distress.[1]

Although the trial had a considerable propaganda effect, it still meant the end of the Communist League. On Marx's suggestion, it dissolved itself soon after the sentences were announced. A few months later, the break-away league also faded out. Its former members had scattered. Heinrich Bauer had emigrated to Australia, Weitling, Ewerbeck and Willich to America. Willich became a brigadier-general in the American Civil War, and was severely wounded at the battle of Murfreesboro' in Tennessee. Engels had gone back to his father's textile factory in Manchester. Marx had started work on *Das Kapital*. When, after another twelve years, the International Working Men's Association began life, its general council included from the former members of the Communist League Marx, Engels, Georg Eccarius, Karl Pfänder and Friedrich Lessner.

1. Karl August Varnhagen von Ense, *Tagebücher*, vol. IX, p. 411, quoted in Obermann, op. cit., p. 125.

7 · The Society of Fraternal Democrats

From 1789 to 1848 the social history of England is a dramatic story of working-class revolt against the terrible exploitation resulting from the Industrial Revolution[1] and also against the political repression to which the workers were subjected.

The first wave of revolt, which found organized expression in the Corresponding Society, was inspired, as we saw, by the cosmopolitan egalitarianism of the French Revolution, embodied so notably in the writings of Thomas Paine. There followed, after a gloomy and desperate interlude of reaction, the revolt of the machine-breakers. After that was suppressed, there developed the co-operative Socialist movement of Robert Owen; after its failure, the rebirth of trade unionism; and, finally, the powerful struggle of the Chartists to win for the workers the right to vote.[2]

These were movements of an immature working class, whose mental horizons were still for the most part those of the villages from which farmers and craftsmen, ruined by enclosures, had migrated to the new industrial towns. There for a number of years they felt, puzzled and helpless, the disintegrating and demoralizing pressures of modern capitalism. By trial and error they sought continuously to find effective means of defending themselves against the punitive, almost slave-like conditions which they experienced in the early factories. Out of this struggle against misery and degradation the working class developed the notions of proletarian solidarity, an idea which stemmed from their growing realization that there was no escape from individual wretchedness save through organized struggle as a class.

1. There is a very impressive description in the first volume of *Das Kapital* by Marx, particularly in chs. 8, 12 and 23. The best account of English working-class conditions during the Industrial Revolution is *The Bleak Age* (London, 1934) by J. L. and Barbara Hammond.

2. For these phases in the history of the British working-class movement, see Max Beer, op. cit., Part 2.

The concept of working-class solidarity in one country contained by implication the idea of solidarity on an international basis: the unity of the oppressed of all countries. This message had been conveyed by the first political movement of the working class in England—the Corresponding Society. Revolutionary developments on the Continent caused the idea to revive.

1

The first impulse came from the revolutions in France in July 1830, and in Poland in 1830 and 1831. On the first anniversary of the July Revolution, the workers' paper, the *Poor Man's Guardian*, called on the London workers to celebrate this 'glorious and immortal deed' in a banquet, as a demonstration of the solidarity of the English and French working classes. 'It must always be borne in mind,' ran the appeal, 'that it is the victory of the working classes in the streets of Paris that we want to immortalize in our memory—this victory which led to the freedom of Belgium, Switzerland and glorious Poland, betrayed but still awaiting a triumphant destiny.'[1]

This appeal, and the mass meeting called by the *Poor Man's Guardian* on 1 August 1831, marked the re-emergence of international solidarity among the English working class. The *Poor Man's Guardian* and, later, the *Northern Star*, the official organ of the Chartists, kept the idea alive. The London Working Men's Association, a political organization of Chartists founded by William Lovett in 1836, also embodied the spirit of international working-class solidarity. 'Our oppressors are united; why should we be divided by national and religious prejudice? . . . Without international agreement we shall never be able to free humanity,' ran one of their statements.[2]

London was at that time a sanctuary for many political refugees from France, Italy, Poland and Germany. They had their own organizations and many of their leaders were in touch and on good terms with leading Chartists such as William Lovett, George Julian Harney and Ernest Jones. On the initiative of Karl Schapper of the League of the Just, and the Polish revolutionary, Colonel Louis Oborski, Lovett founded the Society of the Democratic Friends of All Nations at the beginning of 1845, together with a number of Polish, German and French *émigrés*. This was the first international organization in England.

It did not last long. Lovett, a carpenter by trade, was a highly skilled worker, a convinced Socialist and disciple of Robert Owen. He drafted

1. See Theodor Rothstein, *Aus der Vorgeschichte der Internationale*, supplement to *Die Neue Zeit*, no. 17 (1913), p. 3.
2. Beer, op. cit., vol. I, p. 275.

the series of demands for working-class freedom which came to be known as the Charter, and from which the movement derived its name. Inside the movement, the leadership of which he shared for a time with Feargus O'Connor, Lovett expounded the idea of 'moral force' as an instrument in the fight for freedom, and the tactic of an alliance with the middle class in the campaign for a general extension of the franchise.

The inaugural manifesto of the Society of the Democratic Friends of All Nations which Lovett drew up was in the same spirit. It summoned 'all the oppressed' to a united struggle against 'citadels, armies and prisons'. It appealed to the common humanity of all classes and rejected, in accordance with Lovett's humanitarian, pacifist approach, any revolutionary methods. But this was not the spirit animating the refugees. They aimed at a new revolution and the forcible overthrow of the ruling classes and governments which had exiled them. The revolutionary refugees withdrew from the society. It collapsed soon after it had been formed.

In the same year, however, the Society of Fraternal Democrats was established. Founded on the initiative of Harney, it has gone down in history as a forerunner of the International.[1]

George Julian Harney (1817–97) was one of the most striking figures produced by the British working class. He was an orphan. His father had been a merchant sailor, and he himself felt drawn to the sea. From the age of eleven to fourteen he attended a school for seamen, but could not stand up to the harsh conditions and gave up the sea after his first trip. He became a newspaper-boy on the *Poor Man's Guardian*. But distributing a working-class paper was a hazardous occupation. Henry Hetherington, who founded the paper, published it in defiance of the law. In order to discourage the sale of working-class papers, a stamp duty of 4*d.* was levied on each copy. The *Poor Man's Guardian* appeared unstamped, and at the top of the front page was the announcement: 'Founded contrary to law, to try the power of right against might.' Every copy had to be smuggled to its readers through a network of police agents. Anyone caught distributing the paper went to gaol. When still scarcely seventeen Harney received his first sentence, and at the age of nineteen his third, for a term of six months. Though conditions in English prisons were at that time diabolical, he faced them without fear. At his third appearance before a judge he announced, without trepidation, that he would again distribute the paper illegally on his release. It was his duty to do so, he explained, in the struggle against the 'tax on knowledge' which the ruling class had imposed on the workers.

It was the *Poor Man's Guardian* which made Harney, while still a

1. For the best account in German of the history of the Fraternal Democrats, see Rothstein, op. cit.

young man, into an enthusiastic Socialist. The paper was edited by James Bronterre O'Brian (1805–64), a son of well-to-do parents who had given up a promising career as a lawyer in order to serve the working class. This he did in conditions of deepest poverty. Intellectually, he was the most important of the Chartist leaders. A brilliant writer and an effective speaker, he was the man who first tried to give Chartism a coherent Socialist ideology. Among the Chartists, who held him in high esteem as a philosopher, he was known as 'the schoolmaster'.

Harney admired him greatly. He read every word O'Brian wrote and gladly accepted his intellectual leadership. O'Brian's Socialism was rooted in the Jacobin traditions of the French Revolution. He saw in Robespierre an ideal leader of the people. He wrote an elegy to him and a small fragment of his biography. From the teachings of Babeuf, O'Brian derived his theory of Socialism. He also translated Buonarroti's book on Babeuf and the Conspiracy of the Equals. O'Brian's enthusiasm for the French Revolution was transmitted to Harney, who took Marat, Babeuf and Thomas Paine as his models. In the spirit of these men he founded in 1837 an organization of left-wing Chartism, the London Democratic Association. In the inaugural manifesto which he wrote for the Association, Harney gave as its task the fight for working-class emancipation by 'disseminating the principles propagated by that great philosopher and redeemer of mankind, the immortal Thomas Paine'.[1]

The organization which Harney served as secretary, and which soon embraced thousands of London dockers, weavers and Irish labourers, was to fulfil in his view the same functions as the Jacobin clubs in the French Revolution—that is to say, it was to push forward the broader Chartist movement towards a social revolution. And, as the French Revolution had championed the cause of humanity, Chartism was to be the vanguard of working-class freedom all over the world. The movement's aim, he insisted, must be 'freedom in a world of republics'.

Soon after founding the London Democratic Association, Harney began his extraordinarily swift rise as leader of the Chartist left. Two years later when he was still scarcely twenty-three he was elected delegate to the first Chartist Convention by the workers of three large industrial districts. In 1843 he became editor of the *Northern Star*, and in the same year Engels visited him in the newspaper's office. The two men became friends, and it is clear that Engels, who now began to write for the paper, strengthened the notions of international working-class solidarity and encouraged in the mind of Harney the idea of an international workers' organization—which was to become the Society of Fraternal Democrats.

Harney announced the society's formation at a banquet held on

1. Quoted in A. R. Schoyen, *The Chartist Challenge—a Portrait of George Julian Harney* (London, 1958), p. 14.

22 September 1845 to celebrate the anniversary of the first French Republic. The banquet, which had been called by the Society of the Democratic Friends of All Nations, meeting under the presidency of the Chartist poet Thomas Cooper, had itself a distinctly international character. Speakers included representatives of the French, Polish and German refugees, including Moll and Weitling.

The Society of Fraternal Democrats was formally established on 15 March 1846. To avoid any suggestion that it might be a rival to the Chartist movement, it was first loosely organized and without rules. Its object was 'the mutual enlightenment of its members and the propagation of the great principle, contained in the motto of the society, that "all men are brothers" '. Its programme was formulated by Harney at a meeting to celebrate the first anniversary of its foundation, in the following solemn declaration:

> We renounce, repudiate and condemn all political hereditary inequalities and distinctions of caste; we declare that the earth with all its natural productions is the common property of all; we declare that the present state of society which permits idlers and schemers to monopolize the fruits of the earth and the productions of industry, and compels the working class to labour for inadequate rewards, and even condemns them to social slavery, destitution and degradation, is essentially unjust. . . . Our moral creed is to receive our fellow-men without regard to country, as members of one family—the human race, and as citizens of one commonwealth—the world.[1]

Harney was secretary of the Fraternal Democrats, and as editor of the *Northern Star* he placed this working-class paper at the disposal of the society. He published their declarations, the speeches made at their meetings and the articles of Engels on the Socialist movement in Europe. The paper became, in fact, a powerful means of propaganda for the idea of international working-class solidarity. Harney was no orator, but in spite of this he was one of the most popular speakers among the Chartist leaders. At meetings he campaigned tirelessly to spread the idea of the Fraternal Democrats; he formed local branches and tried to win the co-operation of the Chartist leadership. Philip McGrath, president of the National Charter Association, and two other members of its executive, joined the committee of the Fraternal Democrats, and by the middle of 1847 the society had local branches in more than twenty towns.

The Fraternal Democrats met regularly on the first Monday of each month. Every important revolutionary anniversary such as the storming of the Bastille, the announcement of the first French Republic, and the Polish insurrection, as well as contemporary revolutionary stirrings such as the uprising in Cracow, the revolution in Geneva and the rising of the Portuguese Junta, became occasions for meetings and proclamations

1. Quoted in G. D. H. Cole, *Chartist Portraits* (London, 1941), p. 284.

which were reported far beyond England in the democratic societies and newspapers of Europe.

Once the reputation of the Fraternal Democrats was firmly established, the society developed along more formal lines. The rules agreed to in December 1847 laid down a membership fee of a shilling. The general secretary and the corresponding secretaries of each affiliated national organization formed the executive. The first executive consisted of the corresponding secretaries, Julian Harney for England, Karl Schapper for Germany, Jean Michelot for France, Peter Holm for Scandinavia, August Nemeth for Hungary, Henri Hubert for Switzerland and Louis Oborski for Poland, together with the Chartist leaders Philip McGrath, Ernest Jones, Thomas Clark, Charles Doyle and William Dixon.

In its organizational structure the Society of Fraternal Democrats was a complete prototype of the later, historic International. As later, on the General Council of the First International, the national sections were represented on the central council of the Fraternal Democrats by their corresponding secretaries, each in direct touch with his own section.

In aim and spirit, the organization of the Fraternal Democrats was a true forerunner of the historic International. It was a genuine workers' International, which upheld the ideal of international solidarity. Two years before the publication of the *Communist Manifesto* and two decades before the founding of the historic International, the Fraternal Democrats proclaimed the idea of a militant association of workers throughout the world.

To a meeting of German Communists in February 1848, Harney expounded the Fraternal Democratic conception of international working-class solidarity. 'I appeal,' he declared, 'to the oppressed classes in every country to unite for the common cause.' But what was the common cause? Was it the liberation of Poland from Russian rule, or the freedom of Italy from Austria? Harney explained that 'freedom from the Russian and Austrian yokes is not the end of the matter. We do not need a King Czartoryski.[1] We need no kingdom of Italy. We need the sovereignty of the people in both countries.' But who were 'the people'? The people, he continued, were the workers and peasants, and the cause of the people was 'the cause of labour, of labour enslaved and exploited. . . . In all countries there are people who grow corn and eat potatoes, who make clothes and wear rags, who build houses and live in wretched hovels. . . . Do not the workers of all nations have the same reasons for complaint and the same causes of distress? Have they not, therefore, the same just cause?'

The idea that the cause of the working class in all countries was

1. Leader of the revolutionary Polish aristocracy.

inexorably linked—the idea which inspired the historic International—was vigorously expressed, rather earlier, by the Fraternal Democrats. To a large meeting called in sympathy with the Portuguese revolution, Harney declared: 'A blow against freedom on the Tagus is a blow against all friends of freedom on the Thames; a success for republicanism in France would seal the fate of tyranny in other countries, and the victory of the English democratic Charter would lead to the liberation of millions in the whole of Europe.'

The Society of Fraternal Democrats established a close working relationship with the left-wing revolutionary refugee organizations in London—the German Communist Workers' Educational Society, the Union of French Democrats and the left wing of the Polish Democratic Society. It set up a Democratic Committee for the Regeneration of Poland for the special purpose of popularizing the Polish revolution in England. Harney became secretary, the Chartist leader O'Connor treasurer, and Hetherington and Ernest Jones, as well as Schapper and Oborski, became members.

The first international organization with which the Fraternal Democrats made contact overseas was the Democratic Association (Association Démocratique) in Brussels, which was led by Marx. It was Marx who took the initiative. In the summer of 1847 the first workers' representative, O'Connor, had been elected to the British Parliament. In a letter signed by Marx, Engels and Philip Guigot, the Brussels Democratic Association congratulated the Fraternal Democrats on the election victory and declared their solidarity with the Chartists. In their reply the Fraternal Democrats referred to 'an impending union of the democrats of all nations in the great struggle for political and social equality'. In fact they celebrated the second anniversary of their establishment with an appeal to the democrats of Europe to arrange an international congress of working-class democrats—in opposition to the *bourgeois* International Free Trade Congress which was then meeting. Marx welcomed the proposal. He came over to London as a delegate from the Brussels Democrats to the meeting in commemoration of the Polish rising of 1830 organized by the Fraternal Democrats.

The anniversary meeting took place on 29 November 1847, just before the congress of the Communist League. Schapper read out the message from the Brussels Democrats. Then Marx spoke, to tumultuous applause. He told the meeting that he had been instructed by the Brussels Democrats to propose the calling of a congress, together with their brothers in London, for the following year in Brussels, a 'congress of the workers of all nations to establish freedom throughout the world'. Belgian Democrats and English Chartists were the real exponents of democracy, and if the English could succeed with their Charter,' it would open the way for the freedom of all'. 'Workers of England,' Marx concluded, 'fulfil this mission and you will be praised as the liberators of the whole of humanity.'

In reply to Marx's message, an address from the Fraternal Democrats to the Brussels Democrats declared:

'Your representative, our friend and brother Marx, will tell you with what enthusiasm we welcomed his appearance and the reading of your address.... We accept with the liveliest feelings of satisfaction the alliance you have offered us. . . . We recommended the formation of a democratic congress of all nations, and we are happy to hear that you have publicly made the same proposal. The conspiracy of kings must be answered with a conspiracy of the peoples. . . . We are convinced that we must address ourselves to the real people, to the proletarians, to the men who drip sweat and blood daily under the pressure of the existing social system, if we are to achieve general fraternity.'[1]

2

The international congress which was due to assemble in Brussels on 25 October 1848 on the proposal of the Fraternal Democrats was frustrated owing to the events of that year. The outbreak of revolution in France and Germany in February and March 1848 bore witness to the pressures which had been building up since the spring of 1847. Switzerland was swept by a wave of revolutionary feeling; in Italy there were actual outbreaks; Ireland was simmering; and in England the Chartists were preparing for a decisive battle.

On the day that the revolution broke out in Paris, the Fraternal Democrats were holding a mass meeting to commemorate the Cracow uprising. In London they did not yet know of the developments in Paris. Harney however felt confident enough by then to announce the imminent outbreak of the European revolution. He added that its only worthwhile aim was the emancipation of the workers from economic exploitation. The mass of the people must conquer political power so that 'those who till the soil are also their own masters'. Up to that time, the workers had shed their blood in all revolutions, while the *bourgeoisie* had enjoyed the benefits. The time had come for the rule of the *bourgeoisie* to be overthrown.

The Fraternal Democrats were thrown into feverish excitement by the outbreak of revolution in France. An eye-witness described the scene when, in the middle of their meeting, news of the abdication of Louis-Philippe and the proclamation of the French Republic was brought to them. 'Frenchmen, Germans, Poles, Magyars sprang to their

1. Franz Mehring, *Karl Marx: the Story of His Life* (translated by Edward FitzGerald, London, 1936), pp. 142-3.

feet, embraced, shouted and gesticulated in the wildest enthusiasm. . . . Flags were caught from the walls, to be waved exultantly amidst cries of "*Hoch! Eljen! Vive la République!*" Then . . . the whole assemblage . . . with linked arms and colours flying, marched to the meeting-place of the Westminster Chartists.'[1]

A few days later, a mass meeting called by the Fraternal Democrats met to celebrate the revolution. It decided on a message of congratulations to be sent to the provisional government of France. Harney, Jones and Philip McGrath, president of the Chartist executive, were selected to deliver the message. The delegation, joined by Schapper, Moll and Bauer, representing the Communist League, arrived in Paris on 4 March. Next day it was received in the name of the government by Ledru-Rollin, Louis Garnier-Pagès and Armand Marrast. The delegation also took part in the famous meeting of the German colony, under the chairmanship of Herwegh, on 6 March, when they met Marx.

3

The enthusiasm generated by the French revolution gripped the entire working class. England was suffering from a serious economic crisis in the 1840s, known to social historians as the 'hungry forties'. On the achievement of the Charter—the right of the workers to be represented in Parliament—the workers built their hopes of ending their misery. Twice, in 1839 and in 1842, the government had rejected petitions carrying millions of signatures, calling for the general extension of the franchise. The revolutionary events in Europe touched off once again a powerful movement to secure the Charter. Placards on the walls of London announced meetings in support of the French Revolution under the slogan: 'For the Republic in France, for the Charter in England!' A series of stormy, open-air meetings by night were held in Trafalgar Square in the heart of London, and in fields and open places in the outlying districts, since no meeting-hall in London was big enough to hold the huge crowds which flocked to the demonstrations. Manchester, Glasgow, Plymouth, Newark and other towns saw scenes of tumult during this period. Signatures were again collected for a petition. The executive called a convention in London for 3 April, to consider the next steps.

Forty-two delegates from all parts of England and Scotland attended the Convention. Among them were O'Connor, Harney, Jones and O'Brian. The Convention at once expressed the principles on which the petition was based in the following declaration: 'Labour is the source of all wealth. The people are the source of all political power. The worker

1. Schoyen, op. cit., p. 157.

has the right to the produce of his labour. Taxation without parliamentary representation is tyranny. The resources and economic means of a country are best developed and administered most advantageously by means of laws which are made by the representatives of the working and the industrial classes. In recognition of these principles the Chartists demand that the People's Charter should become the law of the land.'[1]

The Convention then declared itself in permanent session and called on the workers to gather on 10 April at Kennington Common, a large open space in the working-class district in south London, and to march in procession from there to Westminster to hand in the petition.

Both the government and the middle classes were deeply disturbed. All over Europe, from the streets of Calais to the plains of Hungary, the people had risen in revolt. Would the revolutionary flood not spread to England in turn? The middle classes were afraid that the demonstration planned by the Chartist Convention would be the signal for revolution. Lord Campbell, a member of the government, conveyed the mood of the *bourgeoisie* in a letter to his brother the day before the Chartist demonstration: 'This is perhaps the last time I write to you before the Republic is established.'[2]

The government prepared for a decisive battle. On 7 April they issued a proclamation declaring the Chartist Convention an illegal organization, and warned people not to take part in the demonstration. At the same time they declared martial law over London, turning the capital into an armed camp. The troops of the Southern Command were concentrated in London; marines guarding home waters were alerted; reliable elements were given arms, 170,000 volunteers joining the auxiliary police as 'special constables'; the Duke of Wellington, victor at the battle of Waterloo, was given command of the army. The Tower of London, the Bank of England and government offices were fortified with sandbags and the larger shops were closed. Wellington blocked the bridges leading from the working-class suburbs in the south to the centre of the city. On the day before the demonstration, the *Morning Chronicle* warned the Chartists: 'Great masses of cavalry and infantry, supported by artillery battalions, stand ready for a signal to intervene. . . .'

Despite the warning, a crowd of about 100,000 gathered at Kennington Common on 10 April. Before they could open the meeting, however, a police officer arrived. He told O'Connor and McGrath that, while the government did not object to the meeting being held, it could not allow the demonstrators to march on Parliament, since even the suggestion

1. Max Beer, *A History of British Socialism* (London, 1940). The English edition of Beer's *Geschichte des Sozialismus in England* is not a mere translation of the German original but a newly written book with partly different material.
2. Raymond Postgate, *Story of a Year: 1848* (London, 1955), p. 118.

of intimidating Parliament was a punishable offence under existing laws.

There had been a good deal of revolutionary speech-making at the meetings held prior to the demonstration. The crowds assembling at Kennington Common expected revolutionary action. But the Convention had no plans for revolution. The people were unarmed, and in view of the massive display of armed strength by government forces, the Chartist leaders gave up their plans for a mass demonstration. O'Connor, the popular hero, begged the crowd to disperse peacefully, which it did.

The petition, as later revealed by a parliamentary commission, had 1,975,469 signatures. It was taken to Parliament in three carriages by members of the Chartist executive. But Parliament postponed a debate on the matter for fifteen months when, by a majority of 222 to 17, the petition was rejected for the third time.

4

This abject end to the demonstration of 10 April broke the back of the Chartist movement. The third attempt at forcing the Charter through Parliament had failed abysmally, and the disillusion of the workers was intense. In despair, the Chartist leaders tried to rebuild the workers' confidence and inspire them to continue the struggle. They called mass meetings in the provinces, made inspiring speeches and threatened to organize a National Guard. In some places there were violent outbreaks. The government had the Chartist leaders arrested, among them Ernest Jones, who was sentenced to two years' imprisonment for 'incitement'. The Chartist movement, defeated, persecuted, humiliated, and deprived of its leaders, fell to pieces.

Its decline was hastened by the defeat of the revolution in Europe. The English workers had followed with intense interest the course of the revolution in France, Germany, Austria, Italy and Hungary. Its triumph, they fully expected, would be followed by their own. These hopes too were now dashed. During the year or two following 1848, the once victorious leaders of the European revolution were forced to seek asylum in England—among them, Marx and Engels. In the inaugural address which he later wrote for the First International, Marx described the moral effects of the failure of the European revolution on the English workers, as he had seen it at first hand. 'The defeat of the continental working classes . . . soon spread its contagious effects to this side of the Channel. . . . The rout of their continental brothers unmanned the English working classes, and broke their faith in their own cause. . . . Never before seemed the English working class so thoroughly reconciled to a state of political nullity.' As late as 1861, Richard Cobden, one of the pioneers of *bourgeois* radicalism, was found complaining: 'I cannot understand why the workers remain so quiet under the taunts and insults offered them. Have they no Spartacus among them to head a revolt of the slave class against their political tormentors? I suppose it is the reaction from the follies of Chartism which keeps the present generation so quiet.' The collapse of the working-class movement was inevitably a serious blow to the Society of Fraternal Democrats. In addition the government had passed an Aliens Law, directed against the political refugees, empowering the Home Secretary to expel any foreigner without more ado as 'undesirable'. When the executive of the Fraternal Democrats met in May 1848, it found it advisable to change the rules and to formally release foreign members from all obligations towards the society.

Harney, undaunted and tireless, still kept the idea of international working-class solidarity alive in the pages of the *Northern Star*. He was sure, as he wrote in an address to the Fraternal Democrats on the second anniversary of the February revolution in March 1850, that a new revolution on the Continent was very near, a revolution 'which is destined to bring about the destruction of class rule and class slavery'.

But the addresses and meetings of the society were becoming few and far between. The Fraternal Democrats had once been able to fill large halls with their supporters, but by July 1850 their membership had sunk to 261. They had one more success, with a mass rally to welcome Kossuth, who arrived in England as a political refugee in the autumn of 1851. But this was their last effective appearance and the society had ceased to exist by about the end of 1852.

The Society of Fraternal Democrats was the first organized expression of international working-class solidarity, the first international workers' organization to be rooted in England, itself the centre of the strongest Labour movement of the day. Rightly, Theodor Rothstein ends his account of the society's history with the remark that, but for the frustration which stemmed from the triumph of reaction in 1848, the Society of Fraternal Democrats would have developed into the First International.

8 · The International Association

1

The collapse of Chartism played a considerable part in weakening the Fraternal Democrats. A conflict between the two leaders, Harney and Jones, led to its utter ruin.

The conflict, which degenerated into petty personal hostility, was based on the different conceptions held by the two men on the future of the Labour movement. When Chartism collapsed and the hoped-for revival of revolution in Europe failed to materialize, Harney lost faith in the possibility of a purely political working-class movement. He ceased to believe in a future for Chartism, to which he had given so much of his enthusiasm and devotion since his youth. He left the executive in 1852, and soon afterwards broke with the movement completely. A few years later, still scarcely forty, he withdrew from all political activity, first moving to the lonely island of Jersey and finally emigrating to America. But he never abandoned his basic loyalty to Chartism and Socialism. In 1869 he wrote from Boston to the First International's General Council,[1] declaring his adhesion. But for the last forty years of his life, in which the working-class movement gradually rose to new levels of organization and militancy, he played no active part.

In contrast, Jones continued to believe in a Chartist revival. At the end of his two-year sentence in July 1850, and in spite of the fact that his health was broken, he at once flung himself into a propaganda tour of England and Scotland. Everywhere he was received with overwhelming enthusiasm. In Halifax, where he had stood for Parliament and whose workers had sent him as a delegate to the Chartist Convention, a mass demonstration of 10,000 turned out to welcome him. According to a Press report, such an assembly had 'rarely been known in Halifax',[2]

1. Minutes of the General Council, 4 May 1869.

2. John Saville, *Ernest Jones, Chartist* (London, 1952), p. 39. For a short but very sympathetic account of Jones's life, see Cole, *Chartist Portraits*.

and his reception served to strengthen his faith in the future of Chartism.

Ernest Jones (1819–69) was well liked and deeply respected among the working class. He was among other things a poet of quite considerable talent. In their power to move and inspire, his Chartist songs were hardly inferior to the freedom songs of Herwegh and Freiligrath. They were songs of battle, declaimed and sung at hundreds of Labour meetings. The charm, beauty and depth of feeling in Jones's poetry were widely recognized by contemporary critics. But his great reputation among the British working class was not due solely to his gifts as a poet. He was both a brilliant journalist and a powerful public speaker. His writings and speeches conveyed a warmth of feeling for the working-class cause which evoked a deep and genuine response. This was in spite of the fact that Jones was not, by origin, a man of the people. He came from an aristocratic family. His father was a cavalry officer who, after being injured in Wellington's Spanish campaign, had entered the service of the Duke of Cumberland, subsequently King of Hanover. The Duke was Ernest's godfather. He grew up in the atmosphere of high conservatism and court which permeated his home, and was educated at the aristocratic college of St Michael in Lüneburg. When he was eighteen he left Germany, where he had been born, and came to England with his family. He studied law, became a barrister, married the daughter of a rich country gentleman related to the Earl of Derby, was presented to the Queen—in short, lived as a well-to-do gentleman in the world of wealth and power.

By accident he acquired the *Northern Star* at the beginning of 1846, and from that moment was a convert to Chartism. He became a close colleague of O'Connor and was soon one of the most popular among the Chartist leaders. Like a great many of his colleagues he was imprisoned in 1848. He spent two years in solitary confinement shut up in a small cell without table or chair. For nineteen months of the time he was not even allowed books, pen, ink or paper, and was subjected to the barbaric régime of silence then imposed in English prisons. For uttering a word or even for smiling he had to spend three days in the dark cell on bread and water. Two of the Chartists sentenced at the same time died of exhaustion in prison, and a third soon after his release. While he was in the prison hospital, Jones learned that he could earn his release in return for a promise to abandon politics. He refused the offer.

Ernest Jones lived in the deepest poverty. The fortune he had inherited was lost in the *People's Paper*, which he founded in 1852 (Marx, at first, helped him to edit the paper and subsequently wrote for it), and his wife was disinherited by her family. W. E. Adams described in his *Memoirs* how when he saw Jones at a meeting in 1857, 'the pinched face and the threadbare garments told of trial and suffering. A shabby coat buttoned up close round the throat seemed to conceal the poverty to which a too faithful adherence to a lost cause had reduced him.'[1] He declined an income of £2,000 which one of his uncles offered on condition that he gave up his work for the Charter. To his dying breath he remained true to the cause of Socialism and the working class. Both Marx and Engels had a sincere regard for him. The news of his death—he died on his fiftieth birthday in January 1869—caused, as Marx wrote to Engels at the time, 'deep dismay in our household, naturally enough, as he was one of the few old friends'.[2] He died in Manchester, and many thousands of workers marched behind his coffin.

The propaganda tour which Jones had undertaken after his release from prison failed to revive the Chartist movement. The struggling trade unions had lost all faith in political action and after the fiasco of 10 April they wanted to hear nothing more of Chartism. Even the most prominent leaders such as O'Connor, Harney and O'Brian had dropped away. By the end of 1852 Jones remained the solitary leader of the small band still faithful to the movement. He re-formed the executive, provided Chartism with an organ in the *People's Paper*, and in an attempt to organize the working class—Chartists, trade unionists and member of co-operative societies—into one united body, convened a 'Parliament of Labour' in Manchester in March 1854.

The idea he put forward was that the 'Labour Parliament' should function as the political instrument of the working class, as Parliament was an instrument of the ruling class. It should be in permanent session and look after the interests of the workers. It was to direct trade-union and political struggles, finance strikes as acts of working-class solidarity, and develop co-operative societies with the savings of working people.

It was a bold but utopian idea. But even Marx, for whom the failure of the European revolution had been a deeply sobering experience, sent an exuberant letter to the 'Labour Parliament', which elected him an honorary delegate at its opening session. 'The mere assembling of such a Parliament,' he wrote, 'marks a new epoch in the history of the world. The news of this great fact will arouse the hopes of the working classes throughout Europe and America. . . . If the Labour Parliament proves true to the idea that called it into life, some future historian will have to record that there existed in the year 1854 two Parliaments in England, a Parliament in London, and a Parliament at Manchester—a Parliament of the rich and a Parliament of the poor. . . .'[3] These hopes remained unfulfilled, and the 'Parliament of the poor' lapsed after a few weeks.

1. Saville, op. cit., p. 66.
2. *Marx-Engels Briefwechsel*, vol. IV, p. 181.
3. For the complete text of this rather lengthy letter, see Saville, op. cit., pp. 274–5.

But later in the same year the idea of an international organization of the working class was revived. The Crimean War, which started in October 1853 with a declaration of war by Turkey against Russia, stirred England to the depths. Both the *bourgeoisie* and the workers hated Russian despotism. Liberals and Radicals, Chartists and Socialists, Marx and Jones pressed the government to help Turkey in her war against Russia, against the Russia which Marx had been denouncing since 1848 as 'the great bastion of European reaction'. A passionate surge of national feeling forced a reluctant government to declare war on Russia in March 1854.[1] But Britain had as her ally in the war against Russian autocracy the France of Louis Napoleon, the man who had seized power in a *coup d'état*, drowned all protests in blood and erected his throne over the dead body of the French Republic. Up to the signing of the Anglo-French military alliance, he had been regarded by liberal opinion in England as the incarnation of evil. But now that he was an ally, liberal England was ready on the whole to forget his misdeeds and make its peace with him.

However, English Socialists and some at least among the middle-class liberals had not forgotten Napoleon's misdeeds. When it was known in the autumn of 1845 that Armand Barbès, Blanqui's comrade-in-arms, had been pardoned after years of imprisonment, and that Louis Napoleon was about to visit England, Jones called for a committee which would invite Barbès to England and at the same time protest publicly against Napoleon's visit. The new organization was established under the name of the Welcome and Protest Committee. It called a meeting on 4 December, the anniversary of the massacre on the streets of Paris two days after Napoleon's *coup d'état*, to 'welcome a famous refugee and protest against a dishonourable tyrant'. A few weeks later, the Englishmen on the committee were joined by delegates of the Socialist groups of refugees from France, Germany and Poland. This committee was the nucleus of the 'International Association'.[2]

The International Committee made its first public appearance on 27 February 1855 with a mass meeting in St Martin's Hall, the Hall in which the First International was to be founded nine years later. The Russian revolutionary Alexander Herzen, the French Socialist Alfred Talandier, the Chartist leader George Jacob Holyoake, all spoke; and letters from Barbès, Victor Hugo and Stanislas Worzell were read to the meeting. The resolution, which was moved by the leading Chartist,

1. Kingsley Martin in *The Triumph of Lord Palmerston* describes the popular pressure which forced England to undertake the Crimean War against Russia.

2. For a documented account of the origin and history of the Association, see A. Müller-Lehning, 'The International Association, 1855–9', *International Review of Social History*, vol. III (1938).

James Finlen, declared that every alliance 'with despots and criminals such as Franz Joseph of Austria, Louis Napoleon Bonaparte of France and Nicholas of Russia is an infamous disgrace'. It proposed the formation of a permanent International Association, to serve as the core of an 'alliance of peoples', and suggested that an international conference be called 'to proclaim and propagate the principles of a democratic and social republic'.

Jones, who presided at the meeting, appealed in his opening speech to the 'men of Europe'. 'Kings have invented the idea of hostile nationalities so as to split the unity of the peoples,' he declared. 'But democracy shines over all nations like the sun, whose rays never change their colour, irrespective of whether they fall on France or on England, on Germans or on Poles. We are therefore the soldiers of democracy, the vanguard of the world army of liberation.'

Jones then expounded the 'three great and solemn purposes' for which the International Association intended to struggle: 'to protest against alliance with tyrants, and the use of our name in those alliances; to help the oppressed nationalities win their freedom; to proclaim and promote the sovereign rights of Labour, that uncrowned but only legitimate monarch of the world'.

Counter-revolution under the Habsburg Emperor, the Russian Tsar and the King of Prussia had destroyed the national liberation movements of 1848 and 1849 and brought Hungary, Poland and Italy once again under alien rule. In the subject nations, the aristocracy and the *bourgeoisie*, as well as the workers, struggled for freedom against foreign domination. But the aim of the aristocracy and *bourgeoisie* in the national liberation struggle was limited to national independence, with no suggestion of social or democratic reforms. 'Our further duty is to restore the oppressed nations to independence,' continued Jones. 'But what independence? Independence from the aristocrat and the usurer within, as well as the Tsar or Emperor without. Better no Poland than a royalist or aristocratic one.'

Then Jones explained the social significance of national liberation movements. 'For us, nation is *nothing*, man is *all*,' he declared. 'For us the oppressed nationalities form but one: the universal poor of every land, that struggle for life against the nation of the rich, that mighty race of which every man gives health, labour, life unto society. . . . We begin tonight no mere crusade against an aristocracy. We are not here to pull one tyranny down only that another may live the stronger. We are against the tyranny of capital as well.'[1]

1. Saville, op. cit., pp. 58–9.

2

Chief among the refugees' organizations in England which had contributed to the foundation of the International Committee was the Commune Révolutionnaire. It had been formed soon after Louis Napoleon's *coup d'état* by Félix Pyat, a left-republican member of the French National Assembly, in 1848. To this body belonged left-wing Radical republicans, Blanquists and Socialists, including G. Jourdain, Alfred Talandier and Alexander Besson, all of whom later joined the General Council of the First International. The Commune Révolutionnaire was in touch with revolutionary secret societies in France, with the German Communist Workers' Educational Society in London, with the Union of Polish Socialists and with the Chartists. They had a propaganda organ in *L'Homme*, published by Victor Hugo in Jersey and disseminated secretly from there in France.

The International Committee held weekly business meetings; in the tradition of the Fraternal Democrats it organized, together with the Socialist refugee organizations, international rallies to commemorate revolutionary anniversaries. One such meeting held with the Commune Révolutionnaire on 22 September 1855 had an unexpected outcome. Félix Pyat had read out an 'Open Letter' to Queen Victoria, which denounced the misdeeds of Louis Napoleon in scathing terms and protested against England's being allied to the usurper. The letter, which appeared in *L'Homme*, was criticized by *The Times*. This provoked vehement attacks by English Conservatives on the French revolutionary immigrants. The government accordingly ordered the expulsion from Jersey of three men associated with *L'Homme* and the arrest of a Polish refugee for distributing the 'Open Letter' as a leaflet. Victor Hugo, after issuing a manifesto protesting against the expulsion of his colleagues, demonstratively left Jersey for the neighbouring island of Guernsey. Hugo was the most outstanding of the French refugees. When after Napoleon's *coup d'état* he had sought asylum in England, he had been warmly welcomed by English liberals and radicals. These sections of opinion were now appalled by this gross violation of the right of asylum. Edward Miall, the Liberal M.P., called a protest meeting in St Martin's Hall on 12 November at which Ernest Jones made a passionate speech. He published the 'Open Letter' in his *People's Paper*, and the International Committee distributed it as a leaflet. In response to a number of protest meetings, the government stopped its persecution of French refugees and released the arrested Pole.

At the beginning of April 1856 a deputation of French workers arrived in London to deliver an 'Address from the workers of France to their brothers, the workers of England'. They were delegates of a Paris organization, inspired by Proudhon's doctrine of co-operative Socialism. Their address proposed the formation of a 'League of Workers of all Nations', aimed at superseding capitalism by the development of producers' and consumers' co-operative societies. O'Brian welcomed the proposal. He took the chair at a public meeting which decided to send a message of thanks from the British workers to the French workers. A provisional committee was set up with the intention of calling into existence a genuine workers' International. But then nothing happened.

Yet the idea of a workers' International suggested by the French seems to have stimulated the International Committee to form one themselves. A few weeks later, at its first annual conference, the Committee considered transforming itself into an International Association. At a meeting on 10 August 1856, held in conjunction with the French Commune Révolutionnaire, the new international body was established.

The resolution passed at this meeting declared that the French Commune Révolutionnaire, the German Communist Workers' Educational Society, the Union of Polish Socialists and the Society of Chartists had joined together in an International Association, for mutual support in their work for the 'triumph of the universal democratic and social republic'. The four organizations further pledged themselves to 'promote among the people of all nations the organization of national socialist and revolutionary associations; to weld them by all available means into one general association so that international propaganda may from the power of unity . . . derive great gains, so that they could prepare for future revolution. That success was denied them in the past, because they ignored and made no use of the law of solidarity without which neither the individual nor the nation could be emancipated.'

The structure of the International Association was taken over from the Fraternal Democrats and was adopted in its turn by the First International. The Council of the Association, known as the Central International Committee, consisted of five delegates each representing an affiliated national organization. London was the seat of the central committee, which had the responsibility of convening an annual general meeting, to which it submitted a report on its activity. Any ten members —a *décurie*—could form a local branch. The membership fee was 6*d.* a year.[1]

Lehning's account of the Association contains the names of a number of Germans active on the Central Committee. They included Bernard Becker, who later worked with Lassalle and, after the latter's death, was for a short time president of his General Association of

1. For the Statutes of the International Association, see Müller-Lehning, op. cit., pp. 263–6.

German Workers; Hugo Hillmann, later a delegate from Elberfeld-Barmen and Solingen to the foundation congress of the German General Workers' Association at Leipzig; and A. Scherzer, a friend of Weitling and former member of the Paris branch of the Communist League. Rothstein, who reconstructed the history of the association from the files of the *émigré* Press, found Schapper, Lessner and Wilhelm Liebknecht as speakers at nearly all its public meetings. The Polish Socialists, organized in the Polish Revolutionary Society, were represented in the association by Louis Oborski, Zeno Swietoslaski and Henryk Abicht. Jourdain, Talandier and François-David Lardaux, later a member of the French section of the First International, belonged to the French group.

Records of the International Association's activities are scanty. From June 1857 a bulletin edited by Talandier appeared in German, French, English and Polish. It lasted only a year. There were American branches of the Association in New York, Boston, Cincinnati and Chicago. The German Communist League of New York, established in 1857 under the leadership of Marx's friend F. A. Sorge, was affiliated to the Association. (When in 1872 the General Council transferred its seat from London to New York, Sorge became its secretary.) In London and also in New York meetings were held to celebrate revolutionary anniversaries. The last such meeting of which a report is available took place on 24 June 1859 with Lessner and Schapper as speakers.

Prior to this, the International Association had issued two significant manifestos. The first, 'To the Republicans, Democrats and Socialists of Europe', which appeared in English and French in December 1858, was a reply to Mazzini.

Giuseppe Mazzini (1805–72), leader of the secret democratic and unitarian movement in the Italian states, was a formidable revolutionary figure.[1] He inspired the rising in Piedmont in 1833; he organized a revolutionary expedition from France and Switzerland into Savoy; he had a hand in the revolutionary revolts in the Abruzzi in 1841; in Romagna in 1843; in Calabria in 1844; and again in Romagna in 1845. He was an inspiration of the nationalist revolutionary movements in Poland under the domination of Tsarist Russia and in Hungary under the domination of the Habsburg Empire. He was the champion of all oppressed nationalities. The causes of Croatia, Bohemia, Greece he embraced and defended, just as he defended the cause of the unity of Germany—divided as it was into scores of tyrannical kingdoms and principalities—along with the cause of the unity of Italy. He founded the secret association of 'Young Italy' in 1832, and he laid out the constitution of the 'League of Young Europe' in 1834, an association designed

1. For his life and thought, see Bolton King, *Mazzini* (London, 1903).

to link the peoples of the various European nations together in a common crusade against the Holy Alliance, as a 'challenge to the Old Europe of the kings'. He was hounded by the police and government of many a state and was more than once laid under the sentence of death. In despair Metternich complained about him: 'I fought against the greatest soldier of our time; I succeeded in uniting Emperors and Kings, Tsar, Sultan and Pope. But there was no man on earth who made things so difficult for me as that brigand of an Italian, lean, pale, in rags—yet eloquent, like a tempest; ardent, like an apostle; impudent, like a thief; insolent, like a comedian; unrelenting, like a lover; and that man was Giuseppe Mazzini!'

Mazzini's social thought, influenced by Sismondi and Lamennais, was coloured by a vague humanitarian, religious Socialism.[1] Yet he rejected firmly the theory of the class struggle and subordinated the social inspirations of the proletariat under the national and democratic aspirations of oppressed people.

Thus, in 1858, he issued a manifesto appealing to the Democrats and Socialists of Europe not to impede the fight for a union of European republics by raising the 'social question', but rather to join forces with the middle class in one democratic organization.

The manifesto of the International Association rejected Mazzini's suggestion of a united front with the *bourgeoisie*. That class, it declared, wished to overthrow the monarchy merely, as in France in 1848, to replace it with a republic ruled by an oligarchy. The workers, however, had not forgotten 1848. They still remembered the terrible days of June, when the *bourgeoisie* of Paris had had the workers massacred in the streets. If it came to a revolution, the manifesto continued, the workers would take up arms as one man—but for their own ends, not those of the *bourgeoisie*. The International Association, it concluded, strove to unite the working class on the basis of Socialism and aimed at a social instead of a purely political revolution.[2]

The second and last manifesto of the Association, appearing in the spring of 1859, was a comment on the war between Austria and France which was being fought out in Lombardy. It said that the working class had no interest in purely political conflicts between nations. National unification and independence did not by themselves bring freedom to the workers. As long as the existing social system survived, there could be no real freedom.

Meanwhile, at the beginning of January 1859, the International

1. For Mazzini's social thought, see King, op. cit., pp. 283–95; Cole, op. cit., pp. 281–5; Ignazio Silone, *The Living Thoughts of Mazzini* (London, 1939), pp. 26–32.

2. For the text of the manifesto, see Müller-Lehning, op. cit., pp. 274–80.

Association had split. The Polish Revolutionary Society had withdrawn, apparently in protest against the anti-Mazzini manifesto. The Central Committee then dissolved, being replaced by a new Central Committee formed in March and to which the Poles were re-affiliated. There were no further reports of activities from the now feeble organization, apart from the manifesto on the Franco-Austrian War and the public meeting on 24 June 1859, referred to above.

*

The International Association was the last precursor of the historic International. The feeling that the oppressed peoples of the world should join forces on an international scale had sprung directly from the ideas of the French Revolution of 1789, in particular the great central idea of the rights of all men to freedom and equality. It inspired the first political movement of the working class in England—the Corresponding Societies; and the first Socialist movement in France—Babeuf's Conspiracy of the Equals. After the years of reaction it revived once again in the form of Blanqui's Society of the Seasons, the League of the Just, the Communist League, the Society of Fraternal Democrats, the International Committee and, finally, the International Association. The idea of international solidarity among the politically enslaved, in the tradition of Thomas Paine and handed on through generations of Englishmen, developed under Babeuf's influence into the idea of international solidarity among the socially and economically enslaved—the idea of international proletarian solidarity. And from the international, Socialist, *secret* societies in France and Germany there developed the Fraternal Democrats, which already in the mid 1840s assumed the shape of a *public* international working-class movement. The International Committee and its offshoot, the International Association, were only reincarnations of the Society of Fraternal Democrats. They were all precursors of the historic International which, five years after the end of the International Association, started life under the name of the International Working Men's Association.

PART TWO

The First International

9 · The Founding of the Historic International

In spite of its short life, the First International constituted one of the most memorable episodes in the history of Socialism. Its effective existence, from its foundation in 1864 to the Hague Congress in 1872, was a mere eight years. Its membership was inconsiderable and its financial resources almost unbelievably scanty. Yet it succeeded in making a permanent impression on the life of its time. To millions of workers it seemed a legendary power on which they placed boundless hopes. The leading organ of the English middle class compared it to the early Christian church. Governments saw in it a gigantic, menacing, mysterious power. European Cabinets concocted plans for its extermination. In France and Spain it was persecuted under special laws. In the Austro-Hungarian monarchy and in the German Empire it was outlawed as a danger to the state. The Pope condemned it as the 'enemy of God and man'. With the First International, both revered and abused, Socialism stepped on to the stage of history as a world movement.

1

Its founders however had no conception of the historical importance which their project was to attain. The initiative came not from Marx, as reported by legend, but from the working-class leaders in England and France.[1]

We have already seen how from 1789 the English workers responded to revolutions and struggles for freedom abroad. The tradition of international solidarity among the oppressed, which Thomas Paine had

1. For a detailed account of the early history of the International, see D. Riazanov, 'Zur Geschichte der Ersten Internationale', *Marx-Engels Archiv*, vol. I (1925). For an examination of the sources on the origin of the International, see Helmut Hirsch, *Denker und Kämpfer* (Frankfurt am Main, 1955), pp. 131–44.

implanted in their thoughts and feelings, was continually revived whenever the occasion called for acts of solidarity.

Chartism had embodied this spirit since the 1830s. When soon after 1856 the Chartist movement collapsed, the slowly emerging trade-union movement took over the tradition. Italy's fight for freedom evoked the powerful sympathy of the English workers. When Palmerston, using the pretext of Orsini's attempt to assassinate Napoleon III on 14 January 1858, introduced his Conspiracy Bill directed against political refugees, he was deterred by stormy demonstrations. English workers protested strongly against the Treaty of Villafranca (11 July 1859) by which Napoleon sought to establish a confederation, under the honorary chairmanship of the Pope, as an alternative to a united Italy. They followed with enthusiasm every stage of Garibaldi's 'Expedition of the Thousand' in Sicily in 1860. Together with that of the Radicals, their pressure compelled the British government to veto Napoleon's plan for armed intervention against Garibaldi. When Garibaldi arrived in England as a refugee in April 1864, he was given a royal welcome, and when a few weeks later the government forced him to leave the country, a stormy demonstration of London workers ended in clashes with the police. All these activities were organized and led by prominent trade unionists such as Odger, Cremer and Howell.

The reaction of the English working-class movement during the American Civil War (1861–5) was of a quite exceptional nobility. The struggle on the other side of the Atlantic had a disastrous effect on the British economy. Textiles, the key factor of Britain's economic life, depended on raw cotton from the Negro plantations of the Southern States. Blockade by the Northern States, however, prevented cotton from leaving the ports. Almost three fifths of the spindles and looms in Lancashire were stopped and tens of thousands of workers became unemployed. Paralysis spread from the cotton industry to the whole economic life of the country. A section of the middle class, seriously hit by the crisis, called on the government to break the blockade by armed intervention against the Northern States. The demand was supported by the upper classes who identified themselves, naturally, with the outlook and way of life of the southern aristocracy.

Among the workers, however, despite the terrible sacrifices imposed on them by the war, there was a strong feeling of solidarity with the Negro slaves. When the British government seemed to threaten war on the side of the slave-owners, there was considerable resistance from the working-class movement, particularly after Lincoln's Proclamation emancipating the slaves. The textile areas of Lancashire were the hardest hit, yet mass meetings in Manchester as well as in London warned the government against armed intervention and declared in addresses to the

President, Abraham Lincoln, their sympathy with his fight for Negro emancipation. Lincoln, who replied to every one of the addresses, was especially moved by the one from Manchester. 'I know and deeply regret,' he wrote, 'the sufferings which the workers of Manchester are undergoing in this crisis. . . . Under these circumstances their conduct is an exalted example of Christian heroism, which has not been surpassed in any country in any epoch.' Marx also recalled, in the Inaugural Address which he wrote for the International after its foundation in September 1864, this episode in the history of international working-class solidarity. 'It was not the wisdom of the ruling classes,' he declared, 'but the heroic resistance to their criminal folly by the working classes of England that saved the West of Europe from plunging headlong into an infamous crusade for the perpetuation and propagation of slavery on the other side of the Atlantic.' In the north of England the veteran Chartist, Ernest Jones, was in the forefront of the movement. In London the lead was taken by the trade-union leaders, Odger, Cremer and Howell, who were to help found the International, and Applegarth, who became one of its strongest supporters. It was another issue among the different nations, however, which provided the occasion for a renewed attempt at establishing a working-class international.

At the end of January 1863 the Polish people had risen for the third time since 1830 in armed revolt against Russian domination, and had installed a provisional government. It had taken a strong military force, sent by the Tsar's government, over a year of pitiless campaigning before the revolt was crushed. European democrats, particularly in France and England, had a traditional sympathy with the cause of the Polish revolution. In 1848 French workers had called on their government to declare war on Russia, in order to free Poland from the hated tyranny of the Tsar.

The new revolution in 1863 reawakened old sympathies in France and England. In the France of Louis Bonaparte, where all independent working-class initiative was suppressed by the police, such sympathy could not express itself in action. But in England a mass meeting was called by trade-union leaders, to demonstrate their solidarity with the Polish revolution. In the chair was Professor Edward Spencer Beesly, who was also to act as chairman at the foundation meeting of the International. The meeting elected a delegation to demand armed intervention by the British government in support of Poland. When the Prime Minister, Lord Palmerston, received the delegation, he declared that without the support of France it was unthinkable that Britain should intervene. After this the union leaders decided on a further meeting, this time with the participation of French working-class delegates, to increase pressure on the government.

2

Links between the British trade-union leaders and delegates of the French workers had been established at the International Exhibition in London in 1862. The election of a delegation to attend the exhibition was one of the few positive achievements of the French working class under the Second Empire. Napoleon's police state allowed few expressions of independent activity. The formation of trade unions was a punishable offence, there was no right of public assembly and the Press was gagged.

At the same time, Napoleon had tried to reconcile the workers to his *coup d'état* by improving their standard of living. He created industrial councils, subsidized working-class welfare institutions, tolerated mutual-benefit societies, kept down the price of bread and undertook public works on a spectacular scale. This Caesarean policy—a kind of 'imperial Socialism'—was reasonably successful in the economic environment of the 1850s. Most French workers accepted both the prosperity and the régime.

Caesarean illusions were shattered by the economic crisis of 1857–8. Wages fell, and an outbreak of strikes took place in defiance of the law against combination. Working-class unrest forced new concessions from the government. Among these concessions was the right to elect a workers' delegation to the London International Exhibition. Everyone who could prove himself a *bona fide* worker through the possession of a work book was entitled to vote and elected workers' commissions were set up to organize and supervise the voting. In these elections the French workers could act independently for the first time since the *coup d'état*. In Paris alone almost 200,000 voted in the election of 200 delegates; in the provinces and the other towns a further 550 delegates were chosen. To meet the cost of the delegation, the Imperial Exhibition Commission and the Paris Town Council each contributed 20,000 francs; in the workshops another 13,000 francs were raised in voluntary collections. Delegates received an average sum of 200 francs per head.

Although the delegation was genuinely representative of the French working class and had been properly elected, the English trade-union leaders felt no enthusiasm for a group of men who seemed to them to be enjoying the patronage of Napoleon. The French emperor, who was cordially loathed by the working class of England, seemed to be using the delegation as an instrument of policy. It would have seemed natural for the French visitors to be invited by the London Trades Council to share in its celebrations. In fact the only invitation they received came from a committee representing a group of co-operative societies, middle-class politicians and industrialists. The delegation also received a letter of welcome from Lord Palmerston.

Indirectly, however, the visit of the French workers' delegation had significance for the early history of the International. While in London, a group under the leadership of Henri Tolain made contact with English trade-union leaders. In this way the first personal relationship was established between representatives of the English and French working classes. It was through Tolain and his group therefore that an invitation was sent for French workers to attend a second meeting in London in support of the Polish revolution.

Henri-Louis Tolain (1828–97) was at that time the most influential working-class leader in France. He had proposed the election of a delegation to represent the workers of France and together with the president of the Exhibition Commission, Prince Victor Napoleon, a cousin of the Emperor, had forced it through against the resistance of the Paris chief of police. Tolain was in no way an instrument of 'Caesarism'. He was a Republican and, as a convinced Proudhonist, an opponent of Communism and of the 'direct action' against the political régime which was then being advocated by small groups of Blanquists. He thought it possible, by persistent education of the workers, to secure democratic institutions from the régime peacefully and constitutionally, and to overcome the evils of capitalism through the spread of co-operative societies. He was opposed to those workers who placed their main emphasis on political reform. Soon after returning from London, he broke with the bourgeois members of the Commission and became leader of an independent working-class group which, though tolerated by the government, soon freed itself from any suggestion of state sponsorship. In the Paris elections of March 1863, Tolain represented this group as a working-class candidate independent of, and in opposition to, the government.

Tolain accepted the invitation from the English trade-union leaders. He appeared together with some of his Paris comrades at a meeting in support of the Polish revolution, in London, on 22 July 1863. The speakers again included both Odger and Cremer. Tolain also spoke, introducing himself as a 'delegate of the Paris workers'.

On the day following the meeting, the London Trades Council invited the French delegation to a reception. While speeches of welcome were being exchanged, reference was made to the need for closer unity among the workers of all nations. An English committee was formed and instructed to draft an address to the French workers which should include the idea of an international association of the working class.

The meeting of 23 July, therefore, took the decisive step in establishing the historic International. This was made explicit by Odger in drafting the address.

George Odger (1820–77), a shoemaker by trade, was then Secretary of the London Trades Council, to which a number of independent trade unions were affiliated. It had grown directly out of a tremendous struggle by the English building workers for a nine-hour day. This had started with a strike by employees of some of the larger building contractors. The masters replied with a general lock-out and announced that in future they would employ only workers who signed a 'document' renouncing trade-union membership. In this way, the fight which had begun over the shortening of the working day developed into a struggle for a fundamental trade-union principle. The strike lasted for more than six months—from July 1859 to February 1860—and roused the entire working class. The building workers appealed to their comrades in other trades for solidarity, and had a resounding response. Nearly £15,000 was collected in London alone, and over £8,000 came in from 240 provincial centres—sums which evoked surprise among members of the middle class. A committee representing the building workers and members of other unions was formed to organize support and explain to the general public, in a series of mass meetings, the reasons for the strike. Among its most active members were Odger, later president of the International, and W. R. Cremer, its future secretary. Cremer, himself a carpenter, spoke at more than a hundred of these meetings.

The strike ended with a compromise. The contractors withdrew the 'document', thus recognizing the right of the workers to join trade unions. The unions, for their part, ceased their campaign for a nine-hour day.

Despite its equivocal results, the struggle became a turning-point in the history of the British Labour movement. Not only did it give new and powerful impetus to the idea of workers' solidarity; it also gave rise to a new kind of working-class organization. Local committees of trade unionists had been formed to organize collections of money in the workshops. In a number of industrial towns as well as in London these committees developed into the bodies known as trades councils. They soon became important centres of working-class organization, and it was not long before the London Trades Council, founded in July 1860, had won a commanding position in the Labour movement. Its first secretary was George Howell, later a member of the General Council of the International. George Odger succeeded him in 1862.

3

The address which Odger drafted, 'To the Workmen of France from the Working men of England',[1] echoed those earlier appeals to international working-class solidarity which had gone out since the 1840s from George Harney, Ernest Jones, the Fraternal Democrats and their successors. Once again the workers were reminded that the mighty ones of the earth held their own international conferences at which 'successful crimes are justified, and unscrupulous ministers legalize them', while those who fought for national freedom and popular rights met with imprisonment or exile. Such abuse of power could be ended only through international brotherhood. 'Let there be a gathering-together of representatives from France, Italy, Germany, Poland, England and all countries where there exists a will to co-operate for the good of mankind,' the address continued. 'Let us have our congresses; let us discuss the great questions on which the peace of nations depends.'

The address then turned to a very concrete social problem. British employers, it pointed out, had often tried to force down wages by bringing over to Britain lower-paid workers from Belgium, France and Germany. The address was insistent that this had been done 'not from any desire on the part of our continental brothers to injure us, but through a want of regular and systematic communication between the industrious classes of all countries'. Their object must be to raise the general level of wages and to prevent it from being reduced through the playing-off of low-paid against higher-paid workers. This required, above all, international working-class co-operation.

Finally the address called for immediate action in defence of Polish freedom. It proposed a campaign to collect signatures to a petition, launched simultaneously in France and Britain, which would be handed at the same time to the governments of both countries. The petition would demand the granting of belligerent rights to Poland as a nation engaged in a revolutionary war of independence against Russia. 'We must do this,' the address concluded, 'to prevent the intrigues of secret diplomacy (that scourge of nations), by which the devil's tragedy would be played over again—Poland's noblest sons be murdered, her daughters become the prey of a brutal soldiery, making that fair land once more a huge slaughterhouse, to the everlasting shame and disgrace of the civilized world.'

Three months were to pass, however, before the British address was dispatched, and a further eight months before the French reply was received in London. Meanwhile, the Polish revolution had been defeated.

1. For the full text, see Riazanov, op. cit., p. 172.

4

The meeting which was called to hear the exchange of addresses, and at which the historic International was actually founded, met on 28 September 1864 in St Martin's Hall, London. The large meeting-hall was, as Marx reported a few weeks later in a letter to Engels, 'packed to suffocation'.[1] The working-class paper, the *Beehive*, had given the meeting excellent publicity in the London trade-union movement. There were also strong contingents of French, Italian, Swiss and Polish workers in attendance, together with many members of the German Communist Workers' Educational Society. The Paris workers were represented by Henri-Louis Tolain; Charles Limousin, a maker of pillow lace; and Parrachon, a bronze worker. In Paris workshops a subscription of 25 centimes a head had been raised to meet the expenses of the delegation.

Karl Marx had been 'respectfully requested' in a letter from W. R. Cremer to attend the meeting. He had taken no part in the preliminary discussions or in any of the preparations.[2] He had however been notified a few days earlier by his old friend George Eccarius, a German tailor, active in the British trade-union movement and in close touch with Odger about the purposes of the rally. Marx had some reputation, both in London refugee circles and among a section of the former Chartists, as a Socialist scholar and writer. His invitation to the meeting was therefore perfectly natural, although as he told Engels in a letter a few weeks later, he was content to act as a 'mute figure on the platform'.

There was nothing in the nature or the conduct of the meeting, or in the resolutions which it passed, to indicate the birth of a movement of historic significance. After a short opening speech by the chairman, Professor Edward Spencer Beesly, Odger read out the address of the English to the French workers, which, as we have seen, contained the suggestion of an international association.

In the reply from the French workers, read by Tolain on behalf of his delegation (Le Lubez read the English translation), this suggestion was taken up. 'Henceforward,' it declared, 'the people's voice must make itself heard on all the great political and social questions, thus letting the despots know that the end of their tyrannical tutelage has arrived.' The address appealed to the 'workers of all countries who wish to be free' to combine in an international association. It went on to

1. *Marx-Engels Briefwechsel*, vol. III, p. 235. A report of the meeting appeared in *Beehive*, 10 October 1864, reprinted in *Founding of the First International. A Documentary Record*, edited by L. E. Mins (New York, 1937).

2. Friedrich Lessner, 'Vor und nach 1848, Erinnerungen eines alten Kommunisten', *Deutsche Worte*, p. 158; see also Henry Collins and Chimen Abramsky, *Karl Marx and the British Labour Movement* (London, 1965), pp. 30–4.

emphasize that 'by the division of labour, the workman is no more than a mechanical agent', and to warn that 'without the solidarity of labourers' this would 'engender industrial serfdom, more implacable and more fatal to humanity than that destroyed by our fathers in those great days of the French Revolution'. The address concluded with a 'cry of alarm'. 'We, labourers of all countries, must unite to oppose an impassable barrier to a deadly system which would divide humanity into two classes —an ignorant, common people, and plethoric and big-bellied mandarins. Let us save ourselves through solidarity!'

The 'plan of organization' prepared in Paris by the French delegation and read out by Le Lubez, contained no reference to the ambitious social objectives and tasks for the future international association which both addresses had indicated in such high-flown phrases. Its structure was to be modelled on the earlier international organizations. A central commission was to be elected by representatives of the affiliated national groups. It would sit in London and appoint sub-commissions in all the European capitals with which it would correspond. The 'plan' allotted only one task to the central commission: it was to submit questions of interest to workers to the national sub-commissions for consideration and discussion, and then to publish the results of the discussions in several languages. The French 'plan' also proposed, in the course of the following year, to hold the first international working men's congress in Belgium.

These proposals were summarized in a resolution formally moved by the English trade unionists George William Wheeler and William Dell. In the debate which followed, Eccarius spoke on behalf of the German Workers' Educational Society. Other speakers included Major Luigi Wolff, an adjutant of Garibaldi and later Mazzini's secretary, the Frenchman Bosquet and the Irishman Forbes.

The resolution moved by Wheeler, which called the International into existence, declared 'that this meeting having heard the reply of our French brothers to our address, we once more bid them welcome, and as their programme is calculated to benefit the labouring community, accept it as the basis of an international association; and hereby appoint a committee, with power to add to its number, to draw up the rules and regulations for such an association'. The meeting went on to elect a provisional central committee of thirty-two members representing English, French, Italian, Polish and German workers' organizations, and including Odger, Cremer, Howell and, as German representatives, Eccarius and Marx.

So ended the historic meeting, which opened and closed to the strains of music from a German workers' choir. It differed neither in spirit nor in the resolutions which it passed from previous would-be international working-class associations. Since 1789 workers had been aware of a common bond of oppression, and their feelings of solidarity had been voiced at just such meetings on innumerable occasions. Since 1837 attempts had been made to organize an 'International of the oppressed', the 'oppressed' consisting of nations subjected to feudal absolutist régimes, of peoples suffering under foreign rule, and of workers, *petite bourgeoisie* and peasant, economically exploited by capitalism.

But the experience of all the political, social and national revolutions since 1789 had shown that this solidarity of the 'oppressed'—the alliance of the middle and working classes—invariably broke up as conflicts of class interest developed. *Bourgeois* political and national revolutions did not aim at establishing a social democracy with the common people as the ruling class, but at an illusory form of democracy which would conceal the supremacy of the middle class. Their object was capitalism, not Socialism.

What, concretely, should be the objective of this new International, founded in St Martin's Hall? None of the speeches, English or French, contained a clear answer to the question. They repeated the habitual complaints against social and political injustice, expressed in the most general terms. They spoke of freedom and the brotherhood of nations. The English address referred to the common interests of the workers of all countries in struggles for higher wages and better working conditions. The French reply indicted the capitalist system for dividing society into contending classes and enslaving the workers. But the idea of Socialism—a society based on collective property and free from capitalist exploitation—was not expressed. All the speakers appealed to working-class solidarity. But none of them envisaged the future international workers' organization as a political or even a trade-union body. The plan of organization proposed by the French and accepted by the meeting saw the new International as having only one task: to probe and discuss questions of interest to the working class.

The meeting at St Martin's Hall, therefore, gave neither an organizational shape nor a programme of aims, nor even a name, to the new International. These tasks were specially entrusted to the provisional central committee elected at the meeting.

10 · The Principles and Statutes of the First International

1

The fact that Marx participated in the International from the beginning was of decisive importance for its character and its role in history. The English trade unionists and the working-class leaders in France, who came together to establish the International, had the most modest expectations; Marx on the other hand saw in its very existence an important instrument in the workers' struggle for emancipation. For this reason, and although he was hard at work completing the first volume of *Das Kapital*, he had no hesitation in throwing himself into the task of building up the new organization.

After the dissolution of the Communist League in 1852, Marx had withdrawn from political activity.[1] The defeat of the revolution in 1848–9 had not shaken his faith in its return and eventual triumph. But he could see no sign of a revolutionary situation during the 1850s. He recognized quite clearly, as his writings reveal,[2] the social reasons for the defeat of the revolution: it had foundered in the conflict between the middle and working classes. The 'undeveloped frame of the proletariat' had been overpowered by the robust *bourgeoisie* before the revolution could accomplish its historical task. Its defeat had for the time being crippled the forces making for a new revolution.

1. In a letter (of 29 February 1860) to the German poet Ferdinand Freiligrath, Marx wrote: '. . . since November 1852 when, on my suggestion, the [Communist] League was dissolved, I have not belonged to any secret or open society, and thus, the party, in this ephemeral meaning, has not existed for me for the past eight years. . . . I am convinced that my theoretical work benefits the working classes more than participation in any sort of leagues for which the time is past on the Continent. . . . If you are a poet, I am a critic, and I really have enough of the experiments carried out between 1849 and 1852. The League, just like the Société des Seasons of Paris, like the hundreds of other societies, was an episode in the history of the party which is growing spontaneously everywhere on the soil of contemporary society'—Fr. Mehring, 'Freiligrath und Marx in ihrem Briefwechsel', in supplement to *Die Neue Zeit* (1911–12), pp. 42–3.

2. Karl Marx, *Die Klassenkämpfe in Frankreich 1848–50* and *Der Achtzehnte Brumaire des Louis Bonaparte*.

By the beginning of the 1860s, Europe was once again in ferment. In Prussia the liberal middle class was involved in a decisive struggle for power against the ruling feudal aristocracy. The Poles had risen in armed revolt against the Tsar. Garibaldi, at the head of republican guerrilla forces, had stormed through Naples and Sicily, demolishing in a brilliant campaign the decrepit feudal monarchy. In France the elections of 1863 had thrown the Empire into crisis; a revived Labour movement had appeared for the first time since Napoleon III's *coup d'état*. Ireland was seething with revolt. In England, the 'frame of the proletariat' had gained stature and maturity. By the end of the 1850s the large number of tiny trade associations had begun to merge into powerful amalgamated unions. The tremendous struggle of the building workers had made them a more cohesive force, and at the beginning of the 1860s they resumed the campaign for the right to vote. The condition of semi-paralysis into which the democratic and labour movement of Europe had fallen since 1849 had begun to wear off. Marx interpreted these events as symptoms of an approaching revolution which, he assumed, would break out first in France. The revival of the International as an instrument for building in a number of countries a working-class movement, which would be ready for the coming revolution, now seemed to have point and purpose.

The new International rested, moreover, on a different and stronger basis than any of its predecessors. The Society of Fraternal Democrats was based on the Chartist movement, and when the movement declined the society declined along with it. Its successor, the International Association, found no possibilities of growth in the condition of political apathy to which the workers of England and France had been reduced in the mid-1850s. Now, the atmosphere was very different. The International which began life in St Martin's Hall had sprung from the initiative of leaders of British trade unions and French workers' organizations conscious of their growing power. It seemed therefore that the International would establish itself on the firm foundation of an organized working-class movement

In the new conditions Marx saw great possibilities for the International. 'The Association, or rather its Committee, is important,' he wrote to his friend Ludwig Kugelmann, 'because the leaders of the London trade unions are in it, the same people who prepared such a tremendous reception for Garibaldi and who thwarted Palmerston's plan for a war with the United States by "monster meetings" in St James's Hall. The leaders of the Parisian workers are also connected with it.'[1]

1. Karl Marx, *Briefe an Kugelmann*, 29 November 1864 (London, 1936), p. 26.

2

Marx knew perfectly well that he would be co-operating in the International with workers who, however class-conscious, in no way shared his own conception of Socialism. The men who according to the Press responded with greater enthusiasm to the St Martin's Hall decision to found an International were, as Professor Beesly confirmed, 'the most intelligent elements of the working class; but only a few, perhaps not one amongst them, belonged to any Socialistic school. Most of them, I think,' he added, 'would have hesitated to accept the name of Socialist. . . . They joined the International because they felt carried away by a warm fraternal feeling for their working-class comrades on the Continent, with whom they felt themselves more closely united than with the wealthy classes in their own country.'[1]

The English workers in fact, while comparatively indifferent to political theories, recognized in a practical, common-sense spirit the need for political struggle, particularly for the right to vote which would give them influence over legislation. The French workers, by contrast, viewed the state and politics with mistrust, seeking to supplant capitalism by the development of co-operative societies which, as expressions of collective working-class self-help, would come to pervade the whole of society.

Their apostle was Pierre-Joseph Proudhon (1809–65), a fertile if not very profound thinker. If his attacks on the social system were enhanced by a brilliant literary style combined with considerable powers of analysis, his constructive ideas were often confused and contradictory. Born into a poor family in Besançon, Proudhon spent his childhood driving cows to pasture in the vicinity of his home town. He first earned his living as a typesetter, and from adolescence onwards acquired his tremendous knowledge entirely through self-education. With all their defects, his abundant writings made an important contribution to the development of Socialist thinking in France.

Fame came to Proudhon with the publication in 1840 of his first book, *Qu'est-ce que la propriété?* In reply to his own question Proudhon supplied the memorable answer, 'Property is theft'. And since property was, as he had shown, the outcome of theft, violence and injustice, he demanded its abolition. But Proudhon's thinking was dominated by Hegelian dialectics, and in his system, common property or Communism, as the antithesis of private property, was condemned along with its thesis. The synthesis which Proudhon derived from these dialectical

1. Quoted in D. Riazanov, op. cit., p. 192.

contradictions was an even distribution of small property. His was a society of property-owning peasants and craftsmen, with the working class enjoying common property in the form of co-operative societies for production, consumption, mutual aid and insurance, financed by a People's Bank lending money on the basis of 'free credit'. Proudhon advanced the idea of reciprocal services—'Mutualism', as he called it—as a basis for solving the social problem. He rejected every form of Socialism involving state control, since he saw the state was merely a great 'gendarme and executioner'.[1]

Marx had analysed the contradictions and fallacies of Proudhon with pitiless rigour in his *Das Elend der Philosophie* of 1847. Proudhon's system, he showed, left no room for the development of modern industrial society and was a form of utopian Socialism bearing the distinctive trade-mark of the lower middle class. But a large number of French workers who were quite unresponsive to Proudhon's dialectics, which they hardly understood, were fascinated by his scheme for reorganizing France and the whole world on the basis of Mutualism.

Admittedly among the workers of Paris the revolutionary traditions of Blanqui had not been entirely destroyed. In 1859 Blanqui had been released after more than ten years in prison. He gathered round himself from every stratum of society a hard corps of embittered and suffering men for whom his name had become a symbol of emancipation. But police repression prevented the growth of a revolutionary party. In the spring of 1865 Blanqui's follower, Tridon, founded the weekly paper, *Candide*, but it was closed down by the police after its eighth issue. Blanqui managed to avoid arrest only by escaping to Belgium, and did not return to Paris until after the outbreak of the Franco-German War. From Brussels he kept in touch with small groups of supporters whom he tried to organize into a party. But it was not until the Paris Commune of 1871 that his ideas were to have any significant influence. At the time of the International's foundation, the organized workers of France were represented solely by disciples of Proudhon.

The Italian members of the General Council—G. P. Fontana, D. Lama, Aldrovandi, M. Sassinari, C. Setacci and Luigi Wolff (the latter being exposed as a police spy when the French government archives were opened after the fall of Napoleon III)[2]—were, like all the workers' organizations in Italy, completely under the influence of Mazzini, and he, while a fervent revolutionary nationalist, republican and democrat, was strongly opposed to Socialism as Karl Marx conceived it.

1. Karl Diehl, 'P.-J. Proudhon, seine Lehre und sein Leben', Part II, in *Sammlung nationalökonomischer und statistischer Abhandlungen* (1890), vol. VI.
2. Minutes of the General Council, 4 July 1871.

The German working-class movement, which had begun to revive at the beginning of the 1860s, was not directly represented on the General Council until 1868, although Marx in the meantime was acting as corresponding secretary for Germany. On 31 August 1864, a few weeks before the foundation of the International, Lassalle, whose agitation had had a considerable effect on the working class, was killed in a duel. He had established the General German Workers' Association, the first independent and viable workers' party in the country, in 1863. After the death of Lassalle it became known that he had conducted secret negotiations with Bismarck, and had considered supporting him against the middle-class opposition in Germany in return for universal franchise and a measure of social reform. J. B. von Schweitzer (1833–75), who succeeded Lassalle in the leadership of the party, openly advocated an alliance between the workers and the feudal nobility in his journal, *Der Sozial-Demokrat*. This proposition, which Marx repudiated with horror, led to a complete break between himself and Lassalleans in February 1865, and relations were not restored for another three years.[1]

3

For Marx, however, the importance of the International lay not so much in ideology or even in policy, but in its very existence as an international centre of the Labour movement, and he took good care not to endanger it by allowing ideological differences to obtrude. When he drafted the declaration of principles for the International, he was careful to avoid all demands and formulations which might offend any one of the disparate tendencies represented in the new organization. Consequently we do not find, either in the 'Inaugural Address' or in the 'Rules', any statement calling for the nationalization of the means of production, a demand which would have been unacceptable to the Proudhonists. 'It was very difficult,' he told Engels in the letter already quoted (p. 92), 'to frame the thing so that our view should appear in a form acceptable from the present standpoint of the workers' movement. . . . It will take time before the reawakened movement allows the old boldness of speech.'[2]

1. Franz Mehring, *Karl Marx: the Story of his Life* (1936), pp. 330–44, 396–400 For a detailed investigation of the frictions between Marx and the General German Workers' Association, led by Schweitzer, see Roger Morgan, *The German Social Democrats and the First International 1864–1872* (Cambridge, 1965), pp. 43–57.

2. The demand for the common ownership of the means of production had been made explicit by Marx in the *Communist Manifesto* as part of a programme which is still of considerable interest. A number of proposals which must have seemed utopian when they first appeared, have since been realized. It reads: 'The proletariat will use its political supremacy to wrest by degrees all capital from the *bourgeoisie*.

The proposed declaration of principles was discussed as early as the first meeting of the central committee, in what the Minutes described as 'a very long and animated discussion'.[1]

Before the discussion began, the General Council (as the central committee was later to be called) was formally constituted. George Odger was elected chairman; W. R. Cremer, general secretary; and G. Wheeler, treasurer. It was decided to meet every Tuesday evening at eight o'clock. The membership subscription was fixed at 1*s*. a quarter. Later this was found to be too high, and the rate agreed was 1*s*. a year for individual members and 3*d*. a year for members of affiliated organizations. As a temporary measure, the sum of three guineas was collected from the members of the General Council present at the meeting, to defray immediate expenses. With this modest sum in hand, the International began its historic career.

The discussion on the principles of the International ended with the election of a sub-committee, instructed to present a draft statement at the next meeting. The sub-committee consisted of the Englishmen E. Whitlock, John Weston and Pidgeon; the Frenchman Le Lubez; Mazzini's secretary Luigi Wolff; the Pole J. E. Holtorp; and Marx, representing Germany. Odger as chairman and Cremer as secretary were members *ex officio*.

The sub-committee held its first meeting three days later. Marx, who was suffering from carbuncles and in great pain, was unable to

to centralize all instruments of production in the hands of the State, i.e. of the proletariat organized as the ruling class; and to increase the total of productive forces as rapidly as possible. . . . These measures will of course be different in different countries. Nevertheless, in the most advanced countries, the following will be fairly generally applicable:

'(i) Abolition of property in land and application of all rents of land to public purposes

'(ii) A heavy progressive or graduated income tax

'(iii) Abolition of all right of inheritance

'(iv) Confiscation of the property of all emigrants and rebels

'(v) Centralization of credit in the hands of the state, by means of a national bank with state capital and an exclusive monopoly

'(vi) Centralization of the means of communication and transport in the hands of the state

'(vii) Extension of factories and instruments of production owned by the state; the bringing into cultivation of waste lands and the improvement of the soil generally in accordance with a common plan

'(viii) Equal liability of all to labour. Establishment of industrial armies especially for agriculture

'(ix) Combination of agriculture with manufacturing industries; gradual abolition of the distinction between town and country by a more equable distribution of the population over the country

'(x) Free education for all children in public schools. Abolition of children's factory-labour in its present form. Combination of education with industrial production, etc., etc.'

1. Minutes of the General Council, 5 October 1864.

attend. Wolff read out in English his translation of the Statutes of Mazzini's Italian Workers' Societies, suggesting them as a basis for the Statutes of the International. John Weston, an old Owenite—'a very amiable and worthy man', as Marx described him in his letter to Engels—submitted a declaration of principles which he had drafted. But the General Council at its meeting on 11 October referred back both documents to the sub-committee for re-drafting.

Marx had not been notified of the sub-committee's second meeting until too late, and was absent when the documents were duly revised. He learned of the new version only at the General Council meeting on 9 October, and was terrified by what he heard. It was, as he told Engels, an 'appallingly wordy, badly written and utterly undigested preamble, pretending to be a declaration of principles, in which Mazzini could be detected everywhere, the whole being crusted over with the vaguest tags of French Socialism'. The draft contained no fewer than forty paragraphs, and these 'apart from all their other faults, aim at something which is in fact utterly impossible, a sort of central government of the European working classes, with Mazzini in the background, of course'.[1] The General Council was also unhappy about the revised version, and referred it back once again to the sub-committee.

Marx was determined, as he explained to Engels, 'that if possible not one single line of the stuff should be allowed to stand'. He replaced the forty paragraphs of the Statutes by ten, wrote a new preamble, and drafted 'An Address to the Working Classes', which went down to history as the 'Inaugural Address of the Working Men's International Association'.

After two further meetings the sub-committee accepted both the documents drafted by Marx, with a few trivial additions. The second clause in the General Rules, as Marx wrote them, said 'that the struggle for the emancipation of the working classes means not a struggle for class privileges and monopolies, but for the abolition of all class rule'. At the sub-committee's request, the words 'for equal rights and duties, and' were inserted after 'but'. Moreover, to the paragraph in the preamble dealing with the rules of conduct for societies and individuals who joined the International, there was added a phrase stating that 'truth, justice and morality' would be the basis of their relationship to each other. On 1 November the General Council met to consider the 'General Rules' and the 'Inaugural Address'. In the debate which followed Marx's reading of the documents, objection was raised solely to the use of the word 'profitmongers' in the 'Address', and an amendment moved by Worley and Wheeler secured its deletion. After that, both documents were unanimously endorsed and, as Marx proudly reported to Engels,

1. *Marx-Engels Briefwechsel*, vol. III, p. 236.

'with great enthusiasm'. On a motion from Wheeler and Dell the General Council expressed its gratitude for 'so admirable an Address'.[1] Le Lubez undertook to translate the documents into French, Fontana into Italian and Marx, who had written them in English, into German.

4

In force and in the splendour of language the Inaugural Address bears no comparison with the *Communist Manifesto*. It lacks the overpowering vitality of the *Manifesto* with its eloquence and wide-ranging intellectual grasp, embracing at one and the same time a philosophy of history, a critical analysis of Socialist thought and a stirring appeal to revolutionary action.

It opens with a sober account of the blatant contrast between the intoxicating growth of England's wealth and the desperate impoverishment of its working class. It goes on to describe the crippling effects of the defeat of the revolution in 1848, after which 'the short-lived dreams of emancipation vanished before an epoch of industrial fever, moral marasmus and political reaction' and the masses sank into an unprecedented apathy.

Despite all this, the period from 1848 to 1864 was not, in Marx's view, 'without its compensating features'. In particular, working-class progress had been notable for 'two great facts'. The first of these was the Ten Hours Act of 1847, which Marx welcomed in the 'Address', not only because of the 'immense physical, moral and intellectual benefits' which greater leisure brought to the factory workers, but also as 'the victory of a principle; it was the first time that in broad daylight the political economy of the middle class succumbed to the political economy of the working class'.

Marx went on to describe 'a still greater victory of the political economy of labour over the political economy of property', in the growth of the co-operative movement, particularly the co-operative factories. He explained that 'the value of these great social experiments cannot be overrated. By deed instead of by argument, they have shown that production on a large scale and in accord with the behests of modern science, may be carried on without the existence of a class of masters employing a class of hands'; and that 'like slave labour, like serf labour, hired labour is but a transitory and inferior form, destined to disappear before associated labour plying its toil with a willing hand, a ready mind and a joyous heart'. But co-operation, he went on, could be successful

1. Professor Beesly considered the Inaugural Address as 'probably the most striking and powerful defence of the case of the workers against the middle class' (*Fortnightly Review*, November 1870).

as a means for emancipating the working class 'only if it were developed to national dimensions . . . to be fostered by national means'. For this, political power would be needed, and therefore, 'to conquer political power has become the great duty of the working classes'.

Marx then turned to the struggle of the working class for political power. Of the workers, he pointed out that 'one element of success they possess—numbers; but numbers weigh only in the balance if united by combination and led by knowledge'. But past experience had shown too often and too clearly 'how disregard of that bond of brotherhood which ought to exist between the workmen of different countries and incite them to stand firmly by each other in all their struggles for emancipation, will be chastised by the common discomfiture of their incoherent efforts'. That thought, Marx was sure, had moved the meeting in St Martin's Hall to found the International Association.

If the working classes of the various countries were dependent on each other for success in their common struggles, an important political conclusion followed. 'If the emancipation of the working classes requires their fraternal concurrence,' Marx asked, 'how are they to fulfil that great mission, with a foreign policy in pursuit of criminal designs playing upon national prejudices and squandering in piratical wars the people's blood and treasure?' He reminded his readers of how the danger of a British war against the northern states of America had been averted by the resistance of the working class, and in contrast, of the 'idiotic indifference with which the upper classes of Europe have witnessed . . . heroic Poland being assassinated by Russia . . . that barbarous power whose head is at St Petersburg and whose hands are in every Cabinet of Europe.'

These experiences, concluded Marx, reverting a little to the 'old boldness of speech' of the *Communist Manifesto*, 'have taught the working classes the duty to master for themselves the mysteries of international politics; to watch the diplomatic acts of their respective Governments; to counteract them, if necessary, by all means in their power; when unable to prevent, to combine in simultaneous denunciations, and to vindicate the simple laws of morals and justice which ought to govern the relations of private individuals as the rules paramount of the intercourse of nations'. He closed the Address with the same slogan with which he had ended the *Communist Manifesto* of 1848—'Proletarians of all countries, unite!'

The principles of the International were formulated by Marx in the preamble with which he introduced the 'General Rules', the basic proposition being 'that the emancipation of the working classes must be won by the working classes themselves' and would never be obtained, as the utopians liked to delude themselves, from the enlightenment and benevolence of the ruling class.

Marx then identified the central aim of the working-class struggle for freedom. It was not a struggle 'for class privileges and monopolies' but for the total 'abolition of all class rule'. This was derived from Marx's vision of the historical outcome of class struggles in the contemporary world. Since the workers were impelled by their social position to fight for a social order which would rest on the common ownership of the means of production, free, therefore, from exploitation and servitude, they would overcome the division of society into classes and the domination of one class by another.

The next principle enunciated in the preamble embodies the essence of Marx's social philosophy. He explained that since 'the economical subjection of the man of labour to the monopolizer of the means of labour, that is, the sources of life, lies at the bottom of servitude in all its forms, of all social misery, mental degradation and political dependence . . . the economical emancipation of the working classes is therefore the great end to which every political movement ought to be subordinate as a means'.

Finally, the preamble referred to the universal character of the working-class struggle. Up to that time all attempts at emancipation had been foiled by lack of solidarity between the working classes of the world 'and from the absence of a fraternal bond of union between the working classes of different countries'. But the emancipation of the workers was neither a local nor a national but a social problem which embraced all nations where modern society existed. From this there followed the necessity of a workers' International.

Up to this point the principles of the International, as expounded in the preamble to the Rules, while implying revolutionary aims had avoided a direct appeal for revolutionary action. After the preamble the Rules went on to stipulate, in ten paragraphs, the aims of the International and its forms of organization. Its name was the International Working Men's Association. Its aim was to serve as a central medium of communication and co-operation between workers' organizations in different countries. Its supreme authority was to be the annual congress, at which all affiliated bodies would be represented by delegates—one for each body, irrespective of its strength, up to 500 members, with additional delegates for each further 500 members.

The first congress was to meet in Belgium in 1865 to 'proclaim the common aspirations of the working class'. The congress was to elect the General Council and decide on its place of residence. The General Council would elect from among its own members the president, treasurer, general secretary and corresponding secretaries and could add to its numbers through co-option. It had to submit to Congress an annual report of its activities.

The International Working Men's Association was intended to be a genuine brotherhood of toil, and the two concluding paragraphs of the Rules referred to its members as 'united in a perpetual bond of fraternal co-operation' and undertook to provide every member, on removing his domicile from one country to another, with 'the fraternal support of the Associated Working Men'.[1]

1. The Provisional Rules endorsed by the General Council were discussed in detail by the first congress of the International in Geneva (September 1866) and approved with minor changes. The final form of the Rules was decided by the London Conference in September 1871. For the text, see Appendix One.

11 · The Strength of the International–Legend and Reality

1

In the legends of its enemies as well as of its admirers, the International was presented as a vast organization with tremendous financial resources. In the third trial under the French Empire of members of the central committee of the French section (8 June 1870) charged with membership of a secret society, the public prosecutor gave the total membership of the International as 811,513, including 433,785 in France, 45,000 in Switzerland, 150,000 in Germany, 100,000 in the Austro-Hungarian Empire, 80,000 in England and 2,728 in Spain. Its enormous size and the open declaration that its aims 'could be realized only through revolution and only in a democratic and social republic', he added, made the International a 'danger to society'.[1]

A month later, on 4 July 1870, fourteen leading members of the Social Democratic movement in Austria were in court, answering charges of high treason. The public prosecutor began his opening speech with a description of that 'important act of high, if as yet invisible, importance for the working-class movement of the whole world', namely the founding of the International on 28 September 1864. Since then, he went on, the International had 'very quietly developed into a shadow government, a second government in the state, forming a dangerous opposition all the more serious because this second power, this second government, draws its strength and sustenance not from state alone, but from the whole world'.[2] The public prosecutor refrained from giving details of 'this second power's' strength. A few weeks later these details were supplied by the Vienna Police Headquarters in a memorandum to the Home Secretary. After a fairly well-informed

1. Oscar Testut, *L'Association internationale des travailleurs* (Lyon, 1870), p. 310; Edmond Villetard, *Histoire de l'Internationale* (Paris, 1872), p. 313.
2. Quoted in *Der Wiener Hochverratsprozess* (Vienna, 1911), pp. 648–50.

account of the International's history and development, the report concluded that 'it is at present, as has been established, an organization with revolutionary aims and a membership of over 1,000,000, covering the whole of Europe and North America'.[1]

That semi-official organ of the English upper classes, *The Times*, soon improving on the Paris and Vienna estimates, gave the International a membership of about 2,500,000.[2] Even *The Times*'s estimate seems to have been too modest. Oscar Testut, who spent a lifetime studying the International and who published a well-furnished collection of documents on its history as well as a two-volume account of its activities in Europe, reached a figure of 5,000,000.[3] On the financial side, General Friedrich von Bernhardi was able to report 'from reliable sources' a fund of more than £5,000,000 deposited in London and at the complete disposal of the International.[4]

These were accounts by the International's enemies. But its friends' statements were almost equally exaggerated. Johann Philipp Becker claimed a membership of about 30,000 in German Switzerland and César de Paepe a strength of 64,000 in Belgium. Andrew C. Cameron, editor of the *Working Man's Advocate* in Chicago, addressing a congress of the International as a delegate of the National Labor Union, claimed to speak for 800,000 organized workers in America. And *L'Internationale*, the organ of the Belgian section, reported (27 March 1870) that the International 'had already assembled several million workers under its aegis in Europe and America'.[5]

In sober reality the International never disposed of anything like this strength, and accounts of its vast financial resources were even more ludicrously exaggerated.

2

Throughout its existence the International was almost pathetically short of money. The General Council at one of its early sittings had first fixed

1. Quoted in Ludwig Brügel, *Geschichte der österreichischen Sozialdemokratie* (Vienna, 1922–5), p. 46.
2. *The Times*, 5 June 1871.
3. Oscar Testut, op. cit., and *Le Livre bleu de l'Internationale* (Paris, 1871) and *L'Internationale et le jacobinisme au ban de l'Europe* (Paris, 1872). A shortened version of these books appeared in German under the title *Die Internationale, ihr Wesen und ihre Bestrebungen* (Leipzig, 1872).
4. Friedrich von Bernhardi, *Tägebuchblätter aus dem Jahre 1867 bis 1869* (Leipzig, 1901), vol. VIII, p. 406.
5. It seems to be in the nature of politics for leaders of mass movements to exaggerate the number of their supporters so as to enhance their importance. Victor Adler, who was normally anything but a demagogue, once said to Scheidemann: 'You know, I have never been mean with the millions. I have more than once spoken in the name of a few millions, even if only a few hundred people were behind me.' —Philipp Scheidemann, *Der Zusammenbruch* (Berlin, 1921), p. 125.

the annual membership subscription at 1*s.* a head, and 3*d.* a head for members of affiliated unions. The unions regarded this figure as too high and the General Council then reduced it to ½*d.*[1] But even this was too much for the unions and the General Council had to be satisfied with whatever they felt able to contribute on a yearly basis. For example, the Amalgamated Society of Carpenters and Joiners with 9,000 members contributed £2 a year; the Bricklayers with 4,000 members gave £1; the Tobacco Workers paid £1 9*s.*, the Coventry Ribbon Weavers 5*s.* for their 1,000 members, one of the Bookbinders' unions contributed 17*s.* 6*d.*, the Organ-builders 2*s.* 1*d.* and the Birmingham Trades Council £1. No complete statement of the General Council's annual income has been found among its papers. But a report by the treasurer, Cowell Stepney, has been found covering the income of the General Council from individual members' subscriptions for the first six years. The figures were: 1865—£23; 1866—£9 13*s.*; 1867—£5 17*s.*; 1868—£14 14*s.*; 1869—£30 12*s.*; 1870—£14 14*s.* The last financial report submitted by Engels to the Hague Congress for the years 1870–2 showed a deficit of 'more than £25' owed by the General Council to 'members of the General Council and others'.[2] For example, the total income of the General Council for 1869–70 was £51 7*s.* 1*d.* Expenditure for the same year amounted to £47 7*s.* 5*d.*, but there was still £4 0*s.* 4*d.* outstanding in arrears of rent.

Payment of rent and of the general secretary's salary was a source of constant worry to the General Council. The rent, amounting to 4*s.* a week, was hardly ever paid in full, in spite of repeated reminders and threats of legal eviction. 'The General Council owes five weeks' rent and is in debt to its Secretary,' complained Marx in a letter to Engels (24 July 1869).[3] No decision was taken regarding a salary for the secretary before the Geneva Congress of September 1866. Up to then William Randall Cremer served as honorary secretary, without pay. Marx proposed to the General Council that his successor should receive £2 a week, but the Council reduced the figure to £1. But money was rarely available to pay even this modest sum. At the end of May 1867 the General Council reduced the salary to 10*s.* 6*d.* and decided to raise the money by a levy on the members who were present at each meeting. These collections amounted to 11*s.* in the first week and in subsequent weeks to 9*s.*, 8*s.*, 7*s.*, 7*s.* 6*d.*, nil, 6*s.*, nil, 3*s.* and finally 8*s.*, after which the weekly collection was abandoned. As it became continually harder to find 10*s.* 6*d.* a week for the International's secretary,

1. Minutes of the General Council, 9 September 1866.
2. *The First International—Minutes of the Hague Congress of 1872, with related documents*, edited by Hans Gerth (Madison, 1958), p. 123.
3. *Marx-Engels Briefwechsel*, vol. IV, p. 251.

John Hales suggested on 11 October 1870 that the amount be reduced to 5*s*. a week: the motion however was defeated by six votes to one.

With what pitiful resources the general secretary had to work is illustrated by such entries in the Minutes as: 'The sum of 6*d*. was paid to President Eccarius to pay the postage of letters to Germany on the tailors' strike' (27 March 1866); and 'the Secretary was authorized to buy a cash ledger' (2 February 1869). Marx was hardly joking when he told the Executive of the German Social Democratic party in a confidential letter (24 March 1870) that 'the finances of the General Council are below zero, with constantly increasing negative quantities'.[1] General Bernhardi, like so many others, had considerably overestimated the financial resources of the International.

3

As to the organizational strength of the International, it is hard to sift the truth from the innumerable legends about a vast organized army. There are no reliable figures of total membership,[2] but the number of individual members was certainly small. In England, for instance, there were no more than 294 by the end of 1870. In France and Switzerland, though numbers were considerably higher, they cannot have amounted to more than a few thousand. The Paris Central Committee, for example, reported as few as thirty-six local sections in 1870.[3]

It seemed particularly hard to recruit members in Germany. In a letter to Engels on 5 August 1865, Marx complained that Liebknecht 'was unable to form even one branch of the International in Germany with six members'.[4] August Bebel joined only in 1867. Becker, however, was more successful in recruiting members in Germany from his base in Switzerland. Johann Philipp Becker (1809–86) was both emotionally and intellectually a committed revolutionary, who had distinguished himself as a guerilla leader in Baden during the revolution of 1848. His thinking was strongly influenced by Garibaldi, as in the case of Lassalle, and by Marx, as in the case of Bakunin. At the end of 1865 he founded in Geneva the monthly journal, *Der Vorbote*. Intended for Germany as well as Switzerland, the paper was recognized by the General Council as an official organ. In the very first issue of 1 January 1866, Becker

1. *Der Hochverratsprozess wider Liebknecht, Bebel, Hepner* (Berlin, 1894), p. 337.

2. Respecting the list of members, Marx said at the meeting of the General Council, it would not be well to publish what the real strength was as the outside public always thought the active members much more numerous than they really were—Minutes of the General Council, 20 December 1870.

3. Minutes of the General Council, 19 July 1870; E. Dolléans, *Histoire du mouvement ouvrier*, vol. I, 1830–71 (Paris, 1936); G. M. Steklov, *History of the First International* (London, 1928).

4. *Marx-Engels Briefwechsel*, vol. III, p. 337.

appealed to his readers to form local sections of the International with at least three members. Such branches were established in Leipzig, Stuttgart, Solingen, Cologne, Berlin, Magdeburg, Hamburg and other towns in Germany and Switzerland, which together constituted the 'German speaking section' of the International under Becker's leadership. But numbers remained small. For example, the Berlin branch had only six members in January 1866; Stuttgart had only nine in February 1866; and the Cologne branch was only seventeen strong in March 1866. By the end of 1871 the German section of the International contained fifty-eight local branches, about half of them in Germany, with a total membership of only 385.[1] Even after the Eisenach Congress in August 1869 had established the Social Democratic party of Germany, the International's membership failed to grow. '. . . The German labour movement's attitude to the International never really became clear,' complained Engels in a letter of May 1892 to T. Cuno. 'It remained a purely platonic relationship, there was no real membership of individuals either. . . .'[2] 'The number of German workers who joined the International as individual members was always small,' according to Franz Mehring, the historian of German social democracy. 'There were hardly ever more than a thousand members.'[3]

Smaller still was the number of individual members of the International in Austria. This country became a constitutional monarchy, replacing a régime of absolutism, only in 1866, and the first labour organization—the Workers' Educational Society in Vienna—was formed as late as December 1867. Philipp Becker immediately established contacts, and his appeal evoked enthusiastic response. Karl Marx, as well as the General Council of the International, were invited to a rally in September 1868 celebrating the fraternization of the working men of all countries, and the nascent Austrian labour movement was represented at the Fourth Congress of the International in Basle in 1869 by two of its leaders, Heinrich Oberwinder and Ludwig Neumayer.[4] Yet the Austro-Hungarian Foreign Minister, in reply to an inquiry by the British Ambassador, Lord Bloomfield, in July 1871, about affiliations in Austria to the International, informed him in a confidential letter that 'despite the most rigorous police observation, and despite even the treason trial of working-class leaders in 1870, it had been impossible to establish any link with a local section of the International'. He added, however, that the police had discovered membership cards of the

1. Morgan, op. cit., pp. 74–83, 180. Morgan's study contains a wealth of first-hand material.

2. Quoted in Morgan, op. cit., p. 186.

3. Franz Mehring, *Geschichte der deutschen Sozialdemokratie*, vol. III, p. 179.

4. Herbert Steiner, 'Die Internationale Arbeiterassoziation und die österreichische Arbeiterbewegung', *Archiv für Sozialgeschichte*, vol. IV.

International,[1] when searching the houses of 'several of the most active members of the Vienna Workers' Educational Society'.

In Italy the working-class organizations were under the control of Mazzini. The great and only object of his life's work was the achievement of national unity. In struggling for this, he aimed at uniting all classes of the Italian people. Consequently he repudiated Socialism as a workers' movement with narrow, class aims. At first he hoped to use the International to further his aim of a united Italy. When this failed, he became its declared enemy.

In spite of this, the International managed to sink roots in the south of Italy. In May 1866 the Italian Workers' Association in Naples announced its adherence to the International. In the General Council's report to the Basle Congress in 1869, the Italian Society was credited with about 600 members. But it was the Paris Commune in 1871 which stimulated the spread of the International in Italy. The Italian workers had greeted the Commune enthusiastically, but Mazzini, still at the head of the Italian working-class movement, had vehemently denounced it. In contrast, Garibaldi acclaimed the Commune and put his services at its disposal. Soon afterwards, the revolutionary wing of Mazzini's workers' organization, disgusted at his attitude to the Commune, broke away and organized an opposition movement, Il Fascio Operaio, under the leadership of Ludovico Nabruzzi and Ermissio Pescatori, at their congress in Bologna in December 1871. Within a short time, sections of the International began to develop in Bologna, Turin, Milan, Ravenna and Faenza. Benoît Malon, a member of the Paris section of the International up to its suppression after the fall of the Commune, when he had to flee as a leading Communard and take refuge in Italy, spoke of the establishment of about a hundred internationalist and revolutionary groups.[2] Total membership in 1871 was claimed to be 10,000. Cesare Lombroso, however, put it as low as 2,000.

These contrasting figures can be explained by the peculiar social structure of the movement. Leonido Bissolati described the International in Italy at the time as an assortment of intellectuals, eccentrics, poets, enthusiasts, altruists and fanatics with no specific programme or clear-cut aim.[3] They were united only by deeply felt revolutionary sentiments

1. Brügel, op. cit., vol. II, p. 100. According to a report by the intelligence branch of the police to the government, there were only thirty members of the International in Vienna in 1869—Haus-Hof und Staatsarchiv, 592/1869, in Steiner, op. cit., p. 86.

2. Benoit Malon, *Il Socialismo, suo passato, suo presente e suo avenire* (Lodi, 1875), quoted by Robert Michels, 'Proletariat und Bourgeoisie in der sozialistischen Bewegung Italiens', in the *Archiv für Sozialwissenschaft und Sozialpolitik*, vol. XXI, p. 358. See also Richard Hostetter, *The Italian Socialist Movement, 1860–80* (Princeton, 1958).

3. 'In Italy,' wrote Friedrich Engels in a letter to Laura Lafargue, daughter of

and impulses, and formed not so much a distinctive organization as a coalition of heterogeneous forces and bodies linked by vaguely conceived moral objectives. Robert Michels, who quotes this remark of Bissolati in his own work, accepts it only in part. So far as the International was concerned, he insists, its members were recruited from the urban and rural proletariat. However, even the proletariat of Italy was still too immature to develop stable organizations: under the impact of spectacular events or of powerful oratory they came flooding into the branches of the International, but they tended to drift out again after a short time.

In Spain an independent Socialist movement developed only after the first Spanish revolution of September 1868. A month later the General Council of the International issued a declaration, 'To the Workers of Spain', and the Socialists, who had formed until then a wing of the Republican party, broke with them and set up an independent working-class organization. The new body was mainly under Anarchist leadership. In March 1869 a section of the International was founded in Barcelona, and soon afterwards in Madrid. In the revolutionary atmosphere of Spain at the time it soon spread its influence, particularly in Catalonia and Andalusia. Farga-Pellicer, one of the two Spanish delegates to the Basle Congress in September 1869, reported 195 sections in his country with approximately 20,000 members of the International; they included twenty-eight sections with 7,080 members in Barcelona. Engels, however, in his report to the General Council, was less sanguine. The movement in Spain, he believed, was suffering from the internal struggles between Anarchists and Marxists, and was also feeling the effects of government persecution.[1]

In the United States the first German sections appeared as early as 1868. Soon afterwards, American, French, Czech, Irish and Scandinavian sections of the International were formed in New York, Chicago, San Francisco, New Orleans, Newark, Springfield, Washington and Williamsburg—a total of thirty sections with about 5,000 members, in 1871.[2] But in the following year a section consisting mainly of intellectuals broke away from the proletarian elements in the North American Federation of the International, which brought about a sharp drop in membership. At their congress in July 1872 there were only twenty-two

Marx (on 11 March 1872), 'journalists, lawyers and doctors have pushed themselves [into the foreground of the labour movement] so much so that until now we [the International] are unable to get into touch with the workers; now it has begun to change, and we are discovering that the workers, as everywhere, are quite different from their spokesmen'—*Friedrich Engels, Paul et Laura Lafargue. Correspondance*, vol. I: *1868–86* (Paris, 1956), p. 27.

1. Minutes of the General Council, 3 January 1870.

2. Morris Hillquit, *History of Socialism in the United States* (New York and London, 1906), pp. 196–7.

sections, with a total of 950 members—the sections being organized along national lines, twelve of them German, four French, three American, and an Irish, an Italian and a Scandinavian section.[1]

4

There are few surviving sources from which accurate membership figures for the International can be derived, but a careful examination of reports from national sections to the General Council gives us the figures recorded above. In assessing the size and influence of the International, however, it is important to realize that individual members formed only one part of the organization. Much stronger, numerically, was the other part, consisting of affiliated trade-union and political organizations.

The General Council saw as one of its main tasks the winning of the support of the English unions.[2] It sent delegations to meetings of trade-union executives to persuade them to affiliate, or at least give their moral support. It was a major triumph for the General Council when the Conference of Trade Unions at Sheffield in 1866 went on record as 'fully appreciating the efforts made by the International Association to unite in one common bond of brotherhood the working men of all countries' and recommended the 'various societies here represented' to affiliate. By the time of the Basle Congress in September 1869, trade unions with memberships totalling some 50,000 were affiliated to the International.

Such affiliations often took place as the result of bitter industrial disputes. One of the specific tasks which English trade union leaders had allocated to the International at its foundation was the prevention of blackleg labour being brought in from abroad and the organization of solidarity action in support of workers on strike. The General Council acted in this respect as an agency of the British trade-union movement. Half of its members were prominent trade unionists. George Odger, its president, was at the same time secretary of the London Trades Council. The General Council's secretary and treasurer were also active trade unionists, as was the German tailor, Georg Eccarius. At almost every meeting of the General Council, industrial disputes figured on the agenda, with communications or delegations arriving from unions engaged in strikes, requesting the International to use its considerable contacts to prevent the import of foreign blacklegs and to raise money in support of strikers.

1. Hermann Schlüter, *Die Internationale in Amerika* (Chicago, 1918), p. 177. See also John R. Commons, *A History of Labor in the United States*, 2 vols. (New York, 1921).

2. George Howell, *Labour Legislation, Labour Movements and Labour Leaders* (London, 1902); A. W. Humphrey, *Robert Applegarth* (London, 1913).

The General Council did intervene, and with considerable effect, in a good many strikes which were threatened in this way, including strikes by the London wire workers, Edinburgh tailors, London tobacco workers, Manchester tailors, London basket-makers and London tailors. Through its national sections, and through working-class papers in France, Belgium, Holland and Germany, the General Council made contact with workers recruited by agents of English employers, workers who were often unaware that they were intended to serve as blackleg labour. The General Council was often successful in persuading such workers to refuse offers of work in England. 'One of the main indictments in the proceedings against the leaders of the Paris section of the International,' said the General Council in a circular to English unions in July 1869, 'was that they had prevented the departure to England of French workers during the strikes of the English zinc workers, tailors and railway employees.'

Such useful acts of solidarity carried the fame of the International into thousands of working-class families. Most of the men engaged in these disputes would have learned for the first time at strike meetings and from newspaper reports of the existence of a working-class brotherhood which had the power to support the struggles of the workers in Manchester, Edinburgh and London by means of actions in France, Holland and Belgium. It was natural, in the light of such experiences, for such men to feel that they belonged to the International. It was equally inevitable that the occasional strikes which owed their success to the International helped in spreading the legend of its power and ubiquity.

The first major success in this field was the International's aid in the struggle of the Paris bronze workers in February 1867. The employers had locked out about 1,500 workers and threatened to lock out another 4,000 because they had refused to renounce their union, which had recently been established. The workers appealed to the International for help. The General Council at once asked the London Trades Council and the European sections of the International for financial support. Large and small amounts came in: £10 from the London bookbinders, £20 from the London carpenters, £5 from the English tobacco workers; but in addition, £4,000 from a collection among the French unions and a loan of £10,000 from the English hatters' union. This was the first time the International had collected money from workers in more than one country in support of a strike. According to Fribourg, a member of the Central Committee of the Paris section, its impact on both workers and employers was overwhelming.[1] It increased the self-confidence of the

1. E.-E. Fribourg, *L'Association internationale des travailleurs* (Paris, 1871), p. 101.

workers and demoralized the employers. As soon as the employers learned of the arrival of large sums of money from London, they withdrew their demands and reopened their shops. The Paris section of the International shortly had hundreds of working-class recruits.

When in the spring of 1868 the building workers of Geneva struck for a reduction in the working day from twelve to ten hours, the mere rumour that the London General Council had promised the Geneva workers a loan of 40,000 francs a month for the duration of the strike was enough to persuade the employers to discuss a compromise. The strike had aroused the interest of the whole town. The International had triumphed in a head-on collision with the employing class, and about a thousand new members joined the Geneva section.

A similar effect, though on a much larger scale, was achieved by the General Council's intervention in the strike of the silk weavers of Lyon. 'In spite of police intimidation, the workers publicly announced their affiliation to the International,' as the General Council reported to the Basle Congress; 'other groups of workers followed their example and we gained more than 10,000 new members'.

The news of the International's successes spread to many countries. The Minutes of the General Council contain many references to appeals for help from workers engaged in struggle, including the spinners of Rouen, the typesetters of Leipzig, the Paris iron-foundry workers for a loan during a strike, which they obtained from the Amalgamated Society of Engineers in England following a request from the General Council; the paper workers of New York, who requested the General Council to prevent the entry of cheap sweated labour from Europe; the weavers of Vienne in France, the German and later the Belgian tobacco workers, and the Social Democratic party of Germany for a loan to the miners on strike at Waldenburg.

As we have seen, the General Council had no financial resources of its own. Even the unions' funds were small, and none of the International's various sections was either rich or powerful. Some indication of the way in which the International obtained financial aid for workers on strike can be found in the case of the 800 silk dyers and ribbon weavers of Basle whose appeal was presented to the General Council at its meeting on 9 March 1869. The men had been locked out because they had openly affiliated to the International, to the great displeasure of the town's respectable citizens. The General Council transmitted the appeal to its affiliated sections. The first collection raised about £300, including £4 from the General Council, £1 from the London Weavers' Union, £3 7*s*. from the German Communist Workers' Educational Society in London, 30 francs from the Geneva section of the International, 135 francs from a public meeting in Paris and 62 francs from a public meeting in Basle.

It was also reported that the inhabitants of two villages in the neighbourhood of Basle had sent potatoes, apples, green vegetables and firewood to the workers during the lock-out. In the event the workers stood their ground and the employers had to accept the affiliation of the workers to the International.

There were substantial affiliations to the International in Belgium, following the bloody clashes between miners and troops in the mining districts of Charleroi. During an economic crisis in the spring of 1869 the coal barons had reduced the working week in the pits to four days, and at the same time imposed a wage-cut of ten per cent. The miners replied with strikes and demonstrations. Troops intervened, fired at the demonstrators and even pursued the wounded through the streets of Charleroi. There followed the arrest of a number of workers including the leading members of the Belgian section of the International. On 4 May 1869 the General Council issued a manifesto written by Marx, 'To the Workers of Europe and the United States', which denounced the Belgian government before world public opinion in the most scathing terms.[1] At the same time it organized collections for the victims of the struggle, and legal aid for the accused. The events in the mining district had aroused the workers of the entire country, and they affiliated to the International in their thousands.

According to Rudolf Meyer, strikes in France during 1868 and 1869 —of the cotton-workers in Rouen, silk-spinners in Lyon and miners in Saint-Étienne—caused the membership of the International to increase by more than 50,000.[2]

Yet the great majority of those who joined the International in the heat and excitement of battle soon drifted away. But they retained some feeling of identification with the great international workers' organization which had helped them so loyally in their time of need.

5

The relations between the International and the various Socialist parties rested on a rather more solid foundation. But during the period of the First International the elements of Socialist parties on a national scale existed only in Germany and Austria. In Germany there was the General Association of German Workers founded by Ferdinand Lassalle in 1863,

1. For the text of the manifesto, see *Karl Marx und Friedrich Engels über die Gewerkschaften* (Berlin, 1953), pp. 152ff.

2. Rudolf Meyer, *Der Emanzipationskampf des vierten Standes* (Berlin, 1874), vol. I, p. 122. Meyer's work, in two volumes, is the most complete source for documents of the history of the First International and its sections in German. See also Gustav Jaeckh, *Die Internationale* (Leipzig, 1904), and G. M. Steklov, *History of the First International* (London, 1928).

and the Association of German Workers' Organizations led by Wilhelm Liebknecht and August Bebel. At the Eisenach Congress in August 1869 these two organizations came together to form the Social Democratic party of Germany. Neither of these parties joined the International officially, since as Bebel explained at the time of the congress at Eisenach, 'the Social Democratic Party of Germany must first constitute itself as an effective national organization; except on this basis an international organization would be a mere shadow'.[1] But both parties declared their solidarity with the International. The programme adopted by the Eisenach Congress followed almost word for word the declaration of principles in the Rules of the International and stated that 'so far as the law of association permits, we regard ourselves as a branch of the International Working Men's Association'. Moreover, the congress recommended members of the party to join the International as individuals.

The Austrian Social Democratic movement dealt with its relations to the International in much the same way. Austrian Social Democracy originated with the Vienna Workers' Educational Society founded in December 1868 and soon acquiring astonishing support. The Austrian government had officially described the objects of the International as 'a danger to the state'. Any organization which openly affiliated to the International was liable under the penal code to be prosecuted for treason. Formal affiliation was therefore impossible, but unofficially the party acted as though it were in fact a section of the International.[2] This fact was well recognized by the government, which in July 1870 put fourteen leading members of the party on trial, charged with high treason. The indictment did not claim to establish formal affiliation to the International, but supported the charge with evidence that Andreas Scheu and Heinrich Oberwinder, the main accused, had addressed the Eisenach Congress 'on behalf of almost 100,000 Austrians', and had expressed in speeches and newspaper articles not only sympathy with, but their determination to realize, the ideas and principles of the Eisenach programme which embodied the principles of the International.[3] As the accused made no attempt to deny the charges, they were found guilty of high treason and sentenced to six and five years' hard labour.

Although the Austrian party was not affiliated to the International and the number of individual members was very small, and although the figures of '100,000 comrades', in whose name Scheu and Oberwinder

1. Mehring, op. cit., vol. III, p. 368. For a discussion of the tactical considerations which led von Schweitzer as well as Liebknecht to adopt a waiting attitude to the International, see Morgan, op. cit.
2. Steiner, op. cit.
3. *Der Wiener Hochverratsprozess*, pp. 278–9.

greeted the Eisenach Congress, must have been greatly exaggerated, it was still reasonable to conclude that a large number of Austrian workers felt some kind of emotional link with the International. When in the summer of 1872 the governments of Austria-Hungary and Germany called a conference to discuss measures against the International, a memorandum prepared by Schmidt-Zabierow, a high official in the Austrian Civil Service, suggested that in Vienna '20,000 workers could be regarded as active supporters of the International or, rather, of the Social Democratic party, while a further 150,000 were not yet subjected to organized political influence'.[1]

The contrast between the small individual membership of the First International and the emotional response it was capable of evoking from the working class was particularly impressive in France, more especially in Paris, Lyon, Marseille and other large centres. The local French sections of the International contained for the most part small nuclei of activists, though a few had memberships running into hundreds. But through the influence of its members in trade unions, friendly societies, political clubs and other working-class organizations, and favoured by an increasingly revolutionary atmosphere, the International became a mass movement in France, as well as in Belgium and Italy, towards the end of the 1860s.

Typical of the way in which the International's influence could spread in favourable conditions was the story of its American section. Even at its brief zenith this organization contained, as we have seen, only a few thousand members, among them, as Marx reported to the General Council, Wendell Phillips, one of the leaders of the anti-slavery movement.[2] But they enlisted the sympathy of the National Labor Union, a grouping of more than sixty trade unions which had been founded at a congress at Baltimore in 1866 under the leadership of William H. Sylvis. In May 1866 the General Council invited them to send a delegation to the forthcoming Basle Congress of the International. At its congress in Philadelphia in August 1869 the National Labor Union accepted the invitation, and elected A. C. Cameron as representative. As already mentioned, he brought greetings to the Basle Congress in the name of 800,000 American workers. And a year later, at its congress in Cincinnati in August 1870, the National Labor Union declared its 'adherance to the principles of the International Working Men's Association', adding that it would 'join in a short time'.[3] But the promise was not fulfilled, since the National Labor Union succumbed to the pre-

1. For the Memorandum of 8 June 1872, see Brügel, op. cit., vol. II, p. 145.
2. Minutes of the General Council, 15 August 1871.
3. Hillquit, op. cit., p. 181.

vailing apathy among the working class which followed heavy defeats in the widespread strike movement of 1871 and 1872.

But the decline of the American Labour movement did not, apparently, lead to a falling-off of public interest in the International. A typical example of the way in which its prestige was maintained can be seen from a debate in the United States House of Representatives on 15 December 1871, dealing with the appointment of a commission of inquiry into labour conditions. The draft of the Bill was submitted by the Republican Member, R. Hoar, later Attorney-General in the Cleveland administration. Moving the draft Bill, Hoar sought to prove its importance by stating that 'the great International Working Men's Association, an organization which extends over the whole of Europe, which makes its voice heard everywhere and its power felt in all circles, has asked the United States Congress for the measure now before it'. He added that 'the International Association of European and American workers has earned the right to our respect, because it has brought the nations of the earth closer together and because it recognizes a link between man and man, a relationship which springs from the common bond of labour'. And he reminded Congress of 'the dark days of our own war', when the 'ruling classes of England and the Emperor of France' had threatened the North American states with intervention 'which had been prevented only by the angry growls of the workers of Lancashire'. Finally he got the Clerk of the House to read out the resolutions of the International's London Conference of 1871 and its Geneva Congress of 1866, calling for a statistical inquiry into the conditions of the workers in all countries.[1] The House, after repeatedly applauding Hoar, approved the draft and the Senate agreed to appoint a commission of inquiry, though it deferred action on the other part of the Bill which had called for the establishment of a national statistical office.

This is all we have been able to find out about the International's membership and influence at various stages of its history. It does not add up to a complete picture. More detailed figures are simply not available. But at least such evidence as exists shows that the reports of a highly organized army of millions, directed by the General Council of the International from London, are fantasy. The International did not control great masses of working people. It was rather, as the London *Times* described it on one occasion, 'a great idea in a small body'. But it did succeed in making the idea of working-class solidarity live for a large number of people, and it won the support of a good many progressive intellectuals and reformers. This was the source of its strength, which was so feared by the ruling classes of its day.

1. Schlüter, op. cit., pp. 144–5.

12 · Ideological and Political Problems of the International

In the first three paragraphs of the preamble to the Rules, Marx had formulated the leading ideas of the International—ideas based on his own conceptions of history, philosophy and politics.

But the overwhelming majority of the International's members were not Marxist. Admittedly the delegates to the Geneva Congress in 1866 had unanimously adopted the Rules in Marx's draft. They accepted therefore the idea that 'the emancipation of the working classes must be won by the working classes themselves', as stated in the very first sentence of the preamble. They accepted, too, Marx's statement that the economic dependence of the workers on the owners of the means of production lay at the root of social misery and political subordination, and they also endorsed the statement in the Rules that 'the economical emancipation of the working classes is therefore the great end to which every political movement ought to be subordinate as a means'. But these ideas could be interpreted in different ways, and each school of thought in the International interpreted them in terms of its own favourite solution to the social problem.

The International included a very large number of schools of thought, with different and diverse aims. There were the representatives of anti-political, co-operative Socialism; representatives of reformist, syndicalist, revolutionary Anarchist and Utopian ideologies; followers of Proudhon, Fourier, Cabet, Blanqui, Bakunin, Marx—a chaos of mutually conflicting ideas. These differences were fought out at successive congresses in debates on the social and political programme. During the early years the debate centred on the differences between Marxism and Proudhonism, and in the subsequent period between Marxism and Anarchism. The history of the International's congresses is mainly a history of this battle of ideas, in which the movement tried to hammer out a common programme covering both the aims of Socialism and the methods of realizing it.

1

At the foundation meeting in St Martin's Hall it had been decided to hold the first congress of the International in Brussels in September 1865. Marx however was afraid that the chaos of social and political ideas, especially in the French working-class movement, would harm the reputation of the International. He convinced the General Council that it would be better to postpone the congress for another year, holding meanwhile a private conference in London.

This conference met during the last week in September 1865, exactly a year after the foundation meeting. From the beginning, it revealed the movement's organizational weakness. Only four countries—England, France, Belgium and Switzerland—were represented. France was represented only by delegates from workers' organizations in Paris—Tolain, Varlin, Fribourg and Limousin—and by Eugène Dupont, corresponding secretary for France on the General Council. César de Paepe, the delegate from Belgium, and J. P. Becker and François Dupleix from Switzerland, could report only the first beginnings of a movement in their own countries. Germany was not represented at all. Schweitzer, president of the German General Workers' Association, had indeed published the Inaugural Address in his paper the *Sozial-Demokrat*, but his organization did not, as we have seen, formally affiliate to the International. The German element was represented at the conference only by Friedrich Lessner and Karl Schapper, delegates from the German Workers' Educational Society in London, by two corresponding secretaries on the General Council—Marx for Germany itself and Hermann Jung for Switzerland—and by Georg Eccarius, vice-president of the General Council. For Poland, Bobczynski represented the Polish National Society in London, and for Italy there was Major Wolff, Mazzini's secretary. By contrast the English delegation consisted of leading trade unionists such as George Odger and George Howell, Secretary and ex-Secretary respectively of the London Trades Council, and W. R. Cremer of the Carpenters, as well as a number of other prominent trade unionists serving on the General Council.

Differences between Marx and the followers of Proudhon were already apparent at this first conference of the International. It was concerned mainly with questions of organization and finance as well as with preparing the agenda for the congress called for the following year. The General Council had put forward a number of social questions for discussion, such as the length of the working day, female and child labour, trade unions and co-operatives. But the proposed agenda also contained a key political question: the role of Russia in Europe.

Marx saw in Tsarist Russia, that 'barbaric power', the main bulwark of European reaction. To weaken Russia by means of wars and national revolutions such as the Polish uprising seemed to him to be an essential part of the strategy of European democracy and proletarian revolution. He supported every political trend and every European power in conflict with Russia, including the despot power of Turkey during the Crimean War. He had singled out Tsarism for denunciation in his Inaugural Address and it seemed to him natural that at its first congress the International should range itself publicly in opposition to Russia.

The General Council had approved Marx's proposal to submit to Congress a resolution declaring that 'in order to stem the growing influence of Russia in Europe, an independent Poland based on democratic and Socialist principles according to the sovereign right belonging to every nation' should be established. The French delegation opposed the resolution, on Proudhonist grounds. Proudhon had been, on principle, against political action by the working class. Moreover he had opposed the movement of Mazzini and Garibaldi for Italian independence and unity and had repeatedly spoken against the restoration of Poland, even during the rising of 1863. His followers therefore rejected the General Council's resolution, but the conference decided by majority vote that it would go on the agenda for the forthcoming congress.

The General Council supported the resolution on Russian imperialism in a memorandum drafted by Marx as a guide to their delegates at the Geneva Congress which met in September 1866. The Polish question, argued the memorandum, was of the greatest importance in the struggle for working-class freedom, because Tsarism, the 'dark Asiatic power', was the last support of aristocratic and *bourgeois* rule in the face of advancing democracy. The power of Russia, however, could be broken in Europe only by restoring freedom to Poland. The fate of Poland would determine whether Germany would remain an outpost of the Holy Alliance or become an ally of republican France. So long as this great European question remained unsolved, the advance of the working-class movement would be constantly checked and thrown back.

The French delegation at Geneva, supported by the delegates from French-speaking Switzerland, wanted nothing to do with the resolution. E.-E. Fribourg proposed that the congress should not commit itself over this 'complicated question of nationalities', but should confine itself to a general condemnation of despotism. The English delegates had no success in their efforts to persuade the Frenchmen, and an open split seemed likely. To prevent this, Congress finally agreed to a compromise resolution submitted by J. P. Becker. This, while it opened with a denunciation of despotism in general terms, went on to specify Russian imperialism and to call for the restoration of Poland's independence.

2

The Russo-Polish question was the only political issue debated at Congress. So far as social problems were concerned, Marx had drafted a programme which, as he explained in a letter to Kugelmann, was 'deliberately restricted' to 'those points which allow of immediate agreement and concerted action by the workers, and give direct nourishment and impetus to the requirements of the class struggle and the organization of the workers into a class'.[1]

In drawing up this programme, Marx was compelled to take fully into account the theoretical view of the French section. The alliance of the working-class movements in France and England seemed to him of supreme importance for the fate of the revolution which he believed to be on the way. He expected the rapid overthrow of the French Empire and hoped that, as in 1848, a revolution in France would touch off a revolutionary explosion throughout Europe. In an alliance between the workers of England and France he saw a necessary prerequisite to the triumph of the revolution as a whole. The International moreover provided the sole meeting-ground for representatives of the Labour movements in the two countries. It was the only organization which united them, and Marx was careful not to endanger this unity by allowing unnecessary theoretical disputes. The English trade-union leaders, with their pragmatic approach, did not represent a theoretical trend in the International. The French Labour movement on the other hand was still dominated intellectually by the ideas of Proudhon.

The new order of society for which Proudhon strove was based, as he put it, on the idea of justice. But a society based on justice required in his view the end of centralization in political and social life, since he regarded all authority, especially that wielded by the state, as incompatible with the principles of justice. He therefore saw, as he wrote to Pierre Leroux, 'in the abolition of the exploitation of man by man and in the abolition of the government of man by man, one and the same formula'. He did not consider therefore that the principles of justice could possibly be realized in a Communist social order, since Communism was based, as he believed, on the principle of authority. 'Com-

1. Karl Marx, *Briefe an Kugelmann*, p. 31. For the text of the programme submitted to the Geneva Congress under the title 'Instructions for the Delegates of the Provisional General Council: the Different Questions', see *Documents of the First International, 1864–6* (London, 1963), pp. 340–51.

munism and absolutism,' he asserted, 'are the two faces of authority in a reciprocal relationship.'[1] To free the working class from capitalism, he advocated the development of producers' co-operatives; to free the peasants and handicraftsmen from the control of the merchants and bankers, he advocated a system of mutual exchange between small producers on a basis of equality, with free credit supplied by a People's Bank; and to liberate humanity from the authority of the state he proposed a free federation of autonomous communities and societies. It was inevitable that, at some point, the programme submitted by the General Council would arouse the hostility of the French delegation, although Marx hoped to avoid serious conflict by phrasing his programme as innocuously as possible.

The programme did express the main object of the International in the struggle between labour and capital. Its purpose aimed at 'combining and generalizing' the hitherto disconnected struggles of the workers in various countries. Its special task was to 'counteract the intrigues of the capitalists', who tried to play off the workers of foreign countries against their own employees in the event of strikes. 'It is one of the great purposes of the Association,' the programme declared, 'to make the workmen of different countries not only *feel* but *act* as brothers and comrades in the army of emancipation.'

The programme went on to deal with the limitation of the working day. This was another prerequisite for the emancipation of labour, not only 'to restore the health and physical energies of the working class' but also 'to secure them the possibility of intellectual development, social intercourse, social and political action'. The programme called for the legal eight-hour day and the limitation of night-work.

Juvenile and child labour, considered in the next section of the programme, was described as a 'progressive, sound and legitimate tendency' stemming from modern industry, although it became 'distorted into an abomination' under capitalism, 'a social system which degrades the working man into a mere instrument for the accumulation of capital, and transforms parents by their necessities into slave-holders, sellers of their own children'. The programme demanded legal measures to save the children of the working class from 'the crushing effects of the present system'. It propounded an educational policy in which mental education would be combined with physical and technological training so as to develop every side of the human personality.

Marx was sure that the Proudhonists would be up in arms against proposals to secure reforms through legal enactments. In their eyes, every law constituted merely another shackle on personal freedom. It

1. Max Nettlau, *Der Anarchismus von Proudhon bis Kropotkin* (Berlin, 1924), p. 6.

was in combating this view that Marx appealed to the delegates to convert 'social reason into social *force* and, under given circumstances, there exists no other method of doing so than through general laws enforced by the power of the state'. The Proudhonists maintained that even benevolent laws would serve only to enhance the despotic power of the state; but, Marx insisted, 'in enforcing such laws, the working class do not fortify governmental power. On the contrary they transform that power, now used against them, into their own agency. They effect by a general act what they would vainly attempt by a multitude of isolated individual efforts.'

The programme turned next to the role of the unions in the working-class struggle for emancipation. This problem, too, Marx treated as he had treated the other social and political issues in the memorandum drafted for the General Council, as a problem arising out of the existing social system and in relation to his overriding preoccupation—the struggle of the workers against the capitalist system.

Capital, he emphasized at the outset, represented a formidable concentration of social power, whereas the worker, disposing of nothing but his individual power to work, was in a relatively disadvantageous position. The only asset the working class possessed was numbers. 'The force of numbers however is broken by disunion.' Trade unions were necessary therefore to prevent the workers from competing against each other. They were moreover a necessity in the daily conflict between capital and labour, aptly described by Marx as 'guerrilla fights', over decent working conditions, higher wages and shorter hours. But the trade unions had a more far-reaching task, that of serving as '*organized agencies for superseding the very system of wage labour and capital rule*'. The unions must learn to 'act deliberately as organizing centres of the working class in the broad interest of its *complete emancipation*'. They should therefore support every social and political movement which aspired to these aims, and consider themselves 'the champions and representatives of the whole working class', not only of organized labour but also of the great mass of workers who had not yet reached the stage of industrial organization, notably the farm workers. In this way trade unionists would 'convince the world at large that their efforts, far from being narrow and selfish, aim at the emancipation of the downtrodden millions'.

The programme which Marx embodied in his 'Instructions' naturally failed to satisfy the French delegation. They rejected the strike weapon as 'barbarous' and recommended the workers to concentrate rather on developing co-operative associations in which, according to Proudhon's theory, the workers would enjoy 'the product rather than the wages of labour'. They protested in the name of 'freedom of contract' against the proposal for a legally enforcable eight-hour day, on the grounds that it was 'improper' for an international congress to try to 'interfere in the private relations between employer and worker'. With regard to the item on the agenda concerned with female labour, the French delegation had a resolution condemning it 'from the physical, moral and social points of view'. On the subject of trade unions the French proposed an amendment, also embodying the ideas of Proudhon, which stated that 'in the past the workers had experienced slavery, owing to the power of the guilds; in the present they are oppressed by legal obligations, amounting to anarchy; while in the future the worker will be producer, capitalist and consumer at the same time'. And on the General Council's resolution dealing with co-operative societies—based largely on Marx's view, expressed in his Inaugural Address, that co-operation, developed on a national scale and with national resources, could be a means of emancipating the people—the French requested that Proudhon's project of 'free credit' provided by an international People's Bank should be seriously considered.

Before Congress could debate the programme, however, it had first to consider the Provisional Rules endorsed by the General Council. The French delegation had put forward an amendment by which only manual workers would be eligible for membership of the International. This would of course have excluded Marx, though it was not specifically directed against him. It was based on a deep-rooted distrust of intellectuals among the French working class, who considered that they had often been betrayed by middle-class *savants*. Here the peculiar political conditions in France were particularly relevant. There was a vigorous and active Republican party led by middle-class intellectuals and politicians, as well as a conspiratorial movement aiming at a *coup d'état*, under the control of Blanquists. The French delegation at Geneva stood for the development of a working-class movement based on trade unions and co-operatives, and they tried to avoid becoming involved in political questions. If the French section of the International were to take up political issues, they were afraid that the *bourgeois* Republicans or the Blanquists would take over the leadership of the movement.

The French view was completely unacceptable to the English and Swiss delegations. In their countries the Labour movement had long been accustomed to co-operate from time to time with radical *bourgeois* groups and middle-class intellectuals. As recently as February 1865 in England the unions had set up the Reform League with middle-class co-operation, to work for a reform of the franchise. They had co-operated with middle-class organizations in a campaign of public meetings which had rallied hundreds of thousands of workers in support, and was soon, in April 1867, to culminate in a major measure of electoral reform. Marx wrote to Engels, at the time, that he considered the foundation of the Reform League to be a 'great victory' for the International. 'The Reform League is our work,' he informed him. 'In the inner committee of twelve (six middle class and six workers), the workers' representatives are all members of the General Council.' He went on to say that 'should this re-invigoration of the political movement of the English working class succeed, our Association has without much ado already achieved more for the European working class than would have been possible in any other way'.[1] This campaign was of the greatest importance to the English trade-union leaders who were members of the General Council. They could not therefore allow their alliance with the middle-class Radicals to be jeopardized. The French proposal was rejected and the Rules proposed by the General Council were accepted with slight amendments.

After the congress had dispersed, Marx told Kugelmann in the letter already quoted that he had at first 'had great fears for the first congress at Geneva. On the whole however it turned out better than I expected.' He had of course heartily disliked the speeches and proposals of the French delegates. 'The Parisian gentlemen had their heads full of the emptiest Proudhonist phrases. They babble about science and know nothing. They scorn all *revolutionary* action, i.e. action arising out of the class struggle itself, all concentrated social movements, and therefore all those which can be carried through by *political means*, e.g. the *legal* limitation of the working day. Under the *pretext of freedom* and of anti-governmentalism or anti-authoritarian individualism, these gentlemen . . . actually preach the ordinary *bourgeois* science, only Proudhonistically idealized! Proudhon has done enormous mischief.'

But in the event the congress had accepted the essence of Marx's programme. It had acknowledged that the fundamental task of the working class was to destroy the wages system and develop a new social order founded on the power of the workers. It had pledged itself to demand the legal eight-hour day and a public system of popular education. It had accepted the need for working-class political action, and the power of the state as an instrument of social reform. Above all it had gone on record against Tsarism. Even George Odger, the president of the General Council, acknowledged in his report that the results of the congress had far exceeded his expectations. He was particularly enthusiastic about the reception of the delegates by the working people of Geneva.

The reception had indeed been magnificent—the delegation being led in solemn procession by a large crowd with colourful flags to the

1. *Marx-Engels Briefwechsel*, vol. III, p. 315.

building in which the congress was held. Yet in reality the representation at the congress was not particularly impressive. Only three countries—England, France and Switzerland—had been formally represented. Of the total of sixty delegates, thirty-three had been Swiss and sixteen French (including Tolain, Varlin and, for the first time, Benoît Malon). From England the General Council sent six delegates—Odger, Cremer, James Carter, Eccarius, Jung and Dupont. Marx did not attend the congress, being busy completing the first volume of *Das Kapital.*

The Geneva Congress confirmed London as the seat of the General Council and re-elected the existing members. A week later, the General Council reassembled to hear a report from Odger on the congress. It then elected him chairman, with Eccarius as deputy chairman, Peter Fox as general secretary and Dell as treasurer.

The congress received a certain amount of notice in the Press, particularly in the growing number of working-class papers which were beginning to appear in France, Switzerland, Belgium and Germany. By the time the International held its first congress it had four official organs: *The Workman's Advocate* in England; *Der Vorbote* founded by J. P. Becker in Geneva; *La Tribune du peuple,* César de Paepe's paper in Brussels; and the *Journal de l'Association internationale des travailleurs* in Geneva. Besides these, a number of papers were appearing which were in general sympathy with the ideas of the International and carried reports of its first congress. This group included the *Voix de l'Avenir* of Dr Pierre Coullery, a delegate to Congress who published his paper in La Chaux-de-Fonds in French Switzerland; Fribourg's *Courrier français* in Paris; Henri Lefort's *Avenir* in Paris; J. B. von Schweitzer's *Sozial-Demokrat* in Berlin; and *El Obero* in Barcelona. The significance of the congress was also discussed in a number of *bourgeois* papers. The *Journal de Genève* praised 'the truly cosmopolitan spirit which inspired the congress'; and the *Revue des deux mondes* and the *Revue contemporaine*, both highly respected French periodicals, published, as Marx wrote to Engels, 'two detailed articles about the International, in which it and its congress are treated as one of the most important events of the century; similarly in the *Fortnightly Review*'.[1]

3

The International's second congress, which met in Lausanne at the beginning of September 1867, was also reasonably satisfactory from Marx's point of view. Although, in its efforts to bridge the gap, it passed a number of resolutions couched in Proudhonist phraseology and even

1. *Marx-Engels Briefwechsel*, vol. III, p. 441.

embodying a few of the chief Proudhonist ideas, it was mainly a Marxist approach which it brought to the problems under discussion.

At Lausanne there were delegations from Germany, Belgium and Italy, as well as from England, France and Switzerland, which had been represented at Geneva. But of the seventy-two delegates attending the congress, more than half—thirty-eight in fact—came once again from Switzerland. The French delegation comprised nineteen members, and included Charles Longuet for the first time. The six delegates from Germany included Ludwig Kugelmann, a friend of Marx; F. A. Lange, the historian of Materialism; and Ludwig Büchner, the author of a widely-read book, *Kraft und Stoff* (*Energy and Matter*). However, the German delegation represented a few small local groups, and neither of the two large associations of German workers sent representatives. England had two delegates; Belgium one—César de Paepe; and Italy two: Gaspare Stampa and Sebastino Tanari. The General Council was represented by Eccarius, Dupont, Lessner and Carter. Marx once again did not attend.

For the second time there was a sharp expression of the two conflicting positions on the attitude of the working class towards the state. It started with a debate on whether the education of youth should be considered a state responsibility. A number of delegates called for state provision of legal, compulsory and secular education. The French delegation strongly opposed the suggestion. Longuet argued that schools under state control must become, like all state institutions, tools of the ruling class and instruments of political power. Tolain denied, as a matter of principle, that the state had a right to influence the education of children, which was the exclusive concern of their parents. The only exception he would admit was in the case of parents too poor to look after their children's education; in which case it became the state's duty to intervene. It happened, however, that working-class parents were usually too poor to provide for their children's schooling, so that the differences seemed largely academic. Congress therefore agreed on a rather ambiguous resolution which satisfied the Proudhonists in form and the Marxists in content.

There followed a much more vehement debate on a topic which was central to the International and to the development of Socialism—the common ownership of the means of production and hence the economic basis of the future Socialist society.

The resolution before Congress, submitted by the Belgian delegation, dealt with the nationalization of the railways and other branches of the economy under monopoly control. There was naturally no opposition to the proposal that they should be removed from capitalist ownership. But who was to run these industries on behalf of the community? The co-operative societies, split into innumerable, small local groups, were hardly equipped for the task. As to the state, this was the main target of attack from the Proudhonists as a coercive instrument—the arch-enemy of personal freedom. They could not conceivably support a proposal which would actually increase the state's political power through expanding its economic base. The French delegates therefore declared themselves ready to vote for a resolution which called for the transfer of monopolies such as the railways to social ownership, providing that the form of social ownership remained unspecified. At the same time they raised the question of financial monopoly, and demanded that this should be broken by transforming private, capitalist banks into People's Banks operated for the public benefit.

Although the French formulation was accepted by Congress, this by no means ended the discussion on common ownership. De Paepe had called for the question of the public ownership of land to be included in the programme of the International. This was quite unacceptable to the disciples of Proudhon. For them, small landed property was a salutary bulwark of individual freedom, while they considered that agrarian Communism would be, as Coullery put it, 'collective tyranny'. After a vigorous debate, Congress decided to defer a decision until the following year.

The debate on common ownership had of necessity raised the question of the relation between politics and the fight for economic emancipation, and hence the role of the working class in political struggles. For Marx, working-class political action, developing into a struggle for political power, was an inseparable part of the fight against economic exploitation. The Proudhonists, however, saw all political power as necessarily an instrument of tyranny. Their objective was not, as with Marx, the conquest of the state as an organ of concentrated social power, but its complete abolition.

Congress attempted to bridge the gap with two resolutions. The first declared that 'the social emancipation of the workers is inseparable from their political emancipation' and the second that 'the establishment of political freedom is a prime and absolute necessity'. The first resolution could be interpreted *à la Marx* or *à la Proudhon*. The term 'political emancipation' could be taken to mean emancipation from the power of the state, for which the Proudhonists were striving, or the emancipation of the workers from political domination by the propertied classes through conquering the political power of the state, as advocated by Marxists. But while the first resolution was ambiguous, the second implied the necessity of political action, since if political freedom were to be recognized as a 'prime and absolute necessity', how, except through political struggle, could it be secured? Yet both parties considered the

No 5431

INTERNL. WORKING MEN'S ASSOCIN. — ASSOCIATION INTERNLE. DES OUVRIERS

INTERNLE. ARBEITER ASSOCIN. — ASSOCIne. INTERNle. D'OPERAI.

MEMBER'S ANNUAL SUBSCRIPTION CARD.

Frederick Engels was admitted a Member on the First day of January 1865 and paid as his Annual Subscription £

Geo Odger — President of Central Council.

G. W. Wheeler. — Honorary Treasurer.

E. Dupont — Corresponding Secretary for France.

Karl Marx — Germany.

— Italy.

Emile Holtorp — Poland.

H. Jung. — Switzerland.

W R Cremer — Honorary General Secretary.

INTERNATIONAL WORKING ASSOCIATION — CENTRAL COUNCIL LONDON

5a (above) *Engels's membership card for the International Working Men's Association*
5b (below left) *Johann Philipp Becker*
5c (below right) *Henri-Louis Tolain*

6a (above left) *César de Paepe*
6b (above right) *F. Domela Nieuwenhuis*
6c (below left) *Michael Bakunin*
6d (below right) *Édouard Vaillant*

two resolutions to be of supreme importance as a statement of principles, and Congress accepted a further resolution stating that both declarations should be 'solemnly confirmed' at the beginning of every future congress of the International and that it should be particularly brought to the notice of all members.

Before this, Congress had turned to the role of the co-operative societies in the Labour movement. Supporters of co-operative Socialism hoped that they would become the means of peacefully transforming capitalism into a different economic system, based on co-operative values. But, some argued, might not co-operative societies which grew up inside a capitalist framework become in themselves a source of privilege, giving rise to an aristocracy of the working class which enjoyed higher standards of life through the economies of co-operative production? This was precisely the point made by de Paepe in moving a resolution on this subject which was passed by Congress. This warned against the danger of a 'fourth class' emerging from among the members of co-operative societies while the mass of the workers, constituting a 'fifth class', remained poor. This danger could be avoided only if it were stipulated that the profits of co-operative production should be ploughed back into the societies and not distributed to the members.

Congress considered another question which the General Council had agreed to put on the agenda, as to whether the working class could use for their own purposes the credit which, through the banking system, they made available to capitalists and their governments. The French resolution on this topic called for the establishment of People's Banks run on the basis of 'free credit'. The English delegation, however, proposed that trade unions should be asked to put their surplus funds at the disposal of co-operatives, so that the credit which, via the Banks, was put at the disposal of the ruling class, could be used to facilitate their emancipation as a class. If this were considered impracticable, then at least, the English suggested, they might be asked to deposit their funds in co-operative banks.

Finally a political question of some delicacy remained on the agenda. A few days after the end of the International's congress at Lausanne, the League of Peace and Freedom was due to begin its own congress in Geneva. The League's Central Committee had invited the International to participate. The League of Peace and Freedom was an international organization consisting of progressive intellectuals such as Victor Hugo and John Stuart Mill and politicians of the Radical middle class like John Bright; but it was also supported by such revolutionaries as Garibaldi and Alexander Herzen and its membership included the Socialists J. P. Becker, Bakunin and Louis Blanc. Bakunin was actually a member of its Central Committee.

The General Council, which had received the invitation from the League, had already devoted a good deal of time to considering the relationship between the two international bodies. While Marx insisted that the working class should have its own independent political party, he did not rule out in principle its co-operation with the progressive *bourgeoisie* for the achievement of political and social reforms. He welcomed the alliance between trade unions and the Radical middle class in the Reform League's campaign for the franchise. But he saw no point in co-operating with the Peace League, which he considered to be 'impotent'.[1]

Most of the delegates to Congress, however, like the majority of the General Council, favoured co-operation between the International and the Peace League. But they demanded that the League should combine its concern for peace with a struggle for a new social order. Congress therefore passed a resolution declaring that the International was prepared to work with all its strength alongside the Peace League, to abolish standing armies and preserve peace, with the object however of freeing the working class from the rule of capital and founding a confederation of free states in Europe.

The resolution was too moderate for the French delegation. From its point of view, all co-operation with Radical middle-class politicians and with intellectuals was thoroughly undesirable. Tolain, supported by de Paepe, proposed the addition of a clause to the resolution which would make it quite unacceptable to a largely middle-class congress. Congress was to declare that, since the existing economic system with its contrasts between rich and poor was the real cause of wars, it was not enough to dissolve standing armies but it was also necessary to establish a new social system based on a just distribution of property. A delegation led by James Guillaume duly appeared at the Geneva Peace Congress, mandated with this resolution. Contrary to Tolain's expectation it was even carried, with 'tumultuous applause', though the Peace Congress then went on with its business as though nothing had happened, and there was no further reference to the International's resolution in the debates.

Of the two congresses, that at Lausanne was much more widely reported in the Press. The International was already regarded as a force to be reckoned with. It was with a note of triumph that Marx wrote to Engels: 'The lousy *Star* which tried to ignore us completely, said yesterday in its leader that we were more important than the Peace Congress. . . . Apart from the *Courrier français*, the *Liberté siècle*, *Mode*, *Gazette*

1. For details of the attitude of the International to the Peace League, see N. Riazanov, 'Die auswärtige Politik der alten Internationale und ihre Stellungnahme zum Krieg', *Die Neue Zeit*, XXXIII (1915), pp. 463ff.

de France, etc., carried reports of our congress.' In a subsequent letter, Marx referred to reports in the London *Times*. 'Things are on the move,' he added, 'and in the next revolution, which is perhaps nearer than it seems, we (you and I) have this powerful machine in our hands. . . . We can be well satisfied.'[1] In Marx's view, the second congress also signified an advance in the ideological development of the International. It had committed itself to the need for political action by the working class in its struggle for freedom, and had begun a decisive debate on the economic basis of Socialism.

4

The resumption of this debate at the third congress, in Brussels in September 1868, gave the congress particular significance in the history of the International. It was also the largest congress numerically, with a hundred delegates in attendance. More than half the delegates—fifty-six—were from the Belgian section; there were eighteen from France and twelve from the General Council and the English section, including the prominent trade unionist Benjamin Lucraft. There were also eight delegates from Switzerland, four from Germany including Moses Hess, and one each from Italy (Saverio Friscia) and Spain (Sarro Magallan). The General Council had invited J. B. von Schweitzer, President of the German General Workers' Association, to attend the congress, but he was then serving a prison sentence for *lèse-majesté*. Blanqui, however, who had been living in Belgium as a refugee since 1865, attended the Brussels Congress as a visitor.

The great significance of the Brussels Congress lay in its public commitment to the policy of nationalizing the means of production. So far, both in debates on the General Council and in the preparation of congress agendas, Marx had been careful to avoid discussing the issue directly. In all the basic documents which had so far appeared—the Inaugural Address, the Preamble to the Rules and the Instructions to Delegates at the Geneva Congress—there had been no direct attack on private property. For Marx the main thing was to unite the heterogeneous forces co-existing uneasily in the International, to strengthen the idea of working-class solidarity on a world scale, to stimulate by means of the International the development of working-class organizations and to strengthen them to play their historical role in the coming revolution. What happened at congresses was for him less important than 'the main thing', which was that 'congresses are taking place'[2] as a public demonstration of the unity of the international workers' movement. It

1. *Marx-Engels Briefwechsel*, vol. III, p. 500.
2. *Marx-Engels Briefwechsel*, vol. III, p. 504.

was not from Marx, therefore, who was absent from the Brussels Congress, that the initiative came to force a debate on private property, but from César de Paepe, who had first raised the matter at Lausanne in the previous year.

De Paepe's resolution on common ownership was closely argued and had already been thoroughly discussed by the Belgian section. It stated that 'in a well-ordered society' of the kind to which Socialists aspired, the mines, quarries and railways should 'belong to the community, that is, to a new kind of state subject to the law of justice'. These branches of the economy should not be operated directly by the state but by co-operative societies with state assistance. The resolution went on to say that since 'the productive power of the land is the prime source of all wealth . . . the land and soil should be handed over to societies of agricultural workers' and organized on a co-operative basis. Finally the resolution demanded that forests and public transport 'must remain the common property of society'. The delegations from France and French Switzerland naturally opposed what they referred to as 'crude Communism' in a debate of exceptional vehemence. The resolution was nevertheless carried with the support of the Belgians, English and Germans.

In a further resolution carried by Congress the International dealt with the nature of co-operative production, which, under its programme, was to provide the main structure for the new economy. The resolution, which was carried, insisted that co-operative members should derive no privileges from their membership and should get no return in the way of dividend or interest on any capital they may have invested. 'Every society founded on democratic principles,' it stated, 'must reject all claims for a return on invested capital, in the form of rent, interest, profit or any other respect. The worker alone must have the right to the full product of his labour.' By the decisions of the Brussels Congress, the International was committed to the common ownership of land, farms, mines and railways. But these productive forces were to be operated not directly by the state but by co-operative associations of peasants and workers.

The other notable feature of the Brussels Congress was the debate on a question which was to recur throughout the entire history of the International: the attitude of the working class to war. The question was placed on the agenda by the German delegation, in the light of the current threat of war between France and Germany. The resolution stated that such an event would constitute 'a civil war in the interests of Russia'. Workers were asked to resist war by every possible means including, as de Paepe suggested, strikes and refusing to serve. The resolution, drawn up after a discussion between Tolain and Becker and then carried unanimously, called on the workers 'to cease work immediately' in the event of war. The resolution ended with the words: 'Congress counts on the solidarity of the workers in all nations to implement a people's strike against war.'[1]

The middle-class Press treated the Brussels Congress with respect, as representing a force which had now to be reckoned with. Shortly before the congress the London *Times* wrote about the International: 'One has to go back to the time of the birth of Christianity and the rejuvenation of the ancient world by the Germanic nations, to find anything analogous to this workers' movement which seems to perform, in relation to existing civilization, a service comparable to that which the Nordic barbarians rendered in the ancient world.' The aim of the International, said *The Times*, was nothing short of the rebirth of humanity, 'surely the most comprehensive aim to which any institution apart from the Christian Church has ever aspired'. The English, French, German, Swiss and particularly the Belgian Press gave detailed reports of the congress, and discussed with expressions of alarm, which were to be expected, the resolutions dealing with the nationalization of land and mines.

The Belgian government had made strenuous efforts to prevent the congress from meeting in Brussels. The fact that, despite this, the congress was able to assemble and to carry through its business successfully brought the International a good deal of prestige, some of which was reflected in the newspapers. Several thousand workers had joined the Belgian section after the forcible suppression of a miners' strike in Charleroi by the government.[2] The Belgian government was alarmed by this growth of the International. When it was announced that the congress was to be held in Brussels, Bara, the Minister of Justice, asked for a special Act of Parliament against aliens which would have enabled the government to expel foreign delegates. In his speech to the Chamber of Deputies, the Minister described the International as a conspiracy and a threat to the state. After the Bill was rejected by the Chamber, the Brussels section of the International issued an Open Letter to the Minister which was published in a number of papers, thanking him 'for the great service' he had rendered the International, 'in that you, Mr Minister, made the International the subject of a debate in the Chamber and so enabled us to use the official record of Parliament to propagate our ideas'.[3] It is also worth noting that the Brussels Congress paid special tribute to *Das Kapital*, which had been published a year earlier. A resolution which was carried unanimously claimed that 'Karl Marx

1. For a detailed account of the debate on this resolution, see *The International on War*, ch. 21, Part 3.
2. See p. 116.
3. Meyer, *Der Emanzipationskampf des vierten Standes*, vol. II, p. 216.

deserves the very great credit of being the first economist to have subjected capital to a scientific analysis'.

5

At the following year's congress, at Basle in September 1869, the ideological struggle with Proudhonism reached its climax. The General Council had received a protest from the French against the decisions on the common ownership of land which had been reached at the Brussels Congress. There had been no adequate preparation for the debate, the French claimed, and after some discussion on the General Council it was agreed to submit the matter to another congress. The Congress Commission, which prepared the agenda for Basle, divided the subject into two separate resolutions, one declaring that society had the right to establish common ownership of land and the other that it was necessary to do so.

The first resolution was opposed on the grounds that prolonged occupation of land by a family ought to imply some property rights, and that where cultivation had enhanced the value of a farm the increased value belonged by right to the farmer. A majority of the Commission, however, argued that land had originally been common property and had been acquired by private owners only through the ruthless use of political and economic pressure. Society therefore had the right to make good this injustice. Opinions were also divided on the question—apart from the right of society to reassume ownership of the soil—of whether it was necessary. Eventually a resolution was carried by fifty-four against four (with thirteen delegates abstaining), affirming that 'society has the right to abolish private property in land and soil and to transfer it to collective ownership'.

This left open the question of how the commonly-owned lands should be administered. A majority of the Commission recommended that the farms should be run by elected parish councils. A minority wanted them to be controlled by agrarian co-operative societies. Finally, the General Council, represented by Eccarius, suggested that large-scale, mechanized farms should form the basis of a socialized farming system managed by producers' co-operatives. As there was no agreement in sight, the discussion was adjourned to the following year.

The decision of the Basle Congress in favour of common ownership was all the more important as this was the most representative congress ever to be held by the International. For the first time Germany was directly represented by one of the two workers' parties—the Social Democratic Workers' party, founded by Liebknecht and Bebel. This was also the first occasion on which delegates from Austria had been allowed to attend. A delegate had been sent by the National Labor Union, still the most important trade-union association in the United States. Finally, and most significant of all, it was the first congress attended by Bakunin and at which the banner of Revolutionary Anarchism was openly displayed.

Altogether, there were eighty-seven delegates at Basle. Six represented England and the General Council, including the prominent building worker, Benjamin Lucraft, and Robert Applegarth, Secretary of the Carpenters and Joiners Union, one of the largest unions in Britain. There were twenty-five from France, including, besides Henri-Louis Tolain and Eugène Varlin, who had been released from prison a short time earlier, Michael Bakunin representing the section at Lyon. There were twenty-three delegates from Switzerland, including Hermann Greulich, who later established the Swiss Social Democratic party. Twelve delegates attended from Germany, including Wilhelm Liebknecht as well as Moses Hess, and five from Belgium, led by César de Paepe. Henrich Oberwinder and Ludwig Neumayer were there from Austria: they were soon to face a treason trial at home because of their support for the International. The Spanish section was represented by Gaspar Sentinon and Rafael Farga-Pellicer. The Italian section was represented by Stefano Caporusso, and also by Bakunin, with another mandate. The delegate from the National Labor Union in the United States was Andrew C. Cameron, editor of the Chicago working-class paper, the *Working Man's Advocate*.

Before his decision to adhere to the International, Bakunin had tried to win over the Peace League to his brand of Revolutionary Anarchism. One of the chief planks in his platform was the abolition of the right of inheritance. After breaking with the League he tried to win the International for this demand. With the support of the French section the question was placed on the agenda at the Basle Congress.

Michael Bakunin (1814–76), son of a Russian aristocratic landowner, became the most powerful exponent of Revolutionary Anarchism. Of enormous stature and with unusual charm of manner, Bakunin combined immense powers of conviction, an explosive temperament, a taste for macabre conspiracy and a certain naïve truculence. He was happy to sacrifice himself in the cause of freedom.[1] Wherever revolution broke out, Bakunin was likely to be on the scene, and he took part in both the Paris rising of February 1848 and the Dresden insurrection of May 1849. After the defeat in Dresden, Bakunin fled and was captured

1. There is a short and sympathetic biography in German by Georg Steklov: *Michael Bakunin* (Stuttgart, 1913); and a more detailed life in English by E. H. Carr: *Michael Bakunin* (London, 1937). There are a few surviving copies of Max Nettlau's monumental biography, of which one is in the British Museum and another in the International Institute of Social History, Amsterdam.

by Prussian troops. He was twice sentenced to death by courts martial, the first time in Prussia in 1850, the second in Austria in 1851. The Prussians handed him in chains to Austria; the Austrians transferred him, still chained, to the Russians. Imprisoned at Olmütz he spent six months with his hands and feet chained to the walls of his cell. The Tsar kept him in solitary confinement for more than seven years, first in the Peter and Paul Fortress, then in the Schlüsselburg. Finally he was banished to Siberia for life. He escaped in 1861, and after about three years of exile in London he resumed his revolutionary agitation in Italy and Switzerland. With all the glamour of legend, Bakunin appeared—the personal incarnation and symbol of revolution—at the Basle Congress.

In a persuasive speech he defended his demand for the abolition of the right of inheritance. This right, he argued, was the basis which supported the institutions of private property and the state. Once the right of inheritance was abolished, the entire social system resting on private property would break down. The abolition of the right of inheritance was therefore one of the 'fundamental conditions' for the abolition of private property itself. It was the prerequisite of social revolution.

Marx, who did not attend the Basle Congress, had drafted a statement for the General Council which was presented by Eccarius as secretary. The right of inheritance, according to Marx, like the laws of commercial contract, was not the cause but the consequence of a society based on private property. The right to inherit slaves had not been the cause of slavery: the institution of slavery was the reason why slaves could be inherited. If the right of inheritance were abolished, this would in no way destroy an economic system based on private ownership of the means of production. On the other hand, if the means of production were transferred to public ownership, this would be tantamount to abolishing the right of inheritance.

Neither side secured an effective majority. The report of the Congress Commission, which took Bakunin's point of view, received thirty-two votes in favour, twenty-three against; there were thirteen abstentions and seven delegates were absent. The General Council's report received nineteen votes in favour, thirty-seven against; there were six abstentions and thirteen absences. Since neither side had a majority among those eligible to vote, the question remained undecided.

6

The voting however showed the considerable influence which Bakunin had already secured in the International. In Marx's view it was a highly dangerous influence, and he was sure that Bakunin's fantastic aims could only confuse and disorganize the working-class struggle. For Bakunin repudiated all authority and all restrictions on personal liberty. In the omnipotence of the centralized state and its institutions he saw, with Proudhon, the essential denial of freedom. He was convinced that as long as the existing political and social institutions survived there was no possibility of securing economic emancipation for the workers. He therefore preached the destruction of all existing institutions, 'the state, the church, the banking system, the university institutions, the Civil Service, the army, the police—institutions', he claimed, 'which are merely fortresses erected by privilege against the proletariat'. The state itself, he declared, 'be it absolute monarchy, constitutional monarchy or even republic, means domination and exploitation. It means domination of one dynasty, nation or class over another: a manifest denial of Socialism.' However the state may be constituted, however 'embellished with democratic forms, it will always be a prison for the proletariat'. In some ways a democratic republic could be worse than an absolute monarchy. 'Just because of its democratic façade,' he claimed, 'it enables a rich and greedy minority to go on living on the backs of the people in peace and security.' Bakunin's aims, like those of Proudhon which had so strongly influenced him, were 'a free grouping of individuals into communities, of communities into provinces, provinces into nations and, lastly, nations into united states—first of Europe, then of the whole world'.

Bakunin's guiding idea was 'collectivism', in contrast to Marx's 'Communism', which Bakunin called 'State Communism'. 'I am not a Communist,' he explained, 'because Communism, by concentrating all property in the state, necessarily leads to the concentration of all the power of society in the state. I want to abolish the state; my aim is the complete destruction of the very principle of state authority which up to now has meant the enslavement, suppression, exploitation and humiliation of mankind.'

Bakunin rejected all political action by the working class which did not aim directly at social revolution. He opposed participation in parliamentary elections, campaigns for social reforms and all attempts to win influence and power in the state. He condemned all such political activity as a 'betrayal of the revolution', since it gave rise to illusions among the workers that they could be emancipated by means other than revolution. He called on the International to concentrate its efforts entirely on social revolution. His method was the same as Blanqui's: the conquest of power by a *coup*, a *putsch* or an uprising. 'Every revolt is useful, however fruitless it may seem,' he maintained. Proudhon's Anarchism rejected the forcible overthrow of social institutions. Bakunin's Anarchism relied on force.

7

Up to the time of the Basle Congress, the ideological differences in the International had been confined to the two tendencies: the federal, Anarchist anti-collectivism of Proudhon and the centralized Communism of Marx. At Basle a third tendency, Bakunin's federal, Anarchist collectivism, had appeared.

We have seen how the influence of Proudhonism grew less at successive congresses. The Basle Congress gave the final blow by including land nationalization in the programme of the International, in flat contradiction to one of the basic principles of Proudhon. Moreover, in France and particularly in Paris, Tolain's leadership was being challenged with growing success by Eugène Varlin, and Varlin, though still a federalist, had abandoned his earlier Proudhonist views. He had become a collectivist, although he never adopted a fully Marxist position. At Basle, Marx's views were supported completely by the English, German and German-Swiss delegates, while on collectivism he had the additional support of the Belgians and Anarchists from the Latin countries. However, the German delegation represented little real strength at Congress, since neither of the two workers' parties in Germany had affiliated to the International, and its strength both in local sections and in individual membership remained modest. More modest still was the individual membership in Austria, where such working-class movement as there was did not yet constitute a party. In German Switzerland, the workers' associations co-operated with progressive *bourgeois* parties. Bakunin's influence was spreading both in French Switzerland and in the south of France, while his followers had the greatest influence in the Italian and Spanish sections. On most issues, too, the Belgian section led by César de Paepe was closer to Bakunin than to Marx. In the International therefore Marx's position depended only on the support of the English union leaders and the groups of German exiles in London.

Nevertheless, two of Marx's principles had triumphed in the battle of ideas being waged inside the International. Congress had endorsed both the necessity of political action by the working class and the common ownership of the means of production. But the battle of ideas did not end with the adoption of these principles. On the contrary, the future history of the International was to be preoccupied with the clash between Marxism and Anarchism.

During the five years which had passed from the foundation of the International to its Basle Congress, its influence among the workers had spread with unexpected speed. Though its organizational base was feeble it had come to be regarded, by both rulers and ruled, as a power in its own right. Was it, however, really so powerful? And was not its potential being sapped by internal ideological disputes? In the year or so following the Basle Congress, the Franco-German War and the Paris Commune were to subject the International to a crucial test.

13 · The International in the Franco-German War and in the Paris Commune

1

On 12 July 1870 the General Council issued its invitations to the fifth congress. This was to meet at Mainz on 5 September. One item on the agenda which the General Council had prepared for discussion was the question of what the working class could do to prevent wars. A week later, on 19 July, Napoleon III declared war on Prussia.

The International was no longer confronted with the question of how wars could be avoided. The machines of war had begun to turn, and neither French nor German Socialists had the means of stopping them. The Brussels Congress, which had called on the working class to initiate a general strike in the event of the outbreak of war, had lost sight of the real relationships of powers in the world. The International now had the task of identifying those responsible for the war, of keeping alive the feeling of solidarity among the workers of the two warring nations amidst a deluge of jingoism, and of giving a lead to the working class at a turning-point in history.

It was the Paris Federation which spoke first on behalf of the International, since it was in Paris that the war plot had been hatched. A full week before the disaster began to unfold, it issued a manifesto, 'To the Workers of All Nations', directed particularly to the workers of Germany. The manifesto denounced the threatened war as a crime perpetrated by the ruling dynasty. 'A war waged on account of . . . dynastic interests is, in the eyes of the workers, nothing but criminal folly.' It called on the 'brothers in Germany' to recognize that 'a war between us would be a civil war'. It went on to warn the German workers that 'our split would only bring in its wake the complete triumph of despotism on both sides of the Rhine'. And it closed with a solemn declaration that 'whatever the result, for the moment, of our combined efforts, we, the members of the International Working Men's Association, for whom no national frontiers exist, send you in token of our eternal solidarity good wishes and greetings from the workers of France'.

For German Socialists, the war raised rather more complicated questions. French Socialists were justified in denouncing the war as one of Bonapartist aggression. But in Germany the war seemed primarily defensive. Started by Louis Napoleon, it seemed to the overwhelming majority of German workers a clear case of aggression against their country. Could they, in the circumstances, decline the call to defend their fatherland? On the other hand, could the workers be said to have a fatherland at all? Was not every war the result of rivalry between ruling classes and dynasties?[1]

The German workers were divided in their attitude to the war. In its reply to the Paris manifesto, the Berlin section of the International said: 'We earnestly agree with your protest. . . . We solemnly pledge that neither the sound of bugles nor the thunder of cannon, neither victory nor defeat will turn us from our task of making common cause with the workers of all nations.' In line with this statement, mass meetings in Chemnitz, Leipzig, Dresden, Krefeld and Elberfeld denounced the war as a crime by both French and Prussian dynasties. At a meeting in Chemnitz of workers from the province of Saxony, a message to the French workers was adopted which ran: 'In the name of German democracy and, specifically, of workers in the Social Democratic party, we condemn the present war as entirely dynastic. . . . We grasp with joy the hand of brotherhood extended to us by the workers of France. . . . Mindful of the motto of the International Working Men's Association, "Proletarians of all lands, unite!", we shall never forget that the workers of all nations are our friends and the despots of all nations are our enemies.'

However, this was not the dominant mood among German workers. On 16 July a mass meeting in Brunswick said in a message to the French, that while they emphatically rejected all talk of hostility to the French people, since Louis Napoleon had in fact started the war, 'we find ourselves compelled to wage a defensive war as a necessary evil'. It was now their 'prime duty' to resist the man who had irresponsibly destroyed the peace. An even more forthright expression of patriotism was conveyed in a manifesto issued on 24 July by the Brunswick Central Committee of

1. For a detailed account of contrasting attitudes among German Social Democrats during the Franco-German War, see Karl Kautsky, *Sozialisten und Krieg* (Prague, 1937), pp. 188–214; August Bebel, *Aus meinem Leben* (Stuttgart, 1910–14), vol. II, pp. 167–85.

the Social Democratic party. 'So long as French soldiers are so ill advised as to let themselves be dragged in the wake of a Napoleon so that our German lands are threatened with war and devastation,' it declared, 'we are determined to play our full part in the defence of the inviolability of German soil against Napoleonic or any other despotism.'[1] *Volksstaat*, the organ of the Eisenach Social Democrats, saw the struggle as not only one of national defence but also as a war between the two political systems of despotism and democracy. On this interpretation, 'Bonaparte is trying to prop up his shaky throne by humiliating Prussia. The December Empire is the cornerstone of reaction in Europe. If Bonaparte falls, there will fall with him the mainstay of today's class and military régimes. If Bonaparte wins, European as well as French democracy will be vanquished.'

However, it could occur to a German Socialist to ask whether Bismarck's régime was also based on class and military rule, and whether responsibility for the war rested on Bonaparte alone. Might not Prussia's avowed policy of 'blood and iron' be also, in part, responsible?

The North German Parliament met on 19 July to debate on war credits. It contained five Socialist representatives, three from the Eisenach party and two Lassalleans. They had to decide on their attitude to the war. The Lassalleans saw it clearly as a war of defence and had no hesitation in voting for war credits. The Eisenachers, however, particularly Bebel and Liebknecht, were conscious of an acute dilemma. A vote for war credits could well be interpreted as a vote of confidence in Bismarck. On the other hand, a vote against war credits could be taken as condoning the iniquitous policy of Louis Napoleon, and strengthen him in his attempts to suppress the Socialist movement in France.

Bebel and Liebknecht solved their dilemma by abstaining. They defended their attitude in a statement which Bebel read in Parliament. If the existing war was being waged in the interests of the Bonaparte dynasty, it maintained, the war of 1866 had been fought in the interests of the Hohenzollerns. To vote in favour of war credits would amount to a vote of confidence in the Prussian government, 'which, through its actions in 1866, had prepared the ground for the present conflict'. To vote against credits, on the other hand, could be taken as 'approval of the outrageous policy of Bonaparte'. Therefore, 'as Socialists, Republicans and members of the International Working Men's Association, which fights all oppressors without distinction of nationality and which works to unite all the oppressed in a common

1. For the text of this manifesto, see *Der Wiener Hochverratsprozess*, p. 859.

bond of brotherhood, we cannot declare ourselves, directly or indirectly, in favour of the present war'.

2

Four days later, on 23 July, the General Council of the International met to formulate its attitude to the war. Marx had drafted an Address, 'To the Members of the International Working Men's Association in Europe and the United States',[1] which he read to the meeting and which was then unanimously adopted. The Address recognized that 'on the German side, the war is a war of defence'.[2] But this only raised the further question, 'Who put Germany to the necessity of defending herself? Who enabled Louis Bonaparte to wage war upon her? *Prussia!* . . . After her victory [i.e. over Austria in 1866], did Prussia dream one moment of opposing a free Germany to an enslaved France? Just the contrary. While carefully preserving all the native beauties of her old system, she added, over and above, all the tricks of the Second Empire, its real despotism and its mock democratism.'

As to France, the Address contained the prophecy that 'whatever may be the incidents of Louis Bonaparte's war with Prussia, the death-knell of the Second Empire has already sounded at Paris'. But the Germans, in their turn, were sternly warned that 'if the German working class allow the present war to lose its strictly defensive character and to degenerate into a war against the French people, victory or defeat alike will prove disastrous'. The Address concluded with an assessment of the historical significance of the international solidarity expressed in the fraternal exchange of messages between German and French workers.

> The very fact that while official France and Germany are rushing into a fratricidal feud, the workmen of France and Germany send each other

1. For this and the subsequent 'Address of the General Council on the War and the Paris Commune', see Karl Marx, *Der Bürgerkrieg in Frankreich*, with an introduction by Friedrich Engels.

2. It was not known, at the time, that Bismarck had deliberately provoked the war by his 'editing' of the Ems Telegram. Many years later Bebel wrote: 'Bismarck deceived the whole world. He managed to create the impression that Napoleon III provoked the war, and that he, the peace-loving Bismarck, found himself the innocent victim of aggression. . . . The events which led up to the outbreak of war were so confusing that nobody noticed that France, which declared war, was militarily unprepared, while Germany, against whom war was declared, was ready for it down to the last detail, and completed its mobilization without a hitch.' Bebel admitted that if he and Liebknecht 'had known, at the time of the outbreak of hostilities, what we learned during the next few years from official publications and memoirs', they would not have abstained from voting war credits. 'We should have voted directly against them'—August Bebel, *Aus meinem Leben* (Stuttgart, 1910–14), vol. III, pp. 167–8; vol. II (1911), p. 167.

messages of peace and good will, this great fact, unparalleled in the history of the past, opens the vista of a brighter future. It proves that in contrast to old society, with its economic miseries and its political delirium, a new society is springing up whose international rule will be *Peace*, because its national ruler will be everywhere the same—*Labour!* The pioneer of that new society is the International Working Men's Association.

Scarcely six weeks later, the Empire had collapsed. The French army had capitulated at Sedan, Bonaparte was a prisoner of the Germans and two days later, on 4 September, the Republic was declared in Paris. The deputies in the capital constituted themselves a 'Government of National Defence'.

Next day the Central Committee of the German Social Democratic Workers party published a manifesto to the German workers, welcoming the French Republic. It recalled the fact that, for Germany, the war had been primarily defensive, and that it had been forced on the German people by the Emperor and not the people of France. Now the French people were once again in control of their own destiny, and the manifesto demanded an 'honourable peace' with the French Republic. It emphatically opposed the annexation of Alsace-Lorraine, declaring that 'we are conscious of speaking in the name of the German working class. In the common interest of France and Germany, in the interest of peace and liberty, in the interest of Western civilization against Eastern barbarism, the German workmen will not patiently tolerate the annexation of Alsace and Lorraine.' The manifesto ended by pledging that 'we shall faithfully stand by our fellow workmen in all countries, for the common international cause of the Proletariat!' At the same time the Central Committee appealed to local branches throughout the country to organize immediately 'as impressive demonstrations as possible against the annexation of Alsace-Lorraine and for an honourable peace with the French Republic'. Four days later the entire Central Committee of the party (except for Bebel and Liebknecht, who, as deputies, were immune) was arrested and taken in chains to the East Prussian fortress of Boyen near Lötzen. Protest meetings in Leipzig, Berlin, Augsburg and Nuremberg were broken up by the police.

On the same day the General Council of the International issued its second Address on the war, also drafted by Marx, calling on all sections of the International to demonstrate against the proposed annexation of Alsace-Lorraine, and for an honourable peace with the French Republic. In a searching analysis the Address refuted all the arguments—historical, strategic and nationalist—with which the German ruling class sought to justify the annexation of French territory. It warned in advance that such a step would be disastrous. It would without the slightest doubt force France into the arms of Russia and threaten

International Working Mens Association 1

The first Meeting of the Committee elected by the Public Meeting held at St Martins Hall on the 28th of September 1864; was held at 18 Greek St Soho on October 5th 1864 and on the motion of Mr Weston seconded by Mr Whitlock Mr G Odgers was voted to the Chair

The Chairman said the first business was the appointment of a Secretary to the Committee when Dr Marx prop and Mr Whitlock sec that Mr Cremer be appointed. Mr Cremer would prefer the appointment of Mr Le Lubez who was he believed in every way qualified to fill the Office. Mr Le Lubez having for various reasons declined the office Mr Cremer was unanimously elected

The next Question discussed was the Meeting nights of the Committee when several resolutions and Amendments were proposed but ultimately on the Motion of Mr Longmaid sec by Mr Bell it was carried with one dissentient That until the Association is in working order the Committee meet at 18 Greek St every Tuesday evening at 8 o'clock

A Question being asked as to the expenses of Meeting in the Room it was agreed to adjourn the consideration of that matter till the Council of the Universal League had decided on what terms they could allow us the use of the Room

The Question of the rate of Contributions was then discussed when Mr [illegible] prop and Mr Whitlock sec That for the present the rate of Contributions for the Committee be 1s per Quarter but that further Voluntary Contribution be accepted

7 *Minutes of the first meeting of the General Council of the First International*

8a (above) *August Bebel*
8b (below left) *Wilhelm Liebnecht*
8c (below right) *Andrea Costa*

Germany with another terrible but very different war. 'If the fortune of her arms,' said the Address, 'the arrogance of success, and dynastic intrigue lead Germany to a dismemberment of France, there will then remain open to her two courses only. She must at all risks become the *avowed* tool of Russian aggrandisement or, after some short respite, make ready again for another "defensive" war . . . a *war of races*—a war with the combined Slavonian and Roman races.'

Turning to France, the Address welcomed the establishment of the Republic, 'but at the same time we labour under misgivings'. The Republic, it pointed out, had not itself destroyed the throne; it had only occupied the vacant seat. It had been proclaimed not as a social conquest but as a national measure of defence. It was in the hands of a provisional government composed mainly of middle-class reactionaries. However, 'any attempt at upsetting the new government in the present crisis, when the enemy is almost knocking at the doors of Paris, would be a desperate folly'. The French workers, said the Address, should do their duty as citizens without delusions of grandeur or false analogies with previous revolutions. 'Let them calmly and resolutely improve the opportunities of Republican liberty, for the work of their own class organization. It will give them fresh Herculean powers for the regeneration of France, and for our common task—the emancipation of labour. Upon their energies and wisdom hinges the fate of the Republic.'[1]

Meanwhile the Paris Federation of the International addressed a manifesto directly 'to the Social Democrats of Germany'. It appeared in the *Volksstaat* on 11 September. It recalled the solemn pledge made by the King of Prussia when in his Speech from the Throne on the outbreak of war he had insisted that Germany was only fighting a war which had been forced upon her, and that she was waging it against the

1. Fear that the French workers, under the stress of revolutionary and patriotic emotions, would attempt an uprising during the war in an attempt to avert the defeat of France and to establish the 'Social Republic', was a nightmare for Marx. Almost a month before the battle of Sedan, on 8 August 1870, he wrote to Engels: 'What troubles me at the moment is the state of affairs in France itself. The next great battle can hardly fail to turn against the French. . . . If a revolution breaks out in Paris, the question is whether the workers have the means and the leadership to offer a serious resistance to the Prussians.' After Sedan, Engels wrote to Marx on 12 September: 'If anything at all could be done in Paris, a rising of the workers before peace is concluded should be prevented. . . . However the peace may turn out, it must be concluded before the workers can do anything at all. If they were victorious now—in the service of national defence—they would have to inherit the legacy of Bonaparte and of the present lousy Republic, and would be needlessly crushed by the German armies and thrown back another twenty years. . . . But will they not let themselves be carried away again under the pressure of the external attack, and proclaim the Social Republic on the eve of the storming of Paris? It would be appalling if, as their last act of war, the German armies had to fight out a battle with the Parisian workers at the barricades. It would throw us back fifty years. . . .'—*Marx-Engels Briefwechsel*, vol. IV, pp. 430n., 459.

Emperor and not the people of France. The Emperor, the manifesto pointed out, was now a prisoner of the Germans and France was a Republic. 'In the name of 39,000,000 people . . . we repeat what was said to the European Coalition in 1793: the French people will not make peace with an enemy while he occupies their territory.' It called on the Germans to 'go back across the Rhine! Then France and Germany can link hands in friendship across both banks of the river for which they shed their blood. Let us forget the atrocities we have committed against each other at the behest of despots. Let us proclaim freedom, equality and fraternity among all the nations!' Finally, to their fellow Social Democrats in Germany, the manifesto declared: 'The Social Democrats of France are confident that you will work with them to put an end to international hatred and achieve both general disarmament and universal harmony.'[1]

In its reply to the manifesto the *Volksstaat* declared: 'Up to 4 September Germany waged a defensive war. . . . The defensive war is now over. If fighting continues, it will have degenerated into a war of conquest, a war of monarchy against republic, of counter-revolution against revolution—a war waged as much against democratic Germany as republican France'. And when the North German Parliament met again in November to discuss 'the drafting of a Bill to raise the further sums required for the conduct of the war', the deputies of both working-class parties, Lassalleans and Eisenachers, tabled a request to the government 'to make peace as quickly as possible with the French Republic, and to renounce all intention of annexing French territory'.[2]

As soon as Parliament adjourned, Bebel and Liebknecht were arrested on a charge of high treason and sentenced to two years' imprisonment in a fortress. The Social Democratic movement had now lost its entire leadership. At the same time, the French section of the International had been affected by the war and by government repression. Serraillier reported to the General Council that, on his arrival in Paris in September, he had found that 'all members of the organization were either in prison or called up to their various regiments'.[3]

3

France's resistance to the German invasion, organized by her new Government of National Defence, soon collapsed. By 18 September German troops were approaching Paris, and at the end of October the fortress of Metz surrendered. The military situation seemed hopeless,

1. For the text of the manifesto, see *Der Wiener Hochverratsprozess*, pp. 408ff.
2. August Bebel, *Aus meinem Leben* (Stuttgart, 1910–14), vol. III, p. 194.
3. Minutes of the General Council, 28 February 1871.

L'internationale.

C'est la lutte finale.
Groupons nous et demain
L'internationale
Sera le genre humain.

Debout! l'âme du prolétaire!
Travailleurs, groupons nous enfin.
Debout! les damnés de la terre!
Debout! les forçats de la faim!
Pour vaincre la misère et l'ombre
Foule esclave, debout! debout!
C'est nous le droit, c'est nous le nombre:
Nous qui n'étions rien, soyons tout.

C'est la lutte finale,
groupons-nous et demain
L'Internationale
Sera le genre humain.

Il n'est pas de sauveurs suprêmes:
Ni dieu, ni césar, ni tribun.
Travailleurs sauvons-nous nous-mêmes;
Travaillons au salut commun.
Pour que les voleurs rendent gorge,
Pour tirer l'esprit du cachot,
Allumons notre grande forge!
Battons le fer quand il est chaud!

E. Pottier

The manuscript of the 'Internationale', written by Eugène Pottier in June 1871

and on 28 January the provisional government signed an armistice. Bismarck's terms included the surrender of Paris, the resignation of the provisional government and immediate elections for a National Assembly. The French government accepted.

The left in France—Socialists, Internationalists, Jacobins and Blanquists—regarded the capitulation as high treason. They called for the continuation of the struggle, and for a revolutionary-patriotic war on the model of France's revolutionary war of 1793, in which she had secured her freedom, chased the armies of the coalition monarchies from her territory and carried the revolution into their own lands. But the French peasants were no longer revolutionary. They were tired of the war, while the propertied middle class was paralysed by its fear of the workers. The elections on 8 February resulted in a crippling defeat for the left. Among the new Deputies there were only twenty Socialists, and two members of the International: Henri-Louis Tolain and Benoît Malon. About 450 described themselves as Monarchists, almost equally divided between Legitimists and Orléanists. The rest were middle-class Liberals and Republicans.

The government was led by Adolphe Thiers, with Jules Favre as Foreign Secretary. On 13 February the National Assembly met, not in Paris, where the working class was gripped by a fervour of revolutionary patriotism, but in Bordeaux, from where it soon moved to Versailles. Two weeks later Thiers and Favre signed the Peace Treaty, which included the cession of Alsace-Lorraine, a vast war indemnity and the occupation of Paris by the Prussian army. But Paris refused to capitulate. The workers were armed, since the provisional government had itself organized a National Guard as a popular militia, to defend Paris after the proclamation of the Republic. Thus the working class found itself with the physical means of defying the government.

Thiers tried to disarm Paris. On 18 March 1871 regular troops were ordered to attack an artillery position held by the National Guard in Montmartre. The workers of Paris rose under the leadership of Eugène Varlin, the regular troops were repulsed and the government fled to Versailles. Thiers then withdrew the entire apparatus of central and local government from the city, and in order to crush Paris asked Bismarck to release the French soldiers held by the Germans.

The administration's withdrawal left a vacuum. Since the rise of Napoleon I, Paris had been governed not by an elected local authority but by civil servants and officers appointed directly by the government, and although each of the twenty districts of the city had its own mayor, he had scarcely any effective authority. With the withdrawal of the local administration, therefore, there was only one authority left in Paris: the Central Committee of the National Guard. As soon as the Central

Committee found itself in possession of effective power, it decided to call elections for a popular assembly to which it could hand over the government of the city. The local council elected in this way assumed in its proclamation of 28 May the symbolic title of *Commune de Paris*,[1] after the style of the Council of Paris which had been set up during the revolution in 1792.

The Commune was not the result of a conspiracy or of a preconceived plan. It came into existence to fill a vacuum left by the removal of the administrative apparatus by Thiers. With the disappearance of those institutions which had hitherto exercised authority in Paris, a new source of authority based on new institutions became essential if Paris was to be governed at all. And in the circumstances no authority was acceptable other than a council elected by the citizens.

The Commune was elected by universal, direct and equal suffrage. As a great many members of the propertied middle class had fled from the city, it came to represent the workers and the lower middle class. But it was in no way Socialist, and only seventeen of the ninety-two elected representatives were members of the International's Paris Federation. Nor was it, as Lissagaray pointed out, a workers' government; two thirds of its members were *petit bourgeois* in origin. Politically, the Commune was controlled by Blanquists and Jacobins. Its earliest decrees were concerned with political freedom. 'Freedom of thought,' declared one of them, 'is the prime freedom'; and the Commune went on to secure the separation of church and state, and 'considering that the clergy was in reality an ally of the monarchy against freedom', the transfer of hereditary church lands to common ownership. It also ordered the demolition of the Emperor's column in the Place Vendôme—that 'symbol of brute force and infamy' as it was called in the decree of 13 April. Later, after the fall of the Commune, the famous painter Gustave Courbet, a member of both the Commune and the International, was prosecuted by the Versailles government for his part in the demolition.

The Commune announced its social aims in its 'Declaration to

1. The classic, if not very scientific, account of the Paris Commune is P.-O. Lissagaray's *Histoire de la Commune de 1871*. A valuable analysis of political theories prevailing during the Commune is given by Heinrich Koechlin in his *Die Pariser Commune des Jahres 1871 im Bewusstsein ihrer Anhänger* (Basle, 1950). For an excellent examination of the Commune's social and political structure, see G. D. H. Cole, *A History of Socialist Thought—Marxism and Anarchism, 1850–90* (London, 1954), ch. VII. See also N. Lukin, 'Protokolle des Generalrats der Internationalen Arbeiter-Assoziation als Quelle für die Geschichte der Pariser Kommune' in *Unter dem Banner des Marxismus* (1932), Year VI, no. 1, and in particular Karl Marx, *Der Bürgerkrieg in Frankreich*. For a critical treatment, see also E. S. Mason, *The Paris Commune* (New York, 1930); Samuel Bernstein, *The Beginnings of Marxian Socialism in France* (New York, 1933).

the French People' on 17 April, as 'the ending . . . of exploitation, stock-exchange speculation, monopolies and privileges to which the proletariat attributes its slavery, and the fatherland its misery and ruin'. But the decrees passed under the Commune did not aim at the destruction of private property. Their tendency was social reformist, not Socialist. Characteristic were the orders prohibiting night work in bakeries, forbidding employers to make deductions from wages and salaries by way of fines, banning sales of unredeemed articles by pawnshops and suspending rents for a limited period. In only two decrees is it possible to discern Socialist tendencies: the provision of a maximum salary of 6,000 francs a year for public servants and the transfer to co-operative associations of all businesses abandoned by their owners, with payment of compensation. In any event the Commune, with a life-span of only two months, could hardly have achieved a radical transformation of society. Moreover, throughout the entire period, Paris was under siege and her people engaged in a desperate and relentless struggle for survival.

The great historical significance of the Commune, in Marx's view, which he expressed in an Address written for the General Council, lay in its form of organization. It had developed a system of direct democracy in contrast to the central, hierarchical powers of the traditional state. Marx described it as 'the political form, at last discovered, under which to work out the economic emancipation of labour'. Breaking away from the normal parliamentary system with its rigid separation between legislature and executive, it combined both functions in one. Parish councils, which were directly responsible to the electors and could be recalled by them at any time, formed commissions responsible for the various branches of administration which they carried out themselves. All public posts, administrative, judicial and teaching, were elected by universal suffrage, with right of recall. The principle on which the Commune was based was the decentralization of political power. Its programme would have created a French nation formed from a voluntary federation of local communities. In its 'Declaration to the French People' the Commune acknowledged the complete autonomy of every local community: 'Each small section of the nation should be a microcosm of the life of the whole, creating the unity of a beehive rather than of a barracks. The organic cell of the French Republic is the local community, the Commune.'

Contrary to legend, the Paris Federation of the International was in no sense at the head of the working class in this period of revolutionary upheaval. It played no noticeable part in the proclamation of the Republic on 4 September, the uprising of 18 March or the proclamation of the Commune on 28 March. Under the dominant influence of the Proudhonists, who denied the necessity for working-class political activity, its initial attitude to the Republic had been one of suspicion. Organizationally too the Federation was weak. It had been broken up by Napoleon's police shortly before the outbreak of war, and had been only slowly and partially re-established by the beginning of the Commune. 'We are indeed a moral force in Paris, if nowhere else in France,' said Leo Frankel at a sitting of the Paris Federation on 15 February 1871, 'but we are not a material force, for we have no organization.' When on 14 March the General Council of the International considered calling a conference in London, Serraillier opposed on the grounds that the Paris Federation, which was 'scarcely organized', would be unable to send representatives.

Karl Marx, in the 'Second Address' of the General Council, issued five days after the proclamation of the Republic, had urged the French section of the International to concentrate first on re-establishing working-class organization. They should not waste effort in insurrection, since without a strong basis of organization, attempts to overthrow the *bourgeois* government and seize power would undoubtedly end in defeat. Serraillier returned to Paris soon after the Republic had been proclaimed, with these directions from the General Council, and Eugène Dupont, the Corresponding Secretary for France, urged the same course in his letters to the French section. The Paris Federation followed this line and took no part in the Blanquist attempts to seize power on 31 October and 22 January. Leading members of the International in Paris, such as Varlin, Vaillant, Frankel and Malon, joined the Central Committee of the National Guard; after the Commune was established they placed themselves entirely at its disposal. The main political posts in the Commune, however, were taken over by Blanquists and Jacobins. Members of the International, constituting a small minority in the council of the Commune, were allocated to economic and social tasks. Varlin, Beslay and Jourde went to the Finance Commission, Pindy and Duval to the Military Commission, Assi and Chalain to the Commission for Public Security, Frankel to the Commission for Labour and Commerce, Vaillant to Education, Theisz to the Post Office, Camélinat to the Mint and Fontain to Telegraphs.

4

On 18 May the Peace Treaty was ratified by the National Assembly, and three days later the Versailles troops began their attack on Paris. Bismarck had placed 10,000 French prisoners of war at the disposal of the Versailles government for the suppression of the Commune. Thiers could now attack Paris with overwhelming force. The battle for the city opened on 21 May, and lasted for eight days. The Versailles troops had to capture a whole series of barricades, one after the other, against bitter resistance from their working-class defenders. Charles Delescluse, who commanded the Commune's forces, was killed in the street fighting. Eugène Varlin, who took over the command, was captured by government troops on the last barricade and slashed with swords as he was dragged, with one eye hanging out of its socket, to the firing-squad. Bleeding from innumerable wounds, he was shot and his body mutilated. Finally, when the Commune had been drowned in the blood of its defenders, the victors went on killing in cold fury and with a cruelty unequalled in the nineteenth century.[1]

Marx had warned the French workers against the 'desperate folly' of seizing power. From the very inception of the Commune he knew that it was doomed.[2] These forebodings explain the strange fact that the International remained silent during the two-month life of the Commune, the only proletarian revolution to occur during the lifetime of the International; it issued neither an appeal for solidarity nor even an expression of sympathy and support. Marx's powerful 'Third Address'—the *Civil War in France*—was written after the overthrow of the Commune.[3]

Marx read the 'Address' to the General Council at its meeting on 30 May, three days after the fall of the Commune. In the sheer force of its eloquence and passion, it was one of the most impressive documents in the entire range of political literature. It constituted a formidable indictment which 'nailed' the 'exterminators' of the Commune 'to that eternal pillory from which all the prayers of their priests will not avail to redeem them'. It was, at the same time, a memorial to the defenders of the Commune, worthy of the terrible tragedy which consumed them. Historically it is also of considerable importance, since in Lenin's inter-

1. 'Including those killed, wounded and deported, there were 110,000 victims; women, children and aged dependants were left to shift for themselves. . . .' This estimate of the brutality committed after the fall of the Commune was made by the founder of the Catholic trade-union movement in France, Jules Zirnheld, in *Cinquante années de syndicalisme chrétien* (Paris, 1937), p. 19.

2. Some years later he explained the reasons why, in his opinion, the Commune was bound to founder: '. . . apart from the fact,' he observed to Domela Nieuwenhuis, 'that this [the Commune] was merely the rising of a city under exceptional conditions, the majority of the Commune was in no way Socialist, nor could it be. With a modicum of common sense, however, it could have reached a compromise with Versailles useful to the whole people—the only thing that could be attained a the time. The appropriation of the Bank of France alone would have been nough to put a rapid end to the *rodomontades* of the Versailles crowd. . . .'—Marx to Domela Nieuwenhuis, 22 February 1881 (*Marx-Engels, Selected Correspondence*, edited by Dona Torr (1936), pp. 386–7).

3. For an explanation of this 'apparent mystery', see Collins and Abramsky, p cit., pp. 194–8.

pretation it provided the basis for the Bolshevik view of the dictatorship of the proletariat.

The 'Address' did not attempt to provide a critical history of the Commune. It described the events which led to the rising, and the acts of treachery which caused its downfall. It also provided an assessment of its historical significance. Marx saw it as expressing 'a vague aspiration after a Republic that was to supersede not only the monarchical form of class-rule, but class-rule itself'. Its essential secret lay, he said, in its character as 'essentially a working-class government, the product of the struggle of the producing against the appropriating class, the political form at last discovered under which to work out the economic emancipation of labour'.

Thiers, and after him the middle-class press of Europe, had charged the International with responsibility for the Commune. Although Thiers himself had allowed thousands of Paris workers to be slaughtered and their homes to be burned, he accused the International of instigating 'arson'. To this Marx replied that 'the police-tinged *bourgeois* mind naturally figures to itself the International Working Men's Association as acting in the manner of a secret conspiracy, its central body ordering from time to time explosions in different countries. Our Association is in fact nothing but the international bond between the most advanced working men in the various countries of the civilized world. Wherever, in whatever shape, and under whatever conditions the class struggle obtains any consistency, it is but natural that members of our Association should stand in the foreground.' Against the flood of denunciation and slander which poured as from an overflowing sewer against the Commune, Marx concluded his Address with the forthright and uncompromising statement, in the name of the International: 'Working men's Paris, with its Commune, will be for ever celebrated as the glorious harbinger of a new society. Its martyrs are enshrined in the great heart of the working class.'

14 · The Crusade against the International

Adolphe Thiers had made himself responsible for a massive destruction of human life. By removing the apparatus of administration from Paris he had precipitated the establishment of the Commune. But in the Commune he perceived the ghost of that 'Social Republic' which as early as 1848 had thrown the propertied members of the middle class into a paroxysm of fear. In June 1848 the cry of the workers for a Social Republic had been drowned in their blood and Thiers was determined to repeat the performance. No impartial examination of what happened between 13 February and 21 May 1871 can today leave the slightest doubt that this was in fact his intention from the start.

So far as Thiers was concerned, no moral scruples would deter him from executing his plan. According to the estimates of General MacMahon, about 14,000 defenders of the Commune were slaughtered in the streets of Paris or summarily executed; 10,137 prisoners were sentenced by court martial, about half being transported to New Caledonia and the other half imprisoned in France. At the same time Thiers declared martial law over the whole country. He further, on 14 March 1872, passed through Parliament an emergency law directed against the International. It was his intention, as he explained, that the French state should treat the followers of the International as the Spanish Inquisition had treated heretics. In its very first Article the Act declared that 'by the mere fact of its existence, the International . . . represents a threat to public order'. Hence Article 2 provided that everyone who, subsequent to the Law's enactment, 'subscribes to the principles of the International Working Men's Association, joins or remains a member of it' was liable to imprisonment.

In order to justify before world opinion the unusual ferocity with which France was persecuting the International under the inspiration of Thiers, a highly coloured picture was presented of the threat which it constituted to *bourgeois* social order. Even before the Commune had been proclaimed in Paris, the middle class had tended to view the International as a serious threat to its social supremacy. Under the Empire there had been three prosecutions for conspiracy brought against the leaders of the Paris section, and shortly before the outbreak of war the police had arrested all members on whom they could lay hands throughout France, on a charge of conspiring against the Emperor's life. In France, Belgium and Switzerland the *bourgeois* press had held the International responsible for initiating the strike movement of 1868, and scarcely two weeks before the outbreak of war, fourteen leading members of the Social Democratic movement in Austria were found guilty of sympathizing with the aims of the International, and were sentenced by a Viennese court to years of hard labour.

It took the events in France, however, to convince the *bourgeois* world of the terrifying power of the International. Column after column was given over to descriptions of the International, led by its General Council in London, hatching conspiracies at once with Bonapartists and with Bismarck, intervening decisively in the events of the war, plotting insurrections and finally putting Paris to the flames. The *Kölnische Zeitung* alleged that after the setting-up of the French Republic the General Council had decided that the war should continue and had handed over 200,000 francs to the French section to pay for war propaganda. According to the Paris *Figaro* the 200,000 francs had been given to the International by the supporters of Bonaparte. Reuter's reported that the General Council had sent a delegation to the National Assembly in Bordeaux to urge a continuation of the war. On the other hand a number of French papers, including the *Courier de Lyon*, the *Courier de la Gironde* and *La Liberté*, reported secret sessions of members of the General Council in Geneva and Berne, with a Prussian delegate in the chair, planning the Lyon insurrection of 29 September so as to weaken the French Republic's resistance to the German invasion. It was also disclosed in the French Press that Marx had been Bismarck's private secretary and that, with his accomplices in London, he had hatched the plot which led to the establishment of the Paris Commune. A few months later, when the French papers had charged the International with setting fire to Paris, the American Press revealed that the great fire which had reduced Chicago to ashes in October 1871 had been started by the International and the story was telegraphed round the world.[1]

In this way *bourgeois* opinion had been well prepared by the news-

1. Reports by Engels, Marx and Hales to the General Council meetings, 28 February, 21 March and 2 May 1871. See also the General Council's report to the Hague Congress, 1872.

papers for the murderous events of May 1871, and the massacres in the streets of Paris could be applauded as a great victory in the cause of civilization. But the extermination of the International in France had not, apparently, averted the threat to civilization. On 6 June 1871, a few days after the defeat of the Commune, Thiers's Foreign Minister, Jules Favre, released a circular letter to the European powers, warning them, and through them the entire world, of the menace which the International still presented to their way of life. The note denounced the International as 'a society breeding war and hatred. Its foundation is atheism and Communism. Its aim is the destruction of capital and those who possess it. Its medium is the brute force of the masses.' The note concluded with the warning cry: 'Europe is confronted with an agent of destruction aimed at all nations and at the very principles on which civilization depends.' France had done everything which was humanly possible to save civilization. But, the note implied, as the International was a threat to all nations, it was not enough to stamp it out in one country. It had to be annihilated everywhere, and this demanded joint action by the European powers.

The circular was dispatched as a feeler, to test the reactions of other countries to the idea of collaborating in a common effort against the International. Consequently, Jules Favre confined himself for the time being to the question of how the refugees from the Commune should be regarded. Were they entitled to political asylum? The Marquis de Banneville, French Ambassador at Vienna, told the Austro-Hungarian Chancellor, Count Beust, that 'these refugees cannot be allowed to conceal their crimes behind the cloak of political aims; they should be treated as ordinary criminals and given no protection against the justice awaiting them at home'.[1] Jules Favre's circular was given careful consideration by the Cabinets of the main European countries.

Four days after receiving the note, the Austrian Council of Ministers met to decide on 'the question of extradition for those who had fled after taking part in the outrages of the Paris uprising', as it was worded on the agenda of the Council meeting. On this, Count Beust had submitted a memorandum on his conversation with the French Ambassador. It stated that, without wishing to anticipate the decision of the Ministerial Council, Beust suggested, for their consideration, that 'the disaster in Paris did not occur through merely local factors, but was mainly the work of a European conspiracy calling itself the International'. From general, political and humanitarian considerations alike, therefore, it was of supreme importance to avoid giving the impression 'that the supporters of the Commune had only to fly to Austria-Hungary to

1. Ludwig Brügel, *Geschichte der österreichischen Sozialdemokratie*, vol. II, pp. 191ff.

enjoy greater security than in any other country'.[1] Meanwhile Bismarck was preparing to initiate a European-wide campaign against the International. In a memorandum which he submitted to the Cabinets of Europe on 1 July 1871, he proposed a conference of governments to discuss common action and the establishment of a European alliance against the International. 'Such a European alliance,' said Bismarck's journal, the *Norddeutsche Allgemeine Zeitung*, 'is the only possible means of saving the state, church, culture, in a word, everything which makes up the life of European states.' The proposal foundered in the first place in Britain, the seat of the General Council. The British Foreign Minister, Lord Granville, flatly rejected the invitation to join the European alliance, since his country did not feel in any way threatened by the International.

Bismarck, however, did not abandon his project for action against the International on a continental scale. He told the Austro-Hungarian government that he would welcome discussions on 'a common approach towards the subversive activities of the International'. Soon afterwards, Prince Bismarck and Count Beust met at Gastein in order, as Beust later explained in a detailed account, 'to reach an understanding on common measures for defence and struggle . . . against the increasing spread of the International, which exercises a dangerous influence particularly among the working classes, and which is directed against the existing principles of state and society'.[2]

At the Gastein conference, Bismarck and Beust discussed judicial as well as social and political measures against the International. On the legal aspect Beust remarked that, under Austrian law, 'the International, which is led by the General Council in London and, so far as Germany is concerned, by the Executive of the Social Democratic party in Leipzig, is a secret society and therefore has no legal right to exist'. It would therefore be prosecuted as a secret society in Austria. Regarding social policy, Beust wondered whether, in the course of the class struggle, 'it would not be possible to confront the general workers' association with a general association of employers, the solidarity of the propertyless with the solidarity of property', since, he added, 'the power of capital is still a factor making for security and stability in public life'. Finally, Beust and Bismarck agreed that the appropriate Ministries in both countries should work out specific measures to combat the International, and that their recommendations should be submitted to a conference of delegates from the two governments.

1. For the text of the Beust memorandum and the Minutes of the Ministerial Council meeting of 10 June 1871, see Brügel, op. cit., vol. II, p. 191.

2. For the text of the memorandum and the minutes of the ensuing conferences, see Brügel, op. cit., vol. II, pp. 103ff.

After returning from his Gastein conference with Bismarck, Beust secured from his Cabinet a special credit, originally of 3,000,000 gulden, to meet 'the expenses of political intelligence' which had, he asserted, become absolutely necessary 'in view of the dangerous spread of the International over the whole of Europe'.

The Austrian government held its first ministerial conference in Vienna, under the chairmanship of Count Beust, on 1 September 1871. It had before it the circular from Jules Favre and inquiries from the Italian, Russian, British, Belgian and Swiss governments about the measures which the Austrian government had taken against the International. The real purpose of the conference, however, was to work out the guiding principles for a programme of action. At a further conference, under the chairmanship of the Austrian Prime Minister, Prince Adolf Auersperg, in December 1871, Bismarck's suggestion for an all-European conference of governments was considered. Auersperg expressed the view that owing to the 'differences of opinion prevailing in some countries, such as England and Switzerland, regarding the character of the International', it would be expedient to call first of all a conference of Austro-Hungarian and German government representatives to discuss measures 'for the protection of the social order against the attacks of the International'.

At yet another conference of Austro-Hungarian Ministers under the chairmanship of the Foreign Minister, Count Andrassy, on 22 June 1872, it was proposed that the International 'be declared generally harmful by the comity of European states, and that all should refuse to permit the holding and assembling of congresses and of the General Council, on their territory'. Andrassy believed, or at least hoped, that 'England and Switzerland could not stay out of such an international agreement indefinitely'. It was further proposed that in Germany, as in Austria-Hungary, the International should be declared a secret society and prosecuted as such. It was finally proposed 'to treat the activity of the International, in view of its nature and potentialities, as a criminal activity to which extradition agreements would then apply'. Discussions between the two governments on measures to combat the International dragged on until the late autumn of 1872. Finally, on 7 November 1872, the full conference of delegates from the German and Austro-Hungarian governments met in Berlin. They discussed, over fourteen sessions, 'the social question' in all its aspects. Their results were expressed in the following principles:

(i) that the tendencies of the International are in complete contrast with, and antagonistic to, the principles of the *bourgeois* society; they must therefore be vigorously repelled;
(ii) that the International constitutes a dangerous abuse of the freedom of

assembly and, following its own practice and principle, state action against it must be international in scope and must therefore be based on the solidarity of all governments;

(iii) that even if some governments do not intend to pass a special law [i.e. against the International], as France has done, it is still highly desirable that through the adhesion of other governments to the principles and approach on the social question adopted here, the ground should be cut from beneath the feet of the International Working Men's Association and its harmful activities frustrated;

(iv) that it must be regarded as a necessary consequence of this solidarity that other nations should endorse the principles here adopted and refuse to allow the holding of congresses or meetings of the General Council and its related organizations on their territory.

The conference of the two monarchies, however, did not lead in either country to any tightening of the laws against the International. A more stringent interpretation of existing laws was all that was required to ensure its effective suppression. The trials of Scheu and Oberwinder in Vienna, and of Bebel and Liebknecht in Leipzig, showed that mere verbal support for the aims of the International could be construed as evidence of high treason. Both governments were also unwilling to incur the odium, before world opinion, of debasing the machinery of justice in the interests of vengeance, as France had done. Germany and Austria agreed to treat the French proposal for an agreement on extraditing refugees as 'dilatory', hoping that before too long Britain and Switzerland, where political refugees enjoyed rights of asylum, would change their attitude in the cause of solidarity in the fight against the International.

Pope Pius IX attempted to hasten the process of reappraisal, in Switzerland if not in Britain, by an appeal to Christian conscience regarding the right of political asylum. The suggestion of Thiers that the followers of the International should be treated as the Spanish Inquisition had treated heretics, met with his sympathetic approval. In an address to a deputation of Swiss Catholics, he referred to it in the following terms: 'Your government, which is republican, feels obliged to make great sacrifices in the interests of so-called freedom. It grants asylum to characters of the worst kind. It gives free scope to the International, which would like to treat the whole of Europe as it treated Paris. These gentlemen of the International,' concluded His Holiness, 'are to be feared, because they labour in the cause of the eternal enemy of God and mankind. What is to be gained, then, in affording them protection?'[1] An echo of the condemnation of the International by Pius IX occurred in the encyclical, *Quod Apostolici Muneris*, issued by his successor Pope Leo XIII on 28 December 1878. Leo XIII denounced

1. Quoted in the Report of the General Council to the Hague Congress.

the International as 'a criminal organization' which, he said, had set itself the aim of 'destroying the basis of authority in this world'. He condemned Socialism as a 'heresy of the depraved' and he called on the Christian world to 'ensure that no Catholic joins this heretical organization or dares to encourage it in any way'.

Despite the Papal exorcism, however, Catholic Spain was the only one among the European powers prepared to sign an agreement with France on the extradition of Communard refugees. As early as October 1871 the International had been prohibited in Spain by a decree of the Cortes. A few months later, on 16 February 1872, the Spanish Prime Minister, Sagasta, issued a circular to the provincial governors on the operation of the decree. It ordered them to 'treat the International as outside the frame of the Constitution and subject to the criminal law, since it has declared itself to be the enemy of the fatherland, a foe to public safety, and has rejected the state, property and the family'. Therefore, they must 'prevent by all means, including the use of force, all public activity designed to insinuate this criminal organization into our society. Its leaders must be imprisoned at once and handed over to the courts.'[1]

At the same time, the Spanish government took up the idea of joint action on the part of the European powers against the International which Bismarck had proposed in his memorandum of 1 July 1871. The Spanish circular to the governments of Europe on 9 February 1872 called attention to a debate in the Cortes—'perhaps the most important that has ever taken place in a European assembly', was the modest description. This debate, claimed the circular, 'had defined the true nature of the International Working Men's Association'. The Cortes had reached the momentous conclusion that 'this mighty and terrible organization, and its rapid development, must within the next few years attract the attention of all those who are concerned to preserve the social order'. Moreover, the scholarly researches undertaken by or on behalf of the Cortes, had established the fact that the existing social system 'was threatened to its depths by the International', since that diabolical society 'flies in the face of all human tradition, strikes God from the mind, denies family and the principle of heredity, and rejects alike the sublime principles of nationality and civilization'.

The Cortes had then turned to wrestle with the problem of 'how far even the most liberal of political institutions can tolerate the existence of an organization like the International' and had reached the conclusion, after tortuous debate, that it could not be tolerated. But, the note was careful to add, 'it was not enough for one nation to suppress

1. For the full text, see Rudolf Meyer, *Der Emanzipationskampf des vierten Standes*, vol. II, p. 118.

the International by the most stringent means; the problem is not within the jurisdiction of a single nation'. A common approach by all civilized nations was required, especially as it was mainly through the instrumentality of foreigners that the spirit of insurrection was being spread. 'If it is a question,' the note continued, 'of exorcizing the evil, then it is necessary for all nations to unite their efforts in the cause.' Finally, in an oblique reference to Britain, the note concluded: 'A solution would certainly be found more easily if one of the major powers would take the initiative in organizing a common and simultaneous action among the nations of the civilized world.'

The British government, however, responded to the Spanish invitation to join the crusade against the International as it had previously responded to a similar request from Prussia. On this occasion, Lord Granville thought it appropriate to give the Spanish government a lecture, in his note of 8 March 1872, to the effect that 'according to British law, all foreigners have an absolute right to enter the country and to remain; while they are here, they enjoy the same protection from the law as British subjects'. Moreover, foreigners, like British subjects, could be punished only for offences against the law, and only then 'after trial by jury and conviction in accordance with the law and in the light of evidence submitted in open court'. The British government saw no reason to ask Parliament to pass emergency legislation, and its view was, as the note made clear, 'shared by Parliament and public opinion'. To prevent any further time being wasted in futile discussion, Lord Granville made public the Spanish as well as the English version of his note.[1]

The attitude of the British government incurred the strong displeasure of Bismarck. What was the point, wrote the *Norddeutsche Allgemeine Zeitung* on 17 April 1872, of single states such as France and Spain taking 'precautions' against the International, if 'English soil provides free territory from which the other European states may be harassed under the protection of English law'?[2]

The project of a Holy Alliance against the International, suggested by Bismarck and supported by Beust, Thiers, the Pope and Sagasta, had been frustrated by the resistance of England. And the crusade by the

1. *Correspondence between the British and Spanish Governments respecting the International Society* (London, 1872). The Home Secretary used similar arguments in Parliament, on 12 April 1872, in a debate on a motion by a Conservative member, Alexander Baillie-Cochrane, to dissolve the International. Even *The Times* said, commenting on the debate, 'We cannot take arbitrary measures for the suppression of a Society which, so far as we know, is within the pale of our law. . . .'—*The Times*, 15 April 1872, quoted in Collins and Abramsky, op. cit., p. 247.

2. For the texts of the Spanish and English notes, and of the article in the *Norddeutsche Allgemeine Zeitung*, see Meyer, op. cit., vol. I, p. 158.

bourgeois Press and diplomats, intended to destroy the International morally, produced the opposite effect. It provided it with undreamt-of publicity. The International had featured in the deliberations of European Cabinets and Parliaments, and in the Press. The whole world now knew about the International, its aspirations and aims, and its character as a fraternal association of the workers of all nations. The ruling classes, naturally, saw it as a threat to their privileges, wealth and power. But the workers could never see it as a 'menace to society'. However dense might be the tissue of lies with which the *bourgeois* Press surrounded the International, its nature, from its inception, as an association of workers throughout the world to put an end to misery and humiliation, could not be concealed. Moreover, the lies told about the International were too grotesque to be believed, and the denunciation to which it was subjected by the ruling-class Press only strengthened in working-class minds feelings of solidarity with the victims of persecution. Consequently the crusade which was to blacken the name of the International in fact enhanced its prestige, giving it an importance in world politics which bore no relation to its effective power.

15 · The End of the First International

1

In the Franco-Prussian War and in the Paris Commune the International had proved itself not, indeed, as a political power, since it had not the strength to influence the course of events, but as an ideological fraternity whose members had remained true to their principles through one of the crises of history. The Socialists of France and Germany had resisted the flood of chauvinism which the war had unleashed in both countries. They had fraternized across the fighting lines—a 'great fact, unparalleled in the history of the past'. And, after the defeat of the French Empire, the German Socialists had been proud to incur the charge of being 'traitors' by their attitude to the Peace Treaty. They had called openly in Parliament, at mass meetings, in published manifestos and in their Press for an honourable peace with France, and had protested against the seizure of her territory. A delegate conference of the International, meeting in London at the beginning of September 1871, declared in a resolution that 'the German workers had done their duty during the Franco-German War'.

The Paris Federation of the International had no part in the rising of the workers, who seized power against the advice of the General Council. But once the Commune had been proclaimed, the General Council made its cause their own. In the middle of the fight between the Paris Commune and the Versailles government, the International co-operated with other organizations in arranging a mass meeting in Hyde Park on 12 April 1871 to send greetings to the Commune from the workers of London. And after the fall of the Commune, the International had proudly identified itself with its cause, undeterred by the host of enemies which this inevitably provoked.

This spontaneous act of solidarity evoked a tremendously sympathetic response in many sections of the International, particularly in Spain, Italy, Belgium and Germany. After the Belgian Minister of

Justice had insulted the defenders of the Commune in Parliament, and had called for the extradition of the refugees, the Belgian Federation of the International declared on 5 June 1871: 'We solemnly greet the Paris Commune in its hour of temporary defeat. . . . We recognize that the Commune served the cause of all mankind, and that those who fought for it deserve the sympathy and respect of all men of good will.' And when Bismarck derided the Commune in the German Parliament, Bebel, the only Social Democratic representative in the first Parliament of the new-born German Reich, replied: 'You may rest assured that the entire working class of Europe, as well as all those who still care anything for freedom and independence, see, in Paris, their symbol of hope.' That Bebel was expressing the view of his entire party was made clear when, a few days after the defeat of the Commune, while the *bourgeois* Press of Germany was demanding from the Social Democrats a formal repudiation of the 'outrage', the *Volksstaat* wrote: 'We declare our complete solidarity with the Commune and are prepared to defend its actions at any time, against anybody.' After an expression of 'mourning for our fallen brothers', the *Volksstaat* replied to the 'naïve impertinence' of the *bourgeois* Press by printing Freiligrath's 'Song of Triumphant Revolution':

> Once more will I appear before the nations,
> Stand on your necks, your heads, your crowns;
> Liberator, avenger and judge, with sword unsheathed
> I raise a mighty arm to save the world.

2

But hopes of a speedy return of the revolution were doomed to disappointment. With the defeat of the Paris Commune, the only centre of revolutionary power from which the initiative for European revolution could spread had been destroyed. When, after the Lausanne Congress of September 1867, Marx had written to Engels about 'the next revolution, which is perhaps nearer than it appears',[1] it was France which he had mainly in mind. Anticipation of a revolution in France was not at that time a fond illusion of revolutionary dreamers. Many respectable members of the middle class also thought it inevitable. In vain had Louis Bonaparte tried to enlist the sympathies of the workers and the middle class. Workers and *bourgeois*, Orléanists and Legitimists, despised him as a usurper and detested his régime as the embodiment of corruption and police tyranny. The adventurous foreign policy in which the emperor indulged in his neurotic craving for glory was bound one day

1. *Marx-Engels Briefwechsel*, vol. III, p. 500; *Marx-Engels, Selected Correspondence*, op. cit., p. 227.

to involve his régime in crisis. It was widely believed in Paris that when that happened it would bring with it the chance of overthrowing him.

At that time Marx saw other signs of reviving revolutionary pressures. Ireland, in the 1860s, was undergoing a nationalist ferment. In that country the national and social revolutions seemed indissolubly linked. The land—the sole source of livelihood for most of its people—was in the hands of the absentee English aristocracy. Year after year thousands of impoverished and land-hungry Irishmen emigrated to America, or as sweated labour to England. In addition, British sovereignty in Ireland represented the domination of a Protestant ruling class over a Catholic nation. The Irish revolution, for which the Fenians, a secret society of revolutionary nationalists, worked, was intended to free the people from the political as well as the economic domination of foreign heretics.

An uprising had been planned for 1865, but the British government struck first with mass arrests of the Fenians. In spite of this, revolutionary outbreaks occurred in 1866 and 1867. When they were suppressed, the Fenians responded with terrorist activities in England. In September 1867, a few days after the Lausanne Congress, armed Fenians in Manchester attacked in broad daylight a police van carrying two Fenians. They shot the policemen and freed the prisoners. In December, Fenians tried to break into Clerkenwell prison in London by blowing up the walls. Twelve people were killed and over a hundred injured. England was seized by panic. As the real culprits could not be found, some of the large number of arrested Fenians were charged with murder and three of them, despite the lack of any conclusive evidence, were executed.

Marx spoke on the General Council of the need to support the Irish struggle, in spite of the unpopularity which this would inevitably incur. At his suggestion, the General Council called a meeting in London which protested in the name of justice and political wisdom against the intention of executing the Fenians. Marx also proposed an address to the Irish people in which the International would declare its solidarity with their struggle.

Marx's Irish policy was the subject of a vehement debate on the General Council, extending over three sessions.[1] Thomas Mottershead spoke strongly against Irish independence. An independent Ireland, he argued, owing to its geographical position between England and France, would threaten the security of England. An English withdrawal

1. Minutes of the General Council, 16, 26 and 30 November 1869. For a survey of the General Council's debate on the Irish Question, see Collins and Abramsky, op. cit., pp. 132–4, 165–70.

from Ireland would be followed by a French occupation. At a subsequent meeting, a letter from the Chartist veteran, George Julian Harney, who had emigrated to Boston, was read out, in which he protested against the attitude of the International to the Irish Question: 'Ireland,' he wrote, 'is an integral part of the British Empire.'

Marx, however, convinced the General Council that the English working class must in its own interest support the Irish cause. In order to further the social revolution in England, it was in Ireland that the decisive blow had to be struck. Ireland provided the main bulwark for English landlordism; it could not be overthrown in Ireland without succumbing in England too. Such a development would deprive the English landlords not only of substantial revenues but also of considerable prestige as the visible representatives of English domination. On the other hand, by helping to maintain the landlord's power in Ireland, the English workers were making them invulnerable at home. Marx reminded his audience that the English Republic had foundered on Cromwell's Irish policy. 'Finally, what ancient Rome demonstrated on an enormous scale is being repeated in our day in England. The people which oppresses another people forges its own chains.'[1]

Marx did not of course expect any immediate repercussions in the British Labour movement, of Ireland's national struggle. What he did hope for was that the Irish revolution would undermine the power of the English landed aristocracy and that a union of the British working class with the revolutionary Irish would revive the fighting spirit of the British workers, as during the Chartist days. He saw as the immediate task of the British trade-union movement the setting-up of an independent workers' party which, like the Chartists, set its sights on the conquest of political power. The struggle for electoral reform seemed to him most important, since it 'galvanized' the British workers once more and opened the way for their entry through Parliament into the key positions of political power. The revolutionary initiative would, he wrote, be taken by France. But he saw in England the only great power which could serve 'as a lever for a serious economic revolution', because it was the only country in which landed property was concentrated into large units, where capitalist production was completely dominant and where the workers constituted a majority of the population.

3

After the fall of the Commune, however, it was clear that there could be no new revolutionary initiative in France for a considerable time. True,

1. *Briefe an Kugelmann*, p. 108; also pp. 95–6.

the Commune, in going down to defeat, had not involved the International in its ruin. But the terrible bloodshed which the revolutionary movement had suffered in France—its best members killed in battle, executed, deported or compelled to flee the country—and the reign of terror which followed the triumph of the counter-revolution, had destroyed organized Socialism in France, which had been one of the mainstays of the International.

Nevertheless, reaction was powerless to extirpate the idea of the International from the minds of the workers. On 20 July 1872, for example, the Paris correspondent of the Swiss *Revue* reported on the mood of the French workers following their defeat: 'The workers are quiet. They are rebuilding their trade unions, revising the rules in conformity with the law. But their hearts are with the International, in the graveyards [of the Commune's martyrs] with the departed'. In the same month, the Paris correspondent of the Vienna *Neue Freie Presse* reported:

> An active movement is going on in working-class circles. The workers are forming trade-union circles in place of the branches of the International which have been dissolved. They meet diligently in cafés, with room for several thousand people, which are still too small for the numbers present. . . . The speakers display a liveliness, and even a passion, which justifies one in thinking that the optimism which used to prevail among the people of Paris has by no means given way to quiescence.[1]

It was, indeed, the Paris Commune which provided the impetus for the expansion of the International in Italy. Before the proclamation of the Commune, the movement in that country had been feeble. It is true that as early as 1866 Bakunin had gathered round him a circle of young revolutionary idealists—Carlo Gambuzzi, Alberto Tucci, Saverio Friscia, Guiseppe Fanelli and Stefano Caporusso—but Mazzini still controlled the working-class movement. The advent of the Commune shattered the workers' faith in Mazzini. That heroic struggle had fired their enthusiasm; they regarded the cause of the Commune as their own. But Mazzini condemned it in a furious attack in the columns of *La Roma del Popolo*, and condemned the International along with the Commune, for which he held it responsible. With this, Garibaldi ended his long association with Mazzini. Garibaldi had offered his sword to the Commune, and he now paid tribute to the International as the 'sun of the future'. At the same time, Bakunin, in two vigorously worded leaflets,[2] shattered Mazzini's influence over the working-class organiza-

1. Rudolf Meyer, *Der Emanzipationskampf des vierten Standes*, vol. II, p. 734.
2. Michael Bakunin, *Antwort eines Internationalisten an Mazzini* and *Die politische Theologie Mazzinis und die Internationale*. Both leaflets were printed simultaneously in Italian and French in 1871.

tions in northern Italy which transferred their allegiance to the International, constituting its Italian Federation.

Bakunin saw in the rapid expansion of the International in Italy the sure signs of an early revolution. He was, as Alexander Herzen had pointed out, always prone to mistake 'the second month of pregnancy for the ninth'. He now regarded Italy as the leading revolutionary country. In April 1872 he wrote to his Spanish friend, Francisco Mora: 'In Italy they have what other countries lack, a younger generation bursting with energy, without position, without career, without hope, a generation which, despite its *bourgeois* origins, is not yet drained of its intellectual and moral fibre. . . . Today it is throwing itself head over heels into the revolutionary Socialist movement.'[1]

In Spain, which had been in a state of chronic revolution since the end of the 1860s, laws against the International remained ineffective. The organization continued to grow. According to a report delivered at its Córdoba Congress in December 1872, the Spanish Federation embraced 101 local federations, with 332 trade-union branches, 66 other affiliated local groups and 10 sections consisting of individual members.

In Germany, the party's courageous opposition to the Franco-German War had been unpopular with the mass of the people and had led to a decline in membership. When the Eisenach party held its third congress at Dresden in August 1871, it had only 6,225 members from 81 localities. A year previously, at its second congress held at Stuttgart in June 1870, its membership had been 13,147, organized in 113 local branches. Admittedly, the German workers' movement was still suffering from the split between Eisenachers and Lassalleans. Yet both sections united for the elections to the Reichstag called by Bismarck, fresh from the triumph of his Peace Treaty with France, for 3 March 1871. The combined list secured about 100,000 votes—roughly three per cent of the total poll. At the second elections to the Federal Parliament, held in January 1874, the Socialist vote was over 350,000.

On the position in Austria after the fall of the Commune, we have already referred (p. 118) to the memorandum by Schmidt-Zabierow, head of the Civil Service, in June 1872. It said that the 'more decisive attitude of European governments against the entire Labour movement', and the prosecutions of its leaders, had caused it to proceed with 'far more caution'. 'In spite of this,' the memorandum continued, 'it cannot be claimed that the Social Democratic Workers' movement had ceased or declined in Austria.' The memorandum recorded a total of 197 Social Democratic organizations consisting of educational associations, craft

1. Meyer, op. cit., vol. II, p. 192.

societies and trade unions.[1] At the same time, four Social Democratic papers were appearing: *Der Volkswille* in Vienna, *Die Gleichheit* in Wiener Neustadt, *Die Freiheit* in Graz and the *Delnické Listy* in Prague.

Switzerland was hardly touched by the wave of reaction which swamped other European countries after the fall of the Commune. The Labour movement welcomed the establishment of the Commune, followed its struggle with enthusiasm, and after its fall gave hospitality to all refugees who reached Switzerland. They answered Thiers's demand that all Communard refugees be handed back to France as common criminals with mass demonstrations defending the right of asylum. The events in France, and in particular the influx of French refugees, revived the local sections of the International, especially in French-speaking Switzerland.

In Holland the International had been expanding steadily since the end of the 1860s. Its first section, founded in Amsterdam in August 1869, provided it with an organ, *De Standaart des Volks*, and soon afterwards sections were formed in Rotterdam, Arnhem, Haarlem and Utrecht. Two other papers were soon established—*De Werkman* in Amsterdam and *Die Volksblad* in Rotterdam. The white terror unleashed by the counter-revolution in France helped to radicalize the working class of Holland, where the International soon took hold.

In Denmark the fall of the Paris Commune precipitated the formation of the first section of the International. In July 1871 there appeared the first number of a Socialist paper, the *Social-Demokraten*, and a month later the 'International Workers' Association' constituted itself a section of the International.

In only two countries, however, was there evidence of an active mass movement of the working class following the fall of the Commune. These were Belgium and Britain. In Belgium the number of workers who sympathized with the aims of the International ran into tens of thousands, though the number of regular members was of course much smaller. But even these were by no means negligible, since the Social Democratic papers being published at the time in Belgium included *L'Internationale* and *Liberté* in Brussels, *De Werker* in Antwerp, *Le Mirabeau* in Verviers, *Voorruit* in Bruges and *Le Devoir* in Liège.

In England both the number of local branches of the International and its individual membership were small. Its strength, however, rested on its affiliated trade-union membership. Some of the leading trade unionists in Britain had served on the General Council, a fact which brought it considerable political prestige. As early as 1866, a conference of trade unions had recommended organizations affiliated to it to join

1. Ludwig Brügel, *Geschichte der österreichischen Sozialdemokratie*, vol. II, pp. 142–3.

the International. At the Basle Congress in 1869, Applegarth gave the number of trade-union affiliations as twenty-eight. In November 1870, a meeting of the Manchester and Salford Trades Council declared its solidarity with the International and its support for 'all their actions in all countries of the world'. In January 1871, the Birmingham Trades Council also affiliated to the International, declaring in a resolution that it was 'convinced that the realization of the principles of the International would lead to lasting peace among the nations of the world'. The Minutes of the General Council for this period show some evidence that trade-union interest in, and support for, the International might be increasing.

The British trade unions had not as yet set up a working-class political party, and there was no organized Socialist movement. Moreover, organizations affiliated to the International in Britain did not, as in other countries, form their own national federation until the autumn of 1871. Up to that time, the General Council functioned as the executive of both the British section and the world movement. In Britain, therefore, the General Council had fulfilled a political function of the kind which in other countries was performed by federal councils or, as in the case of Germany, by Social Democratic parties. The General Council had helped to initiate the campaign for electoral reform in Britain. After the congress at Basle had come out in favour of the public ownership of land, the General Council in London helped to establish the Land and Labour League in October 1869, to campaign for the Basle decisions. It had also taken the initiative in organizing mass meetings to demand the recognition of the French Republic and the release of the Fenian prisoners, and to oppose the German annexation of Alsace-Lorraine.

Above all, the General Council gave world-wide publicity to the struggles of the British trade unions. Many of these episodes have already been described. Perhaps the most outstanding was the strike of the Newcastle engineers for a nine-hour day in 1871 which led directly to the establishment of the Nine-Hour League. At first the employers had tried to bring in workers from Dundee and London. When both English and Scottish workers refused to act as strike-breakers, the employers' organization sent agents to the Continent. Hundreds of German, Norwegian, Danish and Belgian workers, knowing nothing of the strike, accepted work in Newcastle. The Nine-Hour League approached the General Council, asking it to make use of international connections to stop the influx of foreign labour. The General Council at once sent two of its members, Cohen and Eccarius, to the Continent. With the help of the International's European sections and of their newspapers they stopped the enrolment of foreign strike-breakers. The foreign workers who had already arrived in Newcastle agreed to return home as soon as they learned the facts about the strike.

The struggle of the Newcastle engineers became a national issue. At mass meetings the workers protested against the import of foreign strike-breakers, while the manufacturers defended in the Press their right to employ whom they pleased. The dispute lasted for nearly three months —from 25 May to 11 August 1871—and ended with the complete success of the strikers, who won the nine-hour day. Never again was it possible to bring foreign strike-breakers into England—a success to which the International had powerfully contributed.

4

This brief survey of the state of the International after the fall of the Commune is sufficient to show that the defeat, and even the government prosecutions which followed, had not destroyed its vitality. Admittedly, it had suffered heavy losses, since with the destruction of the movement in France it had lost one of its main centres of power. But in the other continental centres its influence had hardly declined; in England it had actually gained in strength and importance and to the *bourgeois* world in general it still seemed a formidable power.

However, the impression of strength and unity which the International presented was deceptive, and the organization was soon to be undermined by internal schism. In itself, the fact that the General Council's 'Address on the Civil War in France' had started an embarrassing personal conflict on the Council which led to the resignation of George Odger and Benjamin Lucraft, two of its most important members, was of little consequence. The incident was well publicized in the British Press and has been described by many historians as a major crisis. But the Minutes of the General Council for the period do nothing to confirm this. Nor do they confirm the contemporary legend that Marx had tricked the General Council over the Address by adding the signatures of its members without their knowledge.

As the Minutes make clear, the General Council, together with Marx, had taken full responsibility for the document. On 28 March, ten days after the proclamation of the Commune, the Council had instructed Marx to draft an Address to the French people; it had elected an editorial committee—Milner for England, Serraillier for France and Jung for Switzerland—to finalize the Address, and it resolved that the final document was to be signed by all its members. Marx's prolonged illness delayed the draft, which the editorial committee had to discuss at his bedside. It was only on 30 May that Marx was able to submit the Address to the General Council. Moved by Weston and seconded by

Robin, it was carried unanimously and the secretary was instructed to have it printed immediately and to send copies to M.P.s and the Press.

The Address, which hailed the defenders of the Commune as martyrs, provoked a storm of protest in the newspapers. Many of them accused Odger and Lucraft of making common cause with the 'vagabonds and incendiaries' of the Commune. The two trade-union leaders were absent when the Address was discussed on the General Council, but they had been told about it, had approved its general line and had agreed that their names should be included among the signatories. In face of the Press attacks, however, they decided to abandon both the Commune and the General Council. Appearing at the Council's meeting on 20 June, they refused any responsibility for the Address. After a heated debate in which Odger and Lucraft were opposed by all the other English members, they announced their resignation from the Council. Nobody else followed their example. Robert Applegarth, who wrote apologizing for his absence from the meeting, expressed the view that 'the names of the General Council's members are the property of the General Council' and that it was entitled to publish statements in the name of all its members.[1]

After this episode, the General Council continued with its normal agenda. Although the resignation of these two prominent leaders inevitably lessened the International's prestige in trade-union circles, it remained an isolated event. Trade unions continued to avail themselves of the General Council's services as before. When, a few months later, in the autumn of 1871, an English Federal Council was established, a number of branches appeared in some of the main towns of England, Scotland and Ireland.[2] Despite the attacks on the 'Address' from Odger and Lucraft, and widespread denunciations in the Press, the General Council continued to push its sales. The first edition of a thousand copies, published at the beginning of June, was soon sold out. At the end of the month, a second edition of 2,000 copies, and at the end of July, a third edition of a further 1,000, were ordered. The 'Address' was also translated into German, Flemish, French, Dutch, Spanish and Russian and published in Germany, Belgium, Switzerland and the United States. The German translation appeared in the *Volksstaat* as well as in a pamphlet of 8,000 copies.

1. For the debate on the Address, see the Minutes of the General Council, 30 May and 13 June 1871; for the debate with Odger and Lucraft, see the Minutes of 20 and 27 June, 18 July; for Applegarth's letter, see the Minutes of 8 August 1871. At the meeting of 20 June, at which Odger and Lucraft announced their resignation, the English members present were: Boon, Bradnick, Buttery, Hales, Harris, Lucraft, Mottershead, Odger, Robin, Townshend and Weston. Continental members present were: Cohen, Eccarius, Engels, Jung, Kolb, Lessner, Marx and Pfänder.

2. Henry Collins, 'The English Branches of the First International', *Essays in Labour History*, edited by Asa Briggs and John Saville (London, 1960).

5

The crisis to which the International eventually succumbed originated neither in the tragedy of the Commune nor in the resignation of Odger and Lucraft but in the conflict between Anarchism and Marxism, a conflict over the aims of Socialism, the methods of achieving the social revolution and the organizational forms of the International. Moreover, like other ideological conflicts in the history of social and religious movements, this soon degenerated into a bitter personal antagonism between the members of the two wings and became personalized in the form of a struggle between Marx and Bakunin.

It was a battle of Titans, each expressing a powerful messianic urge. In temperament, the protagonists were poles apart. Marx was methodical and realistic, Bakunin exuberant, romantic and an idealist. Marx based his theory of Socialism on the facts of history and on the actual development of capitalist society. Bakunin's Anarchism seemed to him a farrago of muddled utopian fantasy.[1]

For Marx, Socialism was the outcome of highly developed capitalism, which produced, in the form of an intellectually mature and highly organized working class led by a Socialist party, the prerequisites of social revolution. Bakunin, on the other hand, saw even in the semi-feudal economic institutions of Italy, Spain and Russia the ever-present conditions for a social revolution which would germinate out of the poverty and desperation of the agricultural masses in particular. It seemed to him therefore a comparatively simple matter to unleash revolution almost anywhere and at almost any time. He wrote of the Russian people, for example, as being 'in such a desperate state that it would cost no effort to organize an uprising in any selected village'. He did not consider the culturally advanced workers to be good revolutionary material, since they were 'infected with a *bourgeois* outlook'. He placed his hopes on the declassed sons of *bourgeois* parents, on the mass of the peasantry and on that section of the working class which lived in the most degrading poverty in the slums of great cities—the *lazzaronis* in Naples, the *gamins* in Paris—that section of society which Marx called the *Lumpenproletariat*, 'the passively rotting mass thrown off by the lowest layers of the old society', as he had defined it in the *Communist*

1. His programme, Marx wrote on 19 April 1870 to Paul Lafargue, rested 'on a superannuated idealism which considers the actual jurisprudence as the basis of our economical state, instead of seeing that our economical state is the basis and source of our jurisprudence'—*Letters and Documents of Karl Marx*, ed. Bottigelli (Milan, 1958), pp. 172ff., quoted in George Lichtheim, *Marxism. An Historical and Critical Study* (London, 1961), p. 231. Lichtheim's brilliant book is the most stimulating discussion of the complex of ideas current in the First and Second International and beyond.

Manifesto. Like Blanqui, Bakunin was 'a revolutionary of the previous generation'.

The technique of revolution advocated by Bakunin was the armed *coup* or the armed riot. He rejected the political struggle of the workers for state power, as he rejected all political action which did not directly and immediately serve the revolution. He saw the aim of the social revolution as being not the conquest, but the destruction, of state power, and its final outcome as Anarchism, the stateless federation of communes free from all outside coercion and authority.

Marx also envisaged a free, untrammelled community without any form of state power as the ultimate outcome of the class struggle. In the future, he was convinced, there would be no coercive power of the state but only a free, self-governing people enjoying all the benefits of communal freedom, 'an association in which the free development of each is the condition for the free development of all'. But this ideal society could not be established by any sudden dramatic act of revolution on Bakuninist lines. Marx saw the political power of the state as a function of a social system based on private property in the means of production, the outcome of a society divided into classes, an instrument of domination wielded by the exploiting classes. 'Political power, properly so-called,' he had written in the *Communist Manifesto*, 'is merely the organized power of one class for oppressing another.' The state, he argued, would therefore 'wither away' in a classless society, since it would lose its function as an instrument of class domination. 'When, in the course of development, class distinctions have disappeared and all production has been concentrated in the hands of a vast association of the whole nation, the public power will lose its political character.' The working class must therefore, he explained, wrest state power from the ruling classes and then use it as an instrument for destroying class rule before finally dispensing with the state as a political mechanism. When once the working class 'makes itself the ruling class, and as such sweeps away by force the old conditions of production, then it will, along with these conditions, have swept away the conditions for the existence of class antagonisms and of classes generally, and will thereby have abolished its own supremacy as a class'. Later, during his controversy with Bakunin, Marx wrote that 'when once the aim of the proletarian movement to abolish all classes has been realized, there must then disappear the power of the state, which serves to keep the great productive majority under the yoke of a tiny minority of exploiters. The function of government will then change into one of simple administration.'[1]

1. General Council Circular, *Les Prétendues Scissions dans l'Internationale* (Geneva, 1872). In a letter which Engels wrote to Philipp van Patten on 18 April 1883, he explained the attitude of Marx and himself to the Anarchists as follows:

6

The conflict between Marx and Bakunin, however, flared up not on these theoretical disagreements but on the question of how the International was to be organized. When as early as 1847 Marx had discussed with his fellow members of the Communist League the idea of an International, he had thought of it as an integral part of the Labour movement in the various countries, and as a democratic party rather than as a secret society or an insurrectionary conspiracy. He applied the same idea in his work on the General Council. He saw the International as a body which would unite the Labour movements of the world as a federation of regional Socialist and workers' organizations affiliated as sections to the International. On this the General Council based its claim to act as the executive of the world movement.

At first Bakunin had raised no objection to this centralization of authority within the International. At the Basle Congress in 1869 he had even supported an extension of the General Council's authority, voting in favour of its right to suspend sections of the International, subject to ratification by the following congress. But even at this time, Bakunin had already decided to try to use the International as an instrument of his own ideas, and to wrest the leadership from Marx. He made this clear in a letter which he wrote to Alexander Herzen a month after the Basle Congress. Even here he acknowledged the 'vast services' which Marx had given to the 'cause of Socialism, which he has served for more than twenty-five years with intelligence, energy and integrity'.

'Since 1845 Marx and I have held the view that *one* of the ultimate results of the future proletarian revolution will be the gradual dissolution of the political organization known by the name of *State*. The main object of this organization has always been to secure by armed force the economic oppression of the labouring majority by the minority which alone possesses wealth. With the disappearance of an exclusively wealth-possessing minority there disappears also the necessity for the power of armed oppression, or state power. At the same time, however, it was always our view that in order to attain this and the other far more important aims of the future social revolution, the working class must first take possession of the organized political power of the state and by its aid crush the resistance of the capitalist class and organize society anew. . . . The Anarchists put the thing upside down. They declare that the proletarian revolution must *begin* by doing away with the political organization of the state. But after its victory the sole organization which the proletariat finds already in existence is precisely the state. This state may require very considerable alterations before it can fulfil its new functions. But to destroy it at such a moment would be to destroy the only organism by means of which the victorious proletariat can assert its newly conquered power, hold down its capitalist adversaries and carry out that economic revolution of society without which the whole victory must end in a new defeat and in a mass slaughter of the workers similar to those after the Paris Commune'—*Marx-Engels, Selected Correspondence* (1936), pp. 416–17.

If now, as seemed likely, he began a struggle with Marx, this was certainly 'not to attack him personally, but only as a matter of principle, because of the State Communism which he advocates and which the English and Germans, under his leadership, are supporting. This would make it a life-and-death struggle.'

Although Marx can never have seen this letter to Herzen, he did not need it to be convinced of Bakunin's intention to dominate the International. Bakunin's entire attitude to the organization made this only too clear. Soon after its foundation, Bakunin had joined on Marx's invitation and promised to work for it in Naples, when he arrived there from London in the autumn of 1864. Instead of this, however, Bakunin proceeded to found an independent, revolutionary and secret 'International Brotherhood' under his personal control. After moving to Geneva in 1867, he refrained from joining the local section of the International, but instead affiliated, together with his secret society, to the League for Peace and Freedom and tried to use it to further his ideas. Failing there, he founded in the autumn of 1868 a new organization, the International Alliance of Socialist Democracy, which he intended to affiliate to the International as a distinct branch. It would perhaps be unfair to Bakunin to suggest that he founded the Alliance with the deliberate intention of using it as an instrument for controlling the International. When the Alliance formally applied to the General Council for affiliation in December 1868, Bakunin wrote to Marx: 'My fatherland is now the International, of which you are among the most prominent members. You see therefore, my dear friend, that I am your disciple, and proud to be one.'[1]

But the organizational form which Bakunin had given his Alliance increased Marx's misgivings. According to its Rules it was intended to be an International within the International, with its own sections, national officers, central committee and congress. An International which consisted of two rival groups, each with its own separate machinery and structure, could not for long remain a united body. Marx felt justified in concluding that the real object of the Alliance was to enable Bakunin to seize control of the International.

Bakunin's own views on the purpose of the Alliance were expressed in a letter which he wrote to his Spanish supporters in the spring of 1872. The organization was to serve as the General Staff in future revolutions. He did not believe that the International 'was capable of organizing and leading the revolution'. If the aim of the International was to set the army of the revolution in battle-order, the task of the Alliance was 'to provide the International with a revolutionary organization'. To fulfil

1. Franz Mehring, *Geschichte der deutschen Sozialdemokratie* (Stuttgart, 1898), vol. III, pp. 430 and 410.

this role, the Alliance was necessarily organized by Bakunin as a secret society. Its members were to act 'as invisible pilots amid the storm of popular emotion'. The revolution could not be 'led by any visible power; leadership could come only from the collective dictatorship of all members of the Alliance'. Its members must be prepared, said Bakunin, to subordinate their personal freedom to a strict discipline modelled on that of the Jesuits in which 'the individual is lost in the collective will, in the life and activity of the organization'.[1]

In the eyes of the General Council, any Alliance built on lines envisaged by Bakunin could encompass only the ruin of the International. It therefore refused to allow that body to affiliate. Whereupon the Alliance declared itself ready to dissolve as an independent international organization, and to transform its branches into sections of the International. To this, the General Council raised no objection, and the affiliation of the Geneva section, led by Bakunin himself, was agreed to unanimously. In this way, Bakunin was able to attend the Basle Congress as a fully accredited delegate of the Geneva section.

It is pointless to speculate as to whether the Alliance was in fact dissolved, as stated by Bakunin's followers, or whether it continued in secret, as asserted by Marx and his supporters. It was a simple matter for Bakunin, with his magnetic personality, to gather round him at any time a flock of fervent disciples with whom he naturally remained in close personal contact. Bakunin, in effect, came to control the International's sections in Italy through Andrea Costa, in Spain through Francisco Mora and in French Switzerland through James Guillaume.[2] Bakunin's ideas were also disseminated through a number of journals—*Progrès* in Le Locle, edited by Guillaume, *Égalité* in Geneva, which had J. P. Becker on its editorial staff, *Confédération* in Barcelona, *Equalità* in Naples and *Il Fascio operaio* in Bologna.

Bakunin opened his attack on the General Council soon after the Basle Congress in September 1869. *Égalité* and *Progrès* subjected the activities of the General Council to a highly unfavourable examination, while at the same time Bakunin's supporters in French Switzerland were organizing with a view to taking over the Federation. In the course of this struggle the French Federation split at its congress at La Chaux-de-Fonds in April 1870 and, as *Égalité* had turned against him, Bakunin founded a new paper, *Solidarité*, in Neuchâtel, under the editorial control of Guillaume.

1. E. H. Carr, *Michael Bakunin* (1937), pp. 422ff.
2. James Guillaume has left in his four-volume *L'Internationale, documents et souvenirs, 1864–78* (Paris, 1905–10), a source of information on the International which, though strongly hostile to Marx, is of considerable value to historians.

7

The split in the French Federation would, without doubt, have been one of the main subjects for discussion at the congress which had been arranged at Mainz for September 1870. But the opening of the Franco-German War prevented the International from holding its congress, and the persecution to which it was subjected after the defeat of the Commune in France, Spain, Germany, Italy and Austria, gave the General Council good reasons for postponing the congress for a further year. Instead, a private conference was called in London for September 1871.

The London Conference was attended by twenty-three delegates, including six Belgians, one Spaniard and thirteen members of the General Council. It was faced with problems much more serious than the quarrels in the French-Swiss Federation, particularly with the problem of what to do in the face of 'untrammelled reaction'. The resolution on this question—which was later to be violently opposed by the Bakuninists—stated that the workers could act against 'the combined power of the ruling classes' only by establishing a political party of their own which would oppose the entire complex of parties defending the interests of property. Such a party was indispensable for the social revolution, and for its final aim: the abolition of all classes.

The resolution, an important document of the First International which emphasized the imperative necessity of the political struggle of the working class for political power, stated the antithesis of the Bakuninist conception of 'absention' from political struggle. Engels, who had submitted the resolution to the conference, exposed the contradiction in the Bakuninist theory. 'We want the abolition of classes,' he said. 'What are the means to this end? The political power of the proletariat.' Yet the 'absentionists, who call themselves revolutionaries, refuse to recognize that revolution is', he said, 'the supreme action of policy, and if you want it, you must want also the means to achieve it, that is, the political action in preparation of the revolution—the education of the workers for the revolution': political freedom, the rights of assembly and association, the freedom of the Press. These are, he said, 'our weapons, and shall we fold our arms and apply the method of abstention', he concluded, 'if we are to be deprived of them?'[1]

The principle of the resolution—the need of an independent

1. *Karl Marx-Friedrich Engels Werke*, vol. XVII, pp. 416–17. Engels had joined the General Council only after he had sold his share of the family business and had moved from Manchester to London in 1870. He became Corresponding Secretary for Italy. See Minutes of the General Council, 20 September 1870.

working-class party and its struggle for political power—was incorporated as Article 7a of the Statutes by the Hague Congress.

Another resolution adopted at the London Conference was indicative of the new political situation confronting the working class of Europe. It was decided to transfer responsibility for the movement in England from the General Council to a new Federal Council to be elected by the English sections. This move had first been broached in 1869[1] and the idea of it had also been raised in the columns of *Égalité*. At the time, Marx had still believed that the crisis in the French Empire could lead to a revolutionary situation in Europe. He convinced the General Council that it would be foolish to forfeit the influence over the English working class which the General Council possessed in its capacity as head of the English section. In a circular to the Federal Council of French Switzerland on 1 January 1870, the General Council replied to the proposal by *Égalité* which had provoked a lively discussion in that section. The circular maintained that England 'cannot be treated simply as one country among a number of other countries. She must be treated as the metropolis of capitalism.' Owing to its dominant position in the world market, England was 'the only country where every revolution in its economic conditions must react directly on the entire world'. She was, in short, the 'lever of a serious economic revolution' and it would be folly to let control of the lever slip from the hands of the General Council.[2]

By September 1871, however, when the London Conference assembled, the international Labour movement faced a very different situation. In France, counter-revolution had triumphed, and in Germany and Austria the workers' movement was paralysed. For the foreseeable future, no new revolutionary initiative could be expected anywhere in Europe. In England, too, the political development of the Labour movement had belied Marx's hopes of a new revolutionary situation. In the circular to the French-Swiss Federation already quoted, Marx, speaking for the General Council, had maintained that the English possessed all the material prerequisites for a social revolution. 'What they lack,' he added, 'is the spirit of generalization and revolutionary ardour', and it was the task of the General Council to supply the deficiency.

The English workers had shown often enough, and most notably during the Chartist movement of the 1840s, that they were indeed capable of developing along revolutionary lines. After the great defeat of 1848, however, they began to abandon hope of revolution. They tried,

1. Minutes of the General Council, 5 and 19 October 1869. For the history of the English Federation, see Collins, op. cit.

2. For the circular, see Marx, *Briefe an Kugelmann*, pp. 102–10.

by no means without success, to improve their conditions through trade-union pressure. By the 1860s, the struggle for parliamentary reform had galvanized them once again, but it had not turned them back to revolutionary paths. The English ruling class had also learned, from the history of revolutionary movements both in Europe and at home, that the danger of revolution might be averted by reform. To this consideration the English workers owed, in no small measure, their success in the struggle for the Reform Bill of 1867. From this experience, trade-union leaders drew the conclusion that it was possible to raise working-class living standards continuously through trade-union struggles, and that by exerting pressure on middle-class members of Parliament, further concessions could be secured. The Reform Bill gave the franchise to the working class in the towns, and with it an instrument with which they could bring pressure to bear on Parliament. And as the first General Election under the new franchise in 1868 resulted in the defeat of all working-class candidates, the trade-union leaders placed their hopes in an alliance with the progressive sections of the middle class—an alliance which was to last for more than thirty years. Since now and for the foreseeable future England could no longer be considered 'a lever of the proletarian revolution', it was hardly relevant to consider whether, in a revolution which was now recognized to be a long way off, the movement in Britain was to be led by the General Council or an English Federal Council.

Towards the end of the London Conference, some other important decisions were taken on organizational matters. In countries where the International had been made illegal, supporters were recommended to reorganize themselves under another name; at the same time it was strongly emphasized that secret societies were to remain excluded from the International. Conference recommended its supporters in France to organize themselves on a factory basis, while both sections of the French-Swiss Federation were urged to heal the split. The resolution remarked that 'considering the persecution to which the International is at present being subjected, the Conference appeals to the spirit of solidarity and unity which should now more than ever prevail among the workers'.

8

The appeal of the London Conference found no response among Bakunin's supporters. On 12 November 1871, six weeks after the conference, those sections of the French-Swiss Federation which Bakunin controlled—in fact, the old Alliance which was now calling itself the Jura Federation—called a congress of its own in Souvillier. A circular drafted by Guillaume was issued to all sections of the International's Federations in France, Belgium, Spain and Italy, accusing the General Council of exercising usurped and dictatorial powers. The General Council, it declared, had come to consider itself the 'legitimate head' of the International, and some people regarded their membership of the General Council as their 'personal property', giving them the right to force their personal opinions on to the entire movement. 'As they constitute, in their own eyes,' the circular continued, 'a kind of government, it is only natural that their personal views are presented as the official theory of the International, and that the ideas of others appear not as equally legitimate expressions of opinion but as complete heresy.' The General Council was also trying to transform a free association of autonomous sections into a hierarchical organization subject to authoritarian powers. Hence, the circular proceeded with the charge: 'We accuse the members of the General Council of trying to introduce the principle of authority into the International, so as to bring about the triumph of their personal point of view.' It called on the Federations to reduce the status of the General Council at the next congress to that of a mere administrative office and 'to achieve such unity as we may by a free association of autonomous groups instead of by centralization and dictatorship'.

This resolution did not go far enough for the Italian section. At its congress at Rimini, held on 6 August 1872, it called for a complete break with the General Council and for a boycott of the congress of the International which was being called at The Hague in the following month. This resolution repudiated the appeal to the workers, made by the London Conference, to set up their own political party. This was merely an attempt 'to force on the International an authoritarian doctrine, the doctrine of the German Communist party'. But, continued the Rimini resolution, the doctrine of the 'authoritarian Communists' could only 'injure the revolutionary spirit of the Italian proletariat'. The resolution went on to accuse the General Council of 'fraud and slander' and declared 'solemnly, before the workers of the world, that the Italian Federation of the International Working Men's Association renounces from this moment all solidarity between itself and the London General Council'.

The Anarchists in Switzerland and Italy were proposing in effect that the International, beleaguered by the forces of European reaction, should break up into its component parts. Marx's comment on the proposals was that 'they declare that anarchy on the proletarian side is the means of destroying that mighty concentration of political and social power in the hands of the exploiters. Under this pretext they demand that the

International, at a time when the old world is striving to destroy it, should replace its organization with anarchy.'

After the London Conference, Bakunin, as we have seen, declared 'war to the knife' on Marx and Engels. Even before the conference he had declared his intention in a letter to Alexander Herzen of waging a fight 'against their false theories, their dictatorial presumptions and all kinds of underground intrigues, the idle plots of wretched individuals, foul insults and infamous slanders, so characteristic of the political struggles of almost all Germans and which they have now, unfortunately, dragged into the International'. Marx, he believed, was 'as a German and a Jew, an authoritarian from top to toe', while the General Council was a 'pan-German agency', a 'German committee guided by a brain like Bismarck's'.

Although Bakunin's complaints against the methods of his antagonists were not without foundation, he was not entirely free from the sins he attributed to Marx and Engels. This rather unpleasant episode in the war of the Titans belongs to the biographies of the main protagonists rather than to a history of the International. It is sufficient to say that Marx and Engels, with the full agreement of the General Council, stated their full case against Bakunin and Guillaume in the pamphlet already referred to, *Les Prétendues Scissions dans l'Internationale*, in time for the Hague Congress to pass its final verdict.[1]

9

The congress which opened at The Hague on 2 September 1872 had been anticipated with a good deal of tension by the Federations of the International. It was on the advice of the Belgian Federation that the General Council selected The Hague as the place in which to hold the congress, although the local section there was the most recently formed and the smallest in the International; according to Maltman Barry, a congress delegate, it had no more than twenty members. Hardly a centre of industry, The Hague was then a small and rather sleepy town, best known as the seat of the Dutch Court, Parliament and Ministries. The meeting of the 'terrible International', therefore, caused something of a sensation in the town.[2] According to Barry, the children had been warned

1. For a balanced and impartial account of the episode, see Mehring, op. cit., ch. XII: 6, and ch. XIV: 5 and 7. For a criticism of Mehring's approach, see N. Riazanov, 'Sozial-demokratische Flagge und anarchistische Ware', in *Die Neue Zeit*, 32nd year, vol. I, nos. 5, 7–10 and 13. See also Karl Marx and Friedrich Engels, *The Alliance of the Socialist Democracy and the International Working Men's Association* (London, 1873).

2. The French secret police, which had closely shadowed Karl Marx, suspected, as it reported on 14 September 1872, that he had come to The Hague 'to instigate

'not to go into the streets with articles of value upon them' as 'the International is coming and will steal them'. As the delegates arrived in groups, crowds followed them from the station to the hotel, 'the figure of Karl Marx attracting special attention, his name on every lip'. Barry described the huge attendance at the public meeting which concluded the congress:

> An immense crowd blocked the street outside, making the ingress of members a work of no slight difficulty; and whenever the doors were opened it poured in like a flood. Soon every available spot was occupied, and some even that could not legitimately be expected to afford accommodation. Window-sills were not despised, and some lads clustered round the supporting iron pillars. The galleries also were crammed to suffocation.[1]

More countries were represented at The Hague than at any previous congress, the delegates arriving from Germany, Britain, Belgium, France, Switzerland, Holland, Denmark, Austria, Hungary, Bohemia, Poland and Ireland; there were also four delegates, including F. A. Sorge, from the United States. In accordance with the resolutions passed at Rimini, the Italian Federation boycotted the proceedings. The Hague was the first congress in which the Blanquists participated as delegates, and Vaillant, Ranvier, Cournet and Armand, all of them Communard refugees, were there as co-opted members of the General Council. Altogether, the congress accepted the credentials of sixty-one delegates.

To Marx, it seemed that the decision which the congress would have to make on the conflict between the Alliance and the General Council would be decisive for the entire future of the International. He told his friend Kugelmann that it would 'be a matter of life or death for the International; and before I retire I want at least to protect it from disintegrating elements'.[2] Marx himself went as delegate to The Hague—the first congress he had attended since the foundation of the International. Bakunin did not appear, his case being presented by a number of his followers under the leadership of Guillaume.

The debate on the conflict opened with a motion from Marx to expel the Alliance from the International. Congress elected a committee

riots in Holland in order to prepare her annexation by Germany'. The dossier of the Paris police concerning Marx, covering the period 1871–83, contains about twenty-five items on the Hague Congress. The dossier is deposited in the Marx-Engels-Lenin Institute in Moscow. For a brief survey of its contents, see Helmut Hirsch, *Denker und Kämpfer* (1955), pp. 123–8.

1. The best account of the congress is in the Minutes and the reports of Sorge and Barry, from the English and American delegations respectively. These have been published with a number of other documents in *The First International—Minutes of the Hague Congress of 1872, with related documents*, edited by Hans Gerth (Madison, 1958). There is an English translation of the German documents. The volume also contains the facsimile of the Minutes, written in German.

2. Karl Marx, *Briefe an Kugelmann*, p. 132.

of five—three Frenchmen, a German and a Belgian—to examine his charges in detail. There followed discussions on the powers of the General Council, which had submitted a motion empowering it to suspend sections and federations between congresses. A Belgian, Désiré Brimée, was the first to oppose, on behalf of his delegation. He announced that a number of sections in Belgium had gone on record in favour of abolishing the General Council; others wanted to curtail its powers, but none wanted to increase them. Guillaume denied that the International needed any kind of 'head'. 'Has the General Council,' he asked rhetorically, 'ever led a class struggle, or built barricades? And is it likely to do so in the future?' The General Council, he concluded, was useless. Sorge reminded him of the solidarity actions which the General Council had organized in support of the French strikers, and pointed out that an International without a head would belong to a very low class of organism. Morgan then threatened that the Spanish section, on whose behalf he was speaking, would withdraw from the International if congress decided to strengthen the General Council's powers. Its function should be limited to dealing with correspondence.

Marx, replying for the General Council, said that it would be better to abolish the General Council than to degrade its status to that of a 'letter-box'. The General Council's powers of suspending sections and even federations were essential, since police informers and *agents provocateurs* could take control of branches. This had actually happened in France and Austria, and Bismarck was quite capable of doing the same thing in Germany. Since the General Council had no soldiers or armed forces at its disposal, said Marx, it had to rely on moral power based on the confidence of the membership. Even if the General Council were given complete and despotic powers, they would be useless if this confidence were lacking.

By a majority of thirty-two votes to six, with sixteen abstaining, the General Council was voted its extended powers. The German delegation voted solidly in favour, as did six out of the seven French delegates and a majority of the General Council. The Belgian, Dutch, Spanish and most of the English delegates voted against, while the Swiss were evenly divided, with two on each side.

Then Engels, in the name of Marx, Longuet, Serraillier, Dupont, Lessner and other members of the General Council, moved that the seat of the Council be moved to New York. Barry reported the consternation among the delegates as Engels read out his proposal.[1] 'It was

1. The proposal also made some impact on the general public. 'This,' said the Liberal *Manchester Guardian*, reporting the congress on 7 September 1872, 'was at first sight almost as strange as if the Pope had proposed to send the Holy Congregation and the College of Cardinals away from Rome.' See Collins, op. cit., p. 264.

some time before anyone rose to speak. It was a *coup d'état*, and each one looked to his neighbour to break the spell. At length Vaillant rose.' The International, he declared, had prospered exceedingly under the existing leadership and he saw no reason for changing it. Moreover, the seat of the General Council should be close to the fighting-line, that is, within easy reach of France and Germany. If it were moved to the other side of the Atlantic, that could only weaken its influence. Vaillant implored the members of the General Council, whose leadership had 'made the International Society the dread of kings and emperors', to add this one further sacrifice to those they had already made in the cause. When the question as to whether the General Council might move at all was put to the vote, there were twenty-six in favour, twenty-three against and nine abstentions. After that, thirty-one voted for the seat to be in New York, fourteen for remaining in London, and one each for Brussels and Barcelona.

Before the debate on the report by the Commission of Inquiry which had been looking into the affairs of the Alliance, Vaillant spoke strongly in support of the London Conference resolution on the necessity for the working class to set up its own parties and conduct its own independent political activities. The question had gained a certain poignancy from the fate of the revolutionary movement in France. Guillaume, speaking for the Anarchist delegates, protested against political activity by the workers and particularly against their struggling for state power. His characteristic remark on this was: 'We demand the complete destruction of the state as the embodiment of political power.' Longuet replied that if on 4 September 1870 the French workers had been politically organized, Thiers would not have been able to seize power. After that, the resolution was carried by twenty-four votes to four, with nine abstentions.

Next came the report of the Commission of Inquiry on the Alliance. It confirmed—by four votes, with the Belgian delegate as the sole dissenter—that a secret organization had existed, though it could not be conclusively proved that it still did so. It did establish, however, that Bakunin had tried to organize a secret society inside the International. Bakunin was also charged with fraud—unjustifiably, as later research was to show. On a motion by the Commission, Bakunin and Guillaume were expelled from the International. One member of the Commission of Inquiry, van Heddeghem, who had wormed his way into the International in France under the name of Walter, was later exposed as a police spy, as was the delegate d'Entragues, alias Swarm.

10

The Hague Congress was the last to be held by the First International, and in fact prepared the way for its dissolution. Since 1869 the International had been showing symptoms of disintegration. Its Federations in French Switzerland, Spain and Italy were won over to Bakunin and Anarchism, while the Belgian and Dutch Federations were clearly tending in the same direction. The movement in France was destroyed, and most of the Communard refugees who came to represent the French Federation were Blanquists. The triumph scored by the General Council in the voting at the Hague Congress demonstrated weakness rather than strength. It was secured mainly by the sixteen votes of its own members, who had come to the Hague Congress, together with the Germans and the French Blanquists. Even the English section could no longer be relied on for support. And if the Italian Federation had not decided to boycott the congress, it seems likely that the General Council would have lost.

Marx could now count merely on the support of Germany, German Switzerland and the Blanquist refugees from Paris; and even in Germany it was only the Eisenach party which supported him: the Lassalleans did not belong to the International and tended to sympathize with Marx's opponents. In England, where up to now Marx had been able to rely on solid support, first against the Proudhonists, then against Bakunin, an opposition was beginning to develop. Part of the English Federal Council which had been set up after the London Conference in the autumn of 1871, while not going over to the Anarchists, had come out against the centralism in the International's organization for which Marx stood. Moreover, Hales, for a time the secretary of the English Federation, had broken with Marx irreparably.[1]

The crisis in the International was basically a crisis of growth in the European working-class movement. As the Labour movement gained confidence and strength in one country after another, it began to resent the leadership of the General Council as an unwarrantable encroachment on its autonomy. Marx saw the International as the party of the working class in all countries, and the General Council as its leadership. But each of the individual Labour movements began to consider itself an independent party and to develop its own outlook and policy.

Some time before the congress at The Hague, Marx had made up his mind to retire from the General Council. The International had involved him in a tremendous amount of work, over and above the immense

1. For the political and personal background to the split in the English section, see the detailed analysis by Collins, op. cit.

effort he put into finishing *Das Kapital*. He wrote innumerable letters on behalf of the International and drew up memoranda, circulars and addresses. Except when he was prevented by illness he attended all the weekly meetings of the General Council, and was available at all times to anyone wishing to discuss with him the affairs of the International. 'Apart from the boils, which tormented me hellishly, I got to bed last night, for instance, only at 4 a.m. . . , the International takes up an enormous amount of time,' he remarked in a letter to Engels. The International, he complained in another letter, 'weighs on me like an incubus'. In other respects, too, the first five years of the International were among the most gloomy in Marx's life. He suffered painfully from carbuncles and was constantly harassed by financial worries. Work on his book and for the International allowed him scarcely any time or energy for earning a living. 'For two months already I have been living in fact on the pawnbroker and therefore with constantly heavier and daily more unbearable demands and pressures on me,' he wrote to Engels; and several months later he complained that 'the pawnshop—and my wife has pawned so much already that she can hardly go out herself—reminds me of its existence only through continual demands for interest. I therefore had to borrow left and right in London to meet even the barest expenditure. On the other hand the suppliers are threatening, and some have stopped credit and are threatening legal action.' In letter after letter to Engels, Marx repeated the same heart-breaking story. Engels was always ready to help and the friendship between the two men constituted also in this respect, as Mohring said, 'a bond without equal'. But for Marx it was 'indeed depressing to remain dependent half one's life'.[1] Despite all this, Marx did not spare himself and never thought of casting off the 'incubus' so long as there was the hope of doing useful work for the International.

After the Hague Congress this no longer seemed possible. The last task Marx set himself was to protect the International from the 'disintegrating elements', as he put it in his letter to Kugelmann, already quoted. As he saw it, the 'disintegrating elements' were the Blanquists and the Anarchists. Both groups stood for the conspiratorial approach to working-class politics that Marx abhorred, but they took a diametrically opposite view of the General Council. The Blanquists, seeing the Council as the centralized leadership of future revolutions, voted for an expansion of its powers, while the Anarchists would have liked to abolish it. What both groups had in common was a belief in conspiracies and *coups* as a substitute for sustained political activity. Both were equally 'revolutionaries of the previous generation'.

The first necessity for Marx was therefore to remove the General

1. *Marx-Engels Briefwechsel*, vol. III, pp. 304, 357, 332 and 435.

Council from London. Had he not done so, it would without doubt have been taken over, first by the Blanquists—those honoured heroes of the Commune who, after taking refuge in London, had been co-opted on to the General Council—and subsequently in all probability by the Anarchists. Under the direction of either of these groups, Marx feared, the International would be transformed into a conspiratorial clique and discredited for all time. From this fate he was determined to save the International at all costs. But it was far from easy to find a substitute for London as the seat of the General Council. Brussels, Amsterdam and Geneva were out of the question, as their Federal Councils had all opposed the authority of the General Council. In Italy, the Federation had gone further and broken with the Council completely. In France, Spain, Germany and Austria, the International was legally proscribed as a 'danger to the State'. Thus, New York remained the only feasible headquarters for the General Council. It was also Marx's view that the rapid industrial growth which he foresaw taking place in the United States, would create a powerful centre of the International Labour movement.

Some historians have assumed that in arranging for the General Council to move to New York, Marx deliberately planned the International's destruction. But this does not square with his solemn statement to a mass meeting in Amsterdam the day after the conclusion of the Hague Congress. He stressed solidarity as the 'fundamental principle' on which the International was based. 'The revolution must embody the principle of solidarity,' he said, 'and the great example of this is the Paris Commune, which fell because in Berlin, Madrid and the other great European capitals, there was no corresponding revolutionary outbreak to save the proletariat of Paris.' And he ended with the undertaking that 'so far as I am concerned, I shall continue with the task of building this fruitful solidarity of the working class for the future. I have no intention of retiring from the International, and for the remainder of my life, as in the past, I shall dedicate all my efforts to the triumph of those social ideas which will one day, we can be perfectly confident, inaugurate the rules of the working class.'[1]

However, the process of disintegration which had already set in was to prove irreversible. The Blanquist delegates had left The Hague as soon as the vote was taken to remove the General Council to New York. 'Challenged to do its duty, the International failed. To escape from the Revolution, it fled across the Atlantic,' was how the Blanquists justified their secession. And on 15 September, scarcely a week after the Hague Congress, the Anarchists called their own congress at Saint-Imier in

1. For the full text of the speech containing Marx's views on the role of the Revolution, and other important topics, see Meyer, op. cit., vol. I, p. 159.

Switzerland, which was attended by representatives of the Italian, Spanish and Jura Federations. The delegates included Bakunin, Guillaume, Costa, Malatesta and Cafiero. They unanimously repudiated the decisions of the Hague Congress, refused to recognize the General Council it had elected and declared themselves the legitimate representatives of the International Working Men's Association. They were recognized by the Belgian and Dutch Federations and by one of the two groups into which the British Federation had split.

The New York General Council which had been elected at the Hague Congress disavowed the dissident federations and called a congress at Geneva for September 1873. It was, as Marx admitted, a 'fiasco'. The General Council was unable to raise the travelling expenses for even one delegate, and among the twenty-eight who met in Geneva, only two represented foreign parties—an unnamed delegate from the Eisenachers and Heinrich Oberwinder from the Austrian party. The rest were either Swiss or Germans and Frenchmen resident in Switzerland. F. A. Sorge, who had accepted the post of secretary with some reluctance and only out of friendship to Marx, resigned in the following year. At a conference in Philadelphia in July 1876, with only the American Federation represented, the International was formally dissolved. The Philadelphia Conference was the last conference of the Marxist International.[1]

11

In the 'anti-authoritarian' International the process of disintegration was prolonged.[2] It held its first congress in Geneva at the beginning of September 1873, a week before the Marxist congress opened in the same city. Its claim to be the sixth congress of the International (the Hague Congress had been the fifth) was not without foundation, since most of the federations had come out in support, and it had representatives from England (Hales and Eccarius), Spain, France (including Paul Brousse, and L.-J. Pindy, a member of the Paris Commune), Belgium, Holland, Italy (including Andrea Costa) and French Switzerland. Even the Lassallean General German Workers' Association, though it could

1. For the report, see *Internationale Arbeiter-Assoziation—Verhandlungen der Delegierten-Konferenz zu Philadelphia, 15 Juli 1876* (New York, 1876) and Schlüter, *Die Internationale in Amerika* (1918), p. 353. For the state of the International's membership, see the General Council's Circular, 25 June 1876, in Schlüter, op. cit., p. 351. At the time, only two Federations of the International survived, one in North America and one in the canton of Geneva. The General Council had no contact with Spain and Italy, and only loose connections with Germany, Austria, Hungary, France and the Scandinavian countries.

2. For a comprehensive account of the congresses following that at The Hague, see G. M. Steklov, *History of the First International* (London, 1928), Part II.

not affiliate for legal reasons, was favourably inclined. The congress provided the International with a new, 'anti-authoritarian' set of rules; replaced the General Council by a Bureau which had no power and confined its activities to dealing with correspondence; and abolished membership subscriptions.

The 'anti-authoritarian' International was a loose organization, 'without a head' as Guillaume had demanded, without leadership and, it can fairly be said, without a programme. Though created by the Anarchists—in particular by James Guillaume, together with the Spanish and Italian Federations—it contained federations which were not Anarchist but which had revolted against the authority of the General Council. The English, and of course the Lassalleans (who were represented at the second congress of the International by Fromme and Kersten), could be classified as Social Democrats, and the Belgians and Dutch were moving increasingly away from Anarchism towards a Social Democratic outlook. Even Guillaume, who had supported Bakunin so strongly against Marx, while he rejected political and parliamentary activity, was also against the Anarchist tactic of armed uprisings and political *coups*. Guillaume saw the trade unions as the effective instruments of working-class struggle and, at the same time, as the bodies through which the workers could take over the means of production. He was in fact rather a forerunner of syndicalism than an exponent of Bakuninist ideology.

The anti-authoritarian International held three further congresses—at Brussels in 1874, at Berne in 1876 and at Verviers in 1877. Without doubt it represented what was left of the international working-class movement. Its Italian and Spanish sections had become mass organizations; its Belgian section had through bitter and prolonged struggles brought thousands of workers into activity. Even the German Social Democrats, united at their Gotha Congress in 1875, were represented by Julius Vahlteich—at Berne. But once the 'honeymoon period' was over, it became apparent that the leaderless International could satisfy none of its affiliated bodies. The Belgians were soon demanding the re-establishment of the old International, and de Paepe, supported by the Dutch and French, proposed at Berne that a Socialist World Congress should be convened to consider the revival of the International. Against the opposition of the Anarchist Italian and Spanish Federations, the proposal was carried by a majority at the congress.

The Socialist World Congress, which met at Ghent on 9 September 1877, aroused keen hopes and was welcomed by an impressive demonstration of Belgian workers. A procession of 'at least 10,000' marched through the town to celebrate the opening of the congress. At its conclusion, a public meeting was called in the Parnass, which could hold

1,800 people. The assembly rooms and galleries were 'packed to suffocation well before the appointed time'.[1] In the Socialist World Congress at Ghent the Belgian workers saw a reincarnation of the old International.

This was in fact the first congress since the Hague Congress which was in any way representative of international labour. It was attended by delegates from Germany, Hungary and Greece, and by leaders of the stature of Liebknecht, Greulich, de Paepe, Bertrand, Anseele, Hales, Frankel and the Anarchists Costa, Brousse, Guillaume, and Kropotkin, the spiritual leader of Anarchism since the death of Bakunin in the previous year. Unfortunately, however, the main object of the congress, which was to revive an all-embracing International, was thwarted by disagreements between Anarchists and Social Democrats—disagreements concerning both ideology and the tactics of class struggle. The Social Democrats called for a 'pact of solidarity' as a first step towards reviving an International which would represent all sections of the movement. The pact would have put an end to the fratricidal conflicts in the Socialist movement and committed all the factions to working amicably together. The Anarchists saw this as a betrayal of their principles and the congress duly voted down the proposal.

On the same evening the delegates of Germany, Denmark, Belgium, German Switzerland, England, France and Italy, with the Anarchists deliberately excluded, met to consider ways of reviving the International, despite Anarchist obstruction. The result, however, was only a pious declaration about the necessity of unity, the exchange of information, and the moral solidarity of working-class organizations in all countries in their world-wide struggle against the reign of the ruling classes.

Now the 'anti-authoritarian' International was split, with the surviving rump consisting solely of Anarchists. Its last congress met in London in 1881. None of the leading members of the post-Hague International—Guillaume, Costa, Laurent, Verrycken, T. G. Morago—took part. The main actors on this stage were Peter Kropotkin, Malatesta, Most, Peukert, Francesco Saverio Merlino, J. Neves, L. B. Goldenberg, and Louise Michel, heroine of the Paris Commune. The congress received strong support from *La Révolution sociale*, a Paris paper edited by a French police agent. One of its resolutions, which was particularly welcomed by *agents provocateurs*, recommended the organizations and their members to learn chemistry in the interests of the revolution, and to become proficient in forwarding the class struggle by means of the bomb. After London, the Anarchist International held conferences in

1. Daily reports of the Vienna police for 18 and 19 September 1877, from the archives of the Ministry of the Interior (Brügel, *Geschichte der österreichischen Sozialdemokratie*, vol. II, pp. 334 and 338).

Paris (1889), Chicago (1893), Zurich (1896) and a congress in Amsterdam (1907). But the effective existence of the Anarchist International ended after the London Congress. All that remained were a few small groups scattered over a number of countries. The ideological heritage of Anarchism—the concepts of a federal social order without a state, the technique of the general strike, 'direct action' instead of political action by the working class—passed to the revolutionary syndicalists in the trade-union movements of France, Italy and Spain.

Meanwhile, the Belgian Socialist party had continued its efforts to revive the old International. In the summer of 1880 it issued an appeal 'to all Socialists in the Old World and the New', suggesting a congress to discuss 'practical steps for the revival of the International Working Men's Association'. The now unified German Social Democratic party welcomed the proposal, and both parties called an International Congress at Chur in Switzerland, for October 1881. It was not, however, a very representative congress, and delegates came only from Belgium, Germany, France, Denmark and the United States. After long discussions, it too was forced to the conclusion that the time for restoring the International had not yet arrived. The manifesto adopted by the congress declared that working-class parties in France, Belgium, Switzerland, Holland, Spain, Denmark and the United States were still at their formative stage, while those in Germany, Italy and Austria were still under legal threats from their own governments. A vigorous International, however, required lively, responsible parties organized on a national basis and capable of effective action.

These conditions became fulfilled during the 1880s. It was a decade in which, in both Europe and America, old Socialist parties became consolidated and new ones emerged. The Second International, founded at the Paris Congress in 1889, rested on the solid foundation of an international movement now organized firmly in national parties.

The First International represented a phase in the historic emergence and development of a movement capable of representing the working class in all countries. It had evolved the principles which were to serve the working-class movements as a guiding light when the time came for them to be re-formed. It had inspired and stimulated the growth of the Labour movement by giving it a clear, ultimate aim, too daring and ambitious for any previous movement in history: the aim of a rejuvenated humanity living in a classless society, free from all forms of servitude and of the exploitation of man by man. It planted the concept of solidarity firmly in the minds of the workers. It bequeathed to the Labour movement in all countries enthusiasm for a great cause. All this was mainly the work of Karl Marx.

PART THREE

The Second International

16 · Socialism in the 1890s

From the beginning, many writers compared Socialism with Christianity in the days of the early church, before it became established as a state religion. They saw, in Socialism, a new gospel of salvation, and in the Labour leaders the apostles of a new teaching, possessing the same boundless assurance of ultimate success as had fortified the early Christians during the first three centuries of their existence. If one is to make such a comparison, the Second International can be taken as the apostolic period of Socialism, the time of preaching and propagation, preceding the assumption of political power.

In the period of the Second International, Socialism assumed the character of a mass movement. Unlike the First International, which was formed in most countries by none too stable groups of individual members, the Second was based, within a few years of its foundation, on organized mass parties. Their conception of Socialism was, in a general sense, Marxist, though Marxism was by no means the only significant trend. Even after the expulsion of the Anarchists there were revisionists, reformists and working-class radicals who represented powerful conflicting tendencies. But Marxism was, without doubt, the dominant school of thought, and most parties of the Second International had no hesitation in describing themselves as Marxist. In the International's basic statement of principles there were all the leading ideas of Marx, his philosophy of history, his theories of economics, and his attitude to the class struggle, the state and revolution. In its ideology, therefore, the Second International was revolutionary, and its aims included not only a radical transformation of society but a clear view of revolution as the 'midwife of history', the inevitable culminating stage in the struggle to free mankind from capitalism and class rule.

At its foundation, the spirit of the Second International was one of buoyant optimism. The collapse of the capitalist system and the irresistible advance of the new, victorious Socialist society seemed equally inevitable in the fairly near future. At the Erfurt Congress of the German Social Democratic party in 1891, only two years after the revival of the International, August Bebel told his fellow delegates: 'I am convinced that the fulfilment of our aims is so close, that there are few in this hall who will not live to see the day.'[1] It was this confidence of imminent victory which gave the Socialist movement its extraordinary enthusiasm during the period of the Second International.

But this optimism carried the seeds of tragedy. In the twenty-five-year history of the Second International, the Socialist movement became established as a force. In 1914, on the eve of the First World War, membership of Socialist parties, and of trade unions closely connected with them, ran into hundreds of thousands, while in parliamentary elections they numbered their votes, in some countries, by the million. The surprisingly rapid growth of the movement gave rise, in the minds of its supporters, to a fatal over-estimation of the power of Socialism which bore little relation to reality. They chose to overlook the fact that the idea of Socialism had penetrated to only a small section of the working class and that the Socialist parties, in all countries where they existed, were faced with the hostility of an overwhelming majority of the population. They underestimated the power of conservative and nationalist traditions and overestimated the extent to which the revolutionary notion of international working-class solidarity had been accepted, even among the working class. They saw in the International a force capable of averting the threatening war between the Great Powers. They saw, in Social Democracy, a means of arousing revolutionary resistance to war. The Second International was destined to be destroyed by the failure of these hopes and the disillusionment which followed.

1

Optimistic expectations about the historical destiny awaiting them were already pronounced in the Addresses which were read at the opening of the foundation congress,[2] which met in Paris on 14 July 1889—the centenary of the storming of the Bastille. The Salle Petrelle, where the

1. *Protokoll über die Verhandlungen des Parteitages der Sozialdemokratischen Partei Deutschlands—Erfurt 1891* (Berlin, 1891), p. 172.

2. For the pre-history of the Congress and its debates, see *Protokoll des Internationalen Arbeiter-Congresses zu Paris*, with Preface by Wilhelm Liebknecht (Nuremberg, 1890); Victor Adler, 'Die Gründung der neuen Internationale' in *Reden und Aufsätzen*, edited by Gustav Pollatschek (Vienna, 1929), vol. VIII, pp. 58–64; Gustav Mayer, *Friedrich Engels* (Berlin, 1933), vol. II, pp. 391–6; G. D. H. Cole, *The Second International, 1894–1914*, vol. III of *A History of Socialist Thought* (London, 1956), pp. 1–11. See also Leo Valiani, 'Dalla Prima alla Seconda Internazionale 1872–89', in the author's *Questioni di storia del socialismo* (Turin, 1958).

congress took place, was festooned with red cloth, reinforced by red flags. Above the rostrum, in gold letters, shone the closing words of the *Communist Manifesto*, 'Working Men of All Countries, Unite!' An inscription in the foreground announced the central aim in the fight for working-class emancipation: 'Political and Economic Expropriation of the Capitalist Class—Nationalization of the Means of Production'.

The congress was the guest of the Parti Ouvrier Français, the Blanquist Comité Révolutionnaire Central and of the Fédération Nationale des Syndicats Ouvriers de France, the main organization of the French trade unions. The spirit of the French party was admirably expressed on a poster at the rostrum with which they greeted the congress: 'In the name of the Paris of June 1848, and of March, April and May 1871, of the France of Babeuf, Blanqui and Varlin, greetings to the Socialist workers of both worlds.' After the congress was over the delegates organized a march in honour of the revolutionary pioneers. An enormous wreath of everlasting flowers was carried by sixteen men to the grave of the Communards in the Père Lachaise cemetery, and to the grave of Blanqui. The German delegates also marched to the graves of Heinrich Heine and Ludwig Börne in honour, as Liebknecht said in a public oration, 'of the martyrs of freedom and international fellowship'. Paul Lafargue welcomed the delegates, in the name of the Paris organization, as 'apostles of a new idea'. Édouard Vaillant, who together with Wilhelm Liebknecht had been elected president on the first day of the congress, described the congress as 'the first parliament of the international working class', which had assembled, he declared, to conclude a 'sacred alliance of the international proletariat'.

The origin of the Second International was more prosaic than the high-flown speeches with which its inaugural congress opened. After the failure of the efforts to revive the old, comprehensive International at the congress of Ghent in 1877 and that of Chur in 1881,[1] the party of the Possibilists, led by Paul Brousse, had organized two international working-class congresses in Paris in 1883 and 1886. The Possibilists had themselves broken away from the Fédération du Parti des Travailleurs Socialistes, set up in 1880, the programme of which, under the influence of Jules Guesde and Paul Lafargue, had been uncompromisingly Marxist. In opposition to the Guesdists, the Possibilists were committed to an evolutionary Socialism which would be secured through aiming at modest, realizable reforms in alliance with the radical wing of the *bourgeoisie*.

The Guesdists, at loggerheads with the Possibilists from the beginning, boycotted the congresses called by their rivals. Both these

1. See above, pp. 192 and 194.

congresses, however, had been attended by representatives of the British Trades Union Congress (T.U.C.), the leading organization of the British trade unions, whose leaders were themselves in alliance with the Liberal party. The T.U.C. then decided to call an international workers' congress of its own in London in 1888. But representation was limited mainly to trade-union organizations. Socialist parties, such as the German and Austrian, and the two British Socialist bodies, the Social Democratic Federation and the Socialist League, were consequently excluded, and the representatives of the Socialist parties of France, Belgium, Holland and Denmark, who arrived at the congress, were admitted as delegates of their respective trade-union movements, and not of their parties. The congress decided to meet again in the following year, and asked the French Possibilists to arrange for the meeting to be held in Paris.

The Paris Congress, like the London one, was clearly intended for trade unionists and meant to exclude representatives of political parties. The Possibilists, however, invited all the Socialist parties to attend, alongside the trade unions, upon which the Guesdists convened an international congress of their own. To avoid the rather unedifying spectacle of two rival working-class congresses meeting at the same time, the German party tried to persuade the Possibilists and Guesdists to combine their forces. It invited both wings of French Socialism to a conference in The Hague at the end of February 1889, but the Possibilists decided to abstain. The delegates attending in The Hague then decided to call, in their own name, an international congress in Paris for July of the same year, which would have, as the first item on its agenda, the question of bringing the two congresses together.

In this way, two congresses assembled in Paris on 14 July 1889: the Possibilists in the rue Lancre, the Marxists in the rue Petrelle. Though the Possibilist congress, with its 600 delegates, was numerically stronger than the Marxist, with 400, it was the less important of the two and was the last international congress to be held under Possibilist auspices. It was the congress in the rue Petrelle which went down in history as inaugurating the Second International.

It should be said at once that the congress in the rue Petrelle, as soon as it had officially opened, devoted its first two days to a debate on ways of unifying the rival congresses. On a motion proposed by Liebknecht, it delegated Andrea Costa and Amilcare Cipriani to negotiate a unity agreement with the Possibilists. The latter, however, insisted on checking the mandates of the delegates, a gesture reasonably described by Costa as 'an act of mistrust' which caused the negotiations to be broken off.

In spite of this unpromising background, the inaugural congress of the Second International succeeded in uniting representatives of the Socialist and Labour movements in 'both halves of the world'. The French delegation was, naturally, the strongest. It comprised 221 members, including the Blanquist, Édouard Vaillant, who had been a member of the Paris Commune in 1871; the Marxists, Jules Guesde, Charles Longuet and Paul Lafargue, the latter two being sons-in-law of Marx; and Sébastian Faure, representing the Anarchists.

Despite the Anti-Socialist Law, there were eighty-one delegates from Germany, including Wilhelm Liebknecht, Karl Legien, architect of the German trade-union movement, Eduard Bernstein, Georg Heinrich von Vollmar, Hermann Molkenbuhr, Clara Zetkin and Wilhelm Pfannkuch. The German delegation had been elected directly by the workers, partly at 125 public meetings and partly, where such meetings had been prevented by the police, through voting papers passed round the factories and workshops. Interest in the balloting was, according to Vollmar, hardly less than at a normal parliamentary election.

The next strongest delegation, numbering twenty-two members, was the British. It was led by the leading Socialists in the country, including Keir Hardie, founder of the Scottish Labour party and representative of the 56,000 Scottish miners; William Morris, already a celebrated poet and craftsman and founder of the Socialist League; R. B. Cunninghame Graham, great-grandson of the Earl of Menteith, related to the Stuarts and the first Socialist to sit in a British Parliament; Eleanor Marx-Aveling, Marx's youngest daughter and a well-known speaker in the East End of London, and John Burns, a revolutionary trade-union leader who went over to the Liberals in the 1890s and, later, became a Minister—the first worker to sit in a British Cabinet. Only H. M. Hyndman, founder of the Social Democratic Federation, was missing; a rival of William Morris, he attended, despite his strongly Marxist views, the rival Possibilist congress in the same city.

The fourteen delegates from Belgium included the now grey-haired César de Paepe, one of the leading figures in the First International, Édouard Anseele, architect of the Belgian co-operative movement, and Jean Volders, the party organizer. Italy was represented by twelve delegates, among them the two already mentioned—Andrea Costa and Amilcare Cipriani from the First International—and the Anarchist Saverio Merlino. From Austria there was Victor Adler, leading a delegation of eleven.

Working-class parties in Holland, Denmark, Sweden, Norway, Switzerland, Hungary, Bohemia, Poland, Russia, Romania, Bulgaria, Spain, Portugal, the U.S.A. and Argentina were represented by smaller delegations. Some of them, as, for example, the Argentinian delegation, represented the only existing Socialist group or, as in the case of the

Russian and Polish delegations, the only groups of Socialist refugees abroad. Of the five members of the United States delegation, one only represented the Socialist Workers' party, one was a delegate from the 'United Brotherhood' in Iowa, while three were from Jewish trade unions in New York. Admittedly, the congress also received a message of sympathy from the American Federation of Labor, the main organization of trade unionists in the United States, signed by Samuel Gompers. The delegations also included individuals of some historical importance in the international Socialist movement. We have already mentioned a number from France, Germany, Belgium, Austria and Italy. Among the others were such leading figures as G. V. Plekhanov and Peter Lavrov, the leading theorists of each of the two streams of Russian Socialism; Felix Daszynski, leader of the Polish Socialists in Austria; Pablo Iglesias, founder of the Spanish Socialist party; Domela Nieuwenhuis, a celebrated figure in the Dutch Socialist movement; and Willem Hubert Vliegen, architect of the Socialist party in Holland.

The main item on the agenda was the question of international labour legislation. But before this item was reached, congress heard reports from the various delegations on the struggles, setbacks and achievements of the Labour movement in their respective countries. These reports gave a useful and comprehensive picture of the strength of the international working-class movement at the time of the International's revival.

2

The German Socialist party was already the strongest, and it remained so throughout the life of the Second International. At the Gotha Congress, in 1875, both the Marxist and the Lassallean sections of the movement had come together to form a united party. Three years later it was confronted with the Anti-Socialist Law contrived by Bismarck to bring about its destruction. And, in fact, the legislation imposed heavy losses on the party. During the twelve years in which it was in force, 332 labour organizations were dissolved, 1,300 newspapers and periodicals suppressed, about 900 party activists driven from their homes and 1,500 sentenced to a total of 1,000 years' imprisonment.[1] The growth of the party in the face of such severe repression was all the more impressive. In 1881, in the elections for the German Parliament which followed the passing of the Anti-Socialist Law, the party received 310,000 votes. Three years later the figure was 550,000, and by 1887 it had grown to

1. Franz Mehring, *Geschichte der deutschen Sozialdemokratie* (Stuttgart, 1898), vol. III, Part 2, p. 535. Apart from Mehring's *Geschichte* the most important work on the early history of the German Socialist movement is August Bebel, *Aus meinem Leben*, 3 vols. (Stuttgart, 1910–14).

763,000. At the elections of 1890, after the Anti-Socialist Law had expired, the party more than doubled its previous vote, with a total of 1,427,000, about a fifth of all votes cast. Thirty-five Socialist members were returned to the German Parliament. At the same time, the party Press had grown to nineteen daily papers and forty-one weeklies, while the number of trade unionists had reached 120,000.

3

In Britain, the trade-union movement was naturally much stronger and more influential than in Germany. Keir Hardie, in his report to the foundation congress, claimed that of the ten million industrial workers in his country, about a million belonged to trade unions. But the British trade unions were far from being Socialist. Indeed, most of their leaders saw in Socialism merely a utopia, and in the theory of the class struggle a dangerously destructive doctrine. They believed firmly in an ultimate 'harmony of class interests'. Their main concern was to secure, through parliamentary pressure, reforms in trade-union legislation, and in 1871 the T.U.C. established a Parliamentary Committee to organize this pressure and to strengthen the influence of Labour in the House of Commons. They fought elections, however, in alliance with the Liberal party, and the working-class members of Parliament—eleven were elected in 1886 and fifteen in 1892—formed a section of the Parliamentary Liberal party. Only Keir Hardie, John Burns and Cunninghame Graham could be considered in any sense as independent workers' representatives.

However, the trade unions' alliance with the Liberal party proved quite incapable of protecting the workers from the disastrous consequences of the prolonged economic crisis of the 1870s and 1880s. Increasing numbers of unemployed voiced their protests at meetings, public demonstrations and hunger marches, and the agitation spread to the factories and mines, where the employers were trying to cut wages. Keir Hardie, John Burns and other leading trade unionists worked hard to break the alliance with the Liberals and to organize an independent workers' party which, freed from the Liberal party's commitment to capitalism, could represent working-class interests effectively. This radical mood of the workers was also reflected in intellectual circles, and H. M. Hyndman took the initiative in forming a new party, the Democratic Federation, in 1881.

Henry Mayers Hyndman (1842–1921) was a prolific writer and a formidable public speaker, whose private means—his grandfather had made a substantial fortune out of the West Indian slave-trade—enabled him to indulge his intellectual and social interests freely, without having to concern himself with earning a living. The first volume of *Das Kapital*, which he read in 1879, transformed his whole outlook, and through frequent conversations with Marx he became an ardent convert to Socialism. In the year in which the Democratic Federation was founded he published *England for All*, a popularization of Marx's economic theories with particular reference to England. Two years later he published his *Historical Basis of Socialism in Great Britain*, a comprehensive study of the development of capitalism, the Labour movement and Socialism from the fifteenth to the late nineteenth century. His original aim in establishing the Democratic Federation was to revive the Chartist movement, in the traditions of Ernest Jones and Julian Harney, but three years later the Federation acquired a distinctively Marxian socialist outlook and changed its name to the Social Democratic Federation (S.D.F.).[1]

The S.D.F. began as a small body of Socialist intellectuals from the middle and working classes. Its members included William Morris, one of the most attractive figures in the history of British Socialism, and author of the famous utopian *News From Nowhere*, which became a classic of the movement. Other leading recruits were Ernest Belfort Bax, a scholar and writer; Henry H. Champion, the son of a major-general and, like his father, an army officer who, however, resigned his commission in protest against Britain's imperialist war on Egypt; Andreas Scheu, one of the leaders of the Austrian Socialist movement, who had emigrated to England after its split in 1874; J. L. Joynes, a master at Eton and a poet who had translated Herwegh and Freiligrath into English; Walter Crane, whose engravings symbolizing the workers' struggle were reproduced in countless left-wing publications in many countries for several generations; Annie Besant, who later emigrated to India and earned an honoured place in the annals of the Indian nationalist movement; Eleanor Marx-Aveling; and the trade-union leaders, John Burns, Ben Tillett, Tom Mann and Harry Quelch, who started life as a cow herdsman, became a wage-earner, later a trade-union secretary and finally editor of *Justice*.

Justice was the first modern Socialist periodical in England. Appearing for the first time in January 1884 with the subtitle 'Organ of Social Democracy', it soon became the Federation's most important medium of propaganda. It was started with a capital of £300, contributed by the Socialist poet Edward Carpenter. Edited by Hyndman and, later, by Quelch, it included William Morris, Belfort Bax and Andreas Scheu

1. For the history of Socialism in the 1880s and 1890s, see Max Beer, *A History of British Socialism* (London, 1940), Part 4; G. D. H. Cole, *A Short History of the British Working-class Movement, 1889–1927* (London, 1932); Henry Pelling, *The Origins of the Labour Party, 1880–1900* (London, 1954); see also H. M. Hyndman, *Record of an Adventurous Life* (London, 1911).

among its contributors. The Federation published pamphlets, such as *Socialism Made Plain*, which sold 100,000 copies, and evening after evening its members spoke at street-corner and factory meetings. The Federation soon increased its support, and by 1887 it had thirty branches, mainly in London and in the textile districts of Lancashire, but it never succeeded in becoming a mass organization.[1]

After less than a year the S.D.F. experienced its first serious split. Included in its ranks were Socialists of varying points of view, revolutionaries, anti-parliamentarians, reformists and Anarchists. The dictatorial and somewhat erratic leadership of Hyndman gave rise to increasing discontent. At the end of 1884 William Morris, Belfort Bax, Edward and Eleanor Marx-Aveling and others who were critical of Hyndman's personality and tactics left the Federation, together with most of the anti-parliamentarians and Anarchists, to form, under Morris's leadership, the rather ill-assorted Socialist League. A year later the League produced the first number of its organ, *Commonweal*, to which Engels became an occasional contributor. The League had even less success than the Federation in acquiring a mass membership, and when the Anarchists captured the leadership, William Morris, together with the remaining Socialist members, resigned in 1890. After that there was some *rapprochement* between Morris and the S.D.F. The Socialist League soon disintegrated.

At the beginning of 1884 another group of Socialist intellectuals, including the civil servant, Sidney Webb, and the playwright, Bernard Shaw, later to be joined by the novelist, H. G. Wells, formed the Fabian Society. Its declared aim was 'to persuade the English people to democratize completely its political constitution and to nationalize its industry, so that its material life will become completely independent of private capital'. The aim of the society was expressed even more clearly in its programme. The society aimed, it declared, 'at the reorganization of society by the emancipation of land and industrial capital from individual and class ownership, and the vesting of them in the community for the general benefit'.

The Fabians appealed not only to the workers but to all classes of society in their attempt 'to awaken the social conscience by bringing present miseries to the knowledge of society'. One of their chief methods was the production of pamphlets—many of them along lines similar to the first volume of *Das Kapital*, which, as the Fabians said, 'contains a tremendous amount of carefully checked and well-established facts about modern civilization'. These pamphlets—the famous *Fabian Tracts* —and leaflets were distributed in tens of thousands. Like the plays of Bernard Shaw and the social novels of H. G. Wells, they did a great deal

1. In 1884 the membership was 400, but rose hardly to 1,000 in the first ten years.

to permeate the moral and intellectual atmosphere of Britain with Socialist ideas.

Although none of these bodies of Socialist intellectuals succeeded in attracting a large mass of support, their propaganda helped to create an atmosphere which favoured the spread of industrial militancy. This revived once again at the end of the 1880s as the economic crisis receded. There was a considerable fall in unemployment, unskilled workers began to join the unions in large numbers and there was a growing movement to establish an independent party of the working class. At the beginning of 1887 Keir Hardie founded *The Miner*. Changing its name, two years later, to the *Labour Leader*, this soon became one of the most influential Socialist journals in the field. In 1888 Henry Champion's paper *The Labour Elector* and Annie Besant's *The Link* were both started. All these new working-class papers contributed to the growing feeling against the policy of the existing trade-union leadership, for the ending of their alliance with the Liberals and the formation of an independent workers' party. None of the Labour leaders had grasped the need for such a party more clearly or advocated it more persistently than Keir Hardie, a pioneer of Socialism in Britain and a remarkable figure, in some ways reminiscent of the German leader, August Bebel.[1]

Keir Hardie (1856–1915) was born into a very poor working-class family, in Scotland. His father was a ship's joiner who had been incapacitated by an accident, so that the young Hardie had to go out to work as an errand boy at the age of eight. For a time the entire family of father, mother and two children had to live on the 4*s.* 6*d.* a week which the child was able to earn. As he could not attend school, Keir Hardie's mother taught him to read and write in the evenings. At the age of ten he began work in the mines. His first job was that of 'trapper': he had to open and close the ventilation shaft, working for ten hours a day in gloomy solitude, the darkness relieved only by the flickering of his lamp. Encouraged by his mother, who came of farming stock, Keir Hardie acquired through persistence and his own native wit an exceptional knowledge of books. The sources of his Socialism lay in the spirit of democracy and freedom in the poems of Burns, Carlyle's social criticism, the Sermon on the Mount and the outbursts against oppression and injustice which he found in the Hebrew prophets. He despised demagogy and, unlike his contemporary, John Burns, he had no particular gifts as a public speaker. His moral qualities, however, his

1. For an outline of his life, see William Stewart, *J. Keir Hardie* (London, 1921); also D. Lowe, *J. Keir Hardie: From Pit to Parliament* (London, 1913), and *Keir Hardie's Speeches and Writings, 1888–1915*, edited by Emrys Hughes (London, 1928).

disinterestedness and sincerity, won him the lasting affections of the Scottish miners. In 1879, when scarcely twenty-three, he was elected secretary of the Scottish Mineworkers' Union, and in January 1889 he founded the Scottish Labour party, one of the forerunners of the Independent Labour party, which was to become the first mass party of democratic Socialism in Britain.

The year 1889 was, indeed, the turning-point in British labour history, the most outstanding event of the year being the great London dock strike. At the beginning of the year the gas workers in the East End, by merely threatening to strike, had secured an immediate reduction of the working day from twelve to eight hours. This success encouraged the low-paid London dockers to press their wage demands. When these were rejected, 10,000 completely unorganized workers went on strike in August 1889, under the leadership of John Burns, Ben Tillett and Tom Mann. The strike lasted for five weeks, and turned into an impressive demonstration of working-class solidarity. There were no strike breakers, and the general public sympathized with the strike. Collections raised nearly £50,000 and Cardinal Manning offered to mediate. The strike ended with nearly all the demands of the workers being granted.[1]

The two victories of unskilled workers, coming within a few months of each other, gave tremendous impetus to the trade-union movement. The East End of London, that 'immense haunt of misery', had ceased, in Engels's words, to form a 'stagnant pool'. It had 'shaken off its torpid despair',[2] and seen the birth of a new type of trade union, catering specifically for the unskilled worker. During the year of the Second International's foundation in Paris, nearly 300,000 workers joined trade unions, and a further half million in the two years following. During this period, in which the cost of living rose by a little over 4 per cent, the Mineworkers' Union secured a wage-increase of over a third, while trade-union pressure generally raised wages by an average of 10 per cent.

In 1889 the leadership of the trade unions had passed, up to a point, into the hands of Socialists such as Keir Hardie, John Burns, Ben Tillett and Tom Mann. They hoped to establish a Labour party which would be class conscious, independent of the middle class and dominated by a Socialist outlook. On 13 January 1883, this party was set up at a conference in Bradford, with Keir Hardie in the chair. It called itself the Independent Labour party, more generally known as the I.L.P., the main point in its programme being the transfer of the means of production to public ownership. It expanded quickly. According to Keir Hardie, its membership, two years after its formation, exceeded 50,000.[3]

1. See H. H. Champion, *The Great Dock Strike* (London, 1890).
2. Friedrich Engels, *Condition of the Working Class in England in 1844*, Preface to the 1892 edition.
3. Pelling, op. cit., p. 173.

With the establishment of the I.L.P., Socialism for the first time secured a mass basis among the working class. In England, however, unlike continental countries, the Socialist movement did not become preoccupied with ideological disputes. Anarchism was quite foreign to the temperament and traditions of the British people, and from Marxism the English Socialists took only the economic objective of social ownership and control of the means of production. And although some leading intellectuals, such as Hyndman and his circle, expounded and were inspired by the whole range of Marxist ideas, the ideology as such never gained any great influence over the movement. The Socialist outlook which spread from the I.L.P. into the general Labour movement derived its inspiration from Christian ethics and the political traditions of British radicalism.[1]

4

In France, on the other hand, which has some claim to be considered the cradle of Socialism, the movement was split from the very beginning into rival ideological schools. When the movement began to recover from the disaster of the Paris Commune, its leaders were preoccupied with finding the correct theoretical basis. In 1879 the government granted an amnesty which restored freedom to ex-Communards, and in October of the same year a workers' congress, assembled at Marseilles, founded the Fédération du Parti des Travailleurs Socialistes. Jules Guesde, who had been largely responsible for founding the new party, became its first leader.[2]

Jules Guesde (1845–1922) began his career as a radical-republican journalist. During the Commune he became a Socialist, and an article which he wrote in its defence earned him a prison sentence of five years, which he avoided only by escaping to Switzerland. From there he went to Italy, and returned to France in 1876. A year later he founded the Socialist weekly, *Égalité*, the first Marxist periodical in France, which included Wilhelm Liebknecht and César de Paepe among its contributors. The main object of Guesde's paper was the foundation, in France, of its own highly centralized party of Marxian Socialism, on the model of the German Social Democratic party, which he greatly admired. Under

1. For a comprehensive bibliography on the history of Socialism in Britain, see Cole, *A History of Socialist Thought*, vol. III: *The Second International*, Part 2, pp. 978–84.

2. For this period in the history of French Socialism, see Alexandre Zévaès, *Le Socialisme en France depuis 1871* (Paris, 1908); also Édouard Dolléans, *Histoire du mouvement ouvrier*, vol. II (Paris, 1939), pp. 13ff., 89ff.; Aaron Noland, *The Founding of the French Socialist Party* (Harvard University Press, 1956), Introduction, pp. 1–33; Val R. Lorwin, *The French Labour Movement* (Harvard, 1954), chs. 2 and 3.

his leadership the Marseille Congress declared itself fundamentally opposed to the *bourgeoisie*, and in favour of the 'common ownership of land, mines, implements of production and raw materials'. After the congress, Guesde went, together with Paul Lafargue, to London to discuss the programme and constitution of the new party with Marx and Engels. Two documents, embodying their conclusions and drafted jointly by Guesde and Paul Lafargue, were embodied in a resolution adopted by the party's second congress in Paris in 1880.[1]

Only a year later, however, at the congress in Le Havre, the party suffered its first split. It contained within its ranks three incompatible groups. Besides the Marxists there were the followers of Proudhon, believers in Socialism through the development of co-operatives, who rejected both the theory of the class struggle and the desirability of political action. A third group were the Anarchists who, while agreeing with the Marxists in acknowledging the class struggle, opposed all forms of political activity, including parliamentary elections. Both anti-Marxist groups revolted against the party leadership and withdrew.

There was still another section, led by Paul Brousse (1854–1912), which opposed Guesde's theory of revolutionary Socialism by their own ideology of advancing to Socialism in gradual, evolutionary stages. Brousse, a doctor of medicine, had fled to Switzerland after the collapse of the Commune. There he met Bakunin, and worked for a time in the Anarchist Jura Federation. When the amnesty enabled him to return to France, he had become a reformist. However, he joined forces with Guesde and Lafargue, while arguing, in his journal, *Le Prolétaire*, for a theory of municipal Socialism, and for the nationalization of industry by city and provincial governments rather than, as in the Marxist version, by the state. He also advocated an alliance, including election agreements, with middle-class radicals, to secure the greatest possible representation of Socialists on public bodies through which social and political reforms could be implemented.

The party split once again at the congress at Saint-Étienne in 1882. This time it was on questions of theory and tactic. Brousse's supporters, who became known as the Possibilists, won a majority and secured control of the party. They changed its name to the Parti Ouvrier Socialiste Révolutionnaire—despite their decidedly anti-revolutionary views. Guesde and his followers formed the Parti Ouvrier Français, in close liaison with the trade unions represented in the Fédération Nationale de Syndicats.[2]

1. For an outline of the life of Guesde, see Alexandre Zévaès, *Jules Guesde* (Paris, 1929), and the article by Georges Bourgin, 'Jules Guesde', in *Archiv für die Geschichte des Sozialismus und der Arbeiterbewegung*, vol. XIV, 1929.
2. See S. Humbert, *Les Possibilistes* (Paris, 1911).

It was not until 1884, when trade unions became legal, that they began to appear in strength on the French scene. Up to that time their activities had been curbed by the decree passed in the National Assembly in 1790, during the French Revolution,[1] made even more severe by the *Code Napoléon*. The formation of trade unions had been punishable by law and they could be organized only under cover of friendly societies or clubs. 'Our *bourgeoisie*,' complained Guesde at the Congress of the International, 'are more heartless and ruthless than any other, as they showed only too clearly in the massacre of workers in June 1848 and May 1871. They ground the French working class to powder, smashed it to smithereens and, by suppressing trade unionism and freedom of association, deprived it of all possibility of common action.'[2]

Once trade unions had been legalized, they proceeded to establish a joint organization, the Fédération Nationale de Syndicats, which was founded at the Lyon Congress of trade unions in 1886. But within the trade-union movement two opposed factions contended for leadership. The anti-parliamentary faction advanced the policy of 'direct action', by which they meant the achievement of working-class power through the general strike, while those influenced by Proudhon rejected both the general strike and political struggle. Both factions were soon in public dispute with the Parti Ouvrier, whose programme called for political struggle by the working class, while rejecting the general strike as a piece of fantasy. These controversies played their part in splintering the Socialist movement still further. Within a few years the trade unions had completely dissociated themselves from the Socialist party.

Meanwhile, the Possibilists themselves had split. Jean Allemane, a Communard who had been deported to the penal colony of New Caledonia, had joined forces with Brousse on returning to France, but soon opposed him on the question of seeking alliances with middle-class parties. Allemane was also an advocate of the general strike as a key weapon in working-class emancipation. In 1890 he and his supporters broke with the Possibilists and formed the Parti Ouvrier Socialiste Révolutionnaire, whereupon the Possibilists dropped the word 'Révolutionnaire' from the title.[3]

It should also be noted that the Blanquists, who had played a major part in the tragedy of the Commune, had reorganized themselves soon after the amnesty into the Parti Socialiste Révolutionnaire, under the leadership of Vaillant. Reaction, in the period of its triumph, had been quite unable to eradicate Blanquism, with its roots in the spirit of Babeuf and the traditions of the great French Revolution. The Blanquists still

1. See above, p. 24.
2. *Protokoll*, op. cit., p. 38.
3. See M. Chausy, *Les Allemanists* (Paris, 1912) and Jean Allemane, *Mémoires d'un communard* (n.d.).

had a considerable following in Paris and in some of the provincial centres. They were closest to the Parti Ouvrier, but did not fuse with it completely until 1905. At the moment when the International revived, therefore, the French Socialists had disintegrated into six conflicting tendencies, struggling for leadership in the Labour movement—Broussists, Guesdists, Blanquists, Allemanists, Syndicalists and Anarchists.

However, in spite of the numerous schisms, the French Labour movement gained rapidly in influence. The Socialist vote rose from 30,000 in the first elections following the foundation of the party, to 179,000 in the elections following in 1889, and climbed to 440,000 in the 1893 elections.

5

The Belgian Labour movement, like nearly all such movements in the first phase of their development, went through a very similar process of internal conflict and splits, but it recovered more quickly than that in France. Soon after the end of the First International, in which the Belgian Federation, led by César de Paepe, had played an important role, its sections became convulsed in an ideological conflict between the Walloons, who tended to be influenced either by the Anarchists or by the Blanquists, and the Flemish, who were Social Democrats. In 1877 two separate parties appeared, the Socialist party, founded by Édouard Anseele and E. van Beveren, and the Brabant Socialist party among the Walloons. At the inaugural congress of the Belgian Labour party (Parti Socialiste Belge) in Brussels in April 1885, both parties amalgamated, and the split in Belgian Socialism was largely overcome.

Soon, however, there were fresh disagreements on the method by which the party should conduct its campaign for the franchise. A fighting pamphlet in favour of the workers' right to the vote, drafted by the Walloon Socialist, Alfred Defuisseaux, and called *Le Catéchisme du peuple*, sold the surprising number of 260,000 copies. In 1886 it provoked a great and largely spontaneous strike movement in the mining district of Charleroi. The strikes soon spread to Liège and along the Borinage. The government called out police and army against the strikers. 'For some days the province of Hainaut presented the dramatic spectacle of a full-scale war. Martial law was proclaimed in the towns, town halls were occupied by the army, soldiers were camped in the yards of factories and around the pit-heads, squadrons of cavalry patrolled the streets. The shots of the soldiers . . . put down the workers' rising in terror': in these terms the historian Henri Pirenne described the situation in the strike-bound areas.[1] After the failure of the general strike the leaders were prosecuted, some being sentenced to twenty years' solitary confinement. Anseele was given six months in prison for asking mothers of the soldiers to implore their sons not to fire on the workers.

Disappointment at the defeat of the strike combined with disgust at the sentences to bring about renewed struggle between the Blanquist and Social Democratic wings of the party. Led by the brother and the son of Alfred Defuisseaux—Léon and Georges—a new party was formed in 1887, calling itself the Republican Socialist party. It began at once to work vigorously for a general strike and a revolutionary uprising of the workers. But the mass strike which it succeeded in starting at the end of 1888 was also abandoned in failure. This paved the way for a reunification of the two wings at the Louvain Congress in 1889. The conflict of views on the general strike as a weapon in the class struggle was settled at the Namur Congress in April 1892 by a resolution recognizing it as a legitimate instrument in the struggle for the franchise. A few weeks later the party duly called a general strike in the cause of electoral reform. Hundreds of thousands responded to the strike call, and once more there were bloody clashes between the workers and the armed might of the state. The general strike, which had broken out on 1 May, was called off on the 11th, but only after Parliament had agreed to call a constituent assembly to discuss electoral reform.

However, the elections for the constituent assembly gave a majority to the Catholic party, which was against universal suffrage. Upon this the party called another general strike in April 1893. This time it lasted from 11 to 18 April, and again ended in a compromise. The Reform Bill which emerged multiplied the electorate tenfold, but reserved for some privileged sections the right of plural voting in the election of the Chamber of Deputies, while continuing to elect the Senate on a class franchise. At the first election under the new law, in October 1894, the Socialists won 355,000 votes and twenty-eight seats, both Édouard Anseele and Émile Vandervelde being returned. But with the provision for plural voting the party could have no hope of seeing the working class represented in full strength. The struggle for an equal franchise continued. In 1901 the Party Conference at Liège resolved to prosecute the struggle by every means, 'even, if necessary, through the general strike and insurrections'. In April 1902, the party called once more for a general strike, neither for the first nor the last time in the history of the Belgian Labour movement. Eleven years later the party called yet again

1. H. Pirenne, *Histoire de Belgique* (Brussels, 1932), vol. VII, p. 305; and Louis Bertrand, *Histoire de la démocratie et du socialisme en Belgique depuis 1830* (Brussels, 1906).

9 Ferdinand Lassalle

10a (above) *Eduard Bernstein* *10b* (above) *Émile Vandervelde*
10c (below) *G. V. Plekhanov* *10d* (below) *Victor Adler*

for a general strike in the fight for equal voting rights. Reform came only after the First World War.[1]

The Belgian Labour party differed in structure from most other parties in the International. It was not like, for example, the German Social Democratic party, a centralized organization based on individual membership in local groups, but a federation of trade unions, co-operative retail and productive societies, associations of employees in workers' health insurance, and educational, student and Socialist societies of various kinds. It was a party, as Carl Landauer described it, 'which not merely claimed to represent the worker politically, but also to negotiate for him with his employers, to provide him with facilities for buying his food and clothing more cheaply, for insuring him against illness, unemployment, and old age, for providing him with medical treatment and with opportunities for recreation and self-education'.[2] It was, as H. Pirenne remarked, 'more than an ordinary party. It makes the observer think of a state and a church in which the class spirit takes the place of the national or religious spirit'.[3] It depended for its finances on these affiliated societies, which spread rapidly after the foundation by Anseele of the famous co-operative association Vooruit in Ghent in 1880 and which, as Jean Volders reported to the Congress of the International, devoted some of its surplus to building the Socialist Press and the party's cultural institutions. The Belgian party could claim, said Volders, to be one of the best-organized in Europe.[4]

6

The struggle for the vote conducted by the Labour party in Belgium, and particularly its technique of street demonstrations, together with the political general strike, produced a considerable impact on the working people of Austria. In their own fight for universal suffrage, the left wing of the party urged the leadership 'to speak Belgian'.

The Social Democratic Labour party of Austria emerged from a merger between the 'moderates' and the 'radicals' at their conference at Hainfeld in 1888–9, a mere six months before the Congress of the International. It put an end to years of bitter dissension in a Labour movement which had begun promisingly enough at the end of the 1860s. In December 1869, 10,000 Viennese workers had demonstrated in

1. See below, pp. 292–3.
2. Carl Landauer, *European Socialism* (Berkeley, 1959), vol. I, p. 469.
3. Pirenne, op. cit., vol. VII, p. 343.
4. See Émile Vandervelde, 'Die innere Organisation der Belgischen Arbeiterpartei', in *Die Neue Zeit*, vol. XVIII; and Louis de Brouckère and Hendrik de Man, 'Die Arbeiterbewegung in Belgien', in supplement no. 9, *Die Neue Zeit*, vol. XIX (1910–11); Marc-Antoine Pierson, *Histoire du Socialisme en Belgique* (Brussels, 1953).

front of the Parliament building for the right to form legal trade unions. Impressed by the size of the demonstration the government passed a law which permitted the formation of unions. At the same time it stepped up the repression against 'Social Democratic tendencies'. Ten days after the demonstration the Socialist leaders, including Andreas Scheu, Heinrich Oberwinder and Johann Most, were arrested. Six months later they were sentenced to heavy terms of hard labour on charges of high treason. Almost all working-class organizations, including trade unions, were then disbanded. Under the pressure of renewed street demonstrations the police eventually allowed them to re-form, and the imprisoned leaders were released under an amnesty. But the movement and its Press remained under strict police surveillance.

From the beginning the young Austrian Labour movement had modelled itself on the German and considered itself virtually a branch of German Social Democracy. It consequently reflected the controversies which raged in the larger organization. In Austria the dispute became personalized in the struggle between Heinrich Oberwinder (1846–1914) and Andreas Scheu (1844–1927). Oberwinder owed some of his ideas to Lassalle. Claiming that a strong Labour movement could not grow in Austria while the country remained industrially under-developed, he called on the workers to form, for the time being, an alliance with the progressive *bourgeoisie* to fight for democratic and social reform against the ruling aristocracy. His followers described themselves as 'moderates'. Scheu, on the other hand, was a Marxist, demanding an uncompromising class struggle against the *bourgeoisie* as well as the aristocracy for the complete Socialist transformation of society. His followers were called 'radicals'.

As always and everywhere, what began as a genuine difference over principles and tactics soon degenerated into bitter personal antagonism. In 1874 both men abandoned the party, when Scheu left for England and Oberwinder for Germany. In England Scheu joined the Social Democratic Federation and later the Socialist League, working actively, right up to his death, for the ideals which had inspired him as a young man. Oberwinder's development in Germany was much less consistent. After joining the anti-semitic Christian Social party, founded by Stocker, Chaplain to the Prussian Court, he became editor of its paper. He was subsequently a foundation member of the chauvinist Navy League, founded by Admiral Tirpitz, and finished up as one of the main speakers for the 'National Executive', which functioned as a leading section of the reactionary, anti-Social Democratic 'Fatherland Union'.[1]

1. For this period in the history of Austrian Social Democracy, see Heinrich Scheu, 'Erinnerungen', in *Der Wiener Hochverratsprozess* (Vienna, 1911); Andreas Scheu, *Umsturzkeime* (Vienna, 1923); Ludwig Brügel, *Geschichte der österreichischen Sozialdemokratie*, vol. II, pp. 200ff.; Herbert Steiner, *Die Arbeiterbewegung*

After the departure of Scheu, leadership of the radicals fell to Josef Peukert (1855–1910), one of the strangest figures in Austrian Labour history. Genial and impressive, he was adulated by his followers until, after two years, he was suspected of being a police informer.[1] Born in Bohemia, Peukert was an interior decorator by trade, a self-educated man of considerable learning. During his years of travel he came in contact with Anarchist groups in Switzerland and France. After being expelled from France in 1880 he arrived in England, where he established close relations with Most.

Johann Most (1846–1907) was among the leaders of the Austrian Labour movement who were tried for high treason in July 1870, Most being sentenced to five years' hard labour. After a few months, following on a change of government, he and his comrades were released and Most was deported to his native Germany. He had been born in Augsburg, the son of a poor subaltern, and after returning to Germany played a leading part in the Socialist movement for the next seven years. Elected to the German Parliament in 1874 and 1877, Most was sentenced to eighteen months' imprisonment in 1874 for a speech in defence of the Paris Commune. After his release, huge public meetings were held in his honour, and he became editor-in-chief of the Social Democratic paper, *Berliner Freie Presse*. He came to enjoy, according to his friend Eduard Bernstein, 'an immense popularity with the mass of the people'. As soon as the Socialist Laws had been passed, he was expelled from Berlin and settled in London. There he founded, along with a number of members of the old German Communist Workers' Educational Society, the weekly paper, *Die Freiheit*, intended for illegal distribution in Germany.

An exceptionally talented journalist and an impressive public speaker, Most was aptly described by Bernstein as an 'undisciplined genius', impelled mainly by a revolutionary temperament and a messianic conviction that he was destined to be the 'saviour of the revolutionary spirit in Germany'. In this spirit, he used his paper to organize an opposition against the party leadership and the policy of cautious discretion imposed on it by the Socialist Law. In his conflict with the party leaders he gradually moved closer to Anarchism. He even glorified the stupid attempt to assassinate the ageing Kaiser Wilhelm I, which served Bismarck as a welcome pretext for his anti-Socialist legislation.

Oesterreichs 1867–1889 (Vienna, 1964). For a biography of Heinrich Oberwinder, see *Festschrift des Dresdner Anzeigers* (Dresden, 1930). According to Mehring, Oberwinder was exposed in Paris as an agent of the German government during the period of the anti-Socialist laws: *Geschichte der deutschen Sozialdemokratie* (Stuttgart, 1904), vol. II, p. 300.

1. Brügel, op. cit., vol III, p. 229. Peukert tried to clear himself of suspicion; see his *Erinnerungen eines Proletariers aus der revolutionären Arbeiterbewegung*, edited by Gustav Landauer (Berlin, 1913), and Victor Adler, 'Peukerts Erinnerungen', in *Der Kampf*, vol. VII, pp. 302ff.

A party conference in 1880, meeting secretly in Weyden, Switzerland, on account of the Socialist Law, expelled Most, and *Die Freiheit*, originally a foreign organ of the party's radical wing, now passed under the control of the Anarchists.[1]

Most was also sentenced to eighteen months' imprisonment by a London court for an article in *Die Freiheit*, justifying the attempt on the life of Tsar Alexander II in 1881, and recommending similar treatment for all heads of state 'between St Petersburg and Washington'. After his release he was deported from England and emigrated to America. He had a tumultuous welcome as a 'victim of *bourgeois* justice' at a specially convened meeting in New York in December 1882, and his propaganda tour, which took him to the main cities of the United States by the beginning of 1883, resembled a triumphal procession. The Anarchists, who had broken away from the Socialist Labour party of America, rallied to Most, and to *Die Freiheit*, which he again began to publish. There followed the tragedy of Chicago in May 1886 in which, after a bomb attack on a squadron of police who were trying to disperse a demonstration, four of the Anarchist leaders were hanged. This meant the virtual extinction of the Anarchist movement in the U.S.A. and, with it, the political career of Most.[2]

Of all Most's colleagues in London, Peukert had been the closest, and when he returned to Austria in 1881 he was greeted by the radicals as a 'genuine revolutionary'. Nor did he disappoint them. His pamphlets practically dripped blood. But this 'propaganda by deed' had frightful consequences. In July 1882 his supporters tried to rob a shoe manufacturer. In December 1883 they shot two policemen, and in January 1884 they killed and robbed the proprietor of a money-changing bureau. The culprits were arrested and hanged, numerous workers who had copies of Peukert's pamphlets were given heavy prison sentences, and a state of emergency was proclaimed in Vienna and the industrial

1. See Eduard Bernstein, *Sozialdemokratische Lehrjahre* (Berlin, 1928), chs. 14, 19 and 20.

2. For an outline of Most's life, see the Anarchist R. Rocker's *Johann Most, das Leben eines Rebellen* (Berlin, 1924). For the Chicago tragedy, see Morris Hillquit, *History of Socialism in the United States* (New York and London, 1906), pp. 235–45. The trial was a gross example of class justice. The accused, editors of the Anarchist *Arbeiter-Zeitung*—August Spiess, Adolf Fischer, George Engel, Michael Schwab, and Louis Lingg, all of German extraction, the American, Albert R. Parsons, and the Englishman, Samuel Fielden—were sentenced, despite the absence of evidence linking them with the bomb attack, to be hanged for 'incitement to murder by the spoken and written word'. Schwab and Fielden later had their sentences commuted to life imprisonment. Lingg committed suicide in his cell by exploding a cartridge in his mouth. The others were hanged on 11 November 1887. As the noose was put round his neck, Spiess said: 'The time will come when our silence in the grave will be more eloquent than our speeches.' Parsons had escaped arrest, but surrendered voluntarily to the court.

areas of Lower Austria. The same night, according to Victor Adler, 'several hundred comrades were dragged from their beds and deported; those deported were deprived of their citizenship for all time'.[1] The night before martial law was proclaimed, however, Josef Peukert had left for America.

The state of emergency lasted for seven years. Juries for those charged with political offences were abolished, 'suspects' were deported after summary trial, many associations were dissolved and meetings were allowed to take place only with police permission and under police supervision. The régime of repression destroyed a movement which, ten years earlier, in 1873, had had more than 80,000 members and had spread to every part of the Austro-Hungarian Empire.[2]

The Habsburg system of government, however, was described by Victor Adler as despotism mitigated by slovenliness; equally incapable, as he explained to the Congress of the International, 'of just rule and unjust repression, the Government alternated between both courses'.[3] It was this 'slovenliness' which enabled the movement to survive the repression and in 1886 it slowly began to recover. But it was still leaderless and crippled by the sterile strife between its 'moderate' and 'radical' wings—respectively Social Democratic and Anarchist.

Repeated attempts were made to bring the dissident factions together. They were all unsuccessful, until Victor Adler took up the task at the end of the 1880s. He was the real founder of modern Austrian Social Democracy, which came to life in Hainfeld on 1 January 1888.

Victor Adler (1852–1918)[4] came from a well-to do Bohemian Jewish family which had left Prague for Vienna in the 1850s. While still a medical student, he had joined the Democratic German Nationalist movement, which strove to establish a united national state in the spirit of 1848. As a doctor, working among the poor, he was moved by the sheer wretchedness of the poverty he found everywhere, and by the early 1880s his experiences had brought him close to the working-class movement. In the summer of 1883 he came to England to study the system of factory inspection, and after his visit to Friedrich Engels in London the two men formed a lifelong friendship.[5]

In December 1886, Adler used the fortune he had inherited from his father to found the weekly *Gleichheit*, forerunner of the famous *Arbeiter-*

1. Victor Adler, 'Der Weg nach Hainfeld', in *Der Kampf*, vol. II, pp. 145ff.
2. For a statistical survey of the state of the Austrian Labour movement and of its Press in 1873, see Brügel, op. cit., vol. II, pp. 205ff.
3. *Protokoll*, op. cit., p. 43.
4. For a biography, see Julius Braunthal, *Victor und Friedrich Adler* (Vienna, 1965).
5. See the correspondence between Adler and Engels in *Victor Adlers Aufsätze, Reden und Briefe*, edited by Friedrich Adler (Vienna, 1922), vol. I, p. 385.

Zeitung. The paper helped to prepare the ground for a reunited working-class movement. Adler's personality, radiant with wisdom and warmth, won him the confidence of right and left in Austria and in the International. In Austria he enjoyed, right up to his death, a degree of affection and admiration accorded to no other leader of the movement. His prestige in the wider circles of the International was hardly less. Édouard Vaillant, the Blanquist, wrote of him: 'No one else in the International is surrounded with such love and friendship.' Émile Vandervelde, the reformist, testified:

> I have known people who were more well-spoken, in the conventional sense of the term, than Victor Adler; others who have had a more profound effect on the development of Socialist thought; others, again, who were more deeply involved in world affairs and so more effective in a wider sphere of politics. But I have never known anyone—I, repeat anyone—who so combined in his own person all those qualities of character and understanding that go to make up the great party leader. He valued ideals without being blind to reality; he had a thorough grasp of doctrine and also of facts, a wonderful balance of mind and heart, a magnetic power which made him capable of moving the people with composure enough to restrain them in the hour of indignation. Above all, he combined an extraordinary capacity for adapting to circumstances with an inflexible pursuit of the central aim.[1]

The statement of principles adopted at the Hainfeld Congress, on which the factions were able to unite, had been drafted by Victor Adler and revised by Karl Kautsky. It expressed the aim of the movement in terms of Marxist concepts. It acknowledged the need for political struggle, which the Anarchists rejected, and of the fight for social reforms —'palliatives', as they were scornfully called by the Anarchists, who rejected them even more vehemently. But Anarchists could applaud its description of parliamentary government as a 'modern form of class rule', while reformists would welcome its demand for universal suffrage as 'one of the main vehicles of agitation and organization'. It resolved the hotly disputed question on methods of conducting the class struggle, on which the party had split, by declaring that in seeking to accomplish its aims, the party 'will use all means which seem appropriate and which conform to the popular conception of natural justice'—a formula which left the way clear for any method of struggle. It was acceptable to radicals as well as moderates, Social Democrats as well as Anarchists, although, in fact, it sealed the doom of Anarchism in Austria.

1. Édouard Vaillant, 'Ein Glückwunsch aus Frankreich', in *Der Kampf*, vol. v, p. 435; Émile Vandervelde, 'Victor Adler und die Internationale', in *Der Kampf*, vol. XXII, p. 5.

7

In Italy, Anarchism had found a different soil, and one more fertile than in Austria. Italy still had many of the characteristic features of early capitalism, in particular vast estates, owned by a landlord aristocracy and cultivated by semi-servile labour, a large, land-hungry rural proletariat, an urban proletariat living in wretched squalor and a large number of de-classed intellectuals. The Anarchist tactic of fighting poverty by direct action leading to insurrection had a natural appeal to the victims of such a social environment who were beginning to seek an end to their poverty. Moreover, the Anarchists in Italy were building on a tradition, brought there by Bakunin, which had gained considerable strength since the Risorgimento had begun the popular movement for freedom and unity. The tradition of conspiracy and secret societies, the armed *coup d'état* and 'propaganda by deed', was one hallowed by the memories of the patriots who had struggled against Austrian rule, and by the spirit of militant democracy which had been fostered in the underground movements led by Mazzini and Garibaldi. One of the leaders of Italian Anarchism, Errico Malatesta, wrote of the movement that:

> The advocacy of violence was inherited by the Anarchists from democracy. . . . Our Italian Anarchists admired and honoured the armed uprisings of Agesilao Milano, Felice Orsini (both heroes of the Risorgimento) before turning to follow the theories of Bakunin. After affiliating to the International, they learned nothing in this sphere which they had not already learned from Mazzini and Garibaldi.[1]

When the Labour organizations of northern Italy, which had enthusiastically supported the Paris Commune, broke with Mazzini on that issue, they followed the intellectual leadership of Bakunin rather than of Marx. At its Rimini Congress at the beginning of August 1872, the Italian Federation of the International broke off all contact with Marx and the General Council, and refused to send a delegation to The Hague.[2] After that, the Italian Federation became the bulwark of the Anarchist International.

At Rimini one of the most violent advocates of the break with the General Council was the young Andrea Costa (1851–1910) from Imola, whose teacher, Giosuè Carducci, was then one of Italy's leading poets.

1. See Richard Hostetter, *The Italian Socialist Movement* (Princeton, 1958), vol. I: *1860 to 1880*, p. 288; H. L. Gualtieri, *The Labour Movement in Italy, 1848–1904* (New York, 1946); W. Hilton Young, *The Italian Left: A Short History of Political Socialism in Italy* (London, 1940). For a short outline of the history of Italian Socialist thought, see Leo Valiani, 'Die ideologische Entwicklung des demokratischen Sozialismus in Italien', in *Weltstimmen des Sozialismus*, edited by Julius Braunthal (Hanover, 1959).

2. See above, p. 183.

Costa was still studying at the University of Bologna when, swept off his feet by enthusiasm for the Commune, he gave himself completely to the cause of the Socialist revolution. He first helped to build up the Fascio Operaio in Bologna, the organization which, by breaking with the Mazzinist movement and by its subsequent congress in March 1872, had founded the Italian Federation of the International. Costa became secretary of the congress at Rimini and a member of the delegation to the Anarchist Congress at Saint-Imier (September 1872). This was the congress which refused to recognize the General Council elected at The Hague, and which declared itself the only legitimate representative of the International Working Men's Association.[1]

Costa remained in Switzerland for some weeks after the end of the Saint-Imier Congress, planning with Bakunin the future development of the Anarchist International. The Italian Federation was to be transformed into the main instrument of the new International, and the programme which the two men drafted contained a directive which declared: 'Having complete confidence in the instincts of the mass of the people, our revolutionary objective depends on the release of what is usually termed "brutal passions" and the destruction of what the *bourgeoisie* call "public order".'[2]

The subsequent history of the Italian Labour movement under strong Anarchist influence is a story of innumerable attempts to unleash in Italy a social revolution in accordance with the directive. In the years 1873–4 Italy, like Austria and Germany, was in the grip of an acute economic crisis, aggravated by poor harvests. Bread and meat became unobtainable for the continually growing mass of unemployed workers, owing to the rapid rise in prices. A wave of hunger-marches and strikes swept through the country. In the towns of Tuscany, bakeries and grain stores were pillaged, and the government turned troops out against the demonstrators. A 'revolutionary situation' seemed to have arrived.

The leadership of the Italian Federation decided that it was time for action. It set up a secret 'Italian Committee for the Social Revolution', to function as the revolutionary general staff. It was planned to start a rising in Bologna in the middle of August 1874 which would serve as the signal for risings in Tuscany, Romagna and Rome. By the end of July, Bakunin had arrived at Bologna from Locarno in Switzerland to help prepare for revolution.

According to their own figures, the Italian Federation then numbered a membership of 32,450, organized in 151 sections, Bologna being one of the strongest. But instead of the thousands which the general staff were

1. See above, pp. 190–1. For his biography, see P. Orano, *Andrea Costa* (Rome, 1900).
2. Hossetter, op. cit., vol. 1, p. 312.

expecting to turn out at zero hour, there were only a few dozen Anarchists available to seize the arsenals and rouse the masses to insurrection in Bologna, Imola, Florence, Leghorn and Rome. It was easy, therefore, for the police, who had had plenty of advance notice about the planned rising, to nip it in the bud. Not a single shot was fired, and the police picked up the handful of would-be revolutionaries who had been unable to escape. Bakunin, who had been waiting in his Bologna hideout for the revolution to start, fled to Switzerland the same morning, disguised as a parish priest.[1]

The pitiful collapse of the rising led to an opposition inside the party, centring round Enrico Bignami and his paper, *La Plèbe*. It called for the abandonment of Anarchist methods of conspiracy and violence and demanded the formation of a broad-based working-class party to fight for emancipation by legal means. Representatives of this trend came to be known as 'legal Socialists'. But before the party could reach any decision, Cafiero and Malatesta organized another armed uprising.

Cafiero and Malatesta, together with Costa, then formed the triumvirate at the head of the Italian Anarchist movement. All three were selfless idealists, completely devoted to their cause. Carlo Cafiero (1846–83) sprang from the old and wealthy landed aristocracy of Apulia. After studying law at the University of Naples he entered the diplomatic service. He soon gave up his prospects of a brilliant career in diplomacy and moved to London, where he became friendly with Marx and Engels. From the latter he took over the task of building sections of the International in Italy, but when the great split came, he joined not Marx but Bakunin. During his short life he went to prison for his ideals, sacrificed the whole of a considerable fortune for the movement, and died quite destitute.[2]

Errico Malatesta (1853–1932) was also of non-working-class origin. Like Cafiero he had attended a Catholic school and then gone on to the University of Naples. Observing the appalling sufferings of the poor in Naples during the harsh winter of 1868, his heart, as he later described it in his memoirs, 'froze to ice'. 'I called to mind,' he added, 'the Gracchi and Spartacus, and I became aware that my soul was that of a tribune and a rebel.'[3]

1. For a detailed account of the 'Bologna Uprising', see Hostetter, op. cit., vol. I, pp. 321–58.

2. The Anarchist ideal of freedom exercised a particular attraction for gifted idealists in contemporary Italy. For some fine pen-pictures of Anarchist leaders, see James Joll, *The Anarchists* (London, 1965), Peter Kropotkin, *Memoirs of a Revolutionist* (London, 1899), and Ricarda Huch, *Michael Bakunin und die Anarchie* (Berlin, 1922).

3. See M. Nettlau, *Errico Malatesta* (New York, 1922); an autobiographical sketch and some of his writings can be found in *Errico Malatesta. His Life and Ideas*, edited by Vernon Richards (London, 1965).

In the spring of 1877 Cafiero and Malatesta had discussed with Costa their plan for a renewed uprising. Costa opposed the project and refused to participate, but despite his objections, Cafiero and Malatesta went ahead. On 8 April, in the mountain village of Letino near Naples, an armed band of twenty-six men, bedecked with red and black cockades, and under the leadership of Cafiero and Malatesta, hoisted the red and black flag of Anarchism in the market-place, declared King Victor Emmanuel deposed and, to the delight of the peasants, burned the village archives. They then carried the 'revolution' to the neighbouring village. Meanwhile, infantry and cavalry had surrounded the rebel area and soon arrested all the insurgents.

The government had been fully informed of the conspiracy, the leaders of which had assembled several weeks before the uprising in a house rented by Malatesta in the village of San Lupo. They allowed them to proceed, unmolested, so as to catch them in the act and thus secure a pretext for a powerful assault on the entire working-class movement. Developments went according to plan. The Italian section of the Anarchist International was suppressed. 'Legal Socialists' as well as Anarchists were arrested in large numbers.

The fiasco of the conspiracy of San Lupo widened the gulf between the Anarchists and 'legal' Socialists. Andrea Costa had fled to Switzerland as soon as the police raids started. At the congress of the 'anti-authoritarian International' in Verviers, as also at the Socialist World Congress in Ghent, he continued to defend the insurrectionary policies of the Anarchists and denounced the proposed 'solidarity pact' with the Social Democrats.[1] Nevertheless, his confidence in Anarchist doctrine had been shaken. After the attempt on the life of King Umberto in Naples by Giovanni Passanante, in November 1878, a new wave of exceptionally severe police repression against Anarchists and Socialists began. This forced Costa to the conclusion, as he put it, that 'insurrectionism, when put into practice, leads to nothing except the triumph of reaction, and when insurrectionist propaganda is not followed by action, its preachers fall into disrepute'.[2]

After the Ghent Congress, Costa settled in Paris. But, only a few months after his arrival, he was arrested, charged with being a member of the suppressed International, and sentenced to two and a half years in prison. Amnestied after twelve months he broke with the theory and methods of Anarchism. In July 1879 he wrote an open letter from Lugano to his comrades in Italy, in which he rejected both the tactic of insurrection and Bakunin's theory that the state must be destroyed as a first step, so that subsequently a society without a state could arise out

1. See above, pp. 192–3.
2. Hostetter, op. cit., vol. I, p. 410.

of the ruins. Such a society, Costa now believed, would come neith[er] out of a violent revolution nor through the decrees of a revolutionary government. It could emerge only from 'the natural consequences of a never-ending development of the productive forces, together with a new cultural outlook'. It was therefore relegated to the status of 'an ideal for the future'.

In the course of discussions on the revision of Anarchist doctrine, Costa called for the foundation of a workers' party which would aim at converting the masses to Socialism through a propaganda of social reforms such as a shorter working week, the legal protection of working conditions and restrictions on female and child labour. He also recognized the need to use Parliament, if only as an instrument of Socialist propaganda. He appeared, along with Amilcar Cipriani, as a representative of the Italian Socialists at the founding congress of the Second International in Paris.

At this congress, Cipriani played a major part in re-orienting the views of Italian Anarchists. Amilcar Cipriani (1844–1918) personified the revolutionary tradition of the Risorgimento. He had fought with Garibaldi at Aspromonte against the Piedmontese, in Crete against the Turks and in the Paris Commune against the troops of Versailles. There he was taken prisoner and deported to New Caledonia. Six years in the rigours of a penal settlement, however, failed to break his revolutionary spirit. Almost as soon as he arrived back in Italy, he joined in the 1877 conspiracy. But by 1889 he was in Paris, working with the 'legal Socialists' to re-establish the International.[1]

Before the 'Italian Revolutionary Workers' party' proposed by Costa could be founded, the 'Italian Workers' party' (Partito Operaio) was set up in May 1882, under the leadership of Constantino Lazzari and Giuseppe Croce. This party rejected all ideology, seeing as its sole purpose the defence of the social and economic interests of the workers. Another ten years were to pass before an effective Italian Socialist party could be established. The way for it was prepared by the periodical, *La Critica sociale*, edited by Filippo Turati and Anna Kulischov. First appearing at the beginning of 1891, it became the most important organ of Democratic Socialism in Italy. In the same year, Turati founded the Lega Socialisti Milanesi (Milan Socialist League) and in the following year, in August 1892, the two parties agreed at the Genoa Congress to a merger which would exclude the Anarchists. The party founded in Genoa assumed the title of Partito dei Lavoratori Italiano.

The year 1893 saw a serious social unrest in Sicily. The brutally oppressed peasantry of the *latifundia* rose against their masters and occupied the land; the sulphur miners went on strike and there was street

1. See P. Valera, *Amilcar Cipriani* (Milan, 1920).

en demonstrators and troops. At the beginning of 1894, spi, who had taken over the government of Italy with the lism is the enemy', declared martial law. Parliament gh anti-Socialist legislation, and the young party, together ons and other working-class organizations, was disbanded s arrested. But a year later, in January 1895, the party met in Parma for its third congress, assumed the title Partito Socialista Italiano, and at the elections in May 1895, with universal suffrage, almost trebled the earlier vote, increasing from 26,000 to 76,000.

8

Like Italy, Spain was a stronghold of Anarchism. Her economic structure, social and political instability and the tradition of *pronunciamientos* and conspiracies provided a favourable breeding-ground. A vast proportion of the land was owned by feudal landlords and bishops, industry was undeveloped and, except in Catalonia, was still in the pre-capitalist stage. For the millions oppressed by poverty and, in particular, for the masses of land-hungry peasants and urban workers, the revolutionary ideas of Anarchism seemed the perfect expression of their desperate indignation against intolerable economic and social servitude. Moreover, at the end of the 1860s, Spain had been shaken to its foundations by a series of dynastic and constitutional crises, military *coups*, proletarian risings and aristocratic counter-revolutions. There seemed to be all the conditions necessary for a social revolution.

The revolution duly arrived. In Cádiz, on 18 September 1868, the fleet and the army rose on a signal from General Prim. The Spanish Revolution of 1868, however, was, like the French Revolution of 1789, essentially a middle-class one. While at the outbreak peasants and workers united with the middle class against the hated Bourbon monarchy, the domination of the nobility and church, and the régime personified by Queen Isabella II, once the monarchy was overthrown and the Queen had fled, revolutionary unity disintegrated. The upper middle class aimed at a constitutional monarchy, free from clerical and feudal restraints; the middle class strove for a republic; and the working class was disorganized and leaderless.

Marx saw in the convulsions of this *bourgeois* upheaval no sort of preparation for a genuine social revolution. When the revolution broke out, the General Council of the International in London issued an address to the Spanish workers, advising them to organize and then unite with the republican wing of the *bourgeoisie* in the fight for a democratic republic. Bakunin, on the other hand, was sure that Spain was ripe for a social revolution. In November 1868 he sent Giuseppe

Fanelli to Spain, with instructions to organize sections of the International which were to serve as shock troops for the social revolution. The first sections, formed in Madrid and Barcelona in December 1869, provided the basis for the Spanish Federation of the I.W.M.A., which was set up by the Anarchists in the following year, and which remained firmly under Anarchist control.[1]

Marx and Engels tried to destroy Bakunin's influence in the Spanish Federation. To this end, Paul Lafargue, a son-in-law of Marx and a refugee from the Paris Commune, went to Madrid at the end of 1871 and organized a Marxist opposition to the Bakuninist leadership of the Federation. The new group was organized round the journal *La Emancipación*, edited by José Mesa, but Lafargue and the entire opposition leadership, including Pablo Iglesias, José Mesa and Francisco Mora, the historian of Spanish Socialism, were expelled from the Madrid Section in June 1872. After that they organized the New Madrid Section of the International, from which the Spanish Socialist party subsequently developed.

The Spanish Labour movement was consequently split from the outset, both in its political and industrial sections. The Anarchist-led unions were grouped into the Confederación Nacional del Trabajo de España (C.N.T.), and those led by the Marxists into the Unión General de Trabajadores de España (U.G.T.). Most organized workers were in the Anarchist group.

The revolution, after dragging on for nearly five years, reached its peak in 1873. In February, the Cortes declared Spain a republic by an overwhelming majority. At the same time the Legitimists mounted an armed invasion and the workers rose in July, with bloody clashes in Lucar de Barrameda, near Cádiz, and in Alcoy. During the night of 2–3 January 1874, General Pavia, Military Commandant of Madrid, occupied the Parliament buildings, dissolved the Cortes and handed over power to a reactionary government. One of the government's first actions was to re-impose the decree prohibiting the International.[2]

Despite persecution, however, the International was able to continue its activities secretly, and even publicly. When, after an attempt on the king's life in October 1878, the government arrested the Anarchists in droves and installed a régime of terror in Andalusia, the Federation of the International called for terrorist counter-measures. The appeal was followed by bomb attacks and landlords' houses were set on fire.

Pablo Iglesias (1850–1925) and his followers could only look on, as

1. See Max Nettlau, 'Zur Geschichte der spanischen Internationale und Landesföderation (1868–89)', in *Archiv für die Geschichte des Sozialismus und der Arbeiterbewegung*, vol. XIV, 1929.

2. See above, pp. 162–3.

helpless spectators, while successive floods of Anarchism and reaction swept over the political scene. They had established the Spanish Socialist Workers' party (Partido Socialista Obrero Español) at the beginning of 1879. It drew its main support from the Printers Union of Madrid, of which Iglesias, himself a working printer, was a leading member. The party remained underground until, in 1886, it began publishing its official organ, *El Socialista*, and it did not function openly, as a party, until its congress of 1888. When its representatives appeared at the Paris Congress of the International in 1889, its support was still small and only slowly increasing. Its main strength rested in the General Union of Workers (U.G.T.), which it founded and led.

Meanwhile, the Anarchist Federation had disintegrated and its trade-union federation (the C.N.T.) dissolved. All attempts to re-unite the Labour movement failed. The Anarchists founded a new party, based on individual membership, while the trade unions of Catalonia set up a new, syndicalist, trade-union federation, with no party affiliation.

9

Anarchism in Spain and Italy had received its inspiration from Switzerland, specifically from Bakunin's Alliance of Socialist Democracy and from the Jura Federation of the International, which he controlled. But by the time of the Paris Congress, almost all traces of Anarchism had disappeared in Switzerland. Hermann Greulich (1842–1925) had, as a skilled craftsman, left Germany for Switzerland in 1865. He founded the *Tagwacht*, in Berne, and used it to propagate the idea of trade-union unity. By 1873, he had succeeded in uniting the unions into a centralized organization, the Swiss Workers' Association. But the new association remained completely non-party, concentrating its efforts on campaigns for social legislation.

Greulich, who had formed a Social Democratic party as early as 1870, saw it disintegrate after only two years. He then tried, along with Heinrich Scherrer, to win the Grütli Association, the first centralized working-class organization to appear in Switzerland, for Socialism. The Grütli Association had been founded in 1838 on the initiative of Albert Galeer and Dr Niederer, a friend of Pestalozzi, as a workers' educational and sick-benefit society, which also included radically-minded intellectuals and master craftsmen. In 1878 it adopted a programme with slight Socialist tendencies. It was only in 1888 that the Berne lawyer, Albert Steck, succeeded in merging the Union of German Workers, which had been founded on the inspiration of Wilhelm Weitling, together with various local Socialist organizations into a Social Democratic party of

Switzerland. In 1901, this in turn amalgamated with the Grütli Association. By then the party had almost 10,000 members, and three representatives in the National Assembly, which representation it increased to seven at the following elections in 1902.

The party's definitive programme, adopted in 1904 and remaining operative for more than half a century, had been drafted by Otto Lang, a High Court judge from Zurich, and was overtly Marxist in tendency. In mood, however, as well as in political policy, the Swiss party tended towards Reformism, quite contrary to the influences emanating from the lively groups of German, French and Russian refugees who were particularly active in French-speaking Switzerland. Hermann Greulich, the leading figure in the movement, was a follower of Charles Fourier, as was Karl Bürkli (1823–1901), who also helped to establish the exceptionally strong co-operative movement in Switzerland. Another prominent leader of the Swiss party was Leonhard Ragaz (1868–1945), a professor at Zurich University and an influential representative of Christian Socialism in the Swiss Labour movement.[1]

10

In Holland, on the other hand, a movement akin to Anarchism developed more than ten years after it had disappeared in Switzerland. The first Dutch sections of the International were formed towards the end of the 1860s.[2] They were represented at the Hague Congress, where they supported the opposition to Marx, without identifying themselves with the views of the Anarchists. In the period of reaction after 1872, the Dutch Federation disintegrated, and began to revive only under the influence of Nieuwenhuis's journal, *Recht voor Allen*, which first appeared, three times a week, in 1879, and daily from 1889. Under Niewenhuis's leadership the movement united into the Socialist League in 1881.

Ferdinand Domela Nieuwenhuis (1846–1919), who has gone down in history as the father of Dutch Anarchism, developed his ideas not from Bakunin but from the Old Testament and the Gospels. Victor Adler, who met him for the first time at the Paris Congress of the International, described him as a 'man with the head of Christ and the soul of a sectarian fanatic'. Like his father, Domela was a minister and

1. See Robert Grimm, *Geschichte der sozialistischen Bewegung in der Schweiz* (Zurich, 1931); Dr Mario Gridazzi, *Die Entwicklung der sozialistischen Ideen in der Schweiz* (Zurich, 1935); Dr Fritz Giovanoli, *Die sozialdemokratische Partei der Schweiz, Entstehung, Entwicklung, Aktion* (Bern, 1948). For the development of Greulich's ideas, see Werner Kuhn, *Hermann Greulich und Charles Fourier* (Zurich, 1949).

2. See above, p. 171.

a celebrated preacher at the Lutheran church in The Hague, where his congregation had its share of prosperous *bourgeois* members. In a pamphlet expounding the ethical basis of his Socialism, he explained why he had felt obliged to renounce his position in the church in 1879, and devote himself to the cause of the workers.[1] Essentially a romantic idealist, his experience as a Deputy—he was the only Socialist to be elected under the Franchise Act of 1888—confirmed his development into an anti-parliamentarian Anarchist-radical. Parliament, he was now convinced, was dominated by reactionary and capitalist forces and it was a waste for the workers to use their strength in political conflict. Instead, they must organize in anti-political trade unions and free themselves by 'direct action' from the bondage of capitalism.

The Socialist League split over the question of parliamentarism; and in 1894 the 'twelve apostles'—including Pieter Jelles Troelstra (1860–1930), Willem Hubert Vliegen (1862–1947) and H. H. van Kol (1852–1925)—formed the Social Democratic Workers' party, which modelled itself organizationally on the Social Democratic party of Germany and ideologically on that party's Erfurt programme. Its main source of mass support during the early years was the Union of Diamond Workers, organized by Henri Polak (1868–1943), at that time the largest trade union in Holland.

11

While the Dutch Labour movement was thus strongly influenced by Anarchism, there was scarcely a sign of it in the Scandinavian countries. In Norway, the Labour movement began as early as 1848, largely through the efforts of Marcus Thrane (1817–90), a teacher and an enthusiastic Socialist. It was from him that the movement took its name —Thraniterbevegelsen. Within two years of its formation it had 270 local branches and about 30,000 members among the peasants, lumberjacks, artisans and teachers of Norway. It was by no means revolutionary, and concentrated its demands on a redistribution of the land, universal suffrage and education for the children of the poor. The government, however, chose to regard it as a revolutionary menace and suppressed it. Thrane was arrested in 1851, and sentenced in 1855, together with 126 of his followers, for a 'crime against national security'. Thrane received eight years' solitary confinement, since, according to the indictment, he was mainly responsible for the 'revolutionary and socialistic spirit' of the movement.

After his release, Thrane left for America, settled in Chicago and

1. Domela Nieuwenhuis, *Mein Abschied von der Kirche* (Berlin, 1891).

11 Karl Kautsky

12a (above left) *P. B. Axelrod* *12b* (above right) *V. I. Lenin*
12c (below) *Leon Trotsky*

worked in the American Federation of the International. Although his movement in Norway had been stamped out, he had left behind a valuable heritage. He had carried the idea of Socialism into the villages and, since that time, the Norwegian Labour movement has been as deeply rooted in the countryside as in the towns.

The revival did not come for another thirty years, when, in the 1880s, the expansion of industry brought with it an upsurge of trade unionism. In 1883 the Norwegian Trade Union Association was founded; two years later a Social Democratic Union; and in August 1887 came the Norwegian Labour party (Det Norske Arbeiderpartei).

The new party was founded by Christian Holtermann-Knudsen (1845–1929), a printer. He organized the printers, became President of the Union in 1876 and, in 1883, President of the Norwegian Trade-Union Confederation. In the following year he started a small printshop of his own, which produced the movement's new paper—the *Vort Arbeid* (*Our Labour*), the first Socialist paper to appear in Norway. He and his wife wrote, typeset, printed and distributed the journal. In 1885 he founded the Social Democratic Union and his paper changed its name to the *Social-Demokraten*, forerunner of the *Arbeiderbladet* (*Workers' Paper*), which was later the official organ of the Norwegian Labour party. Knudsen's closest collaborator in founding the Social Democratic Union and running the *Social-Demokraten* was the master brush-maker, Carl Jeppesen (1858–1930), who represented his party at the Paris Congress of the International.[1]

12

In Denmark the Labour movement arose directly out of the Paris Commune. Under its inspiration, a young postmaster, Louis Pio (1841–94), published two pamphlets, known as *Socialistike Blade* (*Socialist Papers*), founded the paper, *Social-Demokraten*, in July 1871, and a month later, along with Harald Brix and Poul Geleff, started a section of the International: the International Workers' Club for Denmark.

In the same year the Labour movement came into head-on collision with the forces of the state. In Copenhagen the building workers had called a strike, and the General Council of the International, in London, had appealed for solidarity. The strikers were supported by mass demonstrations in the streets of Copenhagen. Police broke up the

1. See Walter Galenson, *Labour in Norway* (New York, 1951), and *Scandinavian Labour Movement* (Berkeley, 1952); see also Torolf Elster, 'Die ideologische Entwicklung des demokratischen Sozialismus in Norwegen', in *Weltstimmen des Sozialismus*, op. cit., pp. 183–209.

demonstrations; Pio and other Labour leaders were arrested; and the Danish section of the International was suppressed in 1873 by a special emergency law.

Pio received four years' hard labour. After his release he again took over the editing of the *Social-Demokraten* and organized, in June 1876, the first joint congress of local trade-union and Socialist branches. The seventy-five delegates at the congress represented some 6,000 members. But in the following year the young Labour movement received what was justly described as 'a heart-breaking blow'. Louis Pio, the leader who had called it into existence and inspired its early struggles, accepted a large bribe from the police to leave the country permanently. In the spring of 1877, together with Poul Geleff, who had been offered a similar bribe, he emigrated to America. 'There were no new men capable of filling the empty places and the party was too loosely organized, and had too little experience of working together, to remain united. The branches dissolved or quietly faded away.'[1] An attempt to revive the Socialist movement was made in 1880, with the foundation of the Social Democratic party (Socialdemokratisk Forbund i Danmark). According to P. Christensen it had 20,000 members by the time of the Paris Congress of the International, and its organ, the *Social-Demokraten*, had a circulation of 22,000. At the International's Zurich Congress in 1893, the Danish delegation represented 37,000 members of the party and trade unions.

13

In Sweden, the Socialist movement began only in 1882. Its founder was August Palm (1849–1922), a tailor who had worked for a number of years in Germany and Denmark, and returned as an active Socialist in 1881. In the following year he founded, in Stockholm, together with Alex Ferdinand Danielsson (1863–99), the paper *Social-Demokraten*, travelled the whole of Sweden three times on foot, spoke at meetings, which were often held in the forests, distributed leaflets and pamphlets and organized Socialist groups—the first of them in Malmö in 1882. He was soon joined by Hjalmar Branting (1860–1925), a young student, who took over editorship of the *Social-Demokraten* in 1886 and became

1. See Gustav Bang, 'Ein Blick auf die Geschichte der dänischen Sozialdemokratie', in *Die Neue Zeit*, vol. XVI, Part 1, pp. 404–5. See also Rudolf Meyer, *Der Sozialismus in Dänemark* (Berlin, 1875), pp. 13ff; Emil Helms, *Die sozialdemokratische und gewerkschaftliche Bewegung in Dänemark* (1907); and for a short résumé of the history of Danish Social Democracy, see Ernst Christiansen, 'Die ideologische Entwicklung des demokratischen Sozialismus in Dänemark', in *Weltstimmen des Sozialismus*, op. cit., pp. 20–38; for a brief survey of the development of Socialism in Denmark, see Landauer, *European Socialism*, vol. I, pp. 444–9.

the leader of the Social Democratic Workers' party (Sveriges Socialdemokratiska Arbetareparti) when it was founded at its congress in Stockholm in April 1889.

The Swedish party was based on local trade-union branches which affiliated to it collectively. Until the Swedish Trade Union Alliance was established in 1898, the party functioned simultaneously as the central organization of the trade-union movement. At the time of the International's Paris Congress in 1889, the party had barely 7,000 members. In the first five years of its existence it grew very slowly, appeairng as a mass movement only in 1895.[1]

14

Inevitably, under the despotic autocracy of the Tsar, there could be no openly organized Socialist movement in Russia or Poland. There was, nevertheless, a revolutionary ferment in both countries during the 1880s. In St Petersburg, Moscow, Kiev, Odessa and many other towns, underground revolutionary groups developed, led by exiles who supplied them with illegal newspapers and pamphlets. Between 1881 and 1886 tens of thousands of unorganized workers came out on strike. Policemen, Ministers and the Tsar himself fell victim to assassination by groups of revolutionary terrorists. Socialist ideas were eagerly absorbed by young students and intellectuals. Alexander Herzen's paper, *Kolokol*, which was distributed secretly in Russia, published a translation of the *Communist Manifesto* in the 1860s. The first volume of *Das Kapital* was published in Russian as early as 1872—the first foreign translation to appear—and in the 1880s and 1890s the country was almost flooded with the works of Marx, Engels, Lafargue and Guesde.[2]

Russian Socialism divided into two main streams: the agrarian Socialism of the Narodniks, from which the Social Revolutionary party emerged; and Marxism, out of which came the Russian Social Democratic Workers' party, which itself split in 1903 into Menshevik and Bolshevik wings.[3] The main representatives of the Narodniks were

1. For a comprehensive account of the ideological development of Social Democracy in Sweden, see Frans Severin, 'Die ideologische Entwicklung des Sozialismus in Schweden', in *Weltstimmen des Sozialismus*, op. cit., pp. 236–61; also G. Henriksson-Holmberg, 'Die Entwicklungsgeschichte der Arbeiterbewegung in Schweden', in *Archiv für die Geschichte des Sozialismus und der Arbeiterbewegung*, vol. VI (1916); Raymond Fusilier, *Le Parti socialiste suédois, son organization* (Paris, 1965).

2. See Martov and Dan, *Geschichte der russischen Sozialdemokratie* (Berlin, 1926), and Valentin Gitermann, *Geschichte Russlands* (Hamburg, 1949), vol. III, Part 8.

3. The history of the split in Russian Social Democracy and its historical significance is to be discussed in the second volume, covering the years 1914–45.

Nikolai F. Danielson (1844–1918), the translator of *Das Kapital*, and Peter Lavrov (1823–1900), while the leading exponent of Marxism in Russia was Georgi Valentinovich Plekhanov (1856–1918). At the Paris Congress of the International the Narodnik trend was represented by Lavrov and the Marxists by Plekhanov.

Plekhanov, the son of a small landowner, had joined the revolutionary movement while still a student at St Peterburg University, and it was not long before he rose to prominence. In 1880, to escape the Tsarist police, he emigrated to western Europe. With his deep knowledge of philosophy, history, sociology and political economy he was believed to be the most learned man in Europe. His collected works, published by the Russian State Publishing House, run to twenty-four substantial volumes. In September 1883 he founded, in Geneva, together with Paul Borisovich Axelrod (1850–1928), Vera Zasulich (1851–1919) and Lev Grigorevich Deutsch (1855–1941), the Liberation of Labour group. Axelrod came from an extremely poor Jewish family, and became a Socialist as a direct result of the terrible poverty which surrounded him. Deutsch had escaped from Siberia after sixteen years' imprisonment. Vera Zasulich had been sentenced, in her eighteenth year, to two years' imprisonment for her association with a revolutionary group. In February 1878, soon after her release, she tried to assassinate the Head of the St Petersburg police, General Feodor Trepov, who had ordered the flogging of an imprisoned student, Bogolyubov. The jury acquitted her, however, and a large crowd which had assembled outside the courtroom whisked her away from the police, who had had orders to re-arrest her at once. Friends hid her, and soon she escaped to Switzerland.

The group known as the Liberation of Labour formed the nucleus of the Russian Social Democratic Labour party, which was formally established at a secret congress at Minsk in 1898. But as soon as the congress dispersed, all the delegates and most of the leaders of the underground Social Democratic groups in the country were arrested and the party disintegrated. It revived only with the establishment of the journal *Iskra* (*The Spark*) at the end of December 1900.

15

In Tsarist Poland, conditions for the development of a modern Labour movement were much more favourable than in Russia. The industrial revolution had started in Poland in the 1880s. By the turn of the century, as much as a third of the population was concentrated in the towns, and a quarter of all working people were employed as wage-earners in factories, mines and workshops. The working class had inherited the tradition of the Polish revolutions of 1830 and 1863. The aristocracy and the middle classes, which had been at the head of both these revolutions, gradually became reconciled to Tsarism after the defeat of 1863. Consequently, Polish Socialism was from its beginnings a national revolutionary as well as a social revolutionary movement.

The first Socialist secret societies in Poland appeared in 1878, and from 1881 the monthly paper, *Przedswit* (*Dawn*), which was published abroad, was circulated illegally in Poland. In the following year the groups established a Central Committee. Its members, however, were soon arrested and the groups stamped out, four of the organization's leaders being hanged. New groups were formed, and in 1892 they came together at a conference in Paris, to form the Polish Socialist party (Polska Partia Socjalistyczana, or P.P.S.). In March 1894, in Warsaw, the first secret party meeting took place on Polish soil.

Towards the end of 1894 the party's official organ, *Robotnik* (*The Worker*), began to appear, published by an underground press in Warsaw. It was only in 1900, after six years, that the Russian political police, known as the *Ochrana*, discovered the printing works and arrested the editor, Josef Pilsudski. The party which Pilsudski led regarded itself as one section of the Socialist movement of the three provinces—Russian, Austrian and German—into which Poland was divided. In the spirit of the 1830 and 1863 revolutions, the party fought for the re-establishment of a united, independent and democratic Polish republic.

A group of Polish Socialist internationalists in Russia opposed, however, what they considered to be the narrow nationalism of the P.P.S. They thought the Polish Socialists should work for the overthrow of Tsarism in alliance with the working class of Russia. They intended, not to re-establish an independent Poland, but to obtain national autonomy within the framework of a democratic Russian federal republic. They broke away from the P.P.S., and established in 1895 the Social Democratic party of Russian Poland. At their second congress in 1900, they merged with the Social Democratic party of Lithuania to form, under the leadership of Rosa Luxemburg and Leo Jogiches, the Social Democratic party of the Kingdom of Poland and Lithuania. The organ of the new party was the *Sprawa Robotnicza* (*The Cause of the Workers*).[1]

16

In the 1890s there appeared the first Socialist organizations among the Jewish working class of Russian Poland, Lithuania and White Russia. Led by Alexander Kremer and Bronislaw Grosser they united to form,

1. See Paul Frölich, *Rosa Luxemburg. Her Life and Work* (London, 1940).

at their congress in Vilna in 1897, the General Jewish Workers' Union of Russia and Poland, which has gone down to history as the Bund. Like the Polish Social Democratic party, the Bund considered itself to be part of the international Socialist revolutionary movement in Russia. The Bund participated in the formation of the Russian Social Democratic Labour party at its Minsk Congress in 1898, and set up a central organization of the Jewish proletariat in Russia, at once a revolutionary party, a trade-union movement and a cultural organization of Jewish workers, artisans and intellectuals.

The Bund, which was destined to play an important part in the 1905 revolution, was from the very outset subjected to anti-Jewish pogroms instigated by the Tsarist police. The Bund sought, through the Russian revolutionary movement, to free the Jewish workers of Russia, Poland and Lithuania from the double yoke of economic and political discrimination combined with national humiliation. It hoped that a successful revolution would give the Jewish people civil equality and cultural autonomy while destroying the canker of anti-semitism. The Bund saw the future of the Jewish working class as bound up with the cause of democracy and Socialism in Russia.

17

At the turn of the century another movement began, however, which held out to the Jewish working class a national as well as a Socialist aim, the movement known as Poale Zion or Socialist Zionism. The first indication of such a synthesis of Socialism and Zionism appeared as early as 1862 in *Rome and Jerusalem* by Moses Hess. The idea was carried further by Nachman Syrkin in his study of *Die Judenfrage und der sozialistische Judenstaat* (1898), which appeared in instalments in Engelbert Pernerstorfer's *Deutsche Worte*. But the real founder of the movement and the ideology of Socialist Zionism was Ber Borochow (1881–1917). The son of a Hebrew teacher in Poltava, he had been active in the Russian Social Democratic underground while still a high-school student. By the age of nineteen, he later wrote, he and his friends already knew 'Marx's *Das Kapital* by heart'.[1] In accordance with Marx's views he showed the tragedy of the Jewish Labour movement as arising from the anomalous social and economic structure of the Jewish people, whose industrial basis, with its exclusion from basic industry and large-scale production, isolated them from the general Socialist movement. The normalization of the economic and social life of the Jews demanded tremendous energy and statesmanship, and was impossible on the basis of the prevailing Jewish way of life. The Jewish people

1. Ber Borochow, *Sozialismus und Zionismus*, selected writings, edited by Mendel Singer (Vienna, 1932), p. 331.

required a national ideal which would evoke the necessary creative energy. Such an ideal could function only if it had powerful historical associations, and so could only be centred on Palestine. At a conference called by Borochow in September 1900, at Ekatorinoslav, he founded the Poale Zion, consisting at first of some 150 workers and students, the modest beginning of a movement which was to reach fruition in a socialistic Israel.

18

The history of Social Democracy in Hungary goes back to the 1860s when the 'Party of the Disenfranchised' was founded and was represented by Leo Frankel and Károly Farkas at the Geneva Congress of the International in 1866. But the so-called 'party' was merely a small group of Socialists which was soon broken up by the police. A second attempt to found a workers' party was made by Viktor Külföldi and Jakob Schlesinger in 1873, but this too was suppressed by the government. Meanwhile, trade unions had been established which set up their own central organization in 1880 and adopted a Socialist programme. But another ten years were to pass before the foundation of the Social Democratic party of Hungary (Magyaroszâgi Szociáldemokrate Párt) at its congress in December 1890. Its leading members included Ede Baron, István Farkas, Adolf Kiss and the Communard, Leo Frankel, a goldsmith by trade. After the defeat of the Paris Commune, in which Frankel had served as Minister of Labour, he fled to London, became friendly with Marx and was co-opted on to the General Council of the International. In 1876 he returned to Hungary and took over the editorship of the journal, *Arbeiterwochenchronik*. He represented Hungarian Social Democracy at the Ghent Congress in 1877 and at the foundation congress of the Second International.[1]

The Hungarian Social Democrats modelled themselves consciously on the party in Austria, with which they maintained close contact. They felt themselves an integral part of the Socialist movement in the Austro-Hungarian Empire, and when they formally established their party in December 1890, they took over unchanged the Hainfeld Programme of Austrian Social Democracy. Only in 1903 did they adopt their own independent programme, drawn up with the help of Karl Kautsky.

The economic, political and social structure of Hungary severely handicapped the development of Social Democracy. Hungary was almost entirely an agrarian country, with the land in the hands of aristocracy and the tenants and farm-workers virtual serfs. Social

1. For a short biography of Leo Frankel, see Magda Aranyossi, *Leo Frankel* (Berlin, 1957).

Democratic ideas proved quite unable to penetrate to the villages. The party's influence, therefore, was practically confined to Budapest and its immediate sarroundings, the real centre of Hungarian industry. Political control was in the hands of the nobility, which brought its considerable strength to bear against any signs of a democratic movement. While in the Austrian part of the Habsburg domains an electoral reform in 1897 made possible the return of fourteen Social Democrats to Parliament, Hungarian Social Democracy remained completely unrepresented until the revolution of October 1918.

19

Romania, like Hungary, was a land of semi-feudal, large-scale landowners, the Boyars, who held their tenants and employees in a similar state of servitude, and who had reinforced their political domination by a class-differentiated parliamentary franchise. It was an industrially undeveloped country, and so lacked a modern industrial proletariat. The pioneers of Socialism were Russian-Jewish refugees, including Paul Axelrod and, in particular, C. Dobrogeanu-Gherea (1855–1920), an eminent Marxist theoretician, historian and leader of the Romanian literary renaissance.

The first socialist paper, *Bessarabia*, appeared in 1879, and groups of Socialist intelectuals organized themselves round it in the larger towns. The party—the Social Democratic party of the Romanian Workers—was founded at the Bucharest Congress in April 1893. Its adherents were persecuted by the government, and its active members arrested in large numbers; and many of its intellectuals began to despair of the possibility of developing a Socialist movement in a country so economically and politically backward. In their paper, *Lumea Nova*, two members of the party executive, Joseph Nadejde, the editor, and V. Mortzun, argued that the party should dissolve and its members join the Liberal party, working within it for social and democratic reforms. The proposal won a majority at the party's sixth congress in April 1899, and the party was formally dissolved.

The minority which, at the congress, opposed the resolution, organized under the leadership of I. C. Frimu and Gherea in branches which carried on their work inside trade unions and co-operative societies. It was not until 1906 that a conference brought the local Socialist groups together into a common organization, and only in 1910 was the Social Democratic party of Romania (Partidul Social Democrat în România) fully re-constituted.

The party's founder and leader was Christian Rakovsky, who played an important part in the European Socialist movement. Springing from the old aristocracy of great landed proprietors in the Bulgarian Dobrudja, he found himself a citizen of Romania when that country annexed the territory in 1878. At the age of fifteen he was expelled from school for Socialist propaganda, after which he studied in France, became a doctor, mastered the languages of all the Balkan states and four European ones, was a historian and journalist, and at various stages of his life worked in the Socialist movements of France, Germany, Bulgaria, Romania and Russia. Eventually he played a leading part in the Russian Bolshevik revolution and was executed as a member of the anti-Stalinist opposition.[1]

20

Conditions for the development of a Socialist movement were rather more favourable in Bulgaria than in Romania. Although Bulgaria was equally agrarian, the land was owned by free peasants, not aristocratic landowners. The first underground Socialist organization was founded in 1891 by Dimiter Blagoeff (1856–1924) and the young lawyer, Nikola Gabrovsky, but there were soon violent disagreements on the question of forming a political party. Janko Sakosoff (1860–1941), a member of the organization who had studied in London and been impressed by the evolutionary ideas of English Socialism, argued that it was impossible for a Socialist party to develop under the dictatorial régime which Stephan N. Stambulov had created in the country, and moreover, that the working class was not yet mature enough to form its own party. The most urgent task of the Socialists, in his view, was first to organize the workers into trade unions. On the other hand Blagoeff, a Marxist who had led a revolutionary organization in Russia and, after being persecuted by the Tsarist secret police, had returned to his native Bulgaria in 1886, called for the formation of a revolutionary party as well as trade unions—both kinds of organization being enlisted in the service of the revolution.

The fall of Stambulov's reactionary dictatorship in 1893 considerably eased the pressure on the Socialist movement, and improved the prospects of forming a party. At a joint congress in Bosluda in 1894, both wings of the movement agreed to form a Social Democratic party. They won two seats in the elections to the Sobranye in the following year, and six in the elections of 1899. But the success only sharpened the conflict between Sakosoff and his supporters, who advocated a policy of social reform in co-operation with the parties of the democratic middle class, and Blagoeff and his group, who demanded that the Socialists

1. For a brief outline of the history of Romanian Socialism, see Serban Voinea, 'Die Arbeiterbewegung in Rumänien', in *Der Kampf*, vol. XVI (1929).

should work in uncompromising opposition to all *bourgeois* parties. The party split on this issue at its congress in 1903, and the split soon spread to the trade unions, with each wing of the Socialist movement—that of the 'Broads' under Sakosoff and that of the 'Narrows' under Blagoeff—founding its own trade-union organization in bitter conflict with the other.[1]

21

From the western hemisphere, two countries—the U.S.A. and the Argentine—were represented at the Paris Congress. Argentina had two Socialist groups, one of them French-speaking, formed by refugees from the Paris Commune, the other formed by a group of German exiles driven from their country by Bismarck's Anti-Socialist Laws. The French group published the paper, *L'Avenir*, and the Germans the *Vorwärts*. A great public demonstration on May Day 1890 provided the impetus which united both groups together with the trade unions, into the Federación Obrero de la República Argentina. A year later a Socialist Union emerged from the efforts of the Federation and in the middle of 1893 Juan B. Justo (1865–1925), who had translated *Das Kapital* into Spanish, founded the paper *Vanguardia*, which paved the way for the founding of the party at a congress in Buenos Aires in June 1896. The Partido Socialista Argentino was from the very beginning a federation of trade-union and political organizations.

22

Socialism in the United States was also pioneered by German and French refugees. They set up small groups which affiliated, at the end of the 1860s, to the International Working Men's Association.[2] The North American Federation of the International soon split, and some of the former sections established, together with radical working-class organizations in Philadelphia and other towns, the 'Social Democratic Workers' Party of North America', in July 1874. One of its objects was to unite all Socialist organizations in the United States. As a result, a congress was held at Philadelphia in July 1876, which proved a landmark in the history of American Socialism. Delegates attended the congress from the North American Federation of the International (F. A. Sorge and Joseph Weydemeyer), the Social Democratic Working Men's party of North America, the Working Men's party of Illinois and the Social Political Working Men's Society of Cincinnati. The

1. See T. Tchitchovsky, *The Socialist Movement in Bulgaria* (1931).
2. See above, pp. 112–13.

congress set up the 'Working Men's party of the United States', with a programme based on Marxian Socialism. At their second congress they changed their name to the 'Social Democratic Working Men's party of North America'. For more than twenty years they constituted the more important element in the quickly changing movement of American Socialism.[1]

The Working Men's party appeared at a time of acute social tension. Since the financial panic of 1873, the United States had been plagued by a severe economic crisis, which dragged on for five years, reaching its peak in 1877. In that year the number of unemployed was estimated at 3,000,000. Without any means of support they were plunged into the most extreme poverty. At the same time the employers cut wages (on the railways, by 25 per cent between 1873 and 1877). A wave of strikes swept the country, born of the despair of unorganized and undisciplined workers. In July 1877 the railway workers went on strike. The government called out troops to protect strike-breakers. In Maryland, Pittsburg and Reading there was bloody street fighting, freight trains were derailed, railway bridges blown up, coaches and engines destroyed. In Philadelphia alone, the destruction accounted for 600 coaches and 120 engines. In St Louis, the strikers, supported by the mass of the people, took control of the town for a short time.

The crisis favoured the growth of the new party. Enormous numbers attended its meetings and turned out to support its public demonstrations in the industrial centres. Socialist papers had an astonishing circulation. In 1876 and 1877 twenty-one new journals appeared, including eight dailies, in English, German, Czech and Swedish. By the beginning of 1877 the party had enrolled some 10,000 members, organized in about 100 branches distributed over twenty-five states. Inevitably, with the easing of the crisis and the arrival of an economic boom, interest began to wane. A large number of members dropped out and most of the new papers ceased to appear. Of the German daily papers, only the *Philadelphia Tagblatt*, the *Arbeiter-Zeitung*, the *Vorbote* in Chicago and the *New Yorker Volkszeitung* survived the general collapse.

The most interesting of the papers founded during this period was the *New Yorker Volkszeitung*, appearing for the first time at the end of January 1878; it survived for sixty-seven years and ceased publication only in 1945. It was edited by Dr Adolf Douai, one of the leading exponents of Marxism in the United States. While fighting in the German revolution of 1848 he had been captured and held in prison for a number of years. After his release he emigrated to America in 1852 and founded, in San Antonio, Texas, a small paper devoted to the anti-slavery campaign, a paper which he wrote, set up, printed and distributed

1. For an account of its history, see Hillquit, op. cit., ch. II, § 3.

entirely on his own. The white mob detested and harassed him and eventually, after three years, drove him out of town. After working for some years as an itinerant Socialist lecturer, he became editor of the National Labor Union's journal,[1] and after this had collapsed, of the *New Yorker Volkszeitung*. Douai became one of the most prominent Marxists in the country. After his death his place was taken by Hermann Schlüter, the first historian of the International in America.

Already weakened by a substantial drop in membership, the party went on to split at the end of 1880. Its left wing broke away and established, at its Chicago Congress in October 1881, the 'Revolutionary Socialist Working Men's party', and two years later merged with the Anarchists, led by Most, into the 'International Union of the Working People'. Its influence grew rapidly and in a few years Anarchism constituted a powerful current in American radicalism. Its decline set in after the Haymarket 'bomb outrage' in Chicago.[2]

Meanwhile, the Socialist Working Men's party had begun to recover from this set-back. The number of its branches, which had dropped from 100 in 1879 to 17 at the end of 1881, rose to 70 in 1889 and, over the next four years, to 183.

The main section of American Labour, however, was in the trade unions rather than the Socialist party. The first attempt to unite the scattered local organizations of individual trades was made by William H. Sylvis (1828–69) in 1866. He was instrumental in calling a congress with over sixty trade unions participating. This congress established the National Labor Union. Sylvis, a friend of F. A. Sorge, made contact with the General Council of the International in London and tried to infuse the National Labor Union with some of the spirit of working-class internationalism. The National Labor Union sent a delegate to the Basle Congress of the International, declared themselves in agreement with its aims and decided to affiliate.[3] After the death of Sylvis in 1869 it turned to a policy of alliance with middle-class groups, lost its independent working-class character and, after a number of unsuccessful strikes, eventually fell to pieces. No trace of the N.L.U. survived beyond 1874.

Its place was taken by the Noble Order of the Knights of Labor, whose origin constitutes one of the most remarkable episodes in the history of trade unionism.[4] During the 1860s a number of tailoring cutters in Philadelphia had organized a trade union. After a strike, the employers announced that they would no longer employ trade-union

1. See above, pp. 118–19.
2. See above, p. 214.
3. See above, pp. 118–19.
4. Hillquit, op. cit., pp. 289–94.

members. On a suggestion of Uriah Smith Stephens (1821–82), seven members of the union of tailoring cutters met in December 1869 to discuss ways of counteracting victimization by the employers. It was decided to form a secret society for cutters, on the model of the Freemasons.[1] With the assistance of James L. Wright, Stephens drew up a solemn ritual for meetings of the Order, together with a formal oath of initiation. At the meeting which agreed the constitution, Stephens was designated 'Grand Master Workman' and Wright 'Honorable Director and Senior Officer'. The Order was at first confined to tailoring cutters, and at the end of the first year it had sixty-nine members.

In the following year it was decided to admit workers from other trades. Immediately, the Order began to grow rapidly. Within a few months, nineteen branches were started in Philadelphia alone, and the Order spread to Pennsylvania, New Jersey, South Carolina, Connecticut and other states. Up to 1878 the Order had been strictly a secret society, with even its title a carefully guarded secret. But indefinite concealment proved impossible, and its very secrecy made the Order vulnerable to attacks in the Press and from the pulpit as a centre of Communist conspiracy and sedition. For this reason, a congress of the Order in 1878 decided to make its objects and programme public.

The decision increased its membership, especially among the miners, railwaymen and unskilled workers. Its membership, which was 52,000 in 1883, doubled in the next two years, and by 1886 was estimated at between 500,000 and 800,000. The organization even crossed the the Atlantic, with branches in England and Belgium.

The Order of the Knights of Labor was not Socialist, though its programme contained a number of Socialist ideas. It declared its aim to be 'to secure for the workers the full use of the riches created by them' and to set up co-operative workshops 'with the object of replacing the wage system by a system of industrial co-operation'. It also demanded that the nation's land should be made available for colonization by the people, and that telegraph, telephone and railway companies should be nationalized.

The Socialist Labor party tried to win influence inside the Order. Leading members, including its secretary, Philipp van Patten, joined the Knights of Labor as early as 1881, and by 1893 the party controlled

1. Trade-union organization on secret-society lines, with a quasi-masonic ritual, was common in England after Pitt suppressed legal trade unionism in 1799 and 1800. The prohibition of legal trade unionism forced the movement underground. Members were required to take an oath of secrecy on all matters concerning the organization of their union. These methods survived the Repeal of the Combination Acts of 1824, and only ceased in 1834, when six farmworkers in Tolpuddle, who had formed a union, were sentenced to seven years' transportation to the notorious penal settlement of Botany Bay for administering illegal oaths. The memory of the 'Tolpuddle Martyrs' is still alive in the British Labour movement.

the New York District Assembly. The struggle for leadership led to a break between the Knights and the Labor party in 1895. The Socialists withdrew and all links between the two organizations were broken. By this time the Order was already in full decline. For nearly ten years it had been by far the strongest trade-union organization in the United States. But the failure of the strikes in 1886, and the reaction which followed the Chicago bomb attacks, led to the mass withdrawal of disillusioned and terrified members. Besides which, a rival trade-union centre had been established in 1886, the American Federation of Labor, which was soon destined to supplant the Knights of Labor.

The Knights of Labor had attempted to unify the working class in a strongly centralized organization, formed of local branches which cut completely across differences in craft, trade and industry. A group of unions, resenting this extreme centralization, broke away and founded, in November 1881, a new organization, the 'Federation of Organized Trades and Labor Unions of the United States and Canada', from which the American Federation of Labor subsequently developed. The A.F.L., established at a congress in Columbus, Ohio, in December 1886, altered the programme and constitution of the older Federation, and elected Samuel Gompers (1850–1924) as its first President. By its next congress, in 1887, the American Federation of Labor had a membership of 618,000.

From the beginning, some of the leading members of the Socialist Labor party were active in the A.F.L., hoping to win the new Federation for Socialism. But at successive congresses between 1885 and 1898 resolutions moved by the Socialists in favour of independent Labour policies were usually rejected by three quarters of the delegates. Eventually, the congress of 1898 declared itself against the 'recognition or introduction of any party politics'. Nevertheless, the A.F.L. did send fraternal greetings to the Paris Congress of the International, and retained informal contacts with the Second International down to 1914. It considered itself as, in a sense, identified with the world working class, represented by the International, while firmly rejecting all Socialist ideas.[1]

23

Representation at the inaugural congress of the Second International was confined to the Socialist movements of Europe and the American continent. But Socialist ideas had already taken root in one Asian

1. The standard work on Socialism in America is *Socialism and American Life*, ed. Donald D. Egbert and Stow Persons, 2 vols. (Princeton, 1952); for a brief history, see Harry W. Laidler, *Socialism in the United States* (New York, 1952).

country—Japan—during the 1890s. Japan was then undergoing a process of rapid industrialization which created, as everywhere, a modern working class. Many of the medieval trade guilds, like the printers and shipbuilders, transformed themselves into trade unions on the European model, and the workers in some of the newly formed industries also began to organize. At the same time, Socialist groups were developing in intellectual circles.

The pioneer of working-class Socialism in Japan was Sen Katayama (1858–1933). The son of a farmer, he soon acquired an unquenchable thirst for knowledge which led him to learn printing and later, to be nearer the source of learning, to become a doorman at Tokyo University. This did not satisfy his intellectual appetite, and in 1884 he went to California and earned a living while working his way through university. After eleven years he obtained his degree and returned to Japan, to devote himself to the Labour movement. In 1897 he became secretary of the newly formed Metal Workers' Union, founded the paper, *The Labour World*, established the Society for Promoting Trade Unions (Rodo Kunaii Kiseikai) and at the same time, with the help of Professor Isowa Abe, formed a Socialist society in Tokyo. In the following year he founded the Railway Workers' Union and transformed the trade guilds of building workers and wood workers into trade unions.

The development of capitalism in Japan had left its social and political structure still largely feudal. While the rule of the great feudal families—the 'Shogunate'—had been broken in 1868, the 'revolution' had only been dynastic. It had restored the nominal position of the Emperor while leaving the real power in the hands of a small circle of aristocratic families which, as before, commanded the army, controlled the bureaucracy and now monopolized the new industries. The industrial revolution in Japan had overthrown merely the economic basis of society, changing it from a feudalism dominated by big landowners into one dominated by large-scale capital.

However, the process of industrialization had produced a large and rapidly growing middle class which demanded a share of political power. Under their pressure, Japan became a constitutional monarchy in 1899. Under the new constitution, the middle class acquired a very limited amount of influence, but no power. The workers, however, remained completely excluded from all influence on public affairs. In the year in which the new constitution was proclaimed a special law was passed against the rising Labour movement, limiting trade-union rights, making incitement to strike an offence punishable by imprisonment, subjecting the Press to severe censorship and restricting the freedom of assembly.

In this political atmosphere, the foundation congress of the Socialist party of Japan met in 1901, under the leadership of Sen Katayama, Isowa Abe, D. Kotoku (who was hanged, ten years later, for his activities on behalf of the working class) and the novelist, N. Kinoshita. The manifesto issued by the congress was confiscated by the police, and the party immediately suppressed. It was soon re-formed, however, under the name of the Socialist Propaganda Association (Shakai Shugi Kyokai). The following year it founded the daily paper, *Heimin*, in which appeared the first Japanese translation of the *Communist Manifesto*. Predictably the government closed it down. In 1903 a party congress decided to affiliate formally to the International, and delegated Sen Katayama to attend the Amsterdam Congress in the following year as its delegate. Nineteen hundred and four was the year of the Russo-Japanese War, and to demonstrate to the world the solidarity of the Russian and Japanese workers, congress elected Katayama and Plekhanov as its joint Presidents. It was a memorable moment when, to the immense joy of the delegates, these representatives of the working class of two warring countries demonstratively clasped hands on the platform.[1]

The Labour movements of Europe, America and Asia, whose history has here been briefly outlined, provided the basis on which, from the turn of the century, the Second International was to develop.

1. See Sen Katayama, *The Labour Movement in Japan* (Chicago, 1918), and G. D. H. Cole, *A History of Socialist Thought*, vol. III: *The Second International* (London, 1956), pp. 930–40.

17 · Problems of the Second International

1

In the view of its participants, the Paris Congress of 1889 was trying to restore the International which had been founded a quarter of a century before. Between the final congress of the First International in 1872, and the foundation congress of the Second, several international Labour congresses had met. Hitherto, none of them had succeeded in re-establishing the institution. Even the Second International, which came to play such an important role in the history of Socialism, came into existence without even a rudimentary organization. There was no executive committee or secretariat, there were no rules and there was not even a title[1]—the term 'Second International' being informally but widely used by writers and historians, who saw in it a reincarnation of the First.

It will be recalled that, in contrast, the First International had its Provisional General Council elected at the foundation meeting, and that it was duly authorized by that meeting to draft a statement of principles and a body of rules. The Provisional Rules and what came to be known as the Inaugural Address were discussed by the General Council at its first few meetings and adopted in little more than a month. From the start, therefore, the First International had both a constitution and an effective organization.

The Second International, on the other hand, remained for the first eleven years of its existence without any formal organization. Only at its fourth congress, held in London in 1896, was a committee authorized

1. The Second International held its various congresses under a number of different names. The first, in Paris, was known as the 'International Labour Congress'; the Zurich Congress, in 1893, met under the title of the 'International Socialist Labour Congress', while the London Congress, in 1896, was called the 'International Socialist Workers' and Trade-Union Congress'. The title of 'International Socialist Congress' was adopted only at the Paris Congress of 1900 and subsequently.

to investigate the possibility of establishing a central commission, and only at the Paris Congress in 1900 was it finally decided to set up such a permanent body, together with a 'paid international Secretariat'. Until the setting-up of this Secretariat, the Second International had no existence apart from its congresses. The party of the country in which a congress met was responsible for calling and organizing it, and for meeting the not inconsiderable expenses involved. Apart from this, it enjoyed no executive authority. Apart from its congresses, therefore, which met at intervals of two, three or four years, the International, during these first eleven years, had no organization holding together the member parties and, in particular, no body with authority to speak on its behalf.

The International set up such an organization in 1900 in the form of a central commission, which assumed the title of the 'International Socialist Bureau'. Congress entrusted it with the functions of maintaining effective liaison between the parties, and the organization of future congresses, including the preparation of the agenda. In addition, congress required it to 'pronounce publicly on all vital and major issues of the day which affect the interests of the working class'. Victor Adler, who had been partly responsible for the decision to set up the International Socialist Bureau, confirmed that it was a landmark in the development of the International. 'What seemed an unattainable dream at the time of the first congress at Paris in 1889,' he declared, 'has now, as a result, become more nearly a tangible reality. International Social Democracy has developed from a stage of casual contact and mutual sympathy to one of solid organization.'[1]

In addition to setting up the International Socialist Bureau, the Paris Congress also instituted an Inter-Parliamentary Committee, consisting of Deputies from all countries in which the parties enjoyed parliamentary representation, with the object of 'ensuring uniformity of political (i.e. parliamentary) action'.

Each party was represented on the bureau by two delegates, so that its meetings became miniature congresses. The bureau was required by rule to meet annually, but the Executive Committee, elected by the Bureau, had power to convene extraordinary sessions. The congress had chosen Brussels, as the capital of a neutral country, to be the seat of the Secretariat. So as to ensure continuity on the Executive, the bureau entrusted the offices of president, secretary and treasurer to members of the Belgian delegation. Émile Vandervelde (1866–1938), the outstanding leader of the Belgian Labour party, became president, an office which he retained until the collapse of the International during the First

1. *Victor Adlers Aufsätze, Reden und Briefe*, ed. Friedrich Adler (Vienna, 1922), vol. VII, p. 23.

World War. Victor Serwy was secretary until 1905, when he was replaced by Camille Huysmans.

The First International had tried to establish an effective centralization of working-class power, 'so as to be able to concentrate the collective, organized might of the working class at whichever point became the centre of class struggle'.[1] At the same time it had functioned as the central leadership of the international Labour movement, 'the framework of a single, united organization', as Wilhelm Liebknecht described it in his opening speech to the foundation congress of the Second International. The Second International, however, could function only as a loose federation of autonomous and tightly organized national parties.

2

Although the foundation congress of the Second International scarcely touched on the problem of organization,[2] it took one step which, without being intended or planned as such, initiated joint action which made the International a reality in the minds of millions of workers throughout the world. This was the decision 'to organize, for 1 May, a great international demonstration, organized in such a way', declared the resolution, that on the same day 'the workers in all lands and cities will simultaneously demand from the powers-that-be a limitation of the working day to eight hours'.

The question of a mass demonstration in favour of the eight-hour day had already been mooted, in 1888, by the French, American and Belgian Trade Union Congresses. Specifically, the American Trade Union Congress, meeting at St Louis in December 1888, had decided to organize mass demonstrations throughout the United States on 1 May the following year. Raymond Lavigne, the French trade-union leader who brought up the question at the International's congress, suggested that 1 May be fixed as the day for the international demonstration, following the lead of the Americans.

Lavigne's proposal was not on the original congress agenda. It was raised suddenly and without warning shortly before the congress closed, and was carried without debate. It seemed as though none of the delegates grasped, at the time, the significance of the decision. Only after the congress dispersed was the question raised as to what form the demonstration should take. The resolution had not been explicit, saying

1. Gustav Jaeckh, *Die Internationale* (Leipzig, 1904), p. 218.

2. The Spanish delegates, José Mesa and Pablo Iglesias, proposed that a central committee be established, but withdrew the suggestion when Vaillant declared that, in view of the widely differing legal conditions in the various countries, such a resolution would be unacceptable.

merely that the workers should 'organize the demonstration by means and along lines appropriate to their respective countries'. The French and Austrians decided to celebrate 1 May with a general strike, the Germans and British by holding mass meetings on the first Sunday in May and the parties of most other countries with meetings on the evening of 1 May. This was not quite in line with the spirit and wording of the resolution, which called on the workers to display their international solidarity 'simultaneously in all countries on a given day'.

In spite of this, the first May Day meetings in 1890 constituted a turning-point in the history of Socialism. For the first time a resolution passed at a congress of the International had set millions of workers, of both hemispheres, in motion. In France, on 1 May, work stopped in 138 towns and in the mining areas of the *départements* of Allier, Gard and Loire; in Milan, Turin, Leghorn, Lugo and other Italian towns, the workers marched through the streets in close formation; in the towns of Belgium, some 340,000 took part in the demonstrations; in Portugal, 14,000 came out; even in Warsaw and Lodz, despite Tsarist police terror, there were 8,000; in Barcelona, 100,000; in Stockholm, 120,000 attended a mass meeting addressed by August Palm and Hjalmar Branting, and the Socialist paper, the *Social-Demokraten*, appeared in red print.

The May Day demonstrations had a particular significance in the British Labour movement. Friedrich Engels watched the enormous demonstration in Hyde Park, in the centre of London, from the roof of a goods van. 'Around the seven platforms of the Central Committee thick crowds, in countless numbers, approaching with music and flags, more than 100,000 in a column, swelled by almost as many who had come on their own . . . ,' he wrote, adding that 'on 4 May 1890, the English working class joined up in the great international army. . . . Its long winter sleep . . . is broken at last. The grandchildren of the old Chartists are entering the line of battle.'[1]

In Austria, too, the May Day demonstrations 'worked wonders', as Adler recounted. 'Entire layers of the working class, with which we would otherwise have made no contact, have been shaken out of their lethargy. . . . We have drawn new strength from May Day and the demonstrations have been like a plough over virgin lands. The idea of May Day has taken root in the hearts of workers whom we could never have reached with our programmes and speeches, and the impression will never be lost.'[2] The party's propaganda at public meetings and inside the factories for a mass cessation of work on May Day had had a powerful effect. The *bourgeois* Press had been full of the horrors of revolution,

1. Friedrich Engels, 'Der 4 Mai in London', in *Arbeiter-Zeitung*, 23 May 1890; see *Victor Adlers Aufsätze . . .*, vol. I, p. 14.
2. *Victor Adlers Aufsätze . . .*, vol. I, p. 73, and vol. VI, p. 191.

to which, it claimed, the May Day campaign was merely a prelude. The Emperor convened a meeting of the Privy Council to reassure himself that the necessary counter-measures had been taken by the government.[1] The Minutes of the Privy Council, meeting on 8 April 1890, make it clear that 'His Majesty . . . is pleased with the energetic steps taken. . . . The proposal to cease work on 1 May is illegal. . . . His Majesty most graciously wishes to stress that the Government will act decisively . . . [because] it is vital that we meet the suspicious growth of mass unrest with the utmost vigour.' Croatian and Bosnian troops were concentrated in Vienna, Hungarian and Polish troops in Bohemia, German and Czech troops in Polish Galicia, and artillery was trained on the streets of industrial towns. 'The soldiers are prepared, the doors of the houses are locked, families are laying in supplies as though for a siege, the shops are shut tight, women and children are afraid to go out, everywhere there is an oppressive atmosphere of anxiety. . . .'—in these terms a leading Viennese paper described the mood of the middle classes on the eve of 1 May.[2]

This May Day went by in Austria, however, without serious incident; only in the following year did the employers take their revenge for the provocation by locking out the workers in Bohemia, Silesia and Carinthia. In France, on the other hand, the very first May Day demonstrations led to clashes with the authorities and in the following year to street fighting in Fourmies, in the *département du Nord*, in which ten men, women and children were killed and many more wounded. The so-called 'ringleaders' were prosecuted, among them Paul Lafargue, who was given a year's imprisonment.

By contrast, German Social Democracy, the oldest and strongest party in the International, had refused to call on the workers to stop

1. See Ludwig Brügel, *Geschichte der österreichischen Sozialdemokratie*, vol. IV, p. 126. The Emperor William II was also determined, according to a letter from the Austro-Hungarian Foreign Minister, Count Kalnoky, to the Austrian Prime Minister, Count Taaffe, 'to act with the utmost vigour'. Count Kalnoky wrote: 'I consider the newspaper statement that Kaiser Wilhelm has spoken up for the workers in relation to the May demonstration to be a mischievous invention. I hear, on the contrary, that he was most emphatic that, now so much had been done for the betterment of the workers' lot, he would "strike at random" the next time if a workers' movement jeopardized life and property, and that he has already given orders to that effect' (Brügel, op. cit., vol. IV, pp. 124–5).

2. *Neue Freie Presse*, 1 May 1890. The paper added: 'The Saint whose festival is being celebrated in all countries today is called Karl Marx.' It recognized correctly the real meaning of the May Day demonstration when it wrote: '. . . The 1 May sprung from the spirit of the late International. . . . Workers of all countries, unite! This was the call which Karl Marx once has raised, and the 1 May is its echo. Who will let himself be deceived by that demonstration for the eight-hour day! What really is meant is to test the solidarity of the workers. . . . The 1 May is an assault of the Socialist party which aims at the destruction of the present society, at the abolition of capital. . . .' Quoted in Brügel, op. cit., vol. IV, p. 126.

work on May Day, confining itself instead to public meetings on the first Sunday in May. This attitude embittered the French Socialists and caused keen disappointment in Austria. Both parties proposed a resolution at the Brussels Congress in 1891, which pledged all the parties to celebrate May Day on the first of the month. 'The 1 May is the day for joint demonstrations by the workers of all countries,' the resolution declared, 'at which the workers display the solidarity and publicize their demands.' The resolution went on to commit the parties to call strikes on 1 May: 'The day of demonstrations is to be a day on which work ceases, in so far as this is not rendered impossible by conditions in the various countries.'

However, although the Germans (like all other parties, with the exception of the English) voted for the resolution, they still insisted on not calling a strike on May Day, only going so far as to change the date for the demonstrations from the first Sunday in May to the evening of 1 May. Adler tried unsuccessfully to persuade them to alter the decisions at the party congress in Berlin in 1892, which he attended as the Austrian delegate. He reminded the German Social Democrats of the real meaning of May Day. Only through these celebrations, he declared, had the International made its impact on the minds of the people, because 'the knowledge that at a given hour, on the same day, wherever capitalist power prevails, the workers are filled with *one* idea, gives a deeper and more genuinely revolutionary content to the occasion than mere preoccupation with labour legislation'. The moment when the workers of many countries simultaneously defied the might of capital was 'at the same time a religious moment' and 'a moment of enthusiasm'—elements which were very necessary in the development of the movement.[1]

The German party, however, considered that the question of stopping work on 1 May involved deep political issues, since it related to the controversial topic of the general strike as a political weapon—an issue which was later to involve the party in bitter internal disputes. Moreover, the party in Germany felt itself threatened by another wave of reaction. When the Paris Congress assembled in 1889, the Anti-Socialist Law was still in force. It was due to lapse with the dissolution of the Reichstag in October 1890. In the elections for a new Reichstag, the Social Democrats made immense strides, receiving nearly one and a half million out of the seven million votes cast. The Anti-Socialist Law had failed to stem the advance of social democracy. Bismarck now realized that the general franchise, which he had introduced in order to win mass support for his conception of the German national state, was the biggest mistake of his whole career. He intended to devote the remaining years of his life to rectifying the error, and to replace the old

1. *Victor Adlers Aufsätze . . .*, vol. VI, p. 191.

Anti-Socialist Law by a new and much more severe one which would exclude the Socialists from the Reichstag. He intended to introduce by means of a *coup d'état* a new electoral law which would withdraw the right to vote or conduct political activity from all who 'had been proved to harbour revolutionary ideas'; also, in particular, he would withdraw the secret ballot.[1]

Bismarck's plan for a *coup d'état*, which he submitted to the Privy Council on 2 March 1890, was rejected by the Kaiser, who did not want to start his reign with a civil war. But the danger of a *coup d'état* remained latent. Would not a general strike on May Day renew the danger? Bebel made this point in a speech to the Zurich Congress of the International, in which he explained why his party could not vote for a resolution committing them to a May Day strike. Any attempt to honour such a commitment, he maintained, would 'bring about, as nowhere else in the world, a head-on collision with the *bourgeoisie* and the government'. And he added, 'If we want such a struggle, we should prefer to choose our own time.'[2]

The Zurich Congress in 1893 strengthened the earlier Brussels resolution on a May Day demonstration. It pledged the parties to at least 'attempt' strike by the workers on 1 May. But, however great the national and local variations, May Day became, for many generations, an occasion for expressing in world-wide demonstrations the international solidarity of the working class.[3]

3

Besides the controversy over the way in which May Day was to be celebrated, another problem had to be faced at the inception of the Second International—the problem of its relations with the Anarchist movement. What was involved was not only a question of basic

1. See Hans Delbrück, *Regierung und Volkswille* (Berlin, 1914), pp. 61–4; also *Preussische Jahrbücher*, vols. 147 and 153; Egmont Zechlin, *Staatsstreichpläne Bismarcks und Wilhelms II, 1890–4* (Stuttgart, 1929).

2. *Protokoll* (Zurich, 1893), p. 34. 'A Party,' Bebel wrote to Engels on 10 November 1892, defending his attitude, 'should not shed its blood for the sake of a demonstration.' Engels admitted in his reply that a general strike on May Day would have to be paid for with sacrifices in no relation to its gains, but he was afraid it makes 'a bad impression when the strongest party in the world is going to retreat, *noblesse oblige* . . .'. Bebel insisted, however, in his answer to Engels: '. . . We don't want to incur formidable sacrifices for a demonstration whose advantages for us are very small. . . . The power of state and the *bourgeoisie* would gladly accept our challenge, because they know they would be the victors [in that struggle] . . .'—*August Bebel: Briefwechsel mit Friedrich Engels*, ed. Werner Blumenberg (The Hague, 1965), pp. 613, 618, 621. For the history of the conflict, see Mehring, *Geschichte der deutschen Sozialdemokratie*, op. cit., II:2, pp. 328ff.

3. See M. Dommanget, *Histoire du premier mai* (Paris, 1953).

principle; more immediately relevant issues were those of the tactics and methods of working-class struggle, the attitude of the workers towards the state and Parliament, towards the value of political action and social reform. These questions had already been debated at congresses of the First International, which had, in fact, foundered as a direct result of the struggle between Anarchists and 'state Socialists'.

Participation in the Paris Congress of 1889 was not limited to those holding particular views about the nature of Socialism or the ways in which it would be achieved. Invitations went out to all the Socialist workers' organizations and to the trade unions. Anarchist delegates attended, therefore, from France, Italy, Spain, Holland and Germany. Immediately the conflict between the methods and principles of Anarchism and Socialism broke out afresh.

Prominent on the congress agenda was the question of Labour legislation. According to Social Democratic ideas the campaign for such legislation was meaningless without a parallel struggle for influence in parliamentary bodies. The Anarchist speakers—Francesco Saverio Merlino from Italy, Sébastien Faure from France, and Domela Nieuwenhuis from Holland—rejected all forms of working-class political action, including participation in elections and demands for social legislation. The Anarchists saw themselves as a tiny minority, confronting a huge majority of delegates who had no sympathy for their views. The vehemence of their reaction was in inverse ratio to their numerical strength. The most trivial procedural matters provoked them to violent protest, which threatened to reduce the congress to a shambles. The chairman was compelled, with some embarrassment, to order the ejection of the Anarchists from the hall. This in no way solved the problem of Anarchist participation. The expedient adopted at the following congress, at Brussels in 1891, of declaring the Anarchist mandates invalid, came no nearer to a lasting solution. Congress was forced to decide once and for all who was and who was not eligible to attend.

The problem was thrashed out at a preliminary meeting, called to prepare for the Zurich Congress of 1893. Without weakening the universal character of the International, it was impossible to restrict membership to those holding certain approved theories of Socialism. A majority of the Dutch Labour movement, led by Nieuwenhuis, still had Anarchist leanings, most of the French trade unions were syndicalist, while in England the unions were not even nominally Socialist. The Brussels pre-Conference, therefore, proposed to admit trade-union representatives unconditionally to future conferences, while restricting political representation to those parties which acknowledged the 'necessity of political action'. The proposal was put on the agenda for the Zurich Congress.

The Zurich Congress was significant for the participation of an official delegation from the British trade-union movement, led by John Hodge, a representative of the Parliamentary Committee and president of the Trades Union Congress. Friedrich Engels, who also attended, was welcomed with great enthusiasm and elected honorary president at the final session of the congress.

When the congress assembled, it was soon plunged into controversy over the recognition of political action as a condition of future membership. Bebel, Adler, Kautsky and Otto Lang proposed that an explanatory clause should be added to the resolution to the effect that: 'By political action we mean that the workers' parties should make full use of political and legal rights in an attempt to capture the legislative machine and use it in the interests of the working class and for the capture of political power.'

This formulation naturally provoked the violent opposition of the Anarchists, particularly of the two Germans, W. Werner, the printer, and Gustav Landauer, the writer, representatives respectively of two small German groups known as the 'Young Ones' and the 'Independents'. But their arguments failed to carry conviction and the resolution was adopted, with fourteen countries voting in favour and only the two Germans against—France and Poland abstaining. When the vote was announced, the Anarchists in the body of the hall and in the gallery began a storm of protest and tried to rush the platform. Proceedings were suspended while the chairman directed the stewards to remove a number of the Anarchists, including Werner and Landauer, from the hall.

The Anarchists did not let things rest with the decision at Zurich, but demanded at the next congress that the debate on the question of eligibility should be reopened. This congress met in London, at the invitation of the British T.U.C., in July 1896. It was much better attended than any previous congress of the International, with 776 representatives from twenty countries. Of these, however, 465 were from Britain and included all the leading figures in the trade-union and Labour movements: Edward Cowey, President of the T.U.C.'s Parliamentary Committee, who formally opened the congress, Keir Hardie, Chairman of the I.L.P., Ben Tillett of the Dockers and Tom Mann of the Engineers, in addition to Hyndman, Quelch, Lansbury and Belfort Bax of the Social Democratic Federation, Sidney and Beatrice Webb, Bernard Shaw and Ramsay MacDonald from the Fabians—only William Morris was absent, through illness.

The French delegation numbered 133, representing all trends in the Labour movement—Marxists, Possibilists, Allemanists, Blanquists, Anarchists and syndicalist trade unionists under the leadership of

Ferdinand Pelloutier, Raymond Lavigne and Marcel Sembat, in addition to Alexandre Millerand and René Viviani, representing the forty-nine Socialist M.P.s. A comparatively unknown delegate from France, appearing for the first time at a congress, was Jean Jaurès. His first speech, 'repeatedly interrupted by thunderous applause from the entire congress and by the waving of handkerchiefs and hats from the English delegates', according to the Minutes, won him a lasting reputation in the International.[1] The Swedish delegation was led by Hjalmar Branting, the Dutch by P. J. Troelstra and W. H. Vliegen, the Belgians by Louis Bertrand and Émile Vandervelde, the Spanish by Pablo Iglesias and Antonio G. Quejido, General Secretary of the Spanish trade-union movement, and the Swiss by Karl Bürkli and Hermann Greulich. The German delegation of forty-eight was led by Bebel, Liebknecht and Paul Singer, the Austrians by Victor Adler and Karl Kautsky (the latter had a mandate from the Austrian party). The Italians included Constantino Lazzari, Enrico Ferri and Alessandro Schiavi; the Russian Social Democratic party was represented by George Valentinovitch Plekhanov, Paul Axelrod and Vera Zasulich; the thirteen members of the Polish delegation included Felix Daszynski, Josef Pilsudski and Rosa Luxemburg.

Among the Anarchists who came with mandates from trade unions and other *bona fide* Labour organizations there were several leading figures in the movement, including Domela Niewenhuis, Errico Malatesta, who led the Italian Anarchists, Louise Michel, the famous Communard who had fought on the barricades in 1871, served nine years in the penal settlement of New Caledonia and been sentenced to a further six years' hard labour on her return to France, and Gustav Landauer, a major essayist, mystic and visionary who was destined for a martyr's death—a member of the Bavarian Soviet government of 1919. Landauer, like Rosa Luxemburg, was murdered by German army officers.

The London Congress met in the impressive surroundings of the Queen's Hall, and was preceded on the previous day by a mass meeting in Hyde Park, with tens of thousands of workers in attendance. As soon as the congress had been formally opened with the speeches of fraternal greetings, the delegate of the Dutch Anarchist Socialist League, C. Cornelissen, demanded the reopening of the debate on the Zurich resolution. Seeing the chairman's hesitation, the Anarchists began a violent uproar in the hall and galleries, and the session had to be

1. *Verhandlungen und Beschlüsse des Internationalen Sozialistischen Arbeiter- und Gewerkschaftskongresses* (Berlin, 1896), p. 19; our account is also based on the detailed published *Report of Proceedings* (London, 1896) published by the Organization Committee. For a biography of Jaurès, see Margaret Pease, *Jean Jaurès* (London, 1917).

adjourned. The Congress Steering Committee met at once and decided, in order to avoid giving the impression of steam-rollering any section of the congress, to debate the Zurich resolution all over again.

The discussion was opened by Keir Hardie with an appeal for tolerance. He was followed by Tom Mann, pleading that 'no one should be pushed aside because of his opinions'. Then Jaurès and Hyndman spoke in favour of the resolution. Nieuwenhuis, on the other hand, declared that if it were passed all freedom of thought inside the International would disappear. The Anarchists, he insisted, were every bit as good Socialists as the Social Democrats, and their exclusion from congresses would be motivated only by the fear of 'disturbing the fathers of the Marxist church council'. When put to the vote, the resolution was supported by Germany, a majority of the British (223 against 104), Belgium, U.S.A., Australia, Switzerland, Romania, Bulgaria, Russia, Poland, Austria, Bohemia, Hungary, Denmark, Norway, Sweden, Spain and Portugal. Voting against the resolution were a majority of the French (57 to 56) and of the Dutch (9 to 5) delegates. The Italian delegation, being equally divided, abstained.

The fact that nearly a third of the British delegates voted against the resolution in no way indicated any sympathy for Anarchism. It merely expressed the traditional English toleration of (or indifference to) ideological diversity. But the voting did reveal the strength of the Anarchist influence on the Dutch and Italian working class and on the French trade unions. The same influence was displayed in the debate on a resolution drafted by one of the congress commissions and moved by George Lansbury. This sought to define once again what was meant by 'political action'. It said that 'by political action this congress understands all forms of organized struggle for the capture of political power and the use of the legislative and administrative institutions of State and community by the working class, in the interests of its emancipation'.

Joseph Tortelier opposed, on behalf of the French trade unions. He claimed that parliamentarism was widely discredited among the French people, that the workers had nothing to hope for from any parliament and that they could fight effectively for their emancipation only by means of 'direct action'. By direct action Tortelier meant principally the strike weapon, but it could also take other forms—private property in housing, for example, could be ended at once if tenants refused to pay their rent. Jaurès replied with a powerful appeal to the workers to struggle for political power. He described the strike as a method of 'fighting capitalism with folded arms'. Political action was by far the strongest weapon open to the working class, and the most dangerous enemies were those who advised against using this weapon. Bebel then described how, through participating in political activity, including elections, German Social Democracy had advanced from being a small, persecuted and derided sect without prestige or support to being the strongest party in the Reich. 'Ten years ago,' he declared, 'we received less than a hundred thousand votes, while at the last elections the figure was one and three quarter million—a quarter of the total cast. Every economic and political gain secured by the working class in Germany has been due to the activity and pressure of Social Democracy.' Once again the resolution was passed almost unanimously; the Dutch Anarchist delegates had left the congress before the opening of the debate, and there was only a small handful among the French delegates to cast their votes against the resolution.

The congress then decided to settle once and for all the question of Anarchist participation by formally suspending them from membership of the International. With the exception of the French syndicalist delegation everyone voted for a resolution declaring that 'the exclusive right' to attend future congresses should be limited firstly to those organizations 'which stand for the replacement of the capitalist system of property and production by Socialism, and who acknowledge the necessity of participating in legislative and parliamentary activity as a means of achieving this', and, in addition, to 'all trade-union organizations which, without themselves taking part in politics, acknowledge the need for political and parliamentary activity'. The resolution made its point even more explicit by adding, 'Anarchists are hereby excluded.'

As reporter for the commission which had been considering the resolution, Liebknecht explained that Congress felt obliged to take this step because 'we should like to hold our next congress free from the unpleasant scenes which have marred the last two'. The Anarchists had not been satisfied to state their views and then conform with majority decisions, but had persistently tried to sabotage the work of Congress. 'We were therefore compelled to devote whole days to fruitless discussion with those whose only object was to discredit the congress.' The London resolution brought to an end, after nearly thirty years, the struggle between Anarchism and Social Democracy within the confines of a single international movement.

18 · Evolutionary and Revolutionary Socialism

The London Congress of the International had confirmed once again that the object of member parties was to 'transform the capitalist system of ownership and production into Socialism'. It had also decided the controversial question of how the struggle for this aim should be conducted. The overwhelming majority of the parties had rejected Anarchism and Syndicalism. They had acknowledged the necessity of political action and of the struggle for political power to which social democracy was committed. The parties were now confronted with the question of which tactics to pursue in the struggle for agreed aims. Basically, the problem was whether capitalism could be overthrown only by a revolutionary struggle for power culminating in the overthrow of the ruling class, or whether it could be transformed in an evolutionary manner through the growing influence of the working class within the existing social and political framework.

1

The controversy between the revolutionary and evolutionary schools of Socialism had agitated the working-class movement of nearly all countries from the very beginning. An event in France suddenly brought matters to a crisis within the International. On 29 June 1899, a Socialist, Alexandre Millerand, had been invited to join a *bourgeois* government and became the first Socialist to serve under normal conditions in a European cabinet.[1] This event marked a break in the traditions of European Socialism from the time of Marx, and called in question the prevailing theory of proletarian class struggle as interpreted by most parties.

The Waldeck-Rousseau ministry, which Millerand joined, was radical-republican, and had come to power in the course of a crisis

1. Louis Blanc, Millerand's sole predecessor, had joined a government formed as a result of a revolution—that of February 1848.

which shook the French Republic to its depths. The 'Dreyfus Affair'—the campaign to rehabilitate a Jewish captain on the General Staff who had been sentenced to life imprisonment on Devil's Island in 1895 on a false charge of espionage—touched off a tremendous barrage of monarchist and anti-semitic propaganda by the church, the royalist Press and the army, traditionally the deadly enemies of the Republic. Socialists and Radicals had formed a united front in the Chamber against the common danger, and the various Socialist parties into which the French Labour movement had split came together to form an action committee, or 'Vigilance Committee', as it was called in the old Jacobin tradition. Already in 1883 the Socialists had joined forces with the Radicals in an election campaign and had, thanks to the alliance, increased their seats in the Chamber from twelve to forty-nine. They had also, in alliance with the Radicals, won considerable successes in the local elections of 1896.

In May 1898, at the height of the Dreyfus Affair, elections were about to be held for a new Chamber. Once again the Socialists and Radicals formed an electoral alliance, and it triumphed. The victory of the republican forces was complete. But the *bourgeois* left won only a tiny majority in the new parliament. A government of the left could be formed only with the help of the Socialists. René Waldeck-Rousseau, who had been asked to form a government, accordingly asked Millerand to join his cabinet as Minister for Trade and Industry.

Alexandre Millerand (1859–1943), a lawyer with a great reputation among the working class, had been elected to Parliament in 1885 and, like Jaurès, had slowly evolved from radicalism to Socialism. Within the Socialist movement he uncompromisingly supported the evolutionary wing. At a banquet in Saint-Mandé, held to celebrate a victory in the local elections of 1896 and attended by Guesde, Jaurès, Vaillant and other leaders of the diverse trends in French Socialism, Millerand proposed a programme—the famous 'Saint-Mandé Programme'—which he hoped would provide a basis for re-uniting the badly divided movement. Every section of the movement was agreed, he insisted, on replacing the capitalist system by Socialism, but capitalism could hardly be overthrown by revolutionary action in one fell swoop. The abolition of capitalism could be only a gradual process, he explained, through the piecemeal nationalization and municipalization of large industry, the continuous expansion in the economic and social activities of public organizations and a never-ending process of social reform. The instrument for supplanting capitalism, therefore, could never be revolutionary violence but only democracy embodied in the French Republic. Socialists must undertake, he suggested, to win a majority of the people for Socialism, meanwhile seeking joint action with all the progressive elements in society in the struggle for social reform and the nationalization of monopolies.[1]

Millerand, like Jaurès, Viviani, Briand and other Socialist deputies, was a member of the group known as the 'Independent Socialists'. But he joined the government in his individual capacity, without any mandate from his group and without even having consulted either the parliamentary group or the 'Vigilance Committee'. He tried to justify his somewhat surprising decision by pointing to the danger which threatened the Republic. Its preservation in the face of the threat to its existence from the clerical right was, he maintained, at that moment of supreme importance for the working class. And he claimed to be loyal to the Saint-Mandé Programme, promising to work for its objectives from inside the government.

The Waldeck-Rousseau Ministry depended on an alliance of Radicals, the recently formed group of Radical-Socialists and the Parliamentary Socialists themselves. Its slogan was 'No enemies on the left', hence Waldeck-Rousseau's invitation to Millerand to join his government. At the same time, however, he invited General Gallifet, who was responsible for the slaughter of the Communards in 1871, to become Minister of War, as a man who seemed capable of breaking any revolt by the largely monarchist general staff, and to reform the army, which had degenerated into an instrument of reaction.

The surprising news that Millerand had joined the government was greeted with indignation by the whole of the French right, with satisfaction by the followers of Brousse and the Independent Socialists, and with consternation by the Guesdists, Blanquists and Syndicalists. To the Guesdists and Blanquists, Millerand's participation in a *bourgeois* government was a blatant betrayal of the principles of the proletarian class struggle, a betrayal made even more heinous by the presence of Gallifet in the same government. They issued a manifesto repudiating all responsibility for Millerand's action and called a congress to pronounce formally on his behaviour in the name of the French working class. All Labour organizations which acknowledged the class struggle and the principles of international Socialism were invited to the congress, which met in December 1899, with some 800 delegates, representing 1,400 political organizations, trade unions and co-operative societies.

The congress, however, reached no clear decision. It adopted two resolutions. The first, carried by 818 votes against 634, declared that the participation of Socialists in a *bourgeois* government was incompatible with the principles of the proletarian class struggle. The second, how-

1. For the text of the 'Saint-Mandé Programme', see R. C. K. Ensor, *Modern Socialism* (London, 1904), pp. 48–55.

ever, carried by 1,140 votes to 240, said that the Socialist party could consider taking part in such a government under 'exceptional conditions'. It went on to stress that, since the capitalist class must be deprived of its political power before it could be economically dispossessed, the conquest of political power by the workers remained of supreme importance.

The conditions under which Millerand had joined the government were indeed 'exceptional', and the Ministry of Waldeck-Rousseau had in fact repelled the clerical-monarchist attack on the Republic, and implemented a substantial programme of labour-protection laws and social reforms which had been drafted by Millerand. But, as a member of a *bourgeois* government, Millerand was also held responsible for actions of which he disapproved but which he could not prevent—actions which he was even compelled formally to support in order to save the government from being overthrown by the clerical-monarchist right. Socialists were confronted with a Treaty of Alliance between the French Republic and Tsarist Russia, which had been initiated under the previous government, and had the embarrassment of seeing Millerand, as Minister of Trade, accompany the Tsar, who represented the extreme of brutal reaction, on a tour of the Paris World Exhibition, which ended with the solemn award of a Russian decoration to the hapless Millerand. They even had to witness the spectacle of a Socialist demonstration which accompanied the delegates to the International's Paris Congress to the Wall of the Federals in commemoration of the Commune, broken up by police and soldiers on the orders of a government containing a Socialist Minister.

The intolerable contradiction in which the Socialists now found themselves was shown by the events at Chalon in June 1900. The workers had come out on strike, the government had sent troops into the strike-bound area and a bloody clash ensued. The Socialists protested in the Chamber. The Right, seeing an opportunity of overthrowing a government which it detested, proposed a vote of no confidence. In order to save the government, the Independent Socialists, led by Jaurès, voted against the motion, while the Guesdists supported it. This accentuated the conflict between the revolutionary and reformist wings of the movement. By the autumn of 1901 the bitter controversy had resulted in a realignment of the two groups. The revolutionary Socialists—Guesdists, Blanquists and the left wing among the followers of Allemane—united to form the new Parti Socialiste de France; while the reformists—Broussists, Independents and the right wing of the Allemanists—set up the Parti Socialiste Français.[1]

1. For this episode in the history of French Socialism, see A. Zévaès, *Histoire du socialisme et du communisme en France* (Paris, 1947).

2

The excitement over the 'Millerand Affair' spread from France to the Socialist movement of all countries, and, in particular, to Germany. There the smouldering conflict between the revolutionary and reformist wings broke out into the open during the party conference at Hanover in October 1899. The item on the agenda under which the debate took place was entitled 'the attack on the basic views of the party', and the man under indictment for the 'attack' was not Millerand but Eduard Bernstein. Wilhelm Liebknecht, who, in a letter to Victor Adler, had denounced Millerand's entry into the government as a 'great tactical error', suggested that the party should maintain 'the strictest neutrality' in the conflict inside the French Socialist movement.[1] The Bernstein debate at the Hanover Party Congress proved to be a turning-point in the history of German Social Democracy, and had a profound effect on the Socialist Parties of other countries, especially in France.

As in most other countries, controversy between reformist and revolutionary Socialists over tactics had preoccupied the German Labour movement, even during the twelve years when the party was legally suppressed under the Anti-Socialist Law. The fact that the party had been prohibited by the government, and the persecution to which it had been subjected, inevitably strengthened its revolutionary wing. The Anti-Socialist Law had revealed, in the crudest possible way, that the state was an instrument in the hands of the ruling class for the suppression of the workers. The seed of hatred which the state and ruling class had themselves planted sank deep roots in the mind of the working class.[2] The party's reply to the Anti-Socialist Law was the Erfurt Programme of 1891—a programme of revolutionary Socialism in the spirit of Marxism, in sharp contrast to the 'national' brand of Socialism represented by Lassalle and expressed in the Gotha Programme of 1875. The party's deep regard for Lassalle was by no means extinguished. His

1. *Victor Adlers Briefwechsel mit August Bebel und Karl Kautsky*, edited by Friedrich Adler (Vienna, 1954), p. 319.

2. Thirteen years after the repeal of the Anti-Socialist Law, this hatred was still as fresh as ever in the mind of Bebel. In a speech to the Dresden Party Congress in 1903, he described the treatment meted out to the Social Democrats at the time. 'Blows simply rained down on us,' he said, 'and everything was broken up. One city after another, including the surrounding districts, was put into a state of siege. Hundreds and hundreds of our comrades became unemployed and we were driven from our homes like mangy dogs. . . . When I recall,' he continued, 'how we were made to report at the police station, had our measurements taken and were treated generally like criminals, photographed and then given three days to clear out—this was an experience I shall remember as long as I live.' And he went on to say: 'If the day came when I could say to those people, "Now I shall show you what you did to us then", I most certainly should'—*Protokoll über die Verhandlungen des Parteitages—Dresden, 1903* (Berlin, 1903), p. 217.

busts and portraits could be seen in working-class meeting-halls alongside those of Marx and Engels. He was still commemorated in working-class songs. But the Erfurt Programme rejected all identification of the workers with the nationalist state, which had been axiomatic for Lassalle. It asserted the doctrine of irreconcilable antagonism between the working class and the existing state machine; it stressed the international proletarian class struggle in uncompromising terms, and it was drawn up on the assumption of an imminent revolution which would sweep away the capitalist state and the *bourgeois* social order.

However, in the year of the Erfurt Programme, Georg von Vollmar (1850–1922), one of the movement's most respected figures (he came from a Bavarian nobleman's family, had once been a strict Catholic, and, converted to Socialism, had joined the party shortly before the Anti-Socialist Law was enacted), raised the standard of reformism. In the period of the Anti-Socialist Law he had been on the extreme left. In two sensational articles on the tactics of the party under conditions of illegality (they appeared in the *Sozialdemokrat*, the party's official organ, printed, for legal reasons, in Zurich and distributed secretly in Germany), he had declared that the party had no hopes of seeing the Anti-Socialist Law repealed by parliamentary action, and that it would be removed only by revolution. 'The separation of Social Democracy from the existing state and from the present social order,' he wrote, 'becomes continually more complete; the gulf between ourselves and our enemies grows constantly wider, more and more insurmountable. . . . Today Socialism is no longer a matter of theory but simply a question of power, which cannot be solved in any parliamentary situation, but only on the streets and on the field of battle.' He demanded that the party should declare openly 'to our enemies. . . . Yes, we are a danger to the State because we intend to destroy you. We are certainly the enemies of your property, your values, your entire order. . . . We shall meet force with force.'[1]

When, quite contrary to his expectations, the Anti-Socialist Law was removed by parliamentary action, Vollmar renounced the idea of revolutionary violence. While in no sense denying the possibility of political and social revolutions in conditions of crisis, he argued that in more normal conditions the state and *bourgeois* society could be transformed by a process of gradual evolution which the party should assist. It should win the peasants as allies and co-operate with the progressive wing of the *bourgeoisie* for social and political reforms. The fate of the Anti-Socialist Law proved that the middle class was far from being a

1. *Sozialdemokrat*, 12 August 1882, quoted by Eduard Bernstein, *Sozialdemokratische Lehrjahre* (Berlin, 1928). p. 127. For an outline of the life of Vollmar, see R. Jansen, *Georg von Vollmar. Eine politische Biographie* (Düsseldorf, 1958).

solid reactionary mass. The law had been repealed because the centre party and one wing of the Liberals had opposed Bismarck's attempt to make it stronger. In order to increase its influence in Parliament, provincial governments and local councils, the party should be prepared to make electoral alliances with *bourgeois* parties. And in fact, at Vollmar's instigation, the party in 1898 made an electoral alliance with the Catholic Centre party in Bavaria and fought a joint campaign in 1904 to reform the provincial franchise.

Within the party, Vollmar was by no means isolated. But the reformists who rallied to him were opposed to the tactics of the revolutionary Socialists rather than to the principles of the Erfurt Programme. Bernstein, however, had gone much further, and started to call in question the basic concepts underlying the programme. He rejected not only the tactics of the revolutionaries but their fundamental theory. He went beyond empirical reformism to a revision of the entire Marxist outlook.

3

Bernstein's critique of Marxism provoked a storm among the German Social Democrats. Until the publication of his criticism in 1896, he had been regarded as one of the leaders of the party. As editor of the *Sozialdemokrat* he had, for an entire decade of repression under the Anti-Socialist Law, presented the party's views with great effectiveness —'a great service for which we all owe him a debt of gratitude', as Bebel conceded while supporting his indictment at the party congress, 'a man who, up to now, has justly been regarded as one of our leading Marxist theoreticians'.[1] Bernstein had been the confidant and friend of Friedrich Engels, who nominated him, together with Bebel, as his literary executor. He had, said Liebknecht, 'up to then been famous as a guardian of our principles'. Now he was denounced as an apostate in innumerable articles in the party Press. Liebknecht called his critique of Marxism 'a solemn denial of Socialist principles' and Bebel wrote, in a letter to Bernstein, 'For me the decisive fact is that you are no longer in the camp of Social Democracy.' Kautsky, one of Bernstein's friends from his youth, broke off relations with him, and Bebel considered his expulsion from the party.[2]

Eduard Bernstein (1850–1932) had become the international symbol

1. *Protokoll über die Verhandlungen des Parteitages—Hannover, 1899* (Berlin, 1899), p. 95.

2. *Protokoll*, op. cit., p. 192; *Victor Adlers Briefwechsel*, ch. v, 'Aus der Aefangs-zeit des Bernsteinschen Revisionismus'. For a discussion of Bernstein's expulsion from the party, see also the letters from Bebel and Kautsky, pp. 258 and 309; Bernstein's letter to Bebel, p. 258; and Adler's letters, pp. 292, 297–9.

of opposition to the current of revolutionary Socialism, the founder of the Revisionist school. He was not, however, very happy about the role he had come to occupy, a role he had not sought and for which he was temperamentally unsuited. He was impelled on the course he took not by ambition but by sheer intellectual honesty. He was hardly cut out for the role of leader, being much more of an intellectual than a politician. He had amassed his considerable learning entirely by his own efforts. Coming from a *petit bourgeois* Jewish family, he grew up in Berlin under conditions of great poverty.[1] His father was a plumber who later became an engine-driver. But there were fifteen children, and the father's income was hardly enough to save his family from privation. A university education for Eduard, the seventh child, was therefore out of the question. It took a great deal of sacrifice on the part of his family to keep him at grammar school until he was sixteen. Then he had to earn his living. He was apprenticed to a bank and later worked for the Rothschilds. The Paris Commune made him a Socialist. He joined the party and became friendly with Bebel, Liebknecht, Auer and other leading members, who recommended his appointment as secretary to the writer, Karl Höchberg, editor of the Socialist journal, *Die Zukunft*.

The paper appeared in Lucerne in Switzerland, to which Bernstein had moved in 1878. Three years later, the party made him editor of the *Sozialdemokrat*, which was published in Zurich. The German police had issued a warrant for his arrest, and, under pressure from Bismarck, Bernstein and his colleagues were expelled from the country by order of the Swiss Federal government. He removed the paper with him to London. After the lapsing of the Anti-Socialist Law the paper ceased publication, since the party could now publish its own journal legally in Germany. It established in Berlin a central organ with the title, *Vorwärts*. Bernstein, with the warrant against him still outstanding, remained in London as the British correspondent of *Vorwärts*, and also contributed to the *Neue Zeit*, which was edited by Karl Kautsky. During his period of exile he wrote an important study of the Socialist trends in the English revolution of the seventeenth century, the first of a great number of works on history and Socialist theory.[2]

Bernstein insisted that he had not so much abandoned Marxism, as his critics asserted, as subjected some of its hypotheses to critical testing. Far from disparaging Marx, to whom he felt indebted throughout

1. For a sketch of Bernstein's life and an appreciation of his work, see Peter Gay, *Das Dilemma des demokratischen Sozialismus* (Nuremberg, 1954); and Bernstein's reminiscences in *Sozialdemokratische Lehrjahre* (Berlin, 1928) and *Aus den Jahren meines Exils* (Berlin, 1917).

2. Eduard Bernstein, *Sozialismus und Demokratie in der grossen englischen Revolution* (Stuttgart, 1895). For a bibliography of Bernstein's writings, see Gay, op. cit., pp. 374–6.

his life, he tried merely, as he told Bebel, 'to make Marxism conform to reality' and to 'develop' the doctrine further.[1] His criticism was directed primarily against the theory of revolution, which Marx had expounded as part of his philosophy of history and had subsequently elaborated in his analysis of capitalism's laws of development. In Marx's view, capitalism, as it developed, transformed ever greater numbers of people into proletarians, pushed the proletariat into ever-increasing poverty, while at the same time, through its own inherent contradictions, gave rise to repeated and increasingly severe crises which would intensify the class struggle to the point of revolution—revolution, like the eventual triumph of Socialism, being inevitable and resulting equally from the operation of an 'iron law of history'. This theory, which Marx had first outlined in the *Communist Manifesto*, provided the basis for the Erfurt Programme of 1891.[2]

But had the development of capitalism, in the following half-century, confirmed Marx's theories? This was the question which Bernstein posed. He showed that Marx's prediction about the impoverishment of the working class had been falsified by the continuing rise in their standard of living, and that his theory of the inevitable collapse of capitalism was apparently falsified by its continuing expansion and strength. He showed that capitalism had given rise to a new middle class, and displayed an increasing complexity in its social structure, in contrast to Marx's assumption of the polarization of society around two classes, the *bourgeoisie* and the proletariat.[3] From these tendencies, Bernstein

1. *Victor Adlers Briefwechsel*, p. 260.
2. Marx condensed the final conclusions resulting from his analysis in the following terms in *Das Kapital* (Moscow, 1954), vol. I, ch. 32: 'As soon as this process of transformation has sufficiently decomposed the old society from top to bottom, as soon as the labourers are turned into proletarians, their means of labour into capital, as soon as the capitalist mode of production stands on its own feet, then the further socialization of labour . . . takes a new form. That which is now to be expropriated is no longer the labourer working for himself, but the capitalist exploiting many labourers. This expropriation is accomplished by the action of the imminent laws of capitalistic production itself, by the centralization of capital. One capitalist always kills many. Hand in hand with this centralization, or this expropriation of many capitalists by few, develops, on an ever-extending scale, the co-operative form of the labour-process. . . . Along with the constantly diminishing number of the magnates of capital, who usurp and monopolize all advantages of this process of transformation, grows the mass of misery, oppression, slavery, degradation, exploitation; but with this too grows the revolt of the working class, a class always increasing in numbers, and disciplined, united, organized by the very mechanism of the process of capitalist production itself. The monopoly of capital becomes a fetter upon the mode of production, which has sprung up and flourished along with and under it. Centralization of the means of production and socialization of labour at last reach a point where they become incompatible with their capitalist integument. This integument is burst asunder. The knell of capitalist private property sounds. The expropriators are expropriated' (pp. 762–3).
3. On the polarization of society around two classes, the Erfurt Programme stated: 'The number of proletarians is increasing all the time, the army of redundant

drew the conclusion that economic and social development tended to modify class conflicts. In fact, he insisted, there was no sign of a revolutionary situation or an early collapse of *bourgeois* society. Therefore it would be a mistake to persist in preaching a doctrine of revolution and to base the party's tactics on an assumption of imminent catastrophe.[1]

Moreover, Bernstein claimed that the revolutionary aims and language which the party used were in conflict with its actual policy of struggle for social reform, labour legislation and democratic rights. What was worse, the revolutionary ideology alienated whole strata of the middle class and peasantry which the party could win as allies in its fight for social and political reform. The party's influence, he wrote, 'would be far greater than it is today, if Social Democracy could find the courage to free itself from outmoded phraseology and strive to appear as what in fact it now is, a Democratic Socialist party of reform'.[2]

Bernstein developed his criticism a good deal further. He questioned the Marxist theory of Socialism as an imminent 'economic necessity', a theory from which Socialists derived their confidence in inevitable victory. Bernstein, however, conceived Socialism as rather an aim for which the idealism of the worker would lead him to strive, a legitimate moral and cultural objective but in no sense an objective historical necessity. Moreover, Socialism was merely the ultimate aim. Much more important was the movement towards this aim, the Socialist transformation of *bourgeois* society through democratic political reform, by means of which capitalism would develop, in stages, towards Socialism. Bernstein wrote: 'What is generally referred to as the ultimate aim of Socialism means nothing to me; it is the movement itself which means

workers is swelling, the difference between the exploiters and the exploited are becoming ever sharper, the class struggle between the proletariat and the *bourgeoisie* is growing more embittered; it divides modern society into two hostile camps, and it is the common hallmark of all industrial countries.'

1. Bebel had already attacked this view in 1882 in a discussion with Ignaz Auer. He wrote in a letter to Auer: 'The difference does not lie in whether a revolution will start in the next five years. One might discuss this, but it would hardly give rise to a split, and it would be foolish to make it into the cause of a split. The real difference lies rather in the entire conception of the movement as the movement of a class, which has and must have the great aim of transforming the world and can therefore accept no compromise with existing society. If the movement were to reject this standpoint, it would simply perish and subsequently revive in a new form, freed from its present leadership'—August Bebel, *Aus meinem Leben* (Stuttgart, 1910–14), vol. III, p. 226.

2. Eduard Bernstein, *Die Voraussetzungen des Sozialismus und die Aufgaben der Sozialdemokratie* (Stuttgart, 1904), p. 165. The first edition of the book appeared in 1899. Bernstein's critique of Marxism began with a series of articles, 'Probleme des Sozialismus', in *Die Neue Zeit*, 1896–8, which was reprinted in his *Zur Geschichte der Theorie des Sozialismus* (Berlin, 1901), pp. 167–286. For a reply to Bernstein, see Karl Kautsky, *Bernstein und das sozialdemokratische Programm* (Stuttgart, 1899) and Rosa Luxemburg, *Sozialreform oder Revolution?* (Leipzig, 1908).

everything.'[1] With these criticisms Bernstein, as his enemies pointed out in their indictment, had parted company with the basic tenets of German Social Democracy and attacked the very core of its doctrine.

4

The great controversy between Marxists and Revisionists at the Hanover Party Congress ended with a solemn reaffirmation of the party's traditional beliefs, as was inevitable in the circumstances. Marxism had sunk deeper roots in German Social Democracy than in any other country. For the German Social Democrats it was not merely a social and economic theory to which they subscribed, but a body of faith, carrying with it the promise of a new epoch in human history and the vision of a glorious future. Under the banner of Marxism, German Social Democracy had successfully survived the harsh persecutions of the Anti-Socialist Law and had emerged from the period of repression with supporters already running into millions. It seemed therefore ridiculous, at this juncture, to abandon Marxism merely because, here and there, the prophet might prove fallible. Even if Bernstein's critique of the Marxist theory of surplus value had been justified, it could hardly shake the grandiose, novel and exciting picture of the world which emerged from Marx's writings. Who, in any case, apart from a handful of economic specialists, could really assess critically this highly complex analysis of the mechanism by which capital exploited labour? When a man like Victor Adler could admit in a letter to Kautsky: 'I understand nothing of the history of surplus value and, frankly, I don't give a damn,'[2] how much could it mean to the rank and file of the movement? They would agree with William Morris who, when he was asked at a meeting to explain his attitude to Marx and the theory of surplus value, answered with disarming honesty:

> 'Truth to say, my friends, I have tried to understand Marx's theory, but political economy is not in my line, and much of it appears to me to be dreary rubbish. But I am, I hope, a Socialist none the less. It is enough political economy for me to know that the idle class is rich and the working class is poor, and that the rich are rich because they rob the poor. That I know because I see it with my eyes. I need read no books to convince me of it. And it does not matter a rap, it seems to me, whether the robbery is accomplished by what is termed surplus value, or by means of serfdom or open brigandage. The whole system is monstrous and intolerable. . . .'[3]

1. Bernstein, op. cit., p. 169.
2. *Victor Adlers Briefwechsel*, p. 296.
3. John Bruce Glasier, *William Morris and the Early Days of the Socialist Movement* (London, 1921), p. 32.

It was much the same with regard to the interpretation of Marx's theory of impoverishment—the controversy as to how far the working class suffered absolute or relative impoverishment which was sparked off by Bernstein's criticism. It seemed irrelevant since, whatever the theorists might say, the division of capitalist society into property-owners and propertyless, into capitalists and workers, was undeniable, whatever might be happening to the intermediate strata. Moreover, was it really very plausible to claim, with Bernstein, that this division could be bridged through a peaceful process of social and political reform, or that existing society would merge peacefully into the classless society for which Socialists were striving?

Long before Bernstein, the theory that capitalist society would 'grow into' Socialism had been expounded by French, Italian and British Socialists—Malon, Brousse, Millerand and Jaurès in France, Turati in Italy and the Fabians in England. But they were Reformists rather than Revisionists. Jaurès, the leading French Reformist, had occasionally expressed outright criticisms of Marx, but he often tried to defend his Reformist views in terms of Marxist concepts, as when he wrote that 'reforms are not mere palliatives if their tendency is towards facilitating 'revolutionary development', as Marx aptly expressed it. 'Such reforms as those, by undermining the old order, strengthen the forces which will create the new society.' Like the Fabians and the great majority of English Socialists, Jaurès did not see the triumph of Socialism in terms of outright political revolution. Revolution, he said, is a desperate expedient and is used by the forces of history only as a last resort. 'The working class will come to power,' he explained, 'not through a sudden upsurge resulting from political agitation, but by methodical and legal organization under democratic conditions, and by making use of the general right to vote. Our society will gradually develop towards Communism, not through the collapse of capitalism, but by a gradual and inexorable growth of the power of the workers.'[1] What the achievement of Socialism required, therefore, was 'to win over a majority by legitimate means'.[2]

In countries such as Britain and France which enjoyed some form of parliamentary democracy, there was a constitutional basis for theories of evolutionary Socialism, as Engels pointed out in an essay on the draft of the Erfurt Programme in 1891.

> One can envisage [he wrote] that the old society could peacefully grow into the new one in countries where the representatives of the people concentrate all power in themselves, where one can do, constitutionally, whatever one pleases, so long as the majority of the people give their support—in

1. Jean Jaurès, *Theorie und Praxis* (Berlin, 1902).
2. J. Hampden Jackson, *Jean Jaurès* (London, 1943), pp. 68 and 70.

democratic republics such as France and America, or in monarchies like England where the dynasty is powerless against the will of the people. But in Germany [he added], where the Government is almost omnipotent and the Reichstag and other representative bodies for all practical purposes powerless, to proclaim anything like this in Germany would be to remove the fig leaf from absolutism and use it to conceal one's own nakedness.[1]

This was, in essence, the Marxist case against the Revisionists at the Hanover Party Congress. Bismarck had given the German state a constitution which entrenched the political supremacy of the King of Prussia, the aristocratic landowners and the industrial magnates. Germany was not a parliamentary democracy, and the executive power was in the hands, not of a government responsible to the Reichstag, but of an emperor, and more particularly, in the hands of an emperor who was steeped in feudal-absolutist conceptions of government.[2] He regarded the Reichstag as an abomination, and he always considered, as did the landed aristocracy and the army officers, the possibility of abolishing elections to the Reichstag by means of a *coup d'état*.

It seemed hardly conceivable, therefore, that William II, Emperor of Germany and King of Prussia, the army and the wealthy *bourgeoisie* would voluntarily surrender, under working-class pressure, the 'three-class system' of electing the Prussian Parliament, which was such a powerful bulwark of semi-absolutism, against the rising movement of Social Democracy.[3] On the contrary, it seemed only too likely that they

1. Friedrich Engels, 'Zur Kritik des sozialdemokratischen Programmentwurfes 1891', in *Die Neue Zeit*, vol. xx, 1 (1901 2). Marx held also the view, expressed, for example, in his much-quoted speech in Amsterdam on 8 September 1872 after the end of the Hague Congress, that in some countries the working class might be able to achieve its aims by non-violent means. 'We have never asserted,' he said, 'that the roads to our goal are everywhere the same. We know that there must be taken into account the institutions, customs and traditions of the different countries, and we don't deny that there are countries—such as England, America and perhaps Holland—where the workers can attain their goal by peaceful means.' But he also recognized that in most of the countries of the European Continent 'force will be the lever of our revolution'. For the text of the speech, see Meyer, *Der Emanzipationskampf des vierten Standes* (1874), vol. I, pp. 159ff.

2. William II left the German people in no doubt about his attitude to the royal prerogative. At Königsberg, in August 1910, he referred to the coronation of his grandfather, William I, in East Prussia, in the following terms: 'Here my grandfather placed the crown of Prussia on his head by his own right, and clearly pointed out that it had been given him solely by the grace of God, and not by parliaments, popular assemblies or decrees of the people, and that he considered himself to be the chosen instrument of heaven.' He went on to say: 'Considering myself to be the instrument of Him, without regard to any opinions or ideas, I proceed on my way. . . .'

3. The three-class system of election to the Prussian Parliament had been imposed by a *coup d'état* on 30 May 1849. Each class returned the same number of members, and in 1908 the votes were distributed as follows: first class, 293,402; second class, 1,065,240; third class, 6,324,079. In the Prussian parliamentary elections of 1908, the Conservatives won 418,000 votes, but secured 212 seats, while

would use every means in their power to prevent any transition to a parliamentary democracy. In 1914, the Conservative historian, Hans Delbrück, tried to explain to the Social Democrats that 'as far as the human mind can see' there could be no serious possibility of Germany's 'sliding down into a parliamentary democracy'. Power, he explained, rested on strength, and, specifically, on the army, and it was inconceivable that the Prussian Officers' Corps, bound by lifelong tradition to the king, would ever submit to a parliamentary form of government.[1] Only the 'most crushing defeat' in battle, a Sedan on the German side, he wrote, could break the army's resistance. And, in fact, it was broken only when the German army experienced its Sedan at the end of the First World War.

Thus Bernstein was hardly being very realistic in expecting the middle class of the Kaiser's Germany to co-operate with the workers in breaking the Junkers' power—that middle class which, as Liebknecht reminded the Revisionists in the debate, 'could win its own civil liberties from the Junkers neither at the end of the Middle Ages, nor at the end of the eighteenth century, nor again in 1848', and which had capitulated so spinelessly before Bismarck in the constitutional crisis of the 1860s.[2] The vast majority of the German middle class had come to terms, quite satisfactorily, with the existing system. They felt perfectly safe under the German military monarchy, and were in no way disposed

the Social Democrats, with 598,000 votes, won only 7 seats—*Handbuch für sozialdemokratische Wähler* (Berlin, 1911), p. 165.

1. Hans Delbrück, *Regierung und Volkswille* (Berlin, 1914), pp. 136–41. The special role of the German Officers' Corps in the state, as a personal instrument of the monarch, was again stressed in the Reichstag (29 January 1910) by the War Minister, von Heeringen, when he said: 'That an officer occupies a completely different position is clear from the fact that an officer does not take his oath of allegiance to the constitution but solely to the supreme war-lord. . . .' (*Handbuch*, op. cit., p. 156). In a revealing examination of the role of the army, Hugo Preuss showed that it formed 'an extra-territorial enclave of the old order; it has its own system of State law, quite outside the civil code. . . . The boast of the Junkers that a lieutenant and twelve men would be quite sufficient to disperse the Reichstag, therefore was considered very wicked, because it stated, crudely and briefly, exactly what the position was'—Hugo Preuss, *Das deutsche Volk und die Politik* (Jena, 1915), p. 65.

2. *Protokoll*, op. cit., p. 155. The Social Democrats attempted, in fact, to come to an agreement with the Liberals against the Junkers in the elections to the Prussian Parliament in 1903. They met with a refusal. 'It was quite impossible,' wrote Delbrück, 'to bring about any co-operation with the Liberals and the Socialists even in a single constituency; not only did the Liberals forgo the gains which such an alliance would have secured them, they even preferred to let the right-wing Conservatives take all the three seats of Brelau to an agreement with the Socialists which would have secured them one seat'—Hans Delbrück, 'Das Wahlergebnis', in *Preussische Jahrbücher* (October 1903), quoted in Susanne Miller, *Das Problem der Freiheit im Sozialismus* (Frankfurt am Main, 1964), p. 217. The book contains a well-documented analysis of the controversy between Revisionism and Marxism.

to unite with the working class to dismantle the dams which held the Socialist flood—the 'three-class' electoral system and the royal prerogative.[1]

Bernstein had argued that, since Marx's theory of mass pauperization was wrong, the theory that class conflicts would necessarily grow more intense which was derived from it, and the related theory of the catastrophic overthrow of capitalism, must also be false. But he did not take into account the possibility of a social catastrophe arising not out of the struggle between capital and labour, but from a world conflict of rival imperialist powers or, internally, as Bebel insisted, from an attempt by the ruling class to deprive the workers of the hard-earned democratic rights by denying them political equality.

Bebel's reasoning was based on historical experience. In Germany the ruling class had always responded to the growth of Social Democracy with brute force. First, the Anti-Socialist Law had kept Socialism under restraint for twelve years, from 1878 to 1890. Next, in 1894, a new Anti-Socialist Law was proposed in the interests of 'the struggle against subversion'. Then, in 1897, the Parliament of Saxony abolished the equal franchise. Two years later, Major-General von Boguslawski, a leader of the Junkers and of the Prussian Officers' Corps, proposed a *coup d'état* to secure the deportation of the Social Democratic leaders and the abolition of the secret ballot in parliamentary elections. Finally, in 1898, a year before the Hanover Party Congress, the Emperor William proposed a new penal law which would make 'incitement to strike' a criminal offence. Social Democracy lived under a permanent and very real threat of forcible repression.[2]

1. Even the liberal wing of the German *bourgeoisie*, which was politically closest to Social Democracy, believed the royal prerogative to be a necessary safeguard against Socialist legislation. In an article significantly entitled 'Das Allgemeine Wahlrecht ein königliches Recht' ('Universal Suffrage a Royal Prerogative'), in the *Hessische Landeszeitung*, XXIII, no. 25 (1907), Martin Rade defended the system of electing the Reichstag, but solely because 'it is only one link in our constitution'. 'Next above the Reichstag stands the Bundesrat [Federal Council],' he declared, 'and not even the smallest piece of legislation can become effective without the approval of the Chancellor, the Emperor and the Princes. . . . It is therefore laid down that, despite our system of universal suffrage, the trees cannot grow until they reach the heavens. And it is good that we have both bodies in our legislative system.' (Quoted in Robert Michels, *Zur Soziologie des Parteiwesens in der modernen Demokratie* (Leipzig, 1925), 2nd ed., p. 14.) For an analysis of the trends in German middle-class thought in the struggle for parliamentary democracy, see Arthur Rosenberg, *Entstehung und Geschichte der Weimarer Republik* (Frankfurt am Main, 1955), ch. 2.

2. When, during the international tension produced by the Moroccan crisis in 1905, the German government had to consider the possibility of war, William II wrote to the Imperial Chancellor Prince Bernhard von Bülow on 31 December 1905: '. . . I cannot dispense with a single man at a moment when the Social Democracy preaches insurrection. We have first to shoot and behead the Socialists and to render them innocuous—if necessarily by a massacre—and then let's have

In one election after another the Socialists continued to increase their vote, rising from nearly one and a half million in 1890 to more than two million in 1898. One day—and it seemed that it might be close at hand—they would secure a majority in the Reichstag; in which case it seemed only too likely that the government would then 'dissolve Parliament with one lieutenant and twelve men' and summarily abolish the democratically elected Reichstag. Bebel had reason to tell the party congress that: 'Since they are always threatening to resort to a *coup d'état*, and to abolish our existing rights, instead of extending them, I, as a thinking person, can only say: If this sort of thing goes on we have every reason to expect a catastrophe.' And he added: 'The evidence of history is for, not against, the theory of catastrophe.'[1]

A majority of the party was convinced that the German ruling class would not, in fact, permit the workers to use their constitutional rights to achieve power peacefully, without first resorting to a *coup* to destroy those rights and force the workers to fight for power.

> I do not believe [wrote Karl Kautsky in 1904] that they will allow Social Democracy to develop indefinitely along legal lines. . . . The more it increases its political power, the more certain it is that its adversaries will overthrow the constitution, and replace it with a régime in which the workers are violently oppressed, their organizations broken up by force—a régime based on brute force which will require the most vigorous counter-measures.[2]

The party was convinced that some such catastrophe was inevitable and that it would culminate in revolution. Its members were also convinced that the workers would emerge victorious from the revolution, since they believed, with every fibre of their beings, that Socialism was a 'historical necessity'.

It is hard to see what the party would have gained if it had renounced this belief, abandoned its Marxism, disavowed the class struggle, repudiated revolution and followed Bernstein in declaring itself a 'party of Democratic Socialist reform'—a party for which 'the movement is everything, the aim nothing'. It is not even likely that, by thus compromising its ideology and tactics, it would have gained more in the way of social reform for the working class, and it would certainly have done nothing to extend democratic rights. Whatever language the party might choose to speak, Prussia would not have altered her electoral

war! But not before and not *a tempo*!' The letter was published by *Berliner Tagblatt* (14 October 1928), quoted in Karl Anders, *Die ersten hundert Jahre* (Hanover, 1963), p. 27.

1. *Protokoll*, op. cit., pp. 231–2.

2. Karl Kautsky, 'Allerhand Revolutionäres', in *Die Neue Zeit*, vol. XXIII (1904), reprinted in his book, *Der Politische Massenstreik* (Berlin, 1914), pp. 81 and 83.

system, and Germany would not have turned herself into a parliamentary democracy on the British pattern. But, by abandoning the faith in its great historical mission which Marxism gave to the working class, the roots of enthusiasm, which were the source of so much vitality in the Social Democratic movement, would surely have withered. Moreover, such 'loss of faith' would undoubtedly have destroyed the unity of the party and weakened the working class to a disastrous extent.

The key to the attitude of the party's majority in its attack on Revisionism can be found in a remark by Liebknecht which was quoted by a speaker at the Hanover Congress. In a pamphlet criticizing Bernstein, Liebknecht had written: 'Islam was invincible as long as it believed in itself. . . . But the moment it began to compromise . . . it ceased to be a conquering force.' Liebknecht had gone on to say that Islam could not behave otherwise, since 'it was not the true, world-saving faith'. Socialism, however, was just that, 'and Socialism can neither conquer nor save the world if it ceases to believe in itself'.[1]

This faith was a real source of power for German Social Democracy. Even the Revisionists at the party congress voted—no doubt with mental reservations[2]—for the resolution which stated that the party 'now as ever' based itself on the class struggle, that the 'liberation of the working class can be won only by the working class itself' and that the 'conquest of political power' was 'seen as its historical task'. Consequently, there was no reason for the party 'to change either its principles, its basic demands, its tactics or its name'.

5

The Guesdists had naturally welcomed the decision of the Hanover Congress, since it was in line with their own attitude to the 'Millerand Affair'. The French Party Congress, which met at Ivry in the summer of 1900 immediately before the Congress of the International, stated, in the spirit of the Hanover resolutions, that the party was irreconcilably hostile to the class state and that, consequently, 'combined action with *bourgeois* parties' was permissible only in exceptional circumstances and for a limited period.

The controversy over the participation of Socialists in *bourgeois* governments, which had been precipitated by the 'Millerand Affair', was the subject of a debate at the Congress of the International which

1. *Protokoll*, op. cit., p. 149.
2. According to the advice Ignaz Auer, a respected old leader of the party, gave to Bernstein. 'My dear Ed. [Eduard],' he wrote in a letter to him, 'it would be a mistake to adopt by resolution what you suggest, or even to talk about it; the only possible thing is to do it'—quoted in Heinrich Herkner, *Die Arbeiterfrage* (Berlin, 1922), vol. II, p. 392.

began in Paris about the end of September 1900. The item on the agenda was: 'The conquest of State power and the alliance with *bourgeois* parties.' Two resolutions, which had been considered by a commission, were submitted to Congress—a majority resolution, drafted by Kautsky and supported by Vandervelde, and one from the minority, drawn up by Ferri and Guesde.

Enrico Ferri, who spoke for the minority—a professor of criminal law, and the most eminent student of Cesare Lombroso, who founded the science of criminology—represented the revolutionary wing in the Italian Socialist party and was Turati's rival for the leadership. Filippo Turati had tried, from the day he created the 'Milan Socialist League',[1] to win the Italian workers for the evolutionary conception of Socialism. He advocated an alliance with the Liberal *bourgeois* parties—the Republicans and the Radicals—in election campaigns as well as in campaigns for civil liberties and social reforms. Thanks to such alliances the reactionary Crispi ministry was defeated and the election of June 1900 resulted in a great victory for the left; under universal suffrage the party vote rose from 68,000 in 1897 to 175,000, increasing its parliamentary representation from fifteen to thirty-two. This success for Turati's tactics strengthened the reformist tendency in the party. Its congress, which took place a fortnight before the International assembled, had empowered the constituency organizations to conclude electoral pacts with the left *bourgeois* parties.

Kautsky's resolution followed the line adopted at the Guesdist congress on the question of electoral alliances with *bourgeois* parties. It was not opposed since, as Jaurès reminded the delegates, it only conformed to the tactics already employed by the French Socialists in the fight against the clericals and royalists, the Italian Socialists in the struggle against the reactionary cabinet of Crispi, the Belgian Socialists in the campaign for universal suffrage and the German Socialists against the *lex* Heinze, 'by which they ensured', according to Jaurès, 'that the land of Goethe did not become the land of Attila'.[2]

The argument arose, not over alliances with *bourgeois* parties, but over the participation of Socialists in *bourgeois* governments. The resolution supported by Ferri and Guesde rejected it unconditionally, while Kautsky said that it was 'permissible only as a temporary expedient, adopted in exceptional cases under the force of circumstances'. The national parties would have to decide in each particular case whether circumstances made such a dangerous experiment necessary. The question of whether such circumstances existed was one of tactics, not principle, and Congress had no jurisdiction over the tactics

1. See above, p. 221.
2. *Internationaler Sozialististen-Kongress zu Paris 1900* (Berlin, 1900), p. 20.

of member parties. The resolution was careful to add that 'this dangerous experiment' would be justified only if sanctioned by the party, and if the Socialist Minister obeyed his party's mandate while a member of the government.

In its main introduction, Kautsky's resolution said that in a modern democratic state the workers could not take power by a simple *coup d'état*. Power would come only 'as the culmination of a prolonged and complex task of political and economic organization on the part of the workers, together with its physical and moral regeneration, and the gradual increase in the seats held by the party in local councils and central parliaments'. But, since the conquest of political power was an altogether different process which could not 'take place bit by bit', the entry of a Socialist into a *bourgeois* ministry 'is not to be regarded as a normal way of beginning the conquest of political power'.

As it happened, the participation of Socialists in *bourgeois* governments, which took up so much of the congress's time in 1900, seemed, except for the French party, of largely academic interest. But it soon became relevant in Italy also, when the liberal Prime Minister, Giovanni Giolitti, invited Filippo Turati to join his cabinet in 1903, and Leonido Bissolati in 1911. On both occasions, however, the Socialists concerned felt themselves committed by the decisions of the Paris Congress of the International, and when the Italian party decided against entering the government, Giolitti's invitation was turned down.

A few years later the problem appeared in Scandinavia as a result of the electoral successes of the Danish party in May 1913. The Socialists were now the strongest party in the country, and the king invited their chairman, Thorwald Stauning, to form a government. But the party decided at its congress in 1908 to follow the lead of the International and to refuse participation in a *bourgeois* government. Now, however, the Left—the Socialists, together with the Liberals and Radicals—found themselves in a majority in Parliament, and it became possible to change the electoral law of 1866 against which the Socialists had fought from the beginning. For this limited aim the Socialists were prepared to enter a government of the left, but the Liberals refused. The Left-Liberal ministry, formed under Theodor Zahle, now found itself dependent on the Socialists for its majority, and the party was able to force through its reforms while remaining outside the government.

In Sweden, the party decided, in the constitutional crisis of 1914, to join the government. Its congress in 1911 had, in accordance with the International's decision, approved participation in the government only in the case of an acute and exceptional crisis. In 1914 the king had dismissed the Liberal ministry and appointed a Conservative as Prime Minister, in the face of protests from the Liberal and Socialist majority.

The party decided to join the government in order to defend the rights of Parliament against the royal prerogative.

When the International held its congress in Paris in 1900, however, it had only the experience of Millerand's entry into the French government to consider. The resolution on electoral alliances with *bourgeois* parties was carried by acclamation. When Kautsky's resolution came to be decided, Costa announced his support, in the name of a majority of the Italian delegates. Jaurès also pledged support, in the name of the French Broussists and Independents, while Guesde and Vaillant voted against. The delegations of Russia, Poland and the United States also split their votes, and the resolution was finally carried by twenty-nine votes to nine. Irrespective of size, each national delegation had two votes, with Germany, Britain, Austria, Bohemia, Denmark, Norway, Belgium, Holland, Sweden, Switzerland, Spain, Portugal and Argentina in favour, and Bulgaria and Ireland against.

6

The Paris debate on the tactics to be pursued in the struggle for working-class power was only a prelude to the main battle between the revolutionary and reformist trends in the International. The decisive clash came at the Amsterdam Congress in August 1904. Once again, the initiative came from the Guesdists, who at their congress at Lille in September 1903 had called for a discussion on 'the international rules governing Socialist tactics' at Amsterdam and, specifically, to reach a decision on the resolution which had been adopted by the German Social Democrats at their Dresden Congress.

The German Social Democrats had held a congress at Dresden in August 1903, after winning spectacular successes at the elections in June of that year. They had secured over three million votes, a third of the total poll and an increase of 900,000 compared with 1898. With eighty-one delegates in the Reichstag the party now had to consider to what use it would put its greatly enhanced voting power. The party's Reformist wing, to which the trade unions after some hesitation had begun to adhere, decided that in the light of this experience the party should abandon its hostility to the existing state and use its new power to win social and political reforms by parliamentary means. Bernstein had returned to Germany in 1901 after the expiry of the warrant for his arrest, and after living in exile for twenty years. He had been elected to the Reichstag in the following year, and he now proposed that the party should strengthen its influence by demanding that one of its members should become vice-president of the Reichstag, to which it was fully entitled by its numerical strength.

The question of a Social Democratic vice-president, however, was linked with another question which touched the pride of party members. As representatives of the Reichstag, the president and vice-president were equally entitled to attend formal state functions, to some of which they would be officially invited by the Head of State. The Head of State, however, was Kaiser Wilhelm II, who did nothing to conceal his utter loathing and contempt for the Social Democrats, who spoke of them publicly as disaffected subjects deserving punishment and who was always threatening to have them fired on by his soldiers.[1] Bernstein's proposal, therefore, would commit the party to observing court etiquette and involve it in a public display of deference to this crowned Junker who acted as though Germany were his estate and the workers his farm-hands. Moreover, it would expose the party to the risk of public insult from this unpredictable, not to say unstable, autocrat.

Bernstein's proposal, which was supported by Vollmar and his group, was rejected with disgust at party meetings and in most of the party Press.[2] However, the fact that it could be put forward at all was an indication of the growing strength of revisionism in the party, and the whole issue was once again thrown open to debate at the Dresden Congress.

In the electoral successes the Revisionists saw a vindication of the Reformist philosophy which they were pressing on the party. It was the struggle for social and political reforms, they claimed, which had secured hundreds of thousands of new votes, and the more the party could concentrate on specific reforms, free from ideological restraints of Marxism, the more they would succeed in winning over a still greater part of the population.

In the debate, Bebel predicted that if the party were to devote itself exclusively to a struggle for reforms it would be 'beating its head against

1. 'The Republicans are revolutionaries by nature, and are therefore treated as people who deserve shooting and hanging,' wrote Wilhelm II in a letter to Tsar Nicholas II at the end of 1895. 'For us Christian Kings and Emperors it has been allocated as a duty from on High to uphold the principles of Divine Grace'—quoted in Emil Ludwig, *Wilhelm der Zweite* (Berlin, 1926), pp. 175–6. In a speech to his troops on the anniversary of Sedan in 1895, he referred to the Social Democrats as 'a rabble, unworthy of the name of Germans', and called for a struggle 'against this treasonable rabble and to rid ourselves finally of these elements'. In a speech at the swearing-in of guards recruits on 23 November 1891, he said, after referring to the 'internal enemy': 'Lack of faith and demoralization are more than ever raising their heads in the Fatherland, and it is possible that you will be called upon to shoot and bayonet your own relatives, brothers and even parents. . . .' (*Handbuch*, op. cit., p. 25).

2. After the great election victory of 1912, in which the party won 4,250,000 votes, or more than a third of all votes cast, the members decided, nevertheless, to stake a claim for the parliamentary office, and nominated Philipp Scheidemann for the post of vice-president. He was elected, but refused a summons to Court and resigned a few weeks later.

a wall'. The Socialists, of course, had always fought tenaciously for even the smallest concession to the working class and also, whenever it seemed expedient, co-operated with a section of the *bourgeoisie*—notably in second ballots or, in the Reichstag, in voting on certain pieces of legislation. The essential contrast between Marxists and Revisionists was not over the need to struggle for reforms, which was undisputed, but over the spirit in which this was done. Over and above the tedious detail of day-to-day politics, Bebel insisted, the party must not lose sight of its ultimate aim, its historic mission which gave purpose and dignity to its existence. In this lay the essential difference between the Social Democrats and all other parties, and since the party pointed to the future, it embodied in itself the values of the future and in this spirit rallied ever-increasing numbers round its standard. It was unthinkable that the party should abandon its own roots or, to change the metaphor, abandon the path that was manifestly leading it to the heights.

The congress rejected Bernstein's proposal almost unanimously. By 288 votes to 11, it adopted a resolution condemning 'the revisionist attempt to change our policy, which has been gloriously vindicated in every trial, and to replace our struggle to conquer political power by vanquishing the enemy by a policy of acquiescence in the existing social order'. Such an approach, the resolution continued, would change the party from one working for a speedy transformation of a *bourgeois* into a Socialist society, which was, therefore, 'in the best sense of the term, revolutionary', into one which limited itself to tepid reforms within the framework of capitalism. The resolution declared that the party repudiated all responsibility for political and economic conditions arising out of the capitalist mode of production, and hence rejected all methods designed to maintain the power of the existing ruling class. The resolution concluded by reaffirming what Kautsky had successfully put to the Paris Congress of the International, the party's refusal to 'participate in the government of a capitalist society'.[1]

7

It was this which the Guesdists submitted to the Amsterdam Congress of the International. The lines which the Dresden Congress had laid down for the German Social Democrats, the Guesdists wished to make binding for the international Socialist movement. But before their resolution could be submitted to the congress commission, Adler and Vandervelde had submitted a proposal of their own, which, while leaving intact the main content of the Dresden decisions, removed all phrases

1. For the debate and full text of the Resolution, see *Protokoll über die Verhandlungen des Parteitages—Dresden, 1903* (Berlin, 1903).

referring to the conflicts in the German party, in particular, to the condemnation of revisionism and reformism.

In the debate, which lasted for four days—three in committee and one in full congress[1]—no objection was made to the Dresden resolution, which was acceptable to all groups, including even the followers of Jaurès. Controversy arose from the attempt by the Guesdists to internationalize the tactics of the German party. This was strongly opposed by the delegates from Belgium, Switzerland, England and, more especially, from the Scandinavian countries—Branting for Sweden, Knudsen for Denmark, Krieger for Norway—since there the Socialists were temporarily allied, as we have seen, to the Left *bourgeois* parties in campaigns for universal suffrage or against Conservative government. The Guesdists, however, were concerned not with the problems of the Scandinavians, but with their own battle with the followers of Jaurès, who had supported *bourgeois* ministries since Millerand's entry into the Waldeck-Rousseau cabinet.

Admittedly, by the time of the Amsterdam Congress, the 'Millerand Affair' had ceased to be relevant, since the Waldeck-Rousseau government had resigned in 1902 and there were no Socialists in the Combes ministry which had replaced it. Nevertheless, the Jaurès group remained the chief bulwark of the new government. Jaurès had originally supported Millerand to save the existence of the Republic when it was threatened by a clerical-Monarchist assault. But with the advent of the Combes ministry, the struggle entered a decisive phase. Originally destined for the priesthood, Émile Combes had become a teacher of theology and had actually taken the first stage of Holy Orders when he abandoned the church, became a doctor and led a movement which had for its main object the separation of church and state. He had been swept to power on a wave of anti-clericalism and formed his government with the intention of breaking finally the secular power of the church in France. In the tense struggle which ensued, the government relied on the votes of the Socialists in Parliament, and the Jaurès group was convinced that it should give the government its full support.

The struggle between church and state had split society in France for more than a century since the revolution of 1789. The church was fighting against the revolution and its values—against freedom of thought, freedom of teaching and democracy itself. In all the revolutions since 1789—in 1830, 1848 and 1871—the influence of the church had been under attack, and the Paris Commune had formally separated church and state. But in each period of counter-revolution the church had

1. For the discussion in the commission and in full Congress, see *Internationaler Sozialisten-Kongress zu Amsterdam 1904* (Berlin, 1904).

regained and even increased its strength.[1] It was, in fact, a formidable political force, the natural ally of the reactionary forces in society and a deadly enemy of the Republic. It was, moreover, an anti-national force, subordinate to the Papal government of Rome.

Republicans were united in opposing all aspects of clerical domination. They were especially concerned to put an end to the church's control over the schools which had been established by the *Loi Falloux* in 1850. This law was characteristic of the counter-revolutionary mentality, which saw the schools as breeding-grounds of radicalism; but under church control they had been transformed into hot-houses of anti-republicanism. A law passed by the Jules Ferry ministry in 1882, which introduced universal and compulsory education in France, had deprived the state primary schools of their religious character. But at the time of the Dreyfus Affair about two million of France's five million children of school age were being taught in Catholic schools. The royalist revolt against the Republic, which was sparked off by the Dreyfus crisis, supplied a reason for new laws against clerical domination. The church had provoked this move by ordering an army of priests, monks and nuns into action against the Republic.[2] In the elections of 1898 the clerical-Monarchist offensive had been repulsed and Waldeck-Rousseau had no hesitation in erecting new legal bulwarks against the church. The congregations—of which there were 3,216—were placed under supervision by a special law on associations, their very existence being subject to government consent, and no congregation had the right to run schools without special authority. Émile Combes, whose government had, as we have seen, the support of Jaurès, carried the fight against clericalism to new lengths. In July 1904 he introduced a law which deprived all congregations of the right to control schools and in the same month broke off relations between the French Republic and the Vatican. In November 1904 he submitted to the Chamber the draft of a law separating church and state, suspending the ecclesiastical budget and confiscating church property. The law was passed in a somewhat modified form by the Chamber in December 1905.

1. Between the beginning of the Second Empire in 1851 and the year 1878, the number of nuns in France increased from 34,000 to 128,000, while the number of monks rose from 3,000 to 32,000. At the time of the Dreyfus crisis, France had 3,216 congregations with a total membership of about 200,000. The wealth of the religious orders amounted to 581 million gold francs—J. P. Bury, *France, 1814–1940* (London, 1954), pp. 161, 199.

2. It was, apart from the Jesuits, the religious order of the Assumptionists in particular which fought in the forefront against the Republic. 'Through its political daily newspaper, *La Croix*, which served as a model for the papers of the same name published in most dioceses . . . it directed a violent campaign against the Freemasons, the Jews, and the republican government'—Ernest Lavisse, *Histoire de la France contemporaine depuis la révolution jusqu'à la paix de 1919* (Paris, 1921), vol. VII, p. 216.

For Jaurès, the Catholic church was 'the strongest arm of political reaction and social slavery', and the struggle against it was a fight for one of the greatest boons to humanity, freedom of thought. He also regarded the struggle as one to safeguard the foundations of the Republic; like Gambetta, the leader of *bourgeois* democracy, and like Blanqui, the leader of revolutionary Communism, Jaurès saw in anti-clericalism, as he told the congress, the prime task of democracy. It was for this reason that he had joined forces with the Combes government and had created a powerful new weapon in the shape of the paper, *L'Humanité*, which he founded in April 1904.

But the Combes administration, like its predecessor under Waldeck-Rousseau, was unquestionably *bourgeois*. Its parliamentary majority consisted of the 'Left bloc', an alliance of the Socialists under Jaurès with the Radical-Socialists and Radicals. Although the Jaurès group did not formally join the ministry, it became a *de facto* part of the government because of its consistent support in the Chamber. But this was quite incompatible with the Dresden resolution, which, as Bebel pointed out, rejected anything in the nature of a 'permanent alliance' with *bourgeois* parties. A number of speakers at the congress, such as Kautsky, Pablo Iglesias, Rosa Luxemburg, Daniel de Leon, Christian Rakovsky and particularly Jules Guesde, backed up their criticisms of the Jaurès group by referring to the Dresden decisions. But the main prosecution statement came from Bebel, with Jaurès summing up for the defence, a brilliant and, in fact, memorable duel, the echoes of which travelled far beyond the walls of the congress hall, a duel which entered into the life of the Socialist movement of all countries.[1]

Bebel began by making it clear that, if the Dresden resolution had become the subject of a debate at a congress of the International, this was in no way the wish or responsibility of the German party. But since it was down for discussion he had no hesitation in supporting it, because it embodied principles of value, not only for German Social Democracy, but for all Socialist parties. This was because the policies rejected by the Dresden resolution were not confined to Germany, but were international, and existed, said Bebel, in Italy, Austria, Belgium, Holland and, above all, in France. Therefore, the German party believed that the tactical line laid down in the Dresden resolution on relations with *bourgeois* parties and governments should be accepted by the Socialist party in France as well as in other countries. On the other hand, Jaurès painted an altogether different picture of the tactics of his group, justifying in terms of their practical results what Bebel had dis-

1. 'A brilliant display of political eloquence, which will remain permanently in the memories of all those privileged to witness it,' wrote Adler in his report of the congress to the *Arbeiter-Zeitung*. See *Victor Adlers Aufsätze . . .*, vol. VII, p. 41.

paraged on grounds of general principle. 'We succeeded in saving,' he told his fellow delegates, 'the Republican constitution of France at a time when a reactionary *coup d'état* was expected at every hour.[1] We have preserved freedom of thought, checked clericalism, strengthened world peace, repelled chauvinism, nationalism and Caesarism.'

Bebel replied to this by asking whether the Republic which had been saved was worth all the sacrifices of the working class. 'Much as we envy you French your new Republic, we are not keen on having our heads bashed in for its sake,' he declared. Monarchy and *bourgeois* republic were merely two different forms of the class state, two different ways of exercising the class rule of the *bourgeoisie*. And Bebel gave many examples of conflicts between capital and labour in which the government of the French Republic, though depending for its existence on Socialist support, always intervened on the side of capital and always employed the armed power of the state against workers on strike. The only significant difference between a republic and a monarchy, he said, was that in the former the class struggle was waged more openly.

Jaurès, in his reply, pointed to some important differences between the republican and monarchist forms of class state, and, specifically, between the French Republic and the German military autocracy. 'You live under an imperial and feudal régime,' he cried to Bebel, 'while we live in a republican democracy. All our public authorities derive their power from the national will and are responsible to it. Universal suffrage is the basis of our political system.'

Bebel did not deny this. Germany, he admitted, was 'predominantly a feudal, police-controlled country; with the exception of Russia and Turkey she has possibly the most reactionary form of government in Europe'. But if there was a real difference between the constitutions of Germany and France, Jaurès argued, might it not follow that the responsibility of the party differed in the two cases, and that a corresponding difference in tactics might be appropriate? 'In Germany the votes of Social Democratic deputies cannot affect the life of a ministry,' he pointed out. 'But in France the Socialists can sometimes decide

1. Subsequent research has confirmed Jaurès's claim that without the co-operation of the Socialists the Republic would not have been able to meet the threat of reaction. In August 1899, a conspiratorial group consisting of Monarchists, Bonapartists and followers of General Boulanger attempted a *coup d'état*. 'If, in 1899, the Socialists had not made possible the formation of a Left-coalition government, the Right would have formed its own coalition. . . . And if Waldeck-Rousseau and his friends had followed delaying tactics in view of the small size of their majority [in the Chamber] and had failed to arrest the August conspirators, purge the general staff and take energetic measures in the next few months to defend the Republic, the reactionaries would have remained strong enough to emerge successfully from the elections of 1902'—Roger Soltau, *French Political Thought in the Nineteenth Century* (London, 1931), ch. XI.

whether a reactionary or a progressive *bourgeois* government exercises power. The question of co-operation between Socialist and *bourgeois* parties, and of support for *bourgeois* governments, has a quite different aspect in Germany when compared with France, a country in which it is perfectly possible for the workers to participate, directly or indirectly, in parliamentary power.'

In the speech in which he claimed international validity for the Dresden resolutions, Bebel had pointedly criticized some of the domestic policies of French Socialists. In reply, Jaurès claimed the right to subject the internal affairs of the German Social Democrats to the same kind of criticism. For the party, as such, he admitted to having considerable respect. It was a party, he said, 'which has given to international Socialism some of its greatest and most profound thinkers. It has also given us the example of a powerful and highly organized body which shrinks from no sacrifice and is unshakeable in the face of all attacks.' Turning to the German delegates he added, pointedly: 'You are indeed a great party. You are the future of Germany, one of the noblest and most glorious parties of civilized, thinking humanity.'

He went on to say, however, that the size and reputation of the party stood in frightening contrast to its lack of political effectiveness. 'If, in Europe and throughout the world, the questions of peace, of political freedom and of the possibility of Socialist advance are now trembling in the balance, this is not through the alleged compromises or the daring innovations of French Socialists who have allied themselves with other democratic forces to safeguard freedom, progress and world peace, but,' he declared (to what the Minutes described as a 'profound stir' in the body of the congress), 'because of the political weakness of German Social Democracy.' In the June elections, the party had won 3,000,000 votes; that was magnificent. But did it not only serve to underline the frightful contrast between the party's apparent power and its real ability to influence events, a contrast, Jaurès added, which seemed to increase with the growth in the party's electoral support?

Jaurès next raised the question of why the German working class was so incapable of influencing its social and political environment. His answer was that neither its own tradition nor the mechanics of the German constitution permitted the party to transform its tremendous voting power into political action. The German workers, he added, were lacking in revolutionary tradition. Their history showed many instances of devotion and self-sacrifice, but not a single example of successful revolutionary activity. There, universal suffrage had not been won on the barricades; it was a privilege granted from above. But while it was unthinkable to take democratic rights from those who had won them by their own efforts, and could easily win them back again, it was only too possible for the powers-that-be to take back what they had granted only by grace and favour. He went on to remind congress that the party had tamely permitted the curtailment of the franchise in 'your red kingdom, your Socialist kingdom of Saxony'.[1]

The other main source of political weakness in German Social Democracy, according to Jaurès, was the country's constitutional structure. 'Even if you had a majority in the Reichstag,' he told the German delegates, 'your country would be the only one in which you—the Socialists—would not be masters despite that majority, because your parliament is only half a parliament. It does not control the executive and hence has no political power. Its decisions are no more than requests, which the real powers in the State can brush aside whenever they feel inclined.'

Bebel's reply revealed the basic contrast in outlook between the Socialists of France and those of Germany. Jaurès had referred to the weakness of German Social Democracy despite its 3,000,000 votes. 'What did Jaurès expect us to do after our victory and our three million votes?' demanded Bebel. 'Should we have mobilized the three millions, marched them to the palace and deposed the king?' This raised a laugh, but hardly explained the reason for the political impotence of the great German party. Of course, Bebel continued, 'For us three millions are not enough. Let us get seven or eight million votes, and then we shall see. But I do not know what we are expected to do in face of a *bourgeois* majority of about eight million.[2] With these words Bebel implied that the strategy of the German Social Democrats was first to gain a majority in the Reichstag and then use it to abolish the 'three-class vote' in Prussia and autocracy in the country as a whole. But was the ruling class going to wait quietly until the Social Democrats won a majority in the

1. Saxony became known as a 'red kingdom' when the Social Democrats won twenty-two out of the twenty-three constituencies in the Reichstag elections of 1903. The equal franchise to the Parliament of Saxony had been abolished in March 1896 and replaced by a 'three-class vote' after the Prussian model. In the succeeding election the Social Democrats lost nearly half the seats they had won in the previous election under equal franchise.

2. Engels approved Bebel's tactics. In his Preface to Marx's *The Class Struggle in France*, which he wrote shortly before his death in 1895, he admiringly recounted the 'astonishing' successes of German Social Democracy in the elections to Parliament and predicted that the party would, by the end of the century, rally, in addition to the workers, the greater part of the lower middle class and the smaller farmers and thus become 'the decisive power in the country'. He regarded the 'main task' of the party to keep up incessantly the momentum in its growth 'until the day of the decision', that is to say, the day of the seizure of power in the state. There is only one threat to the continual increase of the Socialist army, he went on to explain: an armed clash between the working class and the ruling classes on the scale of the blood-letting of the workers in the struggle between the Paris Commune and Versailles. The ruling classes would like to challenge the workers to such a fight. But, he wrote, 'it would be madness to let ourselves be driven into street fighting'—Friedrich Engels, Preface to *The Class Struggle in France* (Berlin, 1951), pp. 17, 25.

Reichstag? Was it not rather more likely that before that happened they would take away the franchise from the working class?

This had been Jaurès' question, and Bebel's reply was: 'Then we shall take the necessary action', implying that the workers would resort to revolution. But in 1793, 1848 and 1870 the French workers had not waited to win a parliamentary majority, but had earned their freedom by revolutionary street fighting. In fact, however, the German Social Democrats (like all the other sections of the International except the Russians) had, from about the turn of the century, acted as a party of parliamentary democracy. They strove by democratic means to win political power through a parliamentary majority, and then use it to effect the 'social revolution' constitutionally and legally. It regarded itself as a revolutionary party because it genuinely intended to abolish the social and economic bases of capitalism and to establish, through Parliament, a Socialist order of society. It recognized the danger that a counter-attack by the ruling class would force it to defend itself by extra-parliamentary means. But the idea of seizing power in the state by violent revolution no longer formed part of its ideology.

The debate had been conducted throughout, as reported by Vandervelde, 'in a spirit of principled discussion, far removed from any sign of petty personal animosities'. But one remark of Bebel's caused a furore among the French delegates. Stung by Jaurès's reminder that the German workers had not won their right to vote on the barricades but had received it as a gift from above, Bebel replied that the French workers had not established the Third Republic by their own efforts. 'You received your Republic,' he shouted to the French delegation, 'from your enemy, Bismarck, when, after Sedan, he dragged Napoleon III to the Wilhelmshöhe.' The French were visibly shocked—could Bebel really have forgotten the struggles of the Paris Commune?

Before the vote on the resolution was taken, Anseele appealed to the delegates from countries where the party was still weak, such as Russia, Poland, Bulgaria, Spain and Japan, to abstain from voting on a question which was of relevance only to parties with substantial responsibility. The resolution submitted by Adler and Vandervelde, which summarized, except for the explicit condemnation of Reformism, the main tactical principles laid down in the Dresden resolution, was lost, with twenty-one delegates voting each way. Anseele's appeal had had no effect whatever. Those voting for the resolution, with two votes each, were Britain, Australia-Canada-South Africa, Belgium, Austria, Argentina, Denmark, Holland, Sweden and Switzerland, with one vote from France, Norway and Poland. Against were the two votes each from Germany, Bulgaria, Bohemia, Spain, U.S.A., Hungary, Italy, Japan and Russia, together with one vote from France, Norway and Poland.

The Dresden resolution was then carried by twenty-five votes to five, with five abstentions. For it were the two votes from Germany, Austria, Bohemia, Bulgaria, Spain, Hungary, Italy, Poland, Russia, Japan and the U.S.A., plus one vote from Britain, France and Norway. Against were one vote from Britain, France and Norway, plus two votes from the British colonies. Argentina, Belgium, Denmark, Sweden, Holland and Switzerland, with two votes each, abstained entirely.

Jaurès had voted for the compromise Adler-Vandervelde resolution; he had lost and seen the triumph of his rival, Guesde. There remained the problem, vital for both groups, of re-establishing the unity of the movement in France. Congress had appealed, in a special resolution, and with France particularly in mind, for the healing of all splits where these had been allowed to occur. Pierre Renaudel, on behalf of the Jaurès group, and Vaillant, on behalf of the Guesdists and Blanquists, had enthusiastically agreed and pledged their support for reunification. A general congress of all the Socialist groups, meeting in Paris in April 1905, re-established a united party. It took the name of Parti Socialiste and added, on a suggestion from Alexander Bracke and in recognition of its origin, the sub-title Section Française de l'Internationale Ouvrière (S.F.I.O.).

19 · The Debate in the International on the General Strike

1

The idea of a general strike as a method of last resort had long existed inside the Labour movement. It was first proclaimed by the Chartist Convention in February 1839 in a situation of mounting social tension. For nearly twenty years the British workers had fought, in alliance with the middle class, for a wide extension of the franchise, but the fruits of their joint struggle—the Reform Act of 1832—went entirely to the middle class, without the workers securing a single concession. At the height of the campaign, the middle class had employed its own version of the strike weapon by organizing a run on the banks, and had succeeded brilliantly. In contrast, the working class, employing the traditional techniques of meetings, demonstrations and petitions to Parliament, had failed completely. From then on the idea of a general strike began to gain ground. From the earliest days of Chartism in the 1830s it was under discussion as a possible means of bringing pressure to bear on the ruling class. When the first Chartist petition, calling for universal male suffrage, with more than 2,283,000 signatures, was rejected by Parliament, a general strike was in fact proclaimed, but the response was feeble. Three years later, when the second Chartist petition, with over 3,300,000 signatures, was also rejected, a strike broke out among hundreds of thousands of workers in the industrial north.[1]

This was the first large-scale political strike in the history of the Labour movement. It broke out spontaneously, with no preconceived plan. Starting at the beginning of August 1842, it lasted for three weeks. The financial reserves of the unions were too meagre to support the strikers and hunger forced them back to the mines and factories.

1. At the time of the Chartist petition of 1842, the population was under nineteen million, of whom eight million lived in towns. The 3,300,000 signatures represented over half of the adult urban population.

Leading Chartists had foreseen the outcome. Some of them, for this reason, had spoken in Chartist congresses and written in the Chartist Press against calling a strike. Others had supported a strike, in the hope that it would touch off an armed uprising which would usher in the social revolution. Yet others saw in even an unsuccessful strike a useful means of awakening the class consciousness of the masses and so paving the way for revolution. All aspects of the general strike—as an instrument for seizing power, as a lever of insurrection, as a weapon in the fight for immediate political aims, as a 'revolutionary exercise', as a method of 'propaganda by deed'—were, a full half-century before French Socialists discussed such concepts theoretically and Belgian Socialists applied them in practice, discussed by the Chartists. 'There is a decidedly contemporary feel about the situation,' wrote Max Beer in his description of the Chartist debates on the general strike.[1]

2

After the failure of Chartism, the British workers abandoned the idea of the general strike. Its revival in the European Labour movement was the direct outcome of the Anarchist movement in the late 1860s. The question came up at the Brussels Congress of the First International in 1868, as to whether the working class could prevent wars. To the great astonishment of Marx, a resolution introduced by the Belgian and French delegates and passed without a division declared simply: 'Since no society can exist when production is stopped for any length of time . . . it is therefore sufficient to cease work for a war to be made impossible.' It called on the workers, therefore, 'to cease work in the event of war breaking out in their country'.[2]

By the time of the Second International, the problem was beginning to be seen in its full complexity as one requiring considerable thought. It was raised briefly at the Inaugural Congress in Paris in 1889, when a French delegate wanted to add to the resolution on May Day a rider proclaiming it a day of general strike 'to mark the beginning of the social revolution'. The suggestion came shortly before the end of the congress when detailed discussion was impossible. Only Liebknecht referred to it, claiming that it 'was an impossibility', sincc a gcneral strike required a degree of working-class organization 'unattainable in *bourgeois* society'. After that the proposal was withdrawn.

It was only at the following congress, held in Brussels in 1891, that the International began its first serious debate on the problem of the

1. Max Beer, *Geschichte des Sozialismus in England* (Stuttgart, 1913), p. 262, and the chapters following.
2. See above, p. 135.

general strike. And once again the discussion was subordinated by the wider problem—which came up again and again in the history of the International—of whether it was feasible for the working-class movement to prevent war by its own efforts. On this occasion the debate[1] took place on a motion by Domela Nieuwenhuis, who proposed that 'a threatened declaration of war should be answered by an appeal to the people for a general cessation from work'. Thirteen out of the sixteen national delegations present rejected the general strike as a possible means for avoiding wars, with only the Dutch and a majority of the English and French voting for the resolution.

Meanwhile Belgium had experienced a series of exceedingly widespread strikes among the workers, in 1886, 1887, 1891 and 1893. They were distinctive in being political strikes in support of a demand for universal suffrage. The strikes of 1886 and 1887 were spontaneous explosions, touched off by a campaign in Alfred Defuisseaux's militant paper, *Le Catéchisme du peuple*. Those of 1891 and 1893 took place in response to an appeal by the party, which had approved the general strike as a weapon in the campaign for the franchise at its congress in 1891.[2]

The general strikes in Belgium, particularly that of 1893, showed that they were by no means such 'impossibilities' as Liebknecht had imagined. The workers had succeeded in paralysing the country's economy and blasting open the gates which had hitherto kept them out of Parliament. They had proved conclusively that the general strike was a valuable weapon in the armoury of the working class. In the light of this experience, the representatives of French trade unionism asked for the question of a 'world strike' to be put on the agenda of the International's Zurich Congress in 1893.

The proposal went to a commission of the congress for preliminary discussion. A resolution drafted by Kautsky opposed the idea of a 'world strike' on the grounds of impracticability, 'due to the unevenness of economic development in the various countries'. It stated, however, that a general stoppage called in particular industries 'could in certain conditions be a most effective weapon of political as well as economic struggle'. Owing to the pressure of business, this item was not reached on the agenda. Nevertheless, it was on record that a commission of the congress had recognized the mass strike as a legitimate weapon of political warfare.

The French trade-union leaders could hardly be satisfied with the way in which their proposal had been dealt with at Zurich. They there-

1. For an account of which see below, in Chapter 21, 'The International and the War', pp. 325–8.
2. See above, pp. 209–10.

fore put it down for debate at the next congress, in London, in 1896. While admitting that a world-wide strike seemed impracticable, they argued that this did not apply to a general strike called in a particular country, and they insisted that the question be seriously discussed. They proposed that member parties and unions should be asked to study the question and debate it at the following congress. Once again, however, the proposal, which was passed to a commission, was not reached on the congress agenda. Eugène Guérard protested, on behalf of the French trade unions, against the fact that a question of the greatest importance to French workers—since, he said, they considered the general strike to be 'the most revolutionary weapon' they possessed—had not been considered worthy of debate. And he announced that it would again be put down for discussion at the following congress.

3

The question of the general strike was, indeed, of crucial importance to the French trade-union movement. At one congress after another—at Marseille in 1892, Paris in 1893, Nantes in 1894 and Limoges in 1895—the Fédération Nationale des Syndicats Ouvriers had discussed the general strike and supported it with growing emphasis. For the French unions the general strike was not a weapon for securing political objectives. They rejected all forms of parliamentarism, including the revolutionary Marxist version propounded by the Guesdists. The general strike was for them the lever of social revolution.

Syndicalism—the theory that the workers should wage the class struggle entirely by industrial means—was an expression of disillusionment with politics as a means of solving social problems. France was admittedly a parliamentary democracy, with universal and equal franchise for all adult males. But parliamentary democracy was far from having satisfied the revolutionary hopes of the working class, and in their impatience they rejected parliamentarism in its entirety. To them the struggle of the Socialists for parliamentary power seemed not only useless but harmful, since it diverted energy from the class struggle and so weakened the revolutionary impulses of the workers and demoralized the trade unions. Parliamentary activity, they asserted, led inevitably to corruption and opportunism, while all politics provided a jumping-off ground for chatterers, charlatans and careerists. The workers must rely on their own strength, since only 'direct action' based on industrial organization could free them from capitalist domination.[1] Syndicalism

1. 'Direct action' was elevated by the Syndicalists to the status of a 'moral principle which, in contrast to the tactics of discussion, attempts to reach a basis of common understanding with the powers-that-be and the representative system, and has the power of raising the standard of life of the worker in addition to

shared with the Anarchists the view that the power of the state must not be seized, but destroyed. What would follow would be, not a Socialist state, but a Socialist commonwealth without any state, resting on the organization and activity of the unions.

The conflict between revolutionary Syndicalism and Marxism over parliamentarism, the need for political action and the role of the general strike, had been a feature of French trade-union congresses since 1892. It shook and finally destroyed the unity of the French Labour movement. The breach between the unions and the Socialist party was effected at the Nantes Congress in September 1894. The 'indestructible union' between the Socialist movement and the unions which Jules Guesde thought he had established at the Marseille Congress in 1879 had already disintegrated.

At the Nantes Congress, Jules Guesde had gone down after a bitter struggle against Ferdinand Pelloutier, the intellectual progenitor of Anarcho-Syndicalism. Pelloutier (1876–1901) was of middle-class origin. His father had been a post-office official, his grandfather a lawyer and his great-uncle a baron. While still a young man, he had taken to politics with considerable ardour. Beginning as a radical journalist, he soon joined the Guesdists. Disillusioned, however, by the apparent futility and compromise of parliamentarism, he moved closer to the Anarchist ideology. He saw in the unions the germ cells of the coming Socialist order, and in the general strike the lever of the Socialist revolution. In numerous articles and pamphlets he expounded the character and structure of the Socialist community as he envisaged it—a stateless society based on a federation of producers organized in industrial unions. The theory which emerged from his writings became known as Anarcho-Syndicalism.[1]

In 1894 Pelloutier became secretary of the Fédération Nationale des Bourses de Travail—the national federation of trades councils, originally known as labour relations offices, which gradually became the focal points of the social and political life of the Labour movement. When, a

promoting the emancipation of the entire working class from capitalism and centralized control, by means of the opposite principle of direct self-help'—Erich Mühsam, 'Die direkte Aktion im Befreiungskampfe der Arbeiterschaft', in *Generalstreik*, monthly supplement to the *Freier Arbeiter*, vol. I (October 1905).

1. The social aim of the Syndicalists was formulated at the trade-union congress of 1906, in the famous Charter of Amiens, as follows: 'The trade union, which is today a fighting organization, will in the future be an organization for the production and distribution [of goods] and the basis of social renovation'. See Val R. Lorwin, *The French Labor Movement* (Harvard, 1954), p. 30; see also Eugen Naef, *Zur Geschichte des französischen Syndikalismus* (Zurich, 1953); J. Paul Wirz, *Der revolutoinäre Syndikalismus in Frankreich* (Zurich, 1931); also Édouard Dolléans, *Histoire du mouvement ouvrier* (Paris, 1948), vol. II: *1871–1936*. Dolléans had himself been active in the revolutionary Syndicalist movement.

year later, at the Limoges Congress in 1895, the trade unions united to form the Confédération Générale du Travail (C.G.T.), the national federation of trades councils joined the C.G.T. as an autonomous organization, but later merged with it completely at the 1902 congress in Montpellier. The C.G.T. was, from then on, the organized expression of Revolutionary Syndicalism.

In 1898 Victor Griffuelhes (1874–1923) became secretary of the C.G.T. He was a shoemaker by trade, a tough, audacious, class-conscious trade-union leader of Blanquist convictions, who combined Revolutionary Syndicalism with the characteristic Blanquist view of the 'conscious minority' whose mission it was to mobilize and lead the 'dull masses'. His chief colleague was Émile Pouget (1860–1932), who edited the trade-union paper, *La Voix du peuple*. Pouget was a talented journalist of fanatically Anarchist views, and the most important representative of the concept of the 'revolutionary exercise', seeing the C.G.T. as principally a 'training school' for preparation for the revolution.

The trade-union congress at Nantes in 1894 had established a separate committee with its own finances and special powers to prepare for a general strike. According to the Anarcho-Syndicalists the general strike would serve as the final signal for revolution, leading directly to the seizure of factories and mines by the workers and the economic dispossession of the capitalists. Prior to this, however, it was the function of general strikes to train the workers for revolution, to strengthen their class solidarity and militancy—to serve, in fact, as 'revolutionary exercises'. In the 'myth of the general strike', as expounded by Georges Sorel,[1] the Syndicalists discovered a source of inspiration which, they were convinced, could arouse the untapped creative power of the masses. According to Sorel, the motive force of all the great renovating movements in history—the early church, the French Revolution, the Italian Risorgimento—was a social myth, some non-rational concept of perfection which inspired an 'epic state of mind'. The major social changes in history had all resulted from conflicts

1. The general strike is, he stated, 'the myth in which Socialism is wholly comprised, i.e. a body of images capable of evoking instinctively all the sentiments which correspond to the different manifestations of the war undertaken by Socialism against modern society. Strikes have engendered in the proletariat the noblest, deepest, and most moving sentiments that they possess; the general strike groups them all in a co-ordinated picture, and, by bringing them together, gives to each one of them its maximum of intensity; appealing to their painful memories of particular conflicts, it colours with an intense life all the details of the composition presented to consciousness. We thus obtain that intuition of Socialism which language cannot give us with perfect clearness. . . .'—Georges Sorel, *Reflections on Violence*, with an Introduction by Edward A. Shils (Glencoe-Illinois, 1950), p. 145. See also Richard Humphrey, *Georges Sorel. Prophet without Honor* (Cambridge, Mass., 1951).

13 The Amsterdam Congress of the Socialist International, 1904. Rosa Luxemburg is sitting on the platform with Plekhanov on her right and Katayama on her left

14a (above) *Filippo Turati*
14b (above right) *Rosa Luxemburg*
14c (below left) *William Morris*
14d (below right) *Sen Katayama*

between the social values of the myth and those of existing society. In Sorel's doctrine the social myth of the general strike was the essential dynamic which would regenerate society through social revolution and shatter the capitalists and their state. The theory made a deep impression on the minds of the leading Syndicalists.

The Syndicalists had no doubt about the invincible power of the general strike. Despite its enormous physical power, the capitalist state would be unable to withstand such a combined attack by the workers. A detailed illustration of this was provided by Eugène Guérard, speaking in 1896:

> 'In an attempt to defend factories, workshops and warehouses, the army would disperse its forces [he explained]. The mere threat by the workers to destroy railway lines and signalling equipment would compel the government to spread its troops over 39,000 kilometres of the French railway system. An army of 300,000 men defending 39 million metres of railway track would mean one man to every 130 metres, with 130 metres separating each man from his neighbour. In these conditions the government would be unable to protect the warehouses and factories. The factories would be left undefended and the revolutionary workers in the towns would have the field to themselves.'[1]

4

As Eugène Guérard had told the London Congress, the French delegation put the question of the general strike on the agenda once again at the Paris Congress in 1900. In the name of the trade-union representatives, the Allemanists and the followers of Jaurès, they moved a resolution requesting Congress to appeal to 'the workers of the whole world to organize for the general strike', which would serve as a 'lever' for 'exerting pressure on capitalist society indispensable for securing the necessary political and economic reforms'. Under suitable conditions the general strike could also be 'used in the service of the revolution'.

The mover of the resolution at the congress was Briand, a friend of Pelloutier. Briand was an enthusiastic advocate of the idea of the general strike. He had submitted a resolution about it to the trade-union congress at Marseille in 1892 and defended it against Guesde at the Nantes Congress in 1894. He did more than anyone else to introduce the idea of the general strike in the International. He saw in the idea, as he told the Paris Congress, the 'form of revolutionary action' for the entire trade-union movement most appropriate to the conditions of working-class struggle against capitalism. He said in Paris, as at Nantes: 'For me the general strike is a technique of revolution, but of a revolution which offers more guarantees than those of the past, a revolution which will not

1. Quoted in Louis Levine (Lorwin), 'The Labour Movement in France', in *Studies in History, Economics and Public Law* (vol. XLVI, 1912), pp. 89–90.

permit individuals to appropriate the fruits of victory, but will make it possible for the proletariat to take hold of the productive resources of society once and for all.'[1] However, most of the delegates at Congress were more sceptical about the success of a general strike. Karl Legien, the main architect of trade unionism in Germany, replying to Briand, said that the first prerequisite for a general strike was a powerful, mass trade-union organization. 'For the *bourgeoisie*,' he declared, 'a general strike by unorganized masses would be a gift; they would suppress it in a few days, if necessary by force of arms, and so destroy the work of decades.' With a certain condescension he added: 'Let our French and Italian comrades achieve the necessary organization and we shall certainly stand by them.'

The resolution down in the name of Briand, Alleman and Jaurès was supported by only one vote each from France, Italy and Russia and by two each from Portugal and Argentina. The majority resolution endorsed the decision of the commission of the London Congress, which had acknowledged 'strikes and boycotts as necessary means of achieving working-class aims' while rejecting the idea of the international general strike. Both congresses, London as well as Paris, avoided a discussion of the national general strike and its significance for the Labour movement.

5

Meanwhile, in a number of countries, such as Belgium, Sweden and Holland, the general strike had become an acute problem, and once again it was Belgium which supplied the impetus. By the general strike of 1893 the Belgian workers had won the right to parliamentary representation. But the struggle had ended in a compromise based on a system of plural voting which ensured that the working-class representatives would always be outnumbered by the clericals. In the struggle for an equal franchise, the Liège Party Congress in April 1901 agreed to employ 'if necessary, the general strike and street fighting'.

Exactly a year later, on 12 April 1902, insurrections broke out in the streets of Belgian towns. They had broken out spontaneously, without any call from the party, as a result of heated parliamentary debates on electoral reform between working-class and clerical representatives. According to Vandervelde, 'the parliamentary agitation was reflected at

1. *Protokoll*, op. cit., p. 32. Briand also presented the case for the general strike at the Amsterdam Congress of the International in 1904. Two years later he was expelled from the party for entering the Clemenceau government in defiance of its decision. In 1910 he became Prime Minister and suppressed a railway strike in the same year. He ordered troops to occupy the railway stations, called up the strikers into the reserve and then forced them back to work under military orders.

stormy meetings in the main towns. When right-wing deputies came home in the evenings from a parliamentary session they were met at the railway stations by hostile crowds. Everywhere workers poured on to the streets.'[1] In bloody clashes, workers exchanged fire with police and *gendarmerie*, whereupon the party called on the workers to stop the fighting and stay away from work.

The government, however, was well-prepared for the clash. It had reinforced its 60,000 garrison troops by calling up several groups of reservists and mobilizing the civil guard. On the evening of 18 April, when it was announced that the Chamber had rejected the electoral reform bill, there were again stormy demonstrations and clashes between workers and members of the armed forces. In Loewen the civil guard opened fire on demonstrators, killing six and wounding many more.

It was now clear that there was no way of continuing the strike which did not involve starting a civil war, and the party's General Council was faced with the stark alternative of preparing for an armed uprising or calling off the strike. In view of the overwhelming superiority of the armed forces at the disposal of the state, the party could not bring itself to call for revolution; but it had also to face the fact that to break off the general strike would be to admit defeat and could well both demoralize the movement and gravely weaken the party itself. On the other hand, it could not risk the unforeseeable hazards of a civil war, especially in view of its own explicit commitment to legal forms of struggle. On 20 April the party issued a simple request to the strikers to go back to work.

There then occurred one of the most surprising developments in the history of social conflict. The withdrawal from a contest which had engaged the most profound emotions of the workers took place in a calm and orderly manner. At the call of the party the workers resumed work in mine and factory with the same discipline they had shown when they had first downed tools. The party had undoubtedly suffered a defeat, but it was not a catastrophe. Contrary to Legien's fears of the consequences of an unsuccessful general strike, the party was not destroyed. On the contrary, the workers tended, if anything, to draw closer to it.

In the following month the Swedish Social Democrats also employed the general strike in a campaign for the franchise, though in an entirely novel way. The strike was not, as in Belgium, permitted to break out spontaneously. Before it was even announced, the main details of the

1. See Jules Messine, *Émile Vandervelde* (Hamburg, 1948), p. 67. See also Émile Vandervelde, 'Die Belgischen Wahlrechtskämpfe 1902', in *Sozialistische Monatshefte* (1902) and *Le Parti ouvrier belge 1885–1925* (Brussels, 1925).

strike, including its termination, were carefully planned. The decision to use the general strike in this way had been decided as early as the Göteborg Congress in 1894. But at that time the party was still weak and there was no central trade-union body until the Lands-Organisation (L.O.) was established in 1898. At the turn of the century, moreover, the Labour movement in the north of Sweden was preoccupied with severe struggles to secure trade-union recognition.

The movement began to turn its attention once again to the struggle for the franchise when, at the beginning of 1902, the government, acting under pressure of persistent agitation by Social Democrats and Liberals, presented a draft reform bill to the Rigsdag (Parliament). This, while increasing the number of those eligible to vote, still excluded a substantial majority of the workers. The party responded by calling mass demonstrations against the draft, while asking the workers to cease work for the three days beginning on 15 May—the day the bill came before the Rigsdag. As a strike it was a complete success. Industry and transport were paralysed for three days. The strike, which was intended to display the strength and solidarity of the working class, fulfilled its purpose admirably. But as a means of bringing pressure on the Conservative majority in the Rigsdag it failed completely. The general strike of 1902, therefore, was merely an episode in the struggle of the Swedish workers for the right to vote under conditions of universal suffrage—a right they were not to obtain for another seven years.

On the other hand, in Holland, an attempt at a general strike in April 1903 not only ended in failure, but caused a considerable set-back to the already divided Socialist movement. It had begun with a spontaneous strike of railway workers at the end of January, in protest against being required to blackleg in a dock strike. The government, unable to compel railwaymen to replace dockers, withdrew the order. But the success was shortlived. The government immediately introduced a draft law to deprive all workers in state employment, including the railwaymen, of the right to strike.

The proposal met with an angry response from the workers. The two parties into which the Dutch movement had split—the Sociaaldemokratisch Partij in Nederland (S.D.P.) and the Sociaaldemokratisch Arbeid Partij (S.D.A.P.)—set up a joint defence committee which threatened to call out the entire working class of Holland in defence of the freedom to strike. Troelstra, president of the S.D.A.P., who had proposed the resolution at a meeting of the defence committee, called on the workers, in *Het Volk*, to 'make all preparations to respond at once to the appeal of the defence committee with a tremendous strike, which will demonstrate to the world that the Dutch workers would rather go down fighting than be trampled on'. The government seemed unmoved by the threat and the strike was duly called. There followed the most severe clashes between the workers and the state machine in Dutch history. The defence committee was prepared neither to push matters to extremes nor to call off the strike, and the movement accordingly fell to pieces. The defeat worsened and embittered relations between the two Socialist parties and represented a disastrous set-back for the trade-union movement.

6

Experiences in Belgium and Holland had shown the general strike to be a double-edged weapon. In both countries the leadership had soon been faced with the dilemma of either developing the struggle to the point of insurrection or retreating. However, in neither Belgium nor Holland had the leaders of the strike seriously contemplated resorting to illegality, much less calling an armed uprising. But if the fight were to be waged within limits imposed by the law, the government, with its tremendous apparatus of power, was much better placed than the workers. In both cases, therefore, it was the working class and not the government which had withdrawn. From all of which the conclusion was readily drawn that the general strike should be regarded as the *ultima ratio*, the final resort in a crisis, the most extreme measure open to the workers in a pre-revolutionary situation. It should not, therefore, be attempted unless the working class was prepared for a fight to the finish.

These were no doubt the considerations in the minds of most delegations when the general strike again came up for debate at the Amsterdam Congress of the International in August 1904, although the question of legality was not explicitly broached. The Allemanists and the Jaurès group had put the question on the agenda. Jaurès himself had doubts about the value of a general strike. But he was mainly concerned to secure as great as possible a degree of unity between the party and the unions, and since the general strike played such a prominent part in the thinking of the unions in France he voted in favour of a resolution which requested the parties of the International to study 'the rational and systematic organization of the general strike'.

The resolution was formally proposed, both in commission and in open congress, by Briand, who argued that the question of the general strike was simply one of tactics. If Congress approved the tactics of the class struggle, it must necessarily approve the general strike, which was merely, so far as the workers were concerned, its ultimate expression. The general strike was a means of exerting pressure on capitalism to concede reforms, and a means by which the workers could fight when deprived of political rights. 'There is talk of a threat to take away universal suffrage in Germany,' Briand declared. 'In that case what weapon would remain to the working class other than the general strike?'

The resolution supported by a majority of the commission and presented to Congress by Henriette Roland-Holst drew a distinction between general strikes and mass strikes. A 'complete general strike' she believed to be impracticable, 'since it makes the existence of everyone, including the proletariat, impossible'. However, the commission considered a mass political strike to be advisable under certain conditions, but only as 'a last resort, in order to secure important social changes or to resist reactionary attempts on the rights of the working class'. The resolution warned the workers against 'propaganda for the general strike emanating from Anarchist sources' which was intended to 'divert the workers from conducting limited though important struggles by means of trade-union, political or co-operative action'. It appealed to the workers 'to strengthen their unity and attain positions of power in the class struggle through developing their organizations', since it was on organization that the success of a mass political strike would depend, should that be 'found necessary and expedient'. The contorted prose of the resolution hardly served to conceal the doubts felt in many parties about the value of the mass political strike, and their extreme reluctance to think through the implications of such a course to their logical conclusion.

The most emphatic repudiation of the idea of a general strike came from the Dutch and German parties. Experience, so far, declared Vliegen, is strongly against a general strike. 'It is not a means—let alone the only possible means—for securing the aims of the working class.' And Robert Schmidt said, to the enthusiastic applause of the German delegation, that for the German unions with their 900,000 members the question of a general strike was not even 'discussible'. 'The struggle of the proletariat for political and economic power,' he added, 'will not be determined by a general strike but by steady, uninterrupted work in all spheres of political and economic life.'

Support for Briand's resolution came from Jaurès's group and the Allemanists. The French Guesdists voted against, but the Russian Social Revolutionaries and the delegates from Switzerland and Japan also voted in favour. The resolution submitted by the commission was adopted by thirty-six votes to four.

7

No sooner, however, had the Amsterdam Congress risen than Italy experienced a mass political strike which was fiercer and more extensive than any previously known in her decidedly turbulent history. The impetus came from Sicily, where strikes had touched off unrest in many parts of the island, while in Buggaru and Castelluzzi police opened fire on mass demonstrations. When, on 15 September 1904, news of the bloodshed reached the north, the workers of Milan left the factories to demonstrate in the streets. Genoa, Monza, Rome and Leghorn were soon in the grip of strikes and the movement spread like a prairie fire across the whole country.

The signal for strike action had come from the Syndicalist wing of the party, led by Arturo Labriola, and immediately it broke out, the party's executive issued a manifesto declaring that the strike was the concern of the entire working class. The strike movement, however, had not been planned and it remained completely unorganized. An eye-witness, Oda Oldberg,[1] reported that the movement was 'so chaotic yet so overwhelming that it struck all those of us who lived through it as an elemental force which swept over us like an avalanche'. Both in extent and intensity this was indeed a 'total general strike', the first complete general strike in the history of the working-class struggle. It was a spontaneous explosion of class anger against gross injustice, a protest against the misuse of the state's armed forces in an industrial dispute. The workers had not forgotten the famous 'four days of Milan' in 1898, when the government of Antonio di Rudini had called out the army to destroy a mass demonstration against higher bread prices. Nearly 100 were killed and about 500 wounded when the troops opened fire. The working class in Milan was therefore the first to respond to the shootings in Sicily with sympathetic strike action. There was no immediate objective, apart from the implicit decision to stop future armed intervention by governments in industrial disputes. The Liberal Premier, Giolitti, was quick to promise this, as he had been emphatic in refusing to call out the troops,[2] and the strikers returned to work after a few days.

The Italian general strike of September 1904 was mainly a strike of unorganized workers. In spite of this it did not collapse, as Legien was convinced that such strikes must do. The question now was—what exactly had been achieved? The Syndicalists were confident that, in Arturo Labriola's phrase, it 'had proved to the masses that five minutes' direct action was worth as much as four years of empty parliamentary chatter'.[3] The Marxist leadership, led by Constantino Lazzari, saw the main

1. *Die Neue Zeit*, vol. XXIII, Part I (1904).

2. Believing that the strike would weaken the popularity of the Socialists, Giolitti dissolved Parliament soon after the outbreak. The party did, in fact, suffer a set-back in the new elections, with its representation reduced from thirty-three to twenty-seven.

3. See William Salomone, *Italian Democracy in the Making* (Philadelphia, 1945) p. 51.

achievement of the strike as being in its demonstration that, as Oda Oldberg wrote, 'the proletariat . . . in defence of its rights . . . could at any time call out the workers from the factories, mines and building-sites'.

However, the characteristic feature of the Italian general strike was the spontaneous reaction of the masses. They had not been 'called' away from work—they had left of their own accord in a mood of profound resentment. The strike had not been declared, it had erupted as an expression of accumulated anger. It showed that the workers collectively—as individually—were subject to the law of action and reaction. They were 'brought to the boil and transformed into flood and movement only by actual events', as Lassalle had remarked in a letter to Marx in 1854 when, in a period of world-wide reaction, the workers had succumbed to a mood of profound apathy.

8

The law of action and reaction was manifested in spectacular fashion in the Russian revolution of 1905. This broke out a mere five months after the end of the Amsterdam Congress, at which Vliegen, for the Dutch delegation, had rejected out of hand the idea of a general strike, while Robert Schmidt insisted that the question was 'simply not discussible' by the German trade unions. Now Russia presented the imposing spectacle of 'Bloody Sunday', where things were truly 'brought to the boil' with the frightful slaughter of 22 January. After the massacre of unarmed workers, the muted anger of leaderless and unorganized masses built up into tremendous waves which dashed themselves again and again in the form of mass strikes against the structure of Tsarism, until that very stronghold of absolutism began to crumble under the pressure.[1]

It was an unforgettable experience, this first revolutionary uprising of the workers since the Paris Commune of 1871, and, for many contemporaries, the first experience of revolution. To some it seemed that they were living through a turning-point in world history and witnessing the start of a new epoch of European revolutions.[2]

1. A masterly account of the psychological processes at work can be found in Leon Trotsky, *Die russische Revolution 1905* (Berlin, 1923), pp. 63–96. For an analysis of the strikes in Russia, see Rosa Luxemburg, *Massenstreik, Partei und Gewerkschaften* (Hamburg, 1906).

2. Characteristic of the impact of the Russian revolution on the minds of European Socialists is the response to it of Victor Adler, one of the most cool-headed leaders of the International. In a letter to Bebel on 26 December 1904, a week after the outbreak of the revolution, he wrote: '. . . to me, the centre of gravity lies now in Russia. I simply burn of tension, and I believe that there our destiny will be, if not decided, in any case decisively influenced. . . .'—*Victor Adler. Briefwechsel mit August Bebel und Karl Kautsky*, op. cit., p. 445.

These developments brought the problem of mass political strikes back on the agenda of European Socialist parties. Of particular importance was the volte-face in the German party in view of its commanding strength and prestige in the International. It was with reluctance that the German delegates had brought themselves, at the Amsterdam Congress, to vote for the resolution which recognized the mass political strike as a legitimate means, in extreme circumstances, of defending working-class rights. The conference which the party held at Bremen, soon after the Amsterdam Congress, had again refused a suggestion that the mass political strike and its relevance to the struggle of German Social Democracy should be put on the agenda for the forthcoming congress. And the Congress of German Trade Unions, meeting in Cologne at the end of May 1905, once again pronounced the general strike 'undiscussible' and 'hence all attempts to commit us to a particular line of tactics, through propagating the political mass strike, are objectionable'. Theodor Bömelberg, who supported the resolution in the name of the General Council, deprecated the Amsterdam decision to recognize the political mass strike in certain circumstances, declaring: 'We must emphatically put an end to this discussion in the German trade-union movement.'[1]

Now it was impossible to stamp on further discussion. The excitement which spread from Russia to Germany and to the movement in all countries[2] inspired renewed debates on the problems of the mass

1. Karl Kautsky, *Der politische Massenstreik* (Berlin, 1914), p. 117. The book gives a complete account of the discussion on mass strikes in the German Social Democratic movement. See also Elsbeth Georgi, *Theorie und Praxis des Generalstreiks in der modernen Arbeiterbewegung* (Jena, 1908).

2. Evidence of the profound effect of the Russian revolution can be found in the *Protokoll des Parteitages der Sozialdemokratischen Arbeiter-Partei Österreich-Wien, 1905*. In the course of a speech by Wilhelm Ellenbogen the report describes how: 'Comrade Nemec had just handed up a telegram, which had been brought in from the office, to the speaker on the platform. Soon the delegates at the front tables were whispering of "News from Russia". The silence in which Ellenbogen's speech had been heard now gave place to an excited hum of conversation. Ellenbogen suddenly interrupted his speech and began to read the manifesto of the Tsar in a voice trembling with emotion. In no time there was complete silence. But as soon as the first paragraph of the manifesto had been read out, ending with the promise of freedom of the Press and assembly, a deafening cheer broke out in the hall and galleries. "Cheers for the Russian Revolution! Hurrah for the Revolution!" When Ellenbogen resumed reading the telegram the delegates began to stand—it seemed appropriate to stand up on such an historic occasion. The Conference was gripped by an almost religious emotion. As Ellenbogen reached the concluding words of the Tsar's manifesto . . . the delegates instinctively found the appropriate way of expressing their feelings. Suddenly the hall rang with the sound of revolutionary songs. The Czechs and Poles were singing the *Red Flag*, whereupon the Germans responded with the *Marseillaise*. Under the impact of the news the Party Conference decided to call on the workers to down tools on the day Parliament reassembled—28 November—and demonstrate in public meetings for the right to vote. In Vienna 250,000 men and women marched that day along the Ringstrasse

political strike in the German party, its Press, its public meetings and at successive conferences—Jena in 1905, Mannheim in 1906, Magdeburg in 1910 and Jena in 1913.

The problem was essentially whether the German workers could destroy, by legal means, the supremacy of the Junkers which had been maintained over many centuries, making use of the strength of Prussia, her monarchs, armies, bureaucracy, law courts and *bourgeoisie*. The centre of Junker power lay in the methods by which Prussia was ruled and particularly in the three-tier election system on which the entire régime in Germany rested. As long as the Junkers maintained this centre of privilege, there were strict limits to the development of German democracy and working-class power. Until the Prussian Landtag came to be elected by universal suffrage, Junker supremacy would remain untouched. But experience had shown that this was no wall of Jericho, to be thrown down by the blast of trumpets. Up till then, neither speeches, Press campaigns, public meetings nor even street demonstrations had had the slightest effect. The question now posed for the party was whether the political general strike would serve as an effective weapon in the fight for democracy in Prussia.

The debate turned at once on the political implications of a general strike. Bebel was convinced that there was no need for such a strike to develop into a revolution. If it occurred at all it should be regarded 'in every case as a method of peaceful struggle', he declared to the party conference at Mannheim. The majority view, however, voiced by Hilferding, was that if a political general strike were used by the strongest party in Germany against the strongest government and most closely-knit ruling class in the world, this would unquestionably precipitate a decisive struggle for power. 'In Germany,' he declared, 'a general strike, however it starts, must be prepared to meet the most powerful resistance.' In whatever way the party might present the issue—arising, for instance, out of the campaign for electoral reform in Prussia—'the ruling class will inevitably treat it as a question of survival'. The general strike in Germany was therefore a phase in a struggle which would have to be fought through to the finish, or end in disaster for the working class, 'because the enemy would interpret any general strike, however peaceful and legal, as a challenge to its supremacy and as an indication that its own existence was now at stake. It would therefore meet it with every means at its disposal.'[1]

to the Parliament building.' For the influence of the Russian revolution on German Social Democracy, see also the excellent study by Carl E. Schorske, 'German Social Democracy, 1905–1917', in *Harvard Historical Studies*, vol. LXV (1955).

1. Kautsky, op. cit., pp. 161 and 123.

It was this reason—the fact that a political general strike would inevitably become a struggle for the survival of the Socialist movement itself—which made every such discussion the occasion for deep uneasiness in the party and, even more, the trade-union leadership. In the course of half a century the German Labour movement had developed many characteristics of a state-within-a-state. It had won the support of over a third of the electorate. Bebel had become a symbol of the new status of German labour, with a large part of the population regarding him as a kind of 'Counter-Emperor'. He stood at the summit of the largest political party in the world, allied with the world's strongest trade-union movement.[1] Moreover, the German Socialist movement had developed its own elaborate bureaucratic superstructure. Its assets ran into millions, and it controlled a huge number of subsidiary organizations. It owned vast newspapers and publishing houses and great printing works. It had innumerable offices and halls and was often involved in administering building societies and both consumers' and producers' co-operatives. A staff of thousands of secretaries, editors, employees, workers and officials was required to operate this huge Labour movement and administer its manifold enterprises.[2] Together with this enormous growth, the movement had acquired a considerable influence in the state and society. The vast bureaucratic organizations had spawned their own political and trade-union *élites* among the party members, M.P.s, district representatives, local administrators and trade-union general secretaries.

The movement, in fact, had developed its own 'apparatus', obeying its own laws of growth and self-preservation, and members came to regard the movement as an end in itself. Such an apparatus, though

1. The following figures show the strength of German trade unionism within the European Labour movement (Tenth International Report of the Trade Union Movement, 1912).

	Total trade-union membership	*International affiliated membership*
Germany	3,317,271	2,553,162
Great Britain	3,023,173	861,482
France	1,064,413	387,000
Italy	860,502	320,912
Austria	649,082	540,662
Belgium	231,805	116,082

2. The free trade unions alone had a combined annual income of 70 million marks, with assets, in 1914, totalling 80 million marks. See Friedrich Stampfer, *Die vierzehn Jahre der ersten deutschen Republik* (Hamburg, 1947), p. 12. The party had sixty-two printing works, and ninety daily papers with a total circulation of 1,465,212; 10,320 people worked in its publishing houses alone. See 'Bericht des Parteivorstandes an den Parteitag zu Jena 1913', in *Protokoll über die Verhandlungen des Parteitages der Sozialdemokratischen Partei Deutschlands* (Berlin, 1913), pp. 28–9.

originally created to serve the needs of the movement, had by this time produced its own vested interests and its own conservative caste of mind. Concern for the movement's safety and its possibilities of normal development had its own effect on the minds of its responsible officials. The Labour movement had originally created its organization to prepare for social revolution, to sap, undermine and eventually destroy the existing class society. But with the growing strength and influence of its organization, the movement had lost its revolutionary dynamic. The stronger the organization, the more it stood to lose in a decisive struggle for state power. Everything which the working class had created through decades of considerable sacrifice could be lost in a few days or weeks of revolutionary conflict. Admittedly, the organization's existence might be threatened on the initiative of the ruling class itself, but in the depths of its heart the movement hoped that this might somehow be avoided. The stronger the party became, the greater was its popular following and the more dazzling were its electoral successes; and the larger its parliamentary representation, the smaller, it seemed to the leadership, was the danger of the rulers provoking a fight. The party leadership, and above all the top leadership in the unions, was especially concerned not to provoke one. It often recalled the warning of Friedrich Engels, in his well-known introduction, written in 1895, to Marx's *Class Struggles in France*, not 'to let ourselves be driven into street fighting'. The growth of the party 'into the decisive power in the land, before which all other powers will have to bow' was, he believed, irresistible. 'We are thriving,' he added, 'far better on legal methods than on illegal methods and revolt. And there is only one means by which the steady rise of the Socialist fighting forces in Germany could be momentarily halted, and even thrown back for some time: a clash on a big scale with the military, a bloodbath like that of 1871 in Paris.'[1] This was precisely what the leadership of the party and the unions feared—a 'clash on a big scale' with the power of the state. Hence their reluctance to give serious thought to the political general strike. German Social Democracy, revolutionary in its social aims, was by no means revolutionary in its methods of struggle.

The idea of the political general strike as an offensive weapon in the struggle for an equal franchise in elections for the government of Prussia, was supported not only by the Marxist Left—Rosa Luxemburg and her group—but also, more surprisingly, by a section of the Revisionists, led by Eduard Bernstein, Friedrich Stampfer and Kurt Eisner. The overwhelming majority of the party rejected this view of the general strike, tending to agree with the 'Marxists of the centre', represented by Bebel and Kautsky, who acknowledged the general strike only as a defensive weapon—'as one of the most effective means of resisting . . . an attack on

1. See above, p. 282.

the general, equal and direct parliamentary suffrage or the right of assembly'—according to a resolution passed by the Jena Party Conference in 1905. It needed all Bebel's moral authority and diplomatic ingenuity to reconcile the unions to even this tepid endorsement of the political general strike.

9

While the Syndicalist wing of the Labour movement in France and Italy saw the general strike as a weapon of revolutionary attack, it was not destined to be used during the period of the Second International. In both countries, as in Germany, official Socialism saw it essentially as a defensive tactic. In Russia, the Social Democratic party still clung to the political general strike as a weapon of revolutionary attack, despite its failure to halt the counter-revolution which followed soon after the successful revolutionary outbreaks of 1905.

In Finland, the Social Democratic party called a general strike in support of its demand for universal suffrage and a free Press. It lasted from 30 October to 6 November 1905, and was called off only when a manifesto by the Tsar (Finland then being an autonomous part of the Russian Empire) promised a Parliament elected by universal suffrage and the ending of Press censorship. While it lasted, the strike had been almost total. The country had been virtually governed by a central strike committee, with sections responsible for the railways, commerce and industry and the police. The new franchise law became effective only after another year (on 1 October 1906), and then only under the threat of a new general strike.[1]

Three more parties resorted to general strikes during the last ten years of the Second International—the Austrian in November 1905, in a one-day demonstration strike for universal suffrage; the Italian in September 1911, in a twenty-four-hour protest strike against the war in Tripoli, and again in June 1914 in a monumental effort to preserve European peace; and the Belgian in April 1913, as part of the campaign against plural voting, which was called off in a few days when the government undertook to revise the constitution.

In Sweden it was the trade unions, not the Social Democratic party,

1. For a detailed account of this struggle for the franchise, see the Report from the Social Democratic party of Finland to the International Socialist Congress at Stuttgart, in *Die Sozialistische Arbeiter-Internationale* (Berlin, 1907), pp. 191–3. In the course of the campaign, the membership of the Party increased from 16,610 organized in 99 branches at the end of 1904, to 45,298 in 177 branches at the end of 1905, and to 85,027 in 937 branches by the end of 1906. See N.R. af Ursin and Karl H. Wiik, 'Die Arbeiterbewegung in Finnland', in *Archiv für die Geschichte des Sozialismus und der Arbeiterbewegung*, ed. Carl Grünberg, vol. XII (1926), p. 46.

which made use of the weapon of the general strike in 1909 in a counter-attack against an offensive of the well-organized big industrialists. A severe economic depression, which had already set in in 1907, brought about widespread unemployment. Wages were cut and industrial relations grew rapidly worse.

The trade unions attempted to resist and strikes flared up in a number of trades. The central organization of the employers demanded that the strikes should be called off and threatened a general lock-out. The unions decided, however, to resist. Instead of waiting to be locked out, they declared a general strike.

The strike was a trial of strength between the working and the capitalist class. It lasted a month. It was supported with considerable contributions by the trade unions in Denmark and Norway and a number of other countries. But at the end of a month funds were running out, and the strike committee was forced to order back to work those groups who had struck in sympathy with those directly involved. But the ultimate defeat was unavoidable since there was no question of turning the strike into a revolution.

The defeat greatly reduced the numerical strength of the party as well as of the trade unions. The party, which of course had put all its resources into the battle, lost half its members, their number decreasing from 112,000 in 1905 to 55,000 in 1910; and the trade unions lost more than 100,000, their membership falling from 186,000 to 80,000.

But the movement soon recovered, and in the first elections under the new Constitution in 1911, the Social Democratic party doubled its representation in the lower chamber, securing the election of 64 Socialists against 101 Liberals plus 65 members of the right-wing parties.

In all these instances of mass struggles, either with political or industrial objectives, the Socialist parties as well as the trade unions involved were anxious to keep the general strike as a purely legal instrument, to keep the struggle strictly within the bounds of legality and to avoid its being suddenly transformed into a revolutionary operation.

While the International was grappling in this way with the role of the general strike in the broader political movement, it was faced simultaneously with the far-reaching problem of the international general strike as a possible means of averting war. We shall return to this in a later chapter.

20 · The Colonial Question in the International

Two basic principles, embedded deeply in the Socialist tradition, governed the attitude of the International towards the colonial question. There was, first, the principle of the basic equality of all peoples and races in the sense that all had an equal right to dignity and respect, to freedom and national independence. There was, secondly, the idea of solidarity between the oppressed of all countries from which the International itself had sprung.

1

The first expression in the European Labour movement of solidarity between the disinherited members of the white and black races appeared in the attitude of the British workers towards the American Civil War of the 1860s. They saw in the war of North against South a war to liberate the Negro people from slavery. They declared overwhelmingly for the North and protested, at public meetings and in the Press, against the plans of the British government to break the blockade on cotton exports from the South, even though the blockade was forcing tens of thousands of Lancashire cotton workers out of employment.[1]

The First International was established in the course of the war a few weeks before Abraham Lincoln, who had become one of the champions of Negro emancipation, was elected President of the U.S.A. for a second term. One of the first things the General Council did was to send an address of congratulations, drawn up by Marx, to Abraham

1. Marx hailed the solidarity of the British workers with the fight against the American slave-owners. The English working class, he wrote, 'has reaped immortal historical honours by its resistance, expressed enthusiastically in mass meeting, against the repeated attempts of the ruling classes at intervention in favour of the American slave-owners, although the continuation of the American Civil War has inflicted frightful misery and deprivation upon a million workers'—*Marx-Engels Werke*, vol. xv, p. 577.

Lincoln, 'the single-minded son of the working class' who was destined 'to lead the country through the matchless struggle for the rescue of an enchained race and the reconstruction of a social world'. The address assured Lincoln of the solidarity of the European workers and their determination to bear 'patiently the hardships imposed upon them by the cotton crisis', since they had 'understood at once . . . that the slaveholders' rebellion was to sound the tocsin for a general holy crusade of property against labour' and that 'the star-spangled banner carried the destiny of their class'.

The American Civil War was, in a sense, a colonial war, since it involved the future of the quasi-colonial institution of slavery. The 'Address of the International Working Men's Association to Abraham Lincoln' can therefore be considered the International's first pronouncement on a colonial problem.

However, the modern colonial policy of the great powers, and the aggressive phase in their struggle for colonial possessions, started only in the last twenty years of the nineteenth century, and the problem of colonialism, therefore, was a matter for the Second International rather than the First. The London Congress of 1896 demanded, in a resolution proposed by George Lansbury, 'the right of all nations to complete sovereignty', and denounced colonialism as an expression of capitalism. 'With whatever pretexts colonial policies may be justified in the name of religion or civilization,' it continued, 'their sole aim is simply to extend the area of capitalist exploitation in the exclusive interests of the capitalist class.'

2

Only a few years after the London Congress, however, the first doubts regarding traditional attitudes to colonialism began to be expressed in a number of Socialist parties. The impetus for this change in attitude was given by Britain's war against the Boer Republics in South Africa, which began in 1899 and dragged on until 1902. To the great majority of Socialists throughout the world this was merely a classic example of a capitalist colonial war, in which the British ruling class sought to turn the rich gold-fields of South Africa into a sphere for capitalist exploitation. Both the I.L.P. and the S.D.F. campaigned against the war in the spirit of the London Congress resolution, through public demonstrations and Press propaganda. A section of the British Socialist movement, however, strongly represented in the Fabian Society, welcomed and justified the annexation of the Boer Republics, in a manifesto drafted by Bernard Shaw.[1]

1. George Bernard Shaw, *Fabianism and the Empire*, published by the Fabian Society (London, 1900).

15 Keir Hardie

16 Jean Jaurès

Shaw began his case with a statement about the need to protect the natives of the Transvaal from slavery and extermination at the hands of Boer oligarchy. The well-being of the natives in all colonial countries was the concern of the entire civilized world and not only of the particular white ruling class which happened to be in control. Colonialism could be justified morally only in terms of its civilizing influence. 'A State, large or small,' Shaw wrote, 'which hinders the spread of international civilization must disappear.' Furthermore, control of a territory's natural resources could not be handed over to a single nation without due regard for the interests of all nations. The earth was the common property of the whole of humanity, and the common interests of all in having access to the means of life supplied by nature must have priority over the interests of the nation in which the resources happened to be located.

Shaw concluded that the gold-fields of South Africa should be internationalized and exploited in the interests of all peoples. The ideal solution to the problem of native welfare would be to transfer the territories of the Boer Republics to a federative world state. However, since no world state existed as yet, it was realistic for Socialists to support the annexation of the Boer Republics by a great power, such as the British Empire, since 'a great power must, consciously or unconsciously, govern in the general interests of civilization'.

Shaw's pamphlet aroused a storm of indignation in the British Labour movement. His theory was denounced by the I.L.P. and the S.D.F. as a betrayal of the fundamental principles of Socialism. The majority at a Fabian conference, however, including Sidney and Beatrice Webb, endorsed his attitude, and Robert Blatchford, brilliant editor of the *Clarion*, the most widely circulated Socialist weekly, repeated Shaw's argument in justifying the annexation of the Boer Republics.

A point of view similar to Shaw's was expounded, at about the same time, by Eduard Bernstein in his book, *Die Voraussetzungen des Sozialismus* (1899), which criticized the attitude of German Social Democracy to the colonial question. The discussion arose out of the forced leasing of Kiaochow to Germany in 1897, which caused considerable debate in both Reichstag and Press, and constituted Germany's share of the loot of China in her planned partition among the European great powers.[1] The Social Democratic party had protested in the Reichstag against this act of imperialism and denounced all colonialism as incompatible with the 'common principles of Social Democracy'.

It was against just these 'common Social Democratic principles' that Bernstein protested. Though he was at first critical of the way in

1. See below, p. 328.

which the bay of Kiaochow had been obtained, he finally approved of the lease on the grounds that it allowed the German Empire 'a decisive voice' in the partition of China. He did not advocate any further colonial acquisitions, but saw 'no reason to assume that such acquisitions were objectionable in themselves. . . . The important thing is not whether, but how, they are effected.' He defended colonialism as a necessity if the natural resources of the tropics were to be developed. 'Since we enjoy the products of the tropics . . . there can be no real objection to our cultivating the crops ourselves.' Moreover, 'the right of savages to the soil they occupy' could be recognized only as a conditional right. 'In the last resort, the higher culture enjoys the higher right. It is not the conquest but the cultivation of the land that gives the occupier his historical and legal titles.' He supported this position by a quotation from the third volume of Marx's *Das Kapital* which declared that: 'Even a whole society, a nation, or even all simultaneously existing societies taken together, are not the owners of the globe. They are only its possessors, its usufructuaries, and, like *boni patres familias*, they must hand it down to succeeding generations in an improved condition.'[1]

Bernstein's views were rejected by an overwhelming majority of the German Social Democratic party. The party laid down the main lines of its colonial policy at the Mainz Congress in 1900. According to the resolution, colonialism sprang 'in the first instance from the insatiable demands of the *bourgeoisie* to find ever new investment outlets for its continually accumulating capital, as well as from the drive for new markets'. The policy depended 'on the forcible annexation of foreign lands and the ruthless subjugation and exploitation of the indigenous people'. It made 'the exploiting elements' even more savage, and demoralized those 'who strive to satisfy their greed by the most objectionable and even inhuman means'. Against all such 'policies of plundering and exploitation', Social Democracy 'as the enemy of all oppression and exploitation of one people by another would protest as powerfully as possible'. The resolution went on to demand 'that the necessary and desirable cultural contacts between all the peoples of the world should be achieved by means compatible with the preservation of the rights, liberties and independence of those peoples who can be won for modern culture and civilization only by the forcc of teaching and example'.[2]

Bernstein, however, was not the only one to call for a 'realistic' colonial policy. Though it was rejected by most Revisionists, some of the movement's more respected writers, such as Max Schippel, Gustav

1. Bcrnstein, *Die Voraussetzungen* . . ., op. cit., pp. 147–50.

2. For a brief review of the attitude of German Social Democracy to the colonial question, see Karl Kautsky, *Sozialismus und Kolonialpolitik* (Berlin, 1907), and Gustav Noske, *Kolonialpolitik und Sozialdemokratie* (Stuttgart, 1914).

Noske, Richard Calwer, Max Maurenbrecher, Ludwig Quessel and Gerhard Hildebrand, supported from Austria by Karl Leuthner, foreign political editor of the Vienna *Arbeiter-Zeitung*, defended colonialism as necessary for developing the productive resources, extending the civilization and expanding the living-space of the European nations. They stood for the concept of a great German colonial empire.

3

However, the problem of colonial policy could not be viewed in isolation. It was bound up with the whole question of imperialism, including the arms race between the Great Powers, the growth of international tensions and the danger of armed conflict. The fifth congress of the International, meeting in Paris towards the end of September 1900, decided to deal with the problem of colonial policy together with that of world peace and militarism.

The resolution proposed by H. van Kol from Holland on this item of the agenda rejected colonialism without reservation. It declared that colonial expansion was an inevitable accompaniment of capitalism in its latest phase, imperialism. Imperialism involved the threat of a European war, was a source of chauvinism and imposed increasing burdens on the people through military expenditure. The colonial policy of the *bourgeoisie* had, for its sole purpose, according to the resolution, 'an increase in capitalist profit and the maintenance of the capitalist system'. In this way it wasted 'the property and blood of the entire working class' and committed 'crimes and cruelties without number against the native inhabitants of colonies subjugated by force of arms'. The resolution called on the workers of all countries to fight against capitalist colonial expansion, to condemn the colonial policy of the *bourgeoisie* and to put an end to the injustice and cruelty inflicted on the natives, 'victims of capitalism's greed and dishonour'.

The debate on the resolution began with statements from the British delegates about the Boer War, which was still in progress. H. M. Hyndman, chairman of the S.D.F., said that 'as an English Socialist and an inhabitant of the biggest colonial empire in the world', he considered it particularly important to protest, together with the international working class, against the colonial policy of the major powers. Britain's war against the Transvaal filled 'us English Socialists with mourning and shame'. And Quelch declared that, 'to the honour of the British workers', it had proved impossible 'despite all the systematic attempts by capitalist England to corrupt them' to persuade one organized worker, let alone a workers' organization, to express approval of the war. 'The workers,' he said proudly, 'have kept their flag unsullied.'

It was generally felt, however, that it would not be sufficient for Congress merely to denounce colonialism. Richard Géraut, delegate from the Socialist General Council of Guadeloupe, in the French West Indies, proposed that a detailed Socialist programme for the colonies should be worked out, and Congress asked the affiliated parties to give the matter careful study, while also promoting the formation of Socialist parties in colonial territories.

The resolution submitted to the congress by Rosa Luxemburg on world peace and militarism dealt also with the colonial question. Two commissions of the congress, dealing respectively with colonialism and militarism, had met in joint session from the beginning, since Rosa Luxemburg's view was accepted that militarism and colonialism were merely two aspects of a new phenomenon in world politics—a phenomenon whose 'paroxysms had unleashed four bloody wars during the past six years and which threatens the world with a state of permanent war'. Against this danger the working-class parties of the various countries must draw closer together, not only in the everyday struggle against colonialism and militarism but also with regard to the final objective, since 'it is becoming more and more clear', she said, as though with presentiment of the catastrophe that was to break only fourteen years later, 'that the collapse of the capitalist system would take place not through an economic but through a political crisis, resulting from developments in the sphere of world politics'. The workers of all countries must prepare to meet the decisive challenge when it came by international action.

The resolution, which was adopted unanimously without discussion, said that the events since the International had held its previous congress in 1896—the Boer War and the invasion of China by the European Great Powers—had given militarism a new significance. It had become an instrument of policy for colonial expansion, which endangered the normal and peaceful development of society, accentuated rivalry and tensions and 'threatened to bring about a permanent state of war'. The resolution called on all workers' parties in all countries 'to oppose with re-doubled strength and vigour both militarism and colonialism . . . and to reply to the world alliance of *bourgeoisie* and governments for perpetual war with an alliance of the workers of all countries for perpetual peace'. It committed Socialist parliamentary groups 'to vote unfailingly against all estimates for military and naval expenditure or for colonial aggression' and called on the Bureau of the International 'to organize a simultaneous and uniform movement of opposition to militarism'.

4

The Paris Congress of 1900 had requested the member parties to make a study of the colonial problem so as to arrive at a well-considered and viable policy. The first attempt at such a programme came from the colonial commission of the Amsterdam Congress in August 1904. H. van Kol admitted quite candidly that the commission had been unable to agree on many points. 'We must protest against the forcible annexation of colonies,' he said, 'and against all forms of capitalist piracy in colonial areas, since we oppose the atrocities inseparable from such policies, even if we do not consider that it is necessarily bad for a country to be colonized in any circumstances.' In what way, however, were the horrors of colonialism to be in practice alleviated or prevented? Should Socialists try to preserve pre-capitalist conditions in colonial territories, or encourage the development of native forms of capitalism? Kol underlined the dilemma by asking: 'Can we, who defend right and justice, abandon hundreds of thousands to infinite misery, to intellectual and moral degradation, instead of protecting them against capitalism?'

However, the resolution which H. van Kol moved on behalf of the commission avoided the fundamental question which colonialism posed for Social Democracy. He had touched on the question of whether colonialism could be regarded as a blessing or a curse for the people being colonized, whether it was to be opposed in all circumstances or whether its barbarities could be avoided by some form of Socialist colonial policy. The resolution limited itself to pledging the Socialist parties and their parliamentary representatives to oppose all legislation of an imperialist or protectionist character, and to oppose all colonial aggression and all military expenditure for the furthering of colonialist aims. It pledged strong opposition to concessions in the interests of monopolies and plantation-owners and appealed to Socialist parties to denounce publicly all acts of brutality against natives and to demand from their governments specific safeguards for the native peoples against military oppression and exploitation by foreign firms. They should take particular care to see that native peoples were not deprived of their property by force or fraud. Progress in colonial territories must lie in the direction of popular self-government. The resolution demanded, for the peoples of the colonies, 'that degree of freedom and independence appropriate to their stage of development, with the understanding that complete freedom of the colonies must be the ultimate aim'. Finally, the resolution called for foreign affairs to be brought under parliamentary control, so as to counteract 'the private influence of wealthy cliques'.

Before the congress had started to debate the colonial question proper, the colonial commission presented for discussion a resolution from the English delegates on British policy in India. The resolution, which is of some historic importance as an expression of British and International attitudes towards the British Empire, deserves quoting in full. It ran:

> Congress recognizes the right of the inhabitants of civilized countries to settle in lands where the population is at a lower stage of development. However, it condemns most strongly the existing capitalist system of colonial rule and urges the Socialists of all countries to put an end to it. The system results in the oppression of the peoples of Africa, Asia, etc., by the culturally advanced nations of Europe, such as France, Britain, Germany, Belgium and Holland. Since England has had most success in subjugating foreign nations, the effects on British India have been correspondingly greater and more formidable.
>
> This gathering of workers' delegates from the entire civilized world has heard from the representatives of England and India how British rule deprives the Indian people of their means of livelihood, how it exploits and robs them and how more than 200 million Indian people are exposed to the most extreme forms of poverty, misery and famine.
>
> Congress calls on the workers of Great Britain to compel their government to abandon its present infamous and degrading colonial system and to introduce the perfectly practicable system of self-government for the Indian people under English sovereignty.

After reading out the resolution, the president, H. van Kol, asked Congress 'to treat with the greatest reverence the statement of the Indian delegate, an old man of eighty, who had sacrificed fifty-five years of his life to the struggle for the freedom and happiness of his people'. He had come to the congress to present the case of 200 million people in a country 'which could be a paradise on earth but for the avarice of the white race which had transformed it into an area of misery and distress for the vast majority of the population'. According to the Minutes, the president's words produced an immediate and profound effect on the congress. The delegates rose from their seats 'as an expression of sympathy for the sufferings of the Indian people' and greeted the Indian delegate, Dadhabhai Naoroji, founder and president of the Indian National Congress, with 'tumultuous cheers and applause, lasting for several minutes' as he stepped up to the rostrum.

5

In the period between the Amsterdam and Stuttgart Congresses, colonial policies had occupied the centre of debate in both the German and Belgian parties.

In Germany it was the risings in their two African colonies—South-

West Africa, which, after Germany's defeat in the First World War, was mandated to the Union of South Africa, and East Africa, which, as Tanganyika, became a British mandate—that once again brought colonial problems to the fore. The immediate cause for the rising in South-West Africa was the building of a railway from the coast to the mining district of Otavi across the grazing lands of the Herero tribe, which had been allocated to the railway concessionaries. After being driven from their grazing-lands the Hereros revolted. The rising spread and, after a year's fighting, was put down by the German colonial administration with exceptional brutality. At a meeting of the Reichstag on 2 December 1905, Ledebour read out an order from General Trotha—who had been sent to South-West Africa to suppress the rising—calling for the Hereros, including the women and children, to be killed on sight. Many thousands of them had been driven into the waterless desert of Omahene, where they perished from hunger and thirst.[1]

The Social Democrats had denounced the atrocities in Parliament and in the Press. When in December 1906 the government asked Parliament for new credits to finance the campaign against the insurgents, the Social Democrats voted against. The Bill authorizing the credits was defeated, when the Centre party voted against it for personal reasons, upon which the government dissolved the Reichstag and unleashed a flood of nationalist and chauvinist propaganda on the nation. In the ensuing election—the 'Hottentot election'—the party suffered a defeat for the first time since 1884. It lost nearly half its seats in the Reichstag, dropping from seventy-nine to forty-three, and while the number of votes rose by over a quarter of a million, the percentage cast for the Social Democrats declined from 32·6 to 29·5. Kaiser William had triumphed and Social Democracy had been 'ridden down'. The Revisionists attributed the defeat to the 'negative colonial policy' of the party and demanded a more 'realistic and positive' approach.

6

The Belgian Social Democrats faced a colonial problem of a different and more complicated character. The question there was whether Belgium should become a colonial power at all—whether the Belgian

1. The General's order on the Hereros read: 'Within the German borders every Herero, with or without a rifle, with or without cattle, is to be shot. I shall not receive any more women or children; they must be driven back to their people or shot. This is my message to the Hereros—von Trotha, Great General of the Mighty Emperor.' (See Noske, op. cit., p. 112.) The number of Hereros killed under the extermination order was estimated at 60,000 out of a total population of 80,000, while those killed in East Africa numbered 70,000 (*Handbuch*, op. cit., p. 94).

state should take over the huge colonial empire which the king had acquired as a private estate.

The origin of the 'Congo Free State' was indeed, as Lafontaine told the congress of the International in Stuttgart, 'without precedent in world history'. It began in 1876 with a conference of geographers and missionaries, called by King Leopold II in his private capacity, and it seemed only natural that people concerned with African trade should also be invited to attend what was ostensibly a harmless scientific gathering. The conference set up an 'International Society for the Exploration and Civilization of Africa', whose solemnly declared aim was to win 'the black continent' for Christianity and stop the Arab slave-trade. Two years later the society vanished from the scene. Its place was taken by a commission, set up by Leopold—to which he managed to attach the name of the famous explorer, H. M. Stanley—charged with the expansion of Christian civilization, as interpreted by Leopold. By force and a variety of stratagems he secured concessions from the tribal chiefs, giving him sovereignty over vast areas. To exploit the new kingdom which he had created in the heart of Africa, Leopold founded, in 1882, the International Congo Society and, through his family connections with the European Courts, had the Congo Society recognized as a sovereign state by the Great Powers.

The only concession secured by the powers, under the Treaty of Berlin of 1885, was the right to trade freely with the 'Congo Free State', whose independence had been officially recognized. A year later Leopold nominated himself, with the authority of the Belgian Parliament, 'Head of the State established by the Congo Society', and in his will, drawn up in 1889, bequeathed the 'Congo State' to the Belgian state, apart from a huge 'Crown domain', which was to pass to his own heirs. Meanwhile, Leopold, as absolute ruler of the Congo, had issued a decree annexing all land not under regular cultivation, such as woods, deserts and grazing lands, and all mineral land, as well as subjecting the Congolese in the rubber plantations and mines to a system of forced labour little better than slavery. The resulting uprisings had invariably been bloodily suppressed by the use of native troops.[1]

For a time these hideous events were masked by the impenetrable seclusion of the 'black continent'. However, after 1904, news filtered through concerning the system of Christian civilization which Leopold had installed in Central Africa. The English writer, Edmund Dene Morel,[2] exposed the situation in a number of articles, and particularly in

1. Roger Casement, who, when he was British Consul in Nigeria, had been ordered by the British Government to investigate conditions in the Congo, estimated in his report that the population had decreased, in the course of ten years' rule by the Belgian king, by three million.

2. E. D. Morel, a Liberal, joined the I.L.P. in 1914. In 1922, as a member of

two pamphlets, *Leopold's Rule in Africa* (1904) and *Red Rubber* (1906), which changed the course of history. The disclosures were discussed in the British Press and in both British and Belgian Parliaments. Britain and the U.S.A., both signatories to the Treaty of Berlin, protested against the scandal in a joint note. Under moral pressure from the whole civilized world Leopold declared himself ready to transfer his private empire immediately to the Belgian state, in return for a fantastic compensation and except for his 'Royal Estate'.

The draft Bill on the transfer of the Congo appeared before the Belgian Parliament in its final form only in 1906. There was now no more talk of maintaining the 'Royal Estate' as the private property of the royal family, though the Bill continued to provide for a very high level of compensation. But the main question confronting the Belgian Social Democrats was whether, in all the circumstances, they would be justified in voting for annexation. They had denounced the king's appalling régime as a classic expression of capitalist colonialism. Could they now take responsibility for Belgium's becoming a colonial power?

On the other hand, what alternative was there for the Congo? Opinion in the party was divided. It was hardly feasible to propose that the native population, which had hardly advanced beyond the stage of primitive tribalism, should become self-governing. Apart from any other consideration, this would merely hand over the population once again to the mercy of Arab slave-raiders.

A majority in the party came out in favour of transferring power to an international consortium, consisting of all the powers which had signed the Berlin Agreement of 1885. A minority, however, led by Vandervelde, objected that an international régime of capitalist powers would merely perpetuate colonial exploitation, and probably with less restraint than in the case of a single government accountable to a parliamentary assembly. Vandervelde, who made a special trip to the Congo to find out as much as possible about the position, concluded that the annexation of the territory by Belgium would be the lesser evil, providing, of course, that the administration was subject to parliamentary control and that the rights and liberties of the native population were safeguarded by parliamentary legislation.

However, Vandervelde's proposal that the party should vote for annexation, with the safeguards already mentioned, was rejected by the majority. The decisive argument was that as Belgium was unquestionably a capitalist state, the Belgian government would inevitably pursue a normal capitalist colonial policy. If the party were to vote in support of integration in such conditions, it would only saddle itself with the

the Labour party, he was elected to the House of Commons, defeating Winston Churchill.

responsibility of participating in colonial exploitation. But 'the declaration of party principles makes it the duty of every Socialist', the resolution passed by the conference was at pains to emphasize, 'to support all victims of exploitation without regard to race'.

The 'realistic and positive colonial policy' put forward by Vandervelde was incompatible with the thought and feeling of the majority in the party. While no one questioned his moral and intellectual authority, the colonial question brought a majority into conflict with the leadership and for the first and only time they refused to follow him. The resolution passed by Congress abruptly rejected his proposal and declared that Socialist deputies who failed to vote against the annexation of the Congo were 'defying the principles agreed to by congresses of the party and the International'. Vandervelde at once offered his resignation, which, however, Congress declined to accept.

7

While controversies over colonial policy did not affect the unity of the Belgian party, they led in Italy to a decisive split. From the very beginning the history of Italian Socialism was one of acute internal struggles between the revolutionary and Reformist wings. The Reformists, who captured the leadership of the party in 1902, lost it to the 'Integralists' two years later and won it back again at the congress of 1908, whereupon they resumed the policy of co-operation with Left-Liberal governments embarked on in 1902. At the General Election of 1910 the party scored a considerable victory. They won forty-two seats—a net gain of sixteen—and Giolitti, forming his third government in 1911, offered Bissolati a seat in the cabinet. As in 1903, however, when Turati had been invited to join an earlier Giolitti government, the party declined the offer, while co-operating closely with it in Parliament. A crisis occurred in the late summer of 1911, when the government announced its intention of annexing Tripolitania in North Africa and declared war against Turkey on 9 September.

Since the turn of the century, Italy had regarded Tripolitania as a future colony, which she would acquire without a struggle owing to the disintegration of the Turkish Empire. That Empire, however, received a new lease of life from the Young Turk revolution which broke out in 1908 and resulted in the consolidation of Turkey's rule over her Mediterranean provinces. Italy had now to fight for Tripolitania if she wished to wrest it from Turkey.

The establishment of an Italian colonial empire had been a longstanding demand of the Nationalists. When, on 1 July 1911, the German gunboat, *Panther*, anchored off Agadir on the south-west coast of

Morocco, it became clear to the Italian government that they could not conquer Tripoli without provoking resistance from the major European powers. Kaiser William's 'Panther leap' at the port of Agadir, which had been closed to all nations by the Treaty of Algeciras in 1906, was interpreted by Britain and France as a piece of deliberate provocation and involved the Great Powers in a new Moroccan crisis. In Italy the Nationalists urged the government to take advantage of the confusion and seize Tripoli. In influential Catholic circles, too, the idea of conquering the last Turkish province in the Mediterranean was by no means unwelcome, as a final instalment of the Crusades which had begun more than 800 years earlier. Moreover, the Bank of Rome, which was directed by the 'Friends of the Vatican', had invested considerable sums of money in Tripolitania. The war of conquest in Tripolitania on which the government embarked was also popular in wider circles, including the peasants of the over-populated south, who hoped that the conquest of Tripolitania would open up large fertile areas for emigration.

A few weeks after the declaration of war the Socialist party held its congress in Modena. It was faced with a difficult situation. An overwhelming majority of the party condemned the war outright. Shortly before the outbreak, however, Giolitti had introduced a new franchise under which the electorate was increased from three and a half to nearly nine million. Should the party, in protesting against the war, join the opposition to Giolitti? The congress decided to break with the government and vote against war credits, even at the risk of endangering the electoral reform. However, two leaders of the right-wing Reformists, Bissolati and Bonomi, who joined in opposing the war, later voted for the defence budget on the grounds that the war was a *fait accompli* and the nation irrevocably committed.

On the outbreak of war the party, together with the trade unions, called out the workers in a twenty-four-hour strike on 28 September 1911. The break with the government and the proclamation of a general strike reflected the mood of the workers, particularly in the red belt of Emilia-Romagna, Umbria and Tuscany. They saw the war as a frivolous colonial adventure and their anti-war struggles included numerous strikes and attempts to sabotage the movement of troops and munitions, pulling up railway lines and setting fire to stations.

The conflict between this revolutionary trend and the Reformist line of the party leadership came to a head at the congress at Reggio Emilia in 1912. The attack was led by the young Benito Mussolini, editor of a Socialist weekly in his home town of Forli, who had already organized acts of sabotage in the Romagna. In an impassioned speech he charged Bissolati, Bonomi and other defenders of the war with treason to the principles of international Socialism, and demanded that the party expel them and break off all relations with the government. He was completely successful. Bissolati, Bonomi and their followers were expelled, Claudio Treves, Turati's closest colleague, was removed from his post as chief editor of the party's central organ, *Avanti*, and Mussolini was elected his successor. In an effort to preserve unity, Turati and Treves accepted the congress resolutions. Bissolati and Bonomi, on the other hand, formed a new organization, the Reformist-Socialist party, which was joined by seventeen out of forty-two members of the parliamentary fraction.

8

The Amsterdam Congress had requested member parties to set up colonial study-groups in an attempt to clarify the issues. As a result, the Stuttgart Congress, meeting in August 1907 to resume the discussion of the colonial question, was faced with exhaustive memoranda from the British, French, Dutch and Belgian parties on the colonial policies of their respective countries.[1] The debate revolved round the question, first posed by H. van Kol at Amsterdam, as to whether colonialism should be rejected out of hand and on principle, or accepted as an inevitable process for opening up the economies and cultures of underdeveloped areas and for developing the productive powers of mankind.

The resolution presented by van Kol on behalf of the majority of the colonial commission once again rejected capitalist colonial policies on principle. But in two preambles this rejection was carefully qualified. It was made clear that, while 'the usefulness and necessity of colonies in general—especially from the point of view of the working class—has been grossly exaggerated', the Social Democrats 'do not reject all colonial policies in all circumstances, such as those which, under a socialist régime, could serve a civilizing purpose'.

These qualifications provided the main topic for debate, which lasted for three days, one in the commission itself and two at the plenum of the entire congress. The controversy split all the delegations of parties from colonialist countries—the British, German, French, Belgian and Italian. Kautsky and Ledebour opposed Bernstein and David, Quelch spoke against Ramsay MacDonald, Bracke against Rounanet, Wurm against Pernerstorfer, Karski against van Kol.

Those who opposed the majority resolution rejected all colonial policy as incompatible with the basic principles of Socialism. According

1. The English memorandum was drafted by H. M. Hyndman, the Dutch by H. van Kol, the French by Paul Louis and the Belgian by Victor Denis, Lafontaine, L. Furnémont and Émile Vandervelde. The memoranda are contained in the collection published by the International Socialist Bureau, *Anträge und Beschlussentwürfe nebst Begründungen an den Internationalen Sozialistischen Kongress zu Stuttgart* (1907).

to Kautsky, a Socialist colonial policy was a contradiction in terms, since it must necessarily be based on foreign rule, so repudiating the fundamental Socialist concept of the right of every nation to freedom and independence. Even a Socialist colonial régime would represent an alien rule, a benevolent despotism resting on violence and repression.

Was it possible, however, for the world economy to dispense with colonial raw materials? Did not even a capitalist colonial policy develop the productive forces of colonial territories? Must not the colonial peoples pass through a stage of capitalist development before reaching the Socialist goal? These were all questions raised by the advocates of 'positive' Socialist colonialism, such as van Kol, Bernstein and David. David wanted the resolution to state that 'considering that Socialism puts the productive power of the whole world at the disposal of mankind and intends to help all peoples, of all colours and languages, to reach the highest peaks of civilization, Congress sees, in the colonial idea, an essential expression of the Socialist attitude to world culture'.

Congress rejected both the preamble to the commission's resolution and the one sponsored by David. The final resolution, unanimously endorsed, read:

> Congress believes that capitalist colonial policies must, by their nature, give rise to servitude, forced labour and the extermination of the native peoples in colonized territories.
>
> The so-called civilizing mission, in terms of which capitalism seeks to justify its colonial policies, serves merely as a pretext to conceal the will to conquer and exploit.
>
> Only Socialism will offer all nations the possibility of developing freely their own forms of culture.
>
> Capitalist colonial policies, so far from fostering the native economies, destroy the natural wealth of the subjugated territories both by enslaving and pauperizing the native peoples and through the murderously destructive wars engendered by such policies. As a result they retard and frustrate the development of trade and the growth of markets for even the industrial products of civilized nations.
>
> Congress condemns the barbarous methods of capitalist colonialism and demands, in the interests of the development of the productive forces, a policy based on peaceful cultural development and one which develops the world's mineral resources in the interests of the whole of humanity.

The resolution committed all Socialist parliamentary groups to oppose the robbery and subjugation of colonial peoples and to fight for reforms which would better their lot, protect their rights and 'do everything possible to educate them for independence'.

For two decades this resolution was to remain the official statement of Socialist anti-colonialism. Only in 1928 did the International adopt, at its Brussels Congress, a new and more concrete colonial programme calling explicitly for self-government and independence.

21 · The International and the War

It was from the humanist philosophy of the eighteenth-century Enlightenment that Socialism inherited the ideas of international brotherhood and world peace, and the achievement of these ideals represented the ultimate goal of the Socialist International. It sought to unify all national sovereign states in a federal, world Socialist Republic which would eradicate the plague of national hatreds and eliminate war from the earth. It saw in war an extreme expression of the evils of existing society, a barbaric instrument of foreign policies through which ruling classes of the various countries sought to promote, on a world scale, their individual struggles for political and economic power. In fighting to preserve peace, the International saw itself opposing the social system whose end-product was war. Almost every congress of the International was, in part, preoccupied with the question of how the workers of the world could unite to prevent wars.

1

The debate was opened as early as the Brussels Congress of the First International in 1868. This congress took place two years after the Austro-Prussian War—a war in which the Prussian and Habsburg monarchies strove for the domination of the German Confederation, which linked thirty-seven sovereign states under the leadership of Austria. The war had been deliberately provoked by Bismarck with the object of expelling Austria from the German Confederation so as to weld it into a centralized state under Prussian domination.

The war was over with unexpected speed. Scarcely three weeks after the outbreak, Austria was decisively defeated at Königsgrätz. The General Council of the International had devoted five of its meetings to a discussion of the policy which the Labour movement should adopt towards the war. Eventually, the unanimous decision was reached that the conflict was 'one between governments' in which the workers were advised to 'be neutral'.[1]

However, the Austro-Prussian War of 1866 carried within itself the seeds of the Franco-German War of 1870. It was inevitable that Napoleon III would respond to the advance of Prussian power by seeking to prevent the unification of Germany, since this would threaten the predominant position of France on the continent of Europe. In the continuing increase of tension between France and Germany following 1866, the inevitability of war became apparent and the Brussels Congress of the International, held in 1868, anticipated only too accurately the war which was to break out two years later.

In face of the threat, the delegates from German Switzerland, led by Johann Philipp Becker, proposed that the congress should consider 'the attitude of the working class in the event of a war breaking out between two or more great powers, in particular, the policy to be adopted towards the originator'.

The resolution moved by Becker declared 'that the reasons for the precarious character of the peace could only lie in the unjust nature of society, in the jungle conditions of an economic free-for-all . . .; that major wars arise not only from dynastic disputes but also from conflicts of power and of economic interests . . .; and that such a war, of the kind threatening between Germany and France, could only be regarded as a civil war'. The resolution called on the International to organize effectively to nip all such wars in the bud, and to ensure 'that the workers in every country should not only speak out loudly and clearly against all such wars between peoples' but should also 'refuse all work which might contribute to the killing of men or the destruction of property, such as work on military supplies'. Finally, it called for a propaganda campaign to be started immediately, 'so as to make every worker who is obliged to join a standing army clear as to his human rights, and to prescribe to him, in the event of war breaking out, certain principles of conduct'.

However, the idea of a strike against conscription was rejected as probably impracticable. 'If we were really in a position to prevent the working class from undertaking military service,' declared the Belgian delegate, Hirsch, 'the question of war would hardly arise.' The French Proudhonists, on whose behalf Tolain addressed the congress, opposed Becker's resolution, among other reasons because they had only recently and reluctantly admitted the strike to be in any conditions a legitimate method of working-class struggle. In the case of war, they argued that

1. Minutes of the General Council, 19 and 26 June; 3, 10 and 17 July 1866, op. cit., pp. 200–13.

'pressure of public opinion' would be the most effective means of opposition.

Eventually the congress accepted a resolution, moved by César de Paepe and supported by Charles Longuet, which dealt both with the nature of war and with the means of opposing it. Wars between nations, it declared, were civil wars, struggles between 'brothers and comrades'. It regarded economic factors, and, specifically, a 'lack of economic equilibrium', as the 'main cause' of wars. An additional reason, however, lay in 'the conditions arising out of the centralization of power and despotism'. Nations could reduce the number of wars 'in so far as they resist those who initiate and take the lead in wars'. For such resistance, declared the resolution, there existed a 'genuinely effective, legitimate and immediately applicable means'—the general strike. As 'society could no longer exist if production were to cease for any length of time, it would be sufficient', said the resolution, for the workers to stop work 'in order to render impossible all adventures on the part of personal and despotic régimes'. The resolution therefore called on the workers to cease work 'in the event of their country's declaring war'. Becker's proposal of a strike against military service was tacitly dropped.

Marx, who did not attend the congress, was not very happy with that part of the resolution which, on the insistence of de Paepe and the Belgian delegation, appealed to the workers to resist war by general strike; he called it a piece of 'Belgian stupidity'.[1] In letters to Lessner and Eccarius, who represented the General Council at the congress, he advised them to state, in the resolution regarding the general strike as a method of the prevention of war, 'that the working class is not yet sufficiently organized to exert a decisive influence on the course of events; but that Congress protests on behalf of the working class against war and denounces its instigators; and that it declares that a war between France and Germany would be a civil war, ruinous for both countries and Europe altogether'.[2]

2

The Franco-German War, under the shadow of which the Brussels Congress had adopted its resolution, broke out so suddenly and unexpectedly that no one could give the matter much prior thought. In neither France nor Germany was there any suggestion of a strike. In both countries the Socialists confined themselves to protesting against the imminent threat of war, at mass meetings and in public statements

1. Letter to Engels, 16 September 1869, *Marx-Engels Briefwechsel*, vol. III, p. 110.
2. *Marx-Engels: Ausgewählte Briefe*, p. 244 (letter not included in English edition of *Selected Correspondence*).

which reflected the spirit and letter of the Brussels resolution. They condemned it forthrightly as a dynastic war and in the North German Parliament both Liebknecht and Bebel opposed—as 'members of the International Workers' Association'—the government's demand for military credits. But when the war in fact broke out and had all the appearance of an assault by Napoleon III against the German nation, the overwhelming majority of German Social Democrats rallied, along with the rest of the population, to the cause of national defence.[1]

The position of the German Social Democrats was hardly compatible with the International's ideas on war, as embodied in the Brussels resolution. That had called on the workers to resist wars of every kind, with no distinction between those which were aggressive and those which might be described as defensive. The Brussels resolution had taken no account of the possibility that Socialists might feel impelled to defend their country against external aggression.

On the other hand, the General Council, once military operations had started, did recognize a distinction between offensive and defensive wars. It did not question the right of Socialists to defend their country against aggression. It did not view the attitude of the German Socialists, nor that of the French Socialists in the second phase of the war, as a violation of international proletarian solidarity. The first address on the war, written by Marx and signed by all members of the General Council, appeared on 23 July, four days after its outbreak. It recognized that 'on the German side, the war is a war of defence', and the second address spoke with approval of the fact that 'the German working class has resolutely supported the war, which it was not in their power to prevent, as a war for German independence and the liberation of France and Europe from that pestilential incubus, the Second Empire'.

To Engels any other attitude seemed plainly 'impossible'. He had written to Marx on 15 August that 'the whole mass of the German people of every class have realized that this is first and foremost a question of national existence and have therefore at once flung themselves into the fray'. If Germany were defeated, he went on,

> Bonapartism will be strengthened for years and Germany broken for years, perhaps for generations. In that event there can be no more question of an independent German working-class movement either, the struggle to restore Germany's national existence will absorb everything. . . . If Germany wins, French Bonapartism will at any rate be smashed, the endless row about the establishment of German unity will at last be wiped out, the German workers will be able to organize on a national scale, quite different from that prevailing hitherto, and the French workers, whatever sort of government may succeed this one, are certain to have a freer field than under Bonapartism.

1. For a fuller description of the attitude of German and French Socialists and of the International towards the Franco-German War, see Chapter 5.

In Engels's view, the German Social Democrats should

> join the national movement . . . at the same time emphasize the difference between German national and dynastic Prussian interests . . . work against any annexation of Alsace and Lorraine . . . as soon as a non-chauvinist republican government is at the helm in Paris, work for an honourable peace with it . . . constantly stress the unity of interests between the German and French workers, who did not approve of the war and are also not making war on each other.[1]

These ideas were, in fact, decisive in the minds of the German Social Democrats during the war. As long as it remained a defensive war, it had their support. Immediately France was defeated and Napoleon III overthrown, they went into opposition. They issued a manifesto—the famous Manifesto of the Brunswick Committee (which led the Eisenach party) that was to provide the grounds for the subsequent charges of treason against its members—which condemned the continuation of the war, solemnly protested against the proposed annexation of Alsace and Lorraine and demanded an immediate end to the war and the conclusion of an honourable peace. As soon as Bismarck declared in the North German Diet that the war would continue for the conquest of Alsace-Lorraine, the Social Democrats voted against war credits and put down a motion demanding that the government 'effect a speedy peace with the French Republic and renounce any suggestion of annexing French territories'.

French Socialists acted in much the same way. While Bonaparte was in power they opposed the war. But when the war, which had apparently started as an act of French aggression against Germany, changed into a German war of conquest against France, they had no hesitation, after Napoleon's abdication, in joining forces with the new Republican government to resist Germany's war of conquest. Two days after the proclamation of the Republic, Blanqui founded his paper, *La Patrie en danger*, and declared in a statement signed by himself and his principal followers: 'In face of the enemy there must be no party. . . . The government which stemmed from the great popular uprising of 4 September represents the national spirit and the cause of national defence.' A statement from the International—the Second Address of the General Council—called on the French workers to 'perform their duties as citizens' in defence of their country, and begged them not to run the political revolution of 4 September, which had replaced the rule of Napoleon by a *bourgeois* régime, into a Socialist revolution. It issued the clear warning that 'any attempt at upsetting the new government in the present crisis, when the enemy is almost knocking at the doors of Paris, would be a desperate folly'.

1. *Marx-Engels Briefwechsel*, vol. IV, pp. 438–40.

Both German and French Socialists had, in the event, supported the principle of national defence and resistance to aggression against their country, and the International had given the principle its full support.

3

The problem confronting the Second International throughout its existence was not, however, the right of national self-defence, which few thought seriously of denying, but how to prevent nations from getting into the position of having to defend themselves by force. Congress after congress debated the question of how the working class should behave in the event of an outbreak of war. Before very long, however, the question of how to prevent war from breaking out forced itself to the forefront.

The foundation congress of the Second International, in 1889, considered the problem. It opposed outright the institution of standing armies, whose existence, it assumed, constituted in itself a threat to peace. The resolution submitted to the congress by Vaillant repudiated standing armies not only as 'incompatible with any democratic and republican régime', as the military expression of the 'monarchical or oligarchic form of capitalist rule' and as an 'instrument of reactionary *coups d'état* and social repression', but above all as part of the machinery of conquest and hence as an independent cause of war. It called for the replacement of standing armies by a popular militia.

The resolution did not, of course, convey the illusion that such a *levée en masse* would be enough to abolish war. Since war was 'the result of existing economic conditions' it would disappear, the resolution continued, 'only when the capitalist system of production has given way to the emancipation of labour and the triumph of Socialism on an international scale'. But the International believed that the abolition of standing armies and their replacement by popular militias would at least exclude the possibility of wars of open aggression.

At another level the International disbelieved in the possibility of doing away with wars while capitalism survived. The congress which followed at Brussels in 1891 passed a resolution which declared outright that the roots of war were firmly embedded in the capitalist system and that all attempts to preserve peace would be 'futile' until the economic causes of war had been eliminated under Socialism.

But if wars were endemic in capitalist society, was there anything the working class could do, while capitalism survived, to prevent their occurrence? Was any form of mass action likely to be effective? This question dominated the discussion through a succession of congresses which were largely devoted to the problem of war and its prevention.

At Brussels the possibility of various forms of mass action was considered by the commission concerned with the problem of war. In particular, there was a discussion on what action might be appropriate in the face of an outbreak of war—including strike action by reservists or by industrial workers. But as Liebknecht, who reported for the commission, pointed out, all such suggestions were 'immediately and unanimously ruled out by the delegates of the very nations most directly confronted with the challenge of militarism'. The resolution drafted by Vaillant and submitted by Liebknecht, which traced the 'permanent —overt as well as latent—conditions of war . . . to the system of exploitation of man by man and the class struggle which such a system engenders', was content to request the working class 'to protest, ceaselessly and powerfully against the will to war in all its forms, and those alliances which inevitably give rise to wars'.

Domela Nieuwenhuis opposed the resolution on the grounds that it was hardly sufficient to condemn war verbally. The International must make up its mind what it would do if war actually broke out. In the name of the Dutch delegation he proposed that the Socialist parties should 'respond to any declaration of war with an appeal to the peoples for a general cessation of work'. A majority at the congress, however, considered it dangerous to adopt a resolution which the International lacked the power to make effective. Of the sixteen nations represented at Brussels, only the Dutch and a majority of the French and British were prepared to support the resolution.

This spirit of resignation dominated all the International's discussions on war, right down to the actual outbreak in August 1914. The resolution adopted at Zurich, in 1893, had merely emphasized the need for Socialists 'to oppose with all their strength the chauvinist lusts of the ruling class', while it went on to declare that only with the 'total destruction of all forms of class rule would the danger of war be removed', and ended with the statement that 'the overthrow of capitalism will bring world peace'. Once again, in the debate on the resolution, the idea of a general strike and the refusal of reservists to be called to the colours, proposed by the Dutch delegates, was rejected by the majority at the congress. Plekhanov from Russia, Stanislas Mendelssohn from Poland, Liebknecht from Germany, Adler from Austria, Aveling from Britain, Turati from Italy, Rakovsky from Bulgaria, Charles Bonnier from France and Louis Heritier from Switzerland made the point that the mere attempt to call a strike against military service would be crushed by mass executions, while a strike of workers, called on the outbreak of war, would end in bloody defeat for the entire Socialist movement. Daniel de Leon, president of the Socialist Labor party of the United States, was right when he pointed out that a strike against military service could only, from the moment it was called, precipitate a violent revolution. And basically, as was apparent from the debates on the general strike as a weapon in the class struggle, the International was scared of the very idea of revolution. At no stage in the development of the Socialist and Labour movements in western Europe did it feel either the strength or the inclination for a violent clash with the forces of the state.

Plekhanov, who reported for the majority of the commission on war policy, added a new item to the conventional list of arguments against a strike in the armed forces. Such a strike, he alleged, even if it were feasible, would be effective only if it broke out with equal vigour in both camps. The slogan of a military strike against war, therefore, presupposed that Social Democracy had developed with equal strength in all the belligerent countries. But while considerable mass movements had developed in western Europe, there had been no comparable development in industrially backward Russia, languishing under the despotic régime of the Tsars. Yet Russia would be among the most dowerful participants in any future war. A strike against military service, therefore, according to Plekhanov, 'would in the first instance disarm the civilized nations and leave western Europe at the mercy of the Cossacks. The whole of civilization would be swamped by Russian despotism and instead of an era of proletarian emancipation, which the strike was supposed to inaugurate with such brilliance, we should have the rule of the knout. Therefore, what is ostensibly the highly revolutionary proposal of the Dutch delegation, turns out, in practice, to be a recipe for reaction.'

This line was strongly opposed by Domela Nieuwenhuis, who claimed that it reflected a type of chauvinism particularly prevalent among German Social Democrats. He recalled a speech of Bebel to the Erfurt Party Congress of 1891, in which the German leader had declared: 'Should Russia, that land of cruelty and barbarism, that enemy of all human civilization, attack Germany with the object of dismembering and destroying her, we shall resist.'[1] This whole approach, thought Nieuwenhuis, stank of chauvinism, and chauvinism was completely incompatible with the spirit of internationalism for which they stood. At the Brussels Congress he had opposed the attempt to distinguish

1. Bebel's statement was somehow in line with Engels's attitude. A fortnight before the Erfurt Congress, on 1 October 1891, he wrote to Bebel: '. . . a war against Germany by an alliance with Russia is, above all, a war against the strongest and most active Socialist party in Europe. Thus we have no choice but to fight with all our might any aggressor who assists Russia. For either we should be defeated, and then the Socialist movement in Europe will be finished for twenty years, or else we ourselves will get into power. . . .'—*August Bebel: Briefwechsel mit Friedrich Engels*, op. cit., p. 439.

between aggressive and defensive wars, differences which, he asserted, sprang from an essentially chauvinist outlook. Socialists who succumbed to this kind of thinking inevitably betrayed the spirit of international working-class solidarity.

The Dutch resolution was once again rejected by an overwhelming majority. The resolution sponsored by the majority of the commission was passed, with an addendum moved by the Belgians, pledging the working-class representatives in all legislative assemblies 'to vote against military credits, to denounce militarism and to advocate disarmament'.

The London Congress of 1896, which returned to the topic of war, formulated a number of specific proposals designed to avert the threat of war. Like the Paris Congress of 1889 it demanded the abolition of standing armies and their replacement by popular militias. It further proposed the setting up of an international court of arbitration for the peaceful settlement of disputes between nations. Should any government refuse to accept the findings of such a court, the question of war and peace must then be submitted to a national referendum.

4

Soon after the London Congress, the imperialist policy of the major European powers considerably increased the danger of world war. In 1898 a French advance from East Africa into Fashoda in the Sudan brought Britain and France to the brink of war. The Fashoda crisis was followed a year later by the beginning of the Boer War, and in 1900 by a crusade on the part of the Great Powers against China. The carving up of the huge, helpless Asiatic empire had begun in 1894 with the conquest of Korea and Formosa (Taiwan) by Japan. In the course of the next three years Russia occupied Manchuria, Dairen and Port Arthur; Germany secured a lease on the bay of Kiaochow and control over the Province of Shantung; Britain seized the harbour of Weihaiwei and declared the valley of the Yangtze a British sphere of influence; France extorted a lease on the bay of Kwantung and concessions in the Province of Yunnan. A few days before the International assembled for its congress at Paris in August 1900, troops of the major powers had marched into Peking for the bloody suppression of the Boxer Rising—an outbreak born of Chinese resentment at the continuous humiliation and dismemberment to which their country was being subjected by the foreigners.

Since the London Congress of 1896, wars had taken on a manifestly new character. They were no longer, like the Italo-Austrian War of 1859, the Austro-Prussian War of 1866 or the Franco-German War of

1870, purely national in character. The new type of war was overtly imperialist, fought by ruling classes for colonial possessions, markets and spheres of influence in Africa and Asia.

The Paris Congress of 1900 discussed the problem of war in relation to the colonial policy of the Great Powers.[1] It reaffirmed the earlier decisions on working-class policy in the fight against the war danger and recommended particularly 'the education and organization of youth for the fight against militarism'.

5

The idea of systematic anti-militarist propaganda was especially well received in France, and later spread to Germany, Belgium, Italy and beyond. In Germany, the most effective among the early exponents of anti-militarism was Wilhelm Liebknecht's son, Karl, who made a particular point of propagating the Socialist attitude to war among the youth who were eligible for military service and in the armed forces themselves. The propaganda, however, as Liebknecht told a conference of the Young Guard, was 'of course' confined within 'legal limits' and was never intended 'directly or indirectly to incite military disobedience'.[2] Moreover, Liebknecht's anti-militarism did not stray beyond the limits laid down at successive conferences of the German Social Democratic party.

In France, however, anti-militarism spread far beyond the youth movement to the broad mass of working-class activists, where it gave rise to acute controversy concerning the principles as well as the tactics of the party. Gustave Hervé, a leader who had quite early been officially rebuked for his pacifist outlook, advocated not only a general strike among industrial workers and reservists but an armed insurrection in the event of wars being declared. Like Nieuwenhuis, whom he revered on the grounds that he 'kept alive and unsullied the genuine revolutionary Socialist principles of internationalism',[3] he also rejected any distinction between aggressive and defensive wars, and demanded that any international war, no matter who declared it, should be countered by civil war. Since the workers had no country, it was 'immaterial', he

1. See above, p. 311.

2. See the *Handbuch für Sozialdemokratische Wähler* (Berlin, 1911), p. 639. Despite his insistence on the legal nature of his anti-militarist propaganda, Liebknecht was sentenced to eighteen months' imprisonment for 'incitement to treason' in October 1907, after the speech had been published as a pamphlet.

3. Gustave Hervé, *Leur Patrie* (Paris, 1906), p. 201. In this book, which caused a great sensation in France, Hervé explicitly challenged the whole concept of patriotism, as the title suggests. '*Leur Patrie*' meant specifically 'their country'—the country of the rich. The workers had no country and hence no patriotic duties or obligations.

declared in a resolution which he submitted to the Stuttgart Congress of the International in 1907, so far as the workers were concerned, 'which government is calling for patriotic support or who lyingly proclaims the existence of some community of interests among those who happen to live in the same country'.[1]

As in the case of Nieuwenhuis, Hervé's anti-patriotism was rooted in the Proudhonist version of Anarchism. In the days of the First International the Proudhonists had advanced the view that 'all nationalities and even nations were "antiquated prejudices" '—a view which Marx had duly ridiculed when it was raised on the General Council.[2] He had himself declared in the *Communist Manifesto* that 'the working men have no country'. But this widely quoted and widely misunderstood aphorism merely stated a fact—that the workers could reasonably be considered the disinherited stepchildren of the fatherland, those who had been, in Otto Bauer's words, 'abandoned by the nation', shut out from that community of culture that formed the essence of nationhood, allowed no part in the national riches which they produced and denied all right to a say in the nation's affairs. In such conditions the country could fairly be represented in the terms of the *Manifesto* as the property of the ruling classes, the aristocracy and the *bourgeoisie*.[3]

Marx's conclusion had not been that the workers should destroy the nation, but rather that they should take it over. They must themselves, he wrote, immediately following the much-discussed aphorism, 'rise to be the leading class of the nation'. Moreover, Marx assumed, as he went on to explain, that 'national differences, and antagonisms between peoples, are daily vanishing more and more, owing to the development of the *bourgeoisie*, to freedom of commerce, to the world market, to uniformity in the mode of production and in the conditions of life corresponding thereto'. In contrast, Otto Bauer had developed the idea, in his discussion on the sociology of nationalism, that to the extent to which the workers won the right to participate in the benefits of the national civilization and became incorporated in the life of the civilized

1. Hervé founded in 1906 the paper *La Guerre sociale* (*The Social War*) to propagate his views on anti-patriotism and insurrection. However, when war broke out in 1914, he changed the name of his paper to *La Victoire* (*Victory*) and enthusiastically defended both patriotism and the cause of national defence.

2. Minutes of the General Council, 19 June 1866; see also Marx's letter to Engels of 20 June 1866, *Marx-Engels Briefwechsel*, vol. III, p. 408.

3. E. H. Carr, discussing the relation between Marx's theory of nationality and that of the Bolsheviks on the right of national self-determination, in *The Bolshevik Revolution, 1917–23*, describes (vol. I, p. 410) some of the antecedents of the classic Marxist view, including an extract from Robespierre, who declared in his first published speech (*Discours et rapports de Robespierre*, ed. C. Vellay, p. 328): 'In aristocratic States the word *patrie* has no meaning except for the patrician families who usurped sovereignty. It is only under democracy that the State is truly the *patrie* of all the individuals composing it.'

community, nations would diverge more and more in their distinctive characteristics.[1]

Marx, at all events, accepted the nation as a historically constituted entity. For him, therefore, the right to national self-determination as a pre-condition for democracy was beyond question. In the programme which he drafted for the Geneva Congress of 1866, and which was endorsed by the General Council, the right of self-determination for Poland, 'the right of every people',[2] in Marx's words, was demanded. However, if the right of nations to self-determination and independence was recognized as a basic principle of democracy by the International, it was hardly feasible to deny their right to defend that independence. Such a right was asserted by the First International in the General Council's Addresses on the Franco-German War and confirmed by the Second International in the resolution of its London Congress of 1896, which advocated 'the complete autonomy of all nations'.

Hervé's opposition to patriotism, therefore, contradicted the traditional outlook of the International. His agitation was more in line with the Anarcho-Syndicalist tendencies of a section of the French trade-union movement, but found little response in the French Socialist party.

It was, in particular, opposed by Jaurès, who effectively expressed in his own person a fusion between the internationalist currents of Socialism and the modern concept of the nation. He called the paper which he founded for the Socialist movement in 1904 *L'Humanité*—humanity, to whose cause it was dedicated. But, for him, humanity was not a shapeless mass of individuals, but received its highest expression in the nation. He regarded nations as organic entities, formed through a lengthy process of historical development from which had emerged groups of men and women linked together by a common psychology and outlook. The destruction of the nation would mean not only the suppression or annihilation of a great collective existence, but also, as he wrote, 'a reduction of vitality, a spiritual impoverishment, a mental decline and a basic impairment of the individual'. The working class would lose even more than any other group, he added, because it would lose the very medium through which it could conduct its struggle for freedom. 'Even if the conquering nation were to institute Communism in the conquered country, even if it were to abolish capitalist tyranny, it would mean for the working class, thus liberated and violated at the same time, an intolerable suffering, feeling itself enslaved in the very

1. Otto Bauer, *Die Nationalitätenfrage und die Sozialdemokratie* (Vienna, 1907), I, ch. 9.
2. Session of the London Conference of the First International, 27 September 1865, *Documents of the First International* (1964), p. 246.

nature of its apparent economic victory, and unable to taste under the new order of justice the liberty and joy of its own genius.'[1]

Jaurès compared humanity to a crown jewel which derived its lustre from the illuminated facets of the diversity of nations. But he wrote in the first issue of *L'Humanité* that humanity as a genuine organic community did not yet exist, since class distinctions had disrupted the unity of nations, while national selfishness prevented the unity of mankind. To overcome these contradictions was the main task of Socialism. 'Humanity must achieve its genuine, living unity as a free alliance of autonomous and fraternal nations.' Socialism, however, as Otto Bauer pointed out, could be achieved only within the historically constituted framework of the nation. 'Hervé wants to destroy the fatherland,' Jaurès told the Stuttgart Congress. 'We would rather socialize the fatherland for the benefit of the working class, by transferring the means of production into common property. Since the nation embodies the creative spirit of mankind and is the main vehicle for human progress, it is hardly appropriate for the working class to try to destroy it.'[2]

Although the French party charged Hervé with being unpatriotic, his anti-militarist agitation did not go without effect, as became apparent at the Limoges Congress in 1906. The subject of debate was that of the best way of preventing wars. Hervé's proposal of a general strike against war was, of course, turned down. But up to that time a majority of the party, led by Jules Guesde, had also rejected the general strike as a political weapon. Jaurès, however, had conceded that it might be legitimate as a last resort, in face of a fundamental threat to the future of the working class. Such a danger, he now believed, could arise in a war situation, and to meet it all methods of struggle should be considered. He had no hesitation in giving the same warning from the parliamentary rostrum. When the Moroccan crisis was debated in the Chamber of Deputies in December 1905, he said that the Socialist peace policy was governed by the need to 'every day increase the union and effective action of the workers in every country, so as to prevent, by their collective and co-ordinated action, the explosion of wars'. If, in spite of this, a war should break out, he added the warning that the workers would 'reduce to impotence from one end of Europe to another the criminal governments which unleash the tempest'.[3] Jaurès persisted in the belief that it lay within the power of the international working class to prevent wars.

At the Limoges Congress the Marxist wing, led by Guesde, opposed

1. *Petite République*, 24 December 1901, quoted in J. Hampden Jackson, *Jean Jaurès* (London, 1943), p. 132.
2. *Protokoll*, op. cit., p. 89.
3. Jackson, op. cit., p. 126.

these views. The resolution which they submitted to Congress declared both militarism and wars the inevitable results of capitalism. Hence, the evil could be ended only by the destruction of the capitalist system in which it had its roots. Anti-militarist propaganda impeded the fight against capitalism, since it diverted attention from the need to recruit Socialists and so postponed the day when the workers would be sufficiently strong and organized to carry through the Socialist revolution, overthrow capitalism and banish war from the world for all time. As interim measures, however, the resolution recommended the workers to make war 'almost impossible' by struggling to shorten the period of compulsory military service, opposing all credits for the army, navy and colonies and demanding the replacement of standing armies by a mobilization of the entire people.

Guesde's resolution was opposed, at Limoges, by one put forward by Jaurès and Vaillant. The latter also considered militarism to be a phenomenon rooted in capitalist society—'an armed machine organized by the state with the object of keeping the workers under the economic and political yoke of the capitalists'—but it lacked the unqualified pessimism of Guesde's. Jaurès certainly considered capitalism to be the cause of wars. He wrote that 'as the cloud carries lightning and thunder, capitalism is the bearer of war'. But unlike thunderstorms, wars did not arise spontaneously from the clash of elemental forces. Since they sprang from voluntary actions of men and women, they could not be considered inevitable. They could, in fact, be prevented if the working class opposed its own will to that of the rulers. Even in capitalist society, the workers possessed the power to avert the calamity of war. In line with this conviction the resolution called for effective opposition to wars by all means, 'from parliamentary intervention and public agitation to the general strike and the armed uprising'.

In complete contrast to Hervé's anti-patriotic line, however, this resolution recognized that the workers shared in the common destiny of the nation, and it stressed that any threat to national independence must be considered a threat to the working class. Moreover, it declared that the nation had not merely the right to defend its independence against external aggression, but that such defence was an 'imperative duty' which the working class shared fully with the nation as a whole. The principle of national independence was formally adopted and proclaimed by the International. The resolution was also careful to include the corollary that a nation which found its independence threatened enjoyed 'the right to assistance from the workers throughout the world'.

The resolution from Jaurès and Vaillant was approved by a majority at the congress and confirmed, at the following party congress, at Nancy in 1907, by 1,960 votes to 1,174. At the same time it was agreed to submit the resolution for discussion at the forthcoming congress of the International, which was due to meet at Stuttgart in August 1907.

6

The Stuttgart Congress was the seventh to be held by the Second International, and the largest in terms of delegates and national delegations. Twenty-five nations were represented by a total of 886 delegates, a gathering 'more splendid and inspiring', as Bebel claimed in his opening remarks, 'than any other International Socialist congress had been able to achieve'. It was the first congress to be held on German soil and, inevitably, took place beyond the reach of the government of Prussia. It would have been, as Bebel pointed out, a little too risky 'to hold it under the gaze of Prince Bülow and the Berlin police' in the capital of the German Reich.[1]

The problem of 'militarism and international conflicts' came first on the agenda. Discussion, which went on for six days, of which five were taken up by the commission and the sixth in full congress, was based on the two French resolutions, one by Jaurès and Vaillant, the other from Guesde (with an amendment in the name of Hervé), and one submitted by Bebel on behalf of the German Social Democrats.

Bebel's resolution, like Guesde's, saw wars as an expression of capitalist contradictions. They would 'cease only when the capitalist economic system has been superseded or when the magnitude of the sacrifice in men and money needed to maintain and develop the military machine, and the consequent indignation produced by the arms race, brings about the abolition of the system'. The resolution emphasized the duty of the workers, and their parliamentary representatives, to fight with all their power against military and naval armaments and to oppose the granting of money for their maintenance. It also reiterated the earlier demand for the democratization of the armed forces as 'an essential guarantee for a lasting peace'.

Before submitting his own resolution to the commission, Bebel had described the Jaurès-Vaillant resolution as unacceptable to the German delegation, and likely to 'plunge the party into the greatest difficulties and dangers'. Not that he opposed those parts of the resolution which

1. Although the International met outside the sphere of influence of the Prussian police, it was still subjected to a certain amount of interference. The British delegate, Harry Quelch, while Congress was still in session, was expelled by the Wurtemburg government for referring to the governments represented at the Hague Peace Conferencc, which was meeting at the same time, as a 'thieves' kitchen'. His empty seat, adorned with his delegate's badge and a laurel wreath, was placed on the British delegation's table, with a notice saying: 'Here sat Harry Quelch, yesterday expelled by the government of Wurtemburg.'

emphasized the right of the nation and its working class to defend its independence, a right which was questioned by no one except Hervé. What worried him was the passage in the resolution which dealt with the means of preventing wars, and which said that the 'impeding and prevention of war will be achieved by the national and international action of the working class, using every means available, from parliamentary intervention and public agitation to the general strike and the armed uprising'.

Instead of this passage, Bebel proposed to substitute the words: 'If there is a danger of war breaking out, the workers and their parliamentary representatives in the countries concerned are pledged to do everything possible to prevent the outbreak, by whatever means seem most appropriate. If war should, none the less, break out, they should work for its speedy termination.'

The proposal to prevent war by international working-class action was considered to be of such supreme importance that it needed a unanimous vote of Congress and, particularly, the support of the German and French Socialists. Since Europe had divided into two armed camps—the Triple Alliance of Germany, Austria and Italy, and the Franco-Russian Alliance—the question of war or peace was likely to be decided in Berlin and Paris. Only if it should prove possible to bring irresistible pressure on the governments of Germany and France would a European war be prevented. But for this to be even thinkable, an agreement on common action between the Social Democrats of France and Germany was essential.

In developing his case, Jaurès attacked the fatalism which underlay Bebel's resolution. 'We are told,' he exclaimed, 'that it is futile to struggle against war, since capitalism renders war inevitable. But it is also an inherent tendency of capitalism to increase exploitation without limit and to prolong the working day indefinitely. We still fight for the eight-hour day, and with a certain amount of success.' The International ought not to be satisfied with vague generalizations about the means of preventing wars. Means of opposing wars must be expounded with detail and precision so as to prepare the workers for the decisive engagement. Social Democracy must not let the war danger weaken its sense of common struggle. 'To prevent war means to mobilize the workers into an army of invincible strength.' It would be sad, he added, 'if we could not go further than Bebel, if we had to admit that we knew no way of preventing mutual hatred and slaughter among nations'. He recalled that Bebel himself, at the congress of his party at Jena in 1905, had advocated a general strike if the workers were deprived of the right to vote. But was it, then, permissible for the French and German workers to kill each other on the orders of and for the benefit of the capitalists without making just such a supreme effort? 'If we did not, at least, make the attempt, we should be men without honour,' he declared.[1]

Bebel replied that there was no question of unwillingness to make the effort and that his resolution was not meant to rule out any appropriate means of anti-war struggle. But the method proposed in the Jaurès-Vaillant resolution of calling a general strike and a mass uprising was simply 'impossible and undiscussible' in German conditions. He described the situation which would exist in Germany the moment war was declared. Six million men—two million of them Social Democrats—would immediately be called to the colours. 'Where, then, would we get the men for a general strike? . . . Four million families would find themselves plunged into trouble incomparably worse than any general strike. Imagine the mood of the masses in such a situation.' A war, Bebel continued, would precipitate a major economic crisis. 'We depend on imports for a large part of our food supply. The day war was declared, that supply would be cut off. A great deal of our industrial output would remain unsold, because it could not be exported, and so production would cease. This would mean a big increase in unemployment and distress. Prices would begin to climb sky high and there might be danger of famine. . . .' Bebel quoted a German general who had said that, in the mass battles of the future, 'we should not know where to put the wounded or bury the dead'. Bebel continued: 'In a situation like that, could we really play about with the idea of a general strike? Our first attempt would be swept aside with derision.'[2] Resignedly, he concluded: 'We can do nothing but patiently explain, open men's minds, agitate and organize.' German Social Democracy believed in using all methods for fighting militarism and the danger of war. 'But above all we cannot proceed with methods of struggle which could destroy the normal life and, in some conditions the very existence of the party.' He proposed that a sub-committee be elected to find a formula for a resolution which could be accepted by both French and German parties.

1. *Protokoll*, p. 90.

2. *Protokoll*, pp. 83, 100. Four years later, in 1911, Bebel tried to substantiate his case with similar arguments. 'Millions of workers will be taken from their families, who will have nothing to eat or to live on. Hundreds of thousands of small businessmen will go bankrupt, through being unable to carry on their trade. The price of bonds will collapse, leading to the ruin of tens of thousands of hitherto comfortable families. Exports will cease and our extensive world trade will be interrupted. Those numerous factories and industrial concerns not required for war production will have to close. Everywhere there will be mass unemployment and no chance of finding work. The food supply will be partially or totally disrupted. Food prices will become exorbitant. There will be widespread famine. The masses will then demand, not a strike, but work and bread!' (*Protokoll über die Verhandlungen des Parteitages in Jena*).

The resolution which emerged from the sub-committee was a somewhat lengthy document.[1] It declared that war was a phenomenon inseparable from capitalism and pledged the Socialist parties to fight with all their power against the arms race and to educate the working-class youth in the spirit of Socialism and the brotherhood of nations.

The resolution went on to admit that the International was unable 'to lay down rigidly the action to be taken against militarism by the working class in all countries, everywhere and at all times'. Since the time of the Brussels Congress the workers had, on a number of occasions, taken action of various kinds in an attempt to prevent a war or to bring one to an early end. There had been the agreement between the British and French trade unions following the Fashoda crisis, an agreement aimed at maintaining peace and restoring friendly relations between the two countries. There had also been the actions of the Socialist parties in the German and French Parliaments and at public meetings during the Moroccan crisis; the joint rallies in Trieste organized by the Socialists of Austria and Italy to prevent a conflict between the two countries; the efforts of the Socialist workers of Sweden to prevent an attack on Norway; and 'finally, the heroic, self-sacrificing struggle of the Socialist workers and peasants of Russia and Poland in opposition to the war [against Japan] unleashed by Tsarism, to end it and to utilize the nation-wide crisis in the interests of working-class emancipation'. 'All these efforts,' the resolution added, 'were evidence of the growing power of the working class and of its increasing ability to safeguard the preservation of peace by resolute action.'

The resolution ended with the following statement, drafted jointly by Lenin, Luxemburg and Martov, which was to be of supreme importance for the subsequent history of the International. It said:

> If a war threatens to break out, it is the duty of the working classes and their parliamentary representatives in the countries involved, supported by the co-ordinating activity of the International Socialist Bureau, to exert every effort in order to prevent the outbreak of war by the means they consider most effective, which naturally vary according to the sharpening of the class struggle and the sharpening of the general political situation.
>
> In case war should break out anyway, it is their duty to intervene in favour of its speedy termination, and with all their powers to utilize the economic and political crisis created by the war, to rouse the masses and thereby to hasten the downfall of capitalist class rule.

The resolution was passed unanimously, with what the Minutes describe as 'tumultuous, long and continuously repeated applause, with particular enthusiasm from the French delegation'. Congress was convinced, in fact, that the differences between the French and German approaches had been bridged. In the debate it was emphasized that

1. For the wording of the resolution, see Appendix Two.

Bebel's formula of 'the means which seem most effective in the circumstances' for the prevention of war included the general strike, while it must be left to the parties concerned to decide whether this particular weapon should be employed. In any case, all the parties had pledged themselves to resist war by every means in their power.

The last paragraph in the resolution, however, went beyond merely opposing war, or trying to end it quickly once it had broken out. It committed the parties in the belligerent countries to use the crisis resulting from the war to bring about a Socialist revolution. No one drew attention to the significance of this commitment during the debate. Jaurès, for example, who, on his return from Stuttgart, spoke on the resolution to a big mass meeting at the Tivoli-Vaux-Hall in Paris, confined himself to preventive measures.

> 'The International has proclaimed two indivisible truths. Two indissoluble truths. The first is that autonomous nations have the right and the duty to maintain their autonomy with all their energy; the second is that, in order to prevent sudden conflicts, in order to prevent murderous outbreaks in which not only the arteries but the conscience of the workers will bleed, the duty of the workers is to prevent war, and not—you will understand me—by mere verbal maledictions, not by futile grumbling and impotent curses . . . but by the whole force of their action: they must crush out the germ of fatal wars by parliamentary action or by social action.'[1]

It was noticeable, however, that there was now no talk of the 'third truth' which the International had also proclaimed, and no reference to the possibility of responding to world war by revolutionary action to bring about 'the downfall of capitalist class rule'.

7

Fear of war, which had dominated the discussion at Stuttgart, grew as relations between the major powers became steadily worse. The Hague Peace Conference, which had met at the same time, failed when Kaiser Wilhelm refused either to allow the possibility of arms limitation to be discussed or to submit international disputes to arbitration. Britain had also failed in its efforts to reach agreement with Germany on the limitation of naval armaments. Wilhelm was determined to add to his already considerable land force a navy of equal strength. His continual public references to the 'mailed fist' and the 'sharpened sword' were generally taken as an indication that Germany was intent on war. There were, in fact, no conflicts between the major powers which threatened any of their vital interests seriously enough to justify war.

1. Jackson, op. cit., p. 135.

But the frenzied arms race on which the European powers had embarked generated its own atmosphere of hatred, suspicion and mounting tension liable at any time to erupt into war on a continental scale.

The next congress of the International, meeting under the chairmanship of Hjalmar Branting in Copenhagen at the end of August 1910, represented twenty-four national sections with a total of 896 delegates. Its discussions centred on the now dangerous 'Dreadnought' race in which Britain and Germany strove for mastery of the sea,[1] and which introduced a new and dangerous factor into an already explosive situation.

The resolution, drafted by Karl Renner and eventually adopted unanimously, confined itself exclusively to parliamentary activity. It again committed the Socialist representatives in Parliament to oppose the arms race and vote against war credits. It gave a new emphasis, however, to the demand for an international arbitration court to which all disputes between nations were to be referred.

This question had already been discussed at the Stuttgart Congress in the debate on national defence. Jaurès, with the full support of Bebel, had suggested that the position of the Social Democrats in the event of war should depend on the attitude of the respective governments towards arbitration. Any government which refused to submit a dispute to arbitration should be resisted by its working class. On the other hand, full support should be given to a government which was the victim of aggression despite its willingness to refer to arbitration.

The resolution went on to pledge Socialist members of Parliament to 'continuing pressure' for general disarmament and, in particular, for an international agreement on the restriction of naval armaments. Finally, the resolution endorsed the Stuttgart agreement on the action of the workers in the event of war—the last two paragraphs of the agreement being repeated in the text—and instructed the Bureau 'in the event of the

1. Germany's naval construction gave rise to something like panic in Britain, a panic which the jingo Press had done everything to intensify. There was widespread fear of a German invasion. The failure of the British government to reach an agreement with Germany on the limitation of naval armaments led a number of highly esteemed British Socialists—including Hyndman, Belfort Bax and Blatchford—to advocate the naval rearmament of Britain, a course which was strongly opposed by both the I.L.P. and the Labour party. Kautsky tells of a discussion with Hyndman in which he told the latter how much harder his attitude had made the struggle of the German Social Democrats against the Kaiser's naval programme. 'Hyndman asked me,' said Kautsky, 'whether I could guarantee that the German Social Democrats would prevent an invasion of England. I had to tell him that any such undertaking would be irresponsible. We should, of course, do everything possible to prevent an outbreak of war. . . . Right, said Hyndman, as soon as you German Social Democrats are strong enough to prevent a war being waged against us, we in England will oppose the arms programme. But until we can rely on you in this respect we shall have to rely on other factors. . . .'—Karl Kautsky, *Sozialisten und Krieg* (Prague, 1937), p. 398.

threat of war, to take immediate steps to secure agreement, between the workers' parties in the respective countries, on joint action to meet the threat'.

Keir Hardie and Vaillant, however, demanded that the debate on the possibility of direct action by the workers should be resumed. They suggested that Congress should declare a strike in the arms industry, mining and transport, a 'particularly appropriate' technique for preventing wars. In support of the thesis, Vaillant declared that parliamentary means would prove inadequate unless backed up by the extra-parliamentary threat of mass action. Such action could be effective only if prepared for well in advance. 'Our proposal is not so much to declare a general strike as to organize for one,' he explained. And Keir Hardie added that a strike by the miners would, in itself, be enough to prevent a war.

By the time the proposal was debated in full congress, it had already been discussed in the commission and rejected by 119 votes to 58, after Oddino Morgari, for the Italians, had declared that any such resolution would mean 'suicide for the party', and Ledebour, for the Germans, had claimed that it would result in the party's being declared illegal and lead to the 'destruction of the organization'. Eventually, the full congress agreed, at the suggestion of Vandervelde, to refer the proposal to the bureau for examination, and to postpone further discussion until the following congress.

8

It had been agreed at Copenhagen that the next congress of the International would be held at Vienna in the summer of 1913. In fact, however, there were to be no further congresses of the International. A year after the Copenhagen Congress, Italy declared war on Turkey and the Italian workers proved unable to prevent the imperialist attack on Tripoli. Immediately before the outbreak of war, the Socialists had, together with the trade unions, issued a call for a twenty-four-hour general strike, but this 'dignified protest with folded arms, while abstaining from any violent action', as the proclamation of the Socialist party described it, was incapable of preventing the disaster. And, though the workers protested in a number of spontaneous strikes and public demonstrations, the war ran its course for a whole year. It was eventually to precipitate a crisis which, starting in the Balkans, finally unleashed the catastrophe of world war.

Even before the Balkan War had begun, the international situation seemed so threatening that Victor Adler expressed, in a letter to Bebel, his doubts as to whether the congress planned for Vienna in the summer of 1913 would ever take place. Bebel confirmed Adler's fears.

> Looking at the European situation [he wrote to Adler on 6 October 1912] I have felt for some time that next year will probably land us in a European war, resulting from our stupid policy towards England. This has produced an alignment of powers which, only a few years ago, no one would have thought possible, and which is intrinsically most unnatural. The English, it seems to me, cannot allow the situation to last for any length of time and are trying to force a show-down. . . . The whole situation, together with the reasons you mentioned, make it absolutely necessary to postpone the congress. If a conflict with Turkey breaks out, I do not believe that the war will remain isolated. Such developments have their own logic and there are too many seeds of discontent. We are inexorably pushed on, willy-nilly, and the outcome will probably be indescribable.[1]

The conflict with Turkey which Bebel feared came to a head a week later. On 13 October the Balkan states declared war on Turkey—the culmination of a long period of ferment among the Christian peoples of south-eastern Europe. Since the Berlin Congress of 1878, Macedonia and Albania had repeatedly risen in revolt against the hated Ottoman tyranny, and Serbia, Bulgaria and Greece were only waiting for a chance of war which would put an end to Turkish rule in Europe.

Their chance came with the Italian invasion of Libya, though it took a whole year before the governments of the Balkan states could achieve the necessary degree of unity and military preparedness. The war broke out in the first half of October 1912, and to everyone's surprise it took the Balkan armies only a few weeks to reach the Tsataldscha Line at the gates of Constantinople. The end of Turkish power in the Balkans was at hand.

It now seemed, however, that, as Bebel had feared, the Balkan conflict would turn into a European war. The Austrian government had assumed, in Count Bülow's words, that 'Turkey would easily polish off the opposing forces'.[2] The victory of the Balkan states under the leadership of Serbia seemed to Austria a deadly threat to her own empire. She saw in the tiny Serb state of scarcely three million inhabitants her most dangerous enemy, since it served as a magnet to the seven million Yugoslavs under Habsburg domination. To humiliate Serbia and render her powerless with a view, when the time came, to 'cutting out' this 'appendix of Europe', was the main object of Austria's Balkan policy.[3]

1. *Victor Adlers Briefwechsel*, p. 550.
2. Fürst Bernhard von Bülow, *Denkwürdigkeiten*, ed. Franz von Stockhammer (Berlin, 1931), vol. III, p. 112.
3. As early as 1907 the Austrian Chief of Staff, Conrad von Hötzendorf, wrote a memorandum demanding 'the annexation of Serbia, including the central district of Nisch' as the main aim of Austro-Hungarian policy. He argued that 'an independent Serbia acts as a constant incitement for all those aspirations and

In 1908 she annexed the Turkish provinces of Bosnia and Herzegovina, and so permanently alienated the Serbs, who aimed at uniting all the Slav peoples of the Balkans. Russia supported the demands of Serbia while Germany backed Austria, and the Balkan crisis of 1909 threatened to erupt into a general war. However, Russia had not yet recovered sufficiently from the effects of her war against Japan to risk a major armed clash in Europe. She determined, though, to be ready for the next crisis whenever it came.

In 1912 the Balkan crisis flared up again. Serbia had emerged victorious from her war with Turkey and now aimed at securing a port on the Adriatic. Austria was determined to allow no expansion of Serbian territory. She mobilized her army, threatened an invasion and demanded the cession of a corridor—the Sandjak—through Serbia. Once again Tsarist Russia gave her backing to Serbia in her resistance to a Habsburg domination of the Balkans. This time a clash between Austria and Russia, between the Triple and the Franco-Russian Alliances, seemed inevitable. World peace hung in the balance.

9

The Bureau of the International assembled in Brussels on 28 October, a fortnight after the start of the Balkan War. In accordance with the Copenhagen decisions, it convened an extraordinary congress in Basle for 24 and 25 November. At the same time it postponed the normal congress, due to meet in Vienna in 1913, until the following year.

The Basle Congress was little more than a peace demonstration, though perhaps the most impressive in the history of the International. It was formally opened on the Sunday morning in the Hall of the Burgvogtei by Édouard Anseele, with 550 delegates from twenty-three countries. Representatives of the Balkan peoples had come from Romania, Bosnia, Croatia and Bulgaria, including Janko Sakasoff from Sofia, the only member of the Bulgarian Parliament to have protested against the war. He arrived at the congress straight from the battlefields of Macedonia. The Serbian party sent a letter attributing its absence to the war, and beseeching the congress 'to put an end to the bloodshed in the Balkans'.

intrigues aiming at the secession of the South Slav areas'. During the Bosnian annexation crisis of 1908 he had pressed for the annexation to be extended to Serbia. The Austro-Hungarian Foreign Minister, Count Aehrenthal, on the other hand, preferred to wait for 'a favourable European constellation' before attempting anything so ambitious. See Otto Bauer, *Die österreichische Revolution* (Vienna, 1923), p. 12. The opening chapter of the first section of the book provides the best introduction to the Balkan situation in the years leading up to the First World War. See also the same author's *Der Balkankrieg und die deutsche Weltpolitik* (Berlin, 1912).

As the congress was holding its opening session, special trains were arriving in Basle from Baden, Alsace and all parts of Switzerland, and thousands had crowded into the vast Münster, overflowing into the wide squares which surrounded the building. At two o'clock the delegates began to march through the streets of Basle towards the Münster, headed by a group of children in white carrying twigs of birch in front of a forest of red flags. As the demonstration approached the cathedral, church bells began to chime, and as soon as those at the head of the procession passed through the doors the organ struck up the chords of the Bach *Mass in C Minor*.

It was a strange setting for a congress of the Socialist International. Five hundred years before the same high Gothic arches had seen another international congress—the cardinals, bishops and prelates of the Catholic church meeting for the ecumenical council of 1431. Now the Calvinist minister, Taschler, preaching the morning sermon, told how the wardens of the congregation had debated the propriety of admitting the delegates of an international Socialist congress. 'The heads of our community voted unanimously in favour,' he reported, adding: 'It is a gathering filled with the spirit of Christ which will assemble here this afternoon, though the speakers may use a style which sounds strange to our ears. But since it is essentially Christian principles and ideas which will be proclaimed, we welcome with genuine sympathy these men, many of whom have come to us over great distances.'[1]

The proceedings were dominated by the threat which overhung Europe. 'We come from the country,' said Adler, 'whose ruling classes are at this very moment engaged in fateful decisions . . . while we assemble here to defend the cause of peace.' Every speaker was preoccupied with the same question—how could the unspeakable evil be averted? Did the working class possess the strength to ward off the threatening catastrophe? Keir Hardie believed that 'the congress, representing as it does a total of fifteen million Socialist votes, is a powerful bulwark defending the peace of Europe'. More realistically Adler pointed out that: 'It does not, unfortunately, depend on us Social Democrats whether or not a war breaks out. While the international working class is certainly gaining in strength . . . it would be unwise to overestimate our resources. . . .' The best hope seemed to be that the ruling classes would be too scared of revolution to venture on war, and it was this hope which sustained the spirit of the International. According to Adler the governments themselves suspected that 'history itself would punish the perpetrators of a historic crime. . . . If such a crime were committed it would be the beginning of the end for the criminals'

1. *Ausserordentlicher Internationaler Sozialisten-Kongress am 24. und 25. November 1912* (Berlin, 1912), p. 52.

own power.' Jaurès expressed the feelings of the congress in a highly emotional speech. 'The sound of church bells which greeted us on our arrival,' he said, 'seemed to me like a call for reconciliation. It reminded me of the preface which Schiller wrote to his beautiful Song of the Bells: "*Vivos voco, mortuos plango, fulgura frango. . . . Vivos voco* . . . I call the living to the defence of life against the threat of murder! *Mortuos plango* . . . I mourn the uncounted dead whose corpses litter the battle-fields at the other end of Europe, from whom the stench of decay reaches us as remorse for their misdeeds. *Fulgura frango* . . . I shatter the lightning of war which lights up the clouds as a warning of imminent danger!" ' Jaurès concluded his speech with the warning: 'Let governments remember that in conjuring up the danger of war they invite the peoples to make a simple calculation—how much smaller a sacrifice a revolution would involve, when compared with the war they are preparing!'

Next day the congress got down to business. The Chair was taken by Hermann Greulich, a veteran of the International, who forty-three years earlier had represented the Socialists of Switzerland at the Basle Congress of the First International.

At its meeting in Brussels on 28 October the bureau had drafted a long manifesto which differed substantially from previous conference resolutions. It did not merely, as in earlier statements, condemn war and call on the workers to resist in the event of war breaking out. It went further in outlining a specifically Socialist foreign policy designed to meet the threat of war and to facilitate a peaceful solution of the European crisis.

The statement began by endorsing the proposal of the Balkan parties for a democratic federation of the Balkan states. It called on the Socialists of the Balkans to oppose not only all attempts to revive old hatreds among Serbs, Bulgarians, Romanians and Greeks but also all antagonism directed against the Turks and Albanians in the other camp. 'It is the duty of Balkan Socialists,' it declared, 'to fight against every violation of national rights and, against the claims of unbridled chauvinism, to assert the brotherhood of all Balkan nations, including Albanians, Romanians and Turks.'

The manifesto then dealt with the Social Democratic parties of Austria, Hungary, Croatia and Slovenia, Bosnia and Herzegovina. It was their duty to defend Serbia with all their power against the attacks of the Danubian monarchy and oppose all attempts to deprive her of her recent gains by force and to transform her into a colony of Austria. It went on to denounce the intrigues of Tsarism, which, having betrayed the Balkan peoples on a number of occasions, now posed as a liberator of Balkan nations so as to secure her own predominance in this area in the event of war. It called on the workers of Russia, Finland and Poland to oppose every warlike policy of Tsarism and thwart Russia's aggressive designs on Armenia and Constantinople.

The main task, said the manifesto, fell, however, on the Socialist parties of Germany, France and Britain. They must press their own governments to refuse all help to either Austria-Hungary or Russia in their Balkan policies, refrain from all interference in the area and observe strict neutrality. 'It would be criminal folly for the three leading civilized nations to go to war because of a Serbo-Austrian dispute about access to the sea.' However, if the military collapse of Turkey were followed by the break-up of the Ottoman Empire in the Near East it would then be the duty of Socialists in Britain, France and Germany to oppose any attempts by their own governments at territorial expansion, since such attempts would certainly culminate in world war.

But, the document continued, the greatest danger to European peace came undoubtedly from the artificially instigated hostility between Britain and Germany. It urged the Socialists of both nations to strengthen their efforts and secure, if at all possible, an agreement on naval disarmament. To overcome the hostility between Germany on the one hand, and Britain and France on the other, would remove the greatest danger to world peace, considerably weaken the power of Tsarism which exploited this antagonism, rule out the possibility of a surprise attack by Austria-Hungary on Serbia and strengthen the cause of peace. 'All the International's efforts must be devoted primarily to this aim,' the manifesto declared.

The statement ended with a thinly disguised threat of revolution. The ruling powers should not forget, it said, 'that with existing conditions in Europe, including the state of working-class feeling, they would be unable to start a war without endangering their own position'. It reminded the governments that the Franco-Prussian War had been followed by the Paris Commune, that the Russo-Japanese War had triggered off revolution in the Empire of the Tsar and that the current military and naval arms race had raised class conflicts in Britain and on the Continent to a new level of intensity, characterized by widespread strikes. 'It would be madness for governments to lose sight of the fact that the very prospect of such an abomination as a world war would be enough to provoke the indignant hostility of the workers and drive them to revolt.'

The manifesto ended with the solemn declaration: 'The proletariat is conscious of the fact that it carries with it, at this moment, the future of humanity.' In a passionate appeal it called on the international working class 'to prevent the fine flower of the nations from being destroyed, threatened as it is by all the horrors of mass murder, famine and plague', and to demonstrate everywhere and by every means the workers' desire for peace. 'Let the capitalist world of exploitation and mass murder,' it concluded, 'be confronted by the proletarian world of peace and international brotherhood.'[1] The French text was read and approved by Jaurès, the German by Victor Adler and the English by Keir Hardie.

In the debate Hugo Haase spoke for the German party, Frantisek Soukup for the Czech Social Democrats, Troelstra for the Scandinavian, Belgian and Dutch Socialists, Clara Zetkin for the International Women's Movement, Sakasoff for the Balkan Socialists, Vaillant for the French party and Gregorio Agnini for the Spanish, Portuguese and Italian delegations. There was no discussion on the tactical means of preventing war. However, Keir Hardie told the opening meeting of the congress that, if political action proved unable to prevent the outbreak of war, he hoped that the workers would bring into use their economic weapon—'the international revolutionary strike against war'. And Vaillant emphasized that, although the manifesto did not explicitly refer to the question of direct action against war, it 'by no means excluded either an anti-war uprising or a general strike'.

August Bebel spoke at the closing stages of the congress. It was to be his last speech. Already gravely ill, the seventy-two-year-old veteran had barely a year to live. When his name was called and he walked to the rostrum, 'he was cheered', according to the official record, 'for several minutes by the Congress'. Deeply moved, Bebel paid tribute to the gathering, which would go down in the history of the International 'in golden letters' and could never be forgotten by those who had been privileged to take part.

10

Humanity was spared disaster for the time being. But the war-clouds which hovered over Europe did not disperse. Whatever their own intentions towards their neighbours, all the powers felt themselves threatened. The European tensions which had been building up over so many years, and which had not been resolved, continued to breed hatred, mistrust and fear. The armaments of the Great Powers continued to accumulate. Russia went on with the strategic network of roads leading to her western frontier, the French government called on Parliament to extend the period of conscription from two to three years, the German government strengthened its artillery, at the same time building up its fleet, while, for each armoured cruiser Germany added to her navy, Britain built two.

1. For the text of the manifesto, see *Protokoll*, op. cit., pp. 23–7.

An event in the Bosnian capital of Sarajevo the assassination of the Archduke Franz Ferdinand, heir to the Austrian throne, by Serbian conspirators, precipitated the dreaded confrontation of powers. No one guessed, at the time, that the death of a single prince would lead directly to the death of millions still living. Assassinations of royalty in the Balkans were by no means uncommon; the assassins themselves were Bosnians, and thus Austrian subjects; there was no proof that the Serbian government was implicated. Moreover, the Archduke had not been especially popular and even among the ruling Habsburg family few tears can have been shed over his death.

However, the government at Vienna saw, in Serbia, the seat of South Slav irredentism, and the main threat to Habsburg power in the Balkans. The opportunity of removing this threat seemed too good to miss. In 1912 the powers had prevented a show-down with Serbia. This time Austria was determined to let nothing stand in the way. The Sarajevo assassination would be the pretext, not only for humbling Serbia, but also, as Count Berchtold, the Austro-Hungarian Foreign Minister, reported to the Privy Council on 7 July 1914, 'for rendering her permanently harmless by a demonstration of strength'. Berchtold left the Privy Council in no doubt 'that an armed conflict with Serbia could lead to war with Russia'. But since, as he went on to say, he 'felt quite confident of the support of Germany in the event of warlike complications', it seemed a risk worth taking.[1]

It was inevitable that a conflict between Germany and Russia would unleash a European war. Russia had an alliance with France, while Britain could not allow Germany to triumph over France and Russia and so dominate the Continent. In that event Germany would control the entire mainland of Europe from St Petersburg to Brest and so destroy that 'balance of power' on which Britain relied for her security. Although England had no formal bond of alliance with the Franco-Russian bloc, she had let it be understood by both France and Germany that, in the event of a continental war, Britain would fight alongside France and Russia against Germany.[2]

To the Socialist parties, as to everyone else, it seemed incredible that Germany would jump into the abyss of a war against Russia, France and Britain on account of Austria's quarrel with Serbia. They refused to believe that either a European or any other kind of war could develop

1. See *Österreich-Ungarns Aussenpolitik von der Bosnischen Krise 1908 bis zum Kriegsausbruch 1918*, edited by Ludwig Bittner and Hans Übersberger (Vienna, 1930), vol. VIII, p. 343.

2. Viscount Haldane had told Bethmann-Hollweg as early as February 1912 that 'if Germany attacks France, England could give no guarantee' of her neutrality. See Th. von Bethmann-Hollweg, *Betrachtungen zum Weltkrieg*, Part I: *Vor dem Kriege* (Berlin, 1919), p. 53.

out of the incident at Sarajevo. The shots were fired in Sarajevo on 28 June. Regardless of this, Victor Adler's son Friedrich who, as secretary of the Austrian party had been entrusted with the preparation of the International's congress due to take place in Vienna on 23 August, went on with his work quietly. Only three weeks later, on 21 July, when the Austrian censorship deleted those paragraphs from a report in the *Arbeiter-Zeitung* which dealt with the discussions on the Keir Hardie-Vaillant resolution at the French Socialist congress, did Adler express doubts at to whether the Congress of the International, which had the same resolution on its own agenda, would be able to meet in Vienna without police interference. He considered the possibility of changing the meeting-place, but 'hardly any members of the party leadership happened to be in the country at the time'. All those with whom he might have discussed his doubts were enjoying their summer holidays. Only on 23 July was he able to call a meeting to discuss his proposal. However, as Adler records, 'the great majority of my comrades, and Dr Renner in particular, were not prepared even to consider the possibility of war'.[1] Two hours after the meeting closed, Austria's twenty-four-hour ultimatum to Serbia was announced to the world.

Now the leaders of the International, while recognizing the inevitability of a Serbo-Austrian war, convinced themselves that it could be localized. The Executive of the International convened by cable an urgent meeting of the Bureau at Brussels for 27 July. The next day Austria declared war on Serbia. But even then the conference hoped that a European war would be averted. So confident did they feel that, while agreeing to transfer the congress from Vienna to Paris, they announced its opening for 9 August. The Bureau adjourned on 29 July. Three days later, on 1 August, Germany declared war on Russia, and on 3 August on France. The next day Britain entered the war.

11

The war took the Socialists, as it took almost everyone else, by complete surprise. Almost before they could turn round it had broken over their heads.

1. Friedrich Adler, *Vor dem Ausnahmegericht* (Jena, 1923), p. 197. Belief in the unlikelihood of war was strengthened by the attitude of leading statesmen. These were also on holiday, despite the Sarajevo episode—the Austrians and Germans, who were planning war, deliberately intended to lull suspicions, while the French and British did not believe that the crisis would result in war. Kaiser Wilhelm had gone on a pleasure cruise in his yacht to the Norwegian fjords; Conrad von Hötzendorf, the Austrian Chief of Staff, and General von Moltke made a great point of being on holiday. On 15 July Poincaré, President of the French Republic, and the Prime Minister, Viviani, set off on their official visit to St Petersburg and did not return until 29 July. Sir Edward Grey, the British Foreign Secretary, spent the critical weeks trout-fishing in the country.

An example of this complete lack of awareness was provided by the French Socialists, who held an extraordinary congress of their party in Paris on 14 July, a little over two weeks before the outbreak of war. Their discussions were devoted exclusively to the problem of preventing war in general, without reference to the war which was actually brewing almost literally round the corner. The main item on the agenda was the motion from Keir Hardie and Vaillant, which had been referred by the Copenhagen Congress to the following congress of the International, now due to meet in Vienna on 23 August. The conference of the French party considered the problem in the light of a possible war between Germany and France, paying no attention to the role of Tsarist Russia in the international complex of power politics. No one, in the course of the debates, referred to the question of what form of direct action by the Socialist parties could prevent the Austro-Serbian conflict from degenerating into a world war, since only the chanceries of Vienna, Berlin and St Petersburg were aware that this was a serious possibility. The conference spent its time on the more academic question of whether the general strike was an appropriate weapon for preventing wars in general, and whether it would be more effective to call a strike before or after war had been declared.

It is interesting to compare the discussions at the French Conference with those taking place two weeks later at the meeting of the International's Bureau in Brussels. In Paris, Compère-Morel warned the party against taking decisions it had no power to operate. Jaurès, however, believed that the workers would respond to a strike call from the party and that mass action by the working class could prevent war from breaking out. They must not wait for the outbreak of war, however, before calling a strike, 'because in that case the world would already be handed over to the forces of darkness'. The International must call a general strike in the period of war-preparations and in the countries directly involved, and he added that 'we should be prepared to call off the strike in the country which was prepared to submit the dispute to arbitration'. Marcel Sembat agreed that a general strike should be called before the outbreak of war, providing that the workers in the opposing country were also prepared to join in the strike movement. He remained convinced that in the event of a war between France and Germany, a spontaneous strike movement would develop. No one considered, however, what the workers should do in a war which developed out of a Russo-German conflict in which France became involved through her alliance with Russia. Nor did anyone raise the related question of whether the Russian working class, which had risen against Tsarism, been defeated and suffered the destruction of its organizations, would be able to restrain its own government.

The case for the general strike as a weapon against war rested on the assumption that a working-class movement of roughly equal strength existed on both sides of the dividing-line and that the possibilities of strike action were much the same in all the major conflicting countries. If this were not so it would be precisely the country with the more developed Socialist movement which would succumb to the side unhandicapped by a powerful Labour movement. The general strike, said Jules Guesde, would be a danger to those countries where Socialism was more advanced, since 'the better organized country would be destroyed'.[1] If the French party conference failed to discuss the problem of preventing war in the situation which actually existed, and the character of which was to become only too hideously apparent a fortnight later, it was clearly because the idea of the Austro-Serbian dispute escalating into a world war would have seemed too fantastic to merit serious consideration.

The Socialist parties—especially those of Austria and Germany—became dimly aware of the approaching danger only with the publication of the Austrian ultimatum. On the day it appeared, the German Social Democratic M.P.s in Austria released a statement in which, in the name of the working class, they placed the full responsibility for war on those 'who have decided on . . . this fatal step'. 'It is not,' the statement continued, 'in the power of the people to decide the question of war or peace. . . . Parliament, their voice and instrument, is silent. The freedom of public assembly and of the Press has been destroyed. . . .' And, indeed, the text of the manifesto itself was almost entirely suppressed by the censorship.

On the same day the Social Democratic party in Germany published its own manifesto. Since that country was not yet at war, the party could still speak openly, with the advantages of a Press which was still uncensored and a Parliament which, unlike the Austrian, was still free to speak. The manifesto denounces 'the frivolously provocative war policy of the Austro-Hungarian Monarchy' and 'emphatically demands that the German government use its influence with the Austrian government to preserve peace and, should this terrible war now prove unavoidable, itself refrain from any kind of armed intervention'. It called on the workers to demonstrate their will for peace by calling mass meetings immediately. 'A crisis is upon us,' it continued, 'more desperate than for many decades past. The danger of a world war is now imminent.' Three days later, on 28 July, as Austria declared war on Serbia, hundreds of thousands took part in demonstrations in Germany's main towns and in Berlin alone twenty-seven public meetings were held.[2]

1. Alexandre Zévaès, *Le Socialisme en France depuis 1904* (Paris, 1934), p. 54.
2. In a memorandum on 29 July, written in response to a telegram from the

12

On the previous day the Bureau of the International had assembled at the Maison du Peuple in Brussels for the most fateful conference in its history. All the main representatives of the European movement were there: Jaurès, Guesde, Longuet, Adler, Vandervelde, Kautsky, Haase, Rosa Luxemburg, Keir Hardie, Bruce Glasier, Axelrod, Morgari, Angelica Balabanov, Grimm, and many others. They spoke for millions.[1] But they had little confidence in their ability to prevent the threatened war by direct mass action. Though Keir Hardie referred briefly to the possibility of a general strike, it played no other part in the conference discussions.

The first necessity was to clarify the attitude of the Socialist parties in those countries likely to participate in the war—specifically the parties in Austria, Germany, France and Britain. Victor Adler's report, according to his son Friedrich, who was with him at the conference,

Tsar, Kaiser Wilhelm remarked about this peace demonstration: 'The Reds are conducting anti-militarist agitation in the streets; this must not be allowed, especially at present; if there is any repetition I shall declare martial law and have the leaders, one and all, *tutti quanti*, clapped in gaol'—Kautsky, op. cit., p. 441.

1. At the outbreak of war, membership of the Socialist parties in the belligerent powers was as follows:

	Number of members	*Number of votes in the last parliamentary elections before 1914*	*Number of Socialist Deputies*	*Total number of Members of Parliament*
Germany	1,085,905	4,250,329	110	397
France	90,700	1,397,337	101	595
Austria	145,500	1,041,000	82	516
Great Britain	1,559,082	370,802	42	670
Belgium	—	600,000	39	185
Russia	—	800,000	14	442
Serbia	—	25,000	2	166

—*Yearbook of the International Socialist Labour Movement 1956–7*, edited by Julius Braunthal (London, 1956), and *The Socialist Yearbook 1913*, edited by J. Bruce Glasier (London, 1913). In Russia the working class had not yet recovered from its last defeat at the hands of reaction. In 1907 a total of 159 trade unions were dissolved, and in 1908 and 1909 another 100 each; almost all publications of the Labour movement had been suppressed. When Rubanovitch was asked by the Bureau of the International in 1912 to give the number of members of the Russian Socialist party, he replied: 'The only figures I can give you are those of our party members who live as prisoners of the Tsar in fortresses, prisons and places of exile; we estimate their number at about 30,000, including about 10,000 women'—quoted in A. W. Humphrey, *International Socialism and the War* (London, 1915), p. 22. In the elections to the Fourth Duma in 1912 the Socialist parties received about 800,000 votes. Of the 442 deputies, 7 Mensheviks, 6 Bolsheviks and 1 Polish Socialist were returned. At the outbreak of war, Lenin was in Cracow (Galicia). He was immediately arrested, but owing to the intervention of Victor Adler, he was released and allowed to leave for Switzerland.

'breathed a spirit of utter passivity, with a conviction that it was impossible to do anything effective to prevent the war'. 'The war is already with us,' said Victor Adler. 'Up to now we have done what we could to prevent it. . . . There is nothing further we can do. We are at war, our newspapers are suppressed. We are living in a state of emergency, and under the shadow of martial law.' He added: 'I am not here to make speeches at a public meeting but to tell you candidly that any action on our part, when hundreds of thousands are already marching towards the frontier and when we have martial law at home, is completely impossible. . . .' A few years later Vandervelde described how Adler, whose heart disease had grown suddenly worse in the summer of 1914 and who 'had aged ten years in a single day', was continually repeating: 'It is impossible, it is impossible, we should need a miracle. . . .' And the Czech Labour leader, Anton Nemec, from Prague, exclaimed in despair: 'What can we do? Parliament is suspended and public meetings prohibited. Anyone who resists mobilization will be hanged.'

The conference then turned to the position in Germany and was deeply impressed by Hugo Haase's account of the great peace demonstrations. He did something to revive flagging hopes in the possibility of peace with the remark: 'The Kaiser is against the war, not for humanitarian reasons but simply from fear.'

Jaurès shared this optimism. At the closing meeting he assured the delegates that the evil could be averted. 'The governments,' he believed, 'are still undecided. Attila is poised on the very brink of the precipice, but his horse still hesitates, is not yet willing to jump. . . . We must take advantage of the indecision of governments to organize for peace. . . .' About the attitude of his own party he said: 'For us French Socialists the task is very simple. We do not have to force a peaceful policy on our government. It already practises it. I have never been afraid to incur the wrath of our own chauvinists through persistently advocating a Franco-German *rapprochement*. . . . I am, therefore, fully within my rights in assuring you that the French government wants peace.' However, he was careful to add: 'It is our duty to insist that the French government brings strong pressure on Russia, to prevent her from declaring war. And if Russia, unfortunately, refuses to accept this advice, it is our duty to declare that we recognize only one commitment—that which binds us to the human race.'

A similarly optimistic note was struck in Keir Hardie's report. He thought it 'quite out of the question' for Great Britain to be involved in the war. If, nevertheless, the government tried to involve the nation, the trade unions would use every means, including a general strike, to preserve peace.

These reports from the German, French and British delegates

strengthened the conference's belief that it was possible to avoid war. 'Although the terrible threat that the Continent might become engulfed in war provided the main theme in the discussions, no one, not even the German representatives, thought it possible that an immediate breach between the major powers was imminent,' was Bruce Glasier's summary of the mood at the conference. So convinced were they that a European war could be averted that it was decided to convene the Congress of the International in Paris on 9 August. In a final statement the conference called on the workers of all countries threatened by war to organize, in the meantime, a series of peace meetings and to work for a settlement of the Austro-Serbian dispute by arbitration. It declared that 'the German and French workers will bring even greater pressure on their own governments to make Germany exercise restraint on Austria while France persuades Russia to keep out of the conflict'.[1]

The conference ended with a public meeting in the Cirque Royal. There was a demonstration of Brussels workers, thousands of whom marched there in close column, and the city rang with the cry: 'War on War!' Vandervelde, Haase, Hardie and Jaurès spoke from the platform. It was to be Jaurès's last speech. As he had already told the conference, he had done more than enough in France to incur the enmity of the chauvinists, and the right-wing Press had openly called on the 'patriotic forces' to assassinate him. Two days after returning from Brussels, as he was sitting with friends finishing his evening meal at the Café du Croissant, he was shot dead.

13

A few hours before his death, Jaurès had gone with Bracke, Longuet and Marcel Cachin on a deputation to the Quai d'Orsay with the object of persuading the government to bring more effective pressure to bear on Russia. In the absence of the Premier, they were received by the Minister, Abel Ferry. Jaurès expressed his fear that the French government was doing too little to make Russia see reason. According to Cachin Jaurès insisted, 'with quite exceptional power, eloquence and decision', that the government should bring all its influence to bear to prevent Russia from mobilizing. 'Those of us who have, since the beginning of the crisis, constantly defended and never by a single word impeded their faithful activities in support of peace,' he said, 'have the

1. This account of the Brussels Conference is based on Friedrich Adler, op. cit., p. 198; *Victor Adlers Aufsätze . . .*, vol. IX, p. 165; Émile Vandervelde, *Victor Adler und die Internationale, Der Kampf*, vol. XXII (1929), p. 7; Kautsky, op. cit., pp. 370–4; Jackson, op. cit., pp. 179–80; Angelica Balabanov, *Erinnerungen und Erlebnisse* (Berlin, 1927), pp. 55–7; Eduard Bernstein, 'Jean Jaurès', in *Die Neue Zeit*, vol. XXXIII (1915), p. 559.

right to appeal to them now, when dangers are visibly accumulating, even if they should execute us for our pains. . . .'[1] As the deputation left the Quai d'Orsay, news came through that the Kaiser had placed Germany on a war footing. Next morning—1 August—he declared war on Russia, while German troops invaded neutral Luxembourg.

The French party had previously declared that it would not feel bound by 'any secret agreements' which would involve France in a conflict 'with Serbia as the bait'; it would oppose, in fact, a war waged by France in support of Serbia. Even on the day following Germany's declaration of war on Russia (2 August), Vaillant told a mass meeting in the Salle Wagram that the party would support the government in a war only if France herself were attacked. At the same gathering, Longuet gave a report of the International Bureau's meeting in Brussels. He particularly emphasized the speech of Haase, who had solemnly pledged his opposition and that of German Social Democracy to a war against France. 'In the attitude of the German Social Democrats towards France,' said Longuet, 'lies the great hope of reconciliation between our two countries. French Socialists will fight to the end for the maintenance of peace.' He added, however, that 'if France should be attacked, should not the Socialists be the first to spring to the defence of the country of the Revolution, of Democracy, of the Encyclopaedists and of Jaurès? . . .'

The day it returned from Brussels, the British delegation issued a statement, signed by Keir Hardie and Arthur Henderson, calling on the British working class, in the name of the International Socialist Bureau, to keep Britain out of the war through a campaign of 'great public meetings in London and every industrial centre'. 'Let us silence those of our ruling class who would lead us into alliance with Russian despotism. . . . In our time, the success of Russia would be a disaster for the world,' the manifesto declared. Two days later, on 2 August, in accordance with the appeal, great public meetings were held in the main towns. The demonstration in Trafalgar Square was, according to the *Manchester Guardian*, 'the biggest for many years' and was addressed by the leading members of the trade unions and the Labour party, including J. Stokes, Chairman of the London Trades Council, George Lansbury, Will Thorne, Arthur Henderson, Keir Hardie and Cunninghame Graham.

At one such meeting in the provinces, the president of the Miners' Federation, Robert Smillie, said that if it were still possible to prevent the war by general strikes throughout Europe, he would not hesitate to call on the miners to do just this.[2]

1. J. S., 'Die Haltung der französischen Sozialdemokratie beim Ausbruch des Krieges', in *Die Neue Zeit*, vol. XXXIII (1915), p. 577; Jackson, op. cit., p. 182.
2. William Stewart, *J. Keir Hardie* (London, 1921), p. 264.

14

Forty-eight hours later the German Social Democrats in the Reichstag, and the French Socialists in the Chamber of Deputies, voted in favour of war credits. These acts struck a mortal blow to the International. It fell, the first victim of the world war. It had been conceived as a brotherhood, uniting the workers of all countries in a spirit of solidarity for the joint struggle against the ruling classes. Now the Socialist parties of the belligerent countries were making common cause with their own ruling classes, which bore the sole responsibility for the war, against peoples of other lands who had had war forced on them. The bond of brotherhood between the nations had been broken and the spirit of international solidarity of the working classes superseded by a spirit of national solidarity between the proletariat and the ruling classes.

Up to the last moment the Socialist parties had done what they could to oppose the war and the struggle had, for many years, absorbed most of their energies. Their stubborn efforts to win the mass of the people to the Socialist cause, so as to strengthen the influence of the movement in state and society, had been inspired by the idea that only a strong Social Democratic movement could prevent war. Now social democracy had lost its race against time. To continue the struggle by calling for an uprising once war had broken out, seemed beyond its strength. Moreover, the war crisis had developed with incredible speed, and in the disastrous clash between the two groups of Great Powers, the workers in each camp saw themselves faced with the danger of invasion by one or other of the dreaded bulwarks of reaction—in Germany and Austria by Tsarist Russia, in France, Belgium and Britain by Prussian militarism. The war stemmed from the imperialist conflicts of the ruling classes and served only their narrow imperialist aims. But the Socialist parties saw it not merely as an inter-imperialist conflict of capitalist ruling classes, but also and especially as a fight for national survival.

The International saw in the approach of war a terrible and perhaps fatal threat to the values for which the movement stood, a denial of everything they felt to be hopeful and creative for the future of mankind. But when war arrived, the Socialist parties did not withhold their support for a contest they lacked the power to prevent. On the contrary, they gave their enthusiastic support, both morally and politically, to the war effort. The International, which had served for so long as the symbol and expression of working-class unity, could not survive.

The world war marked the end of a distinctive phase in Socialist history. The fifty years which elapsed between the foundation of the International in 1864 and the outbreak of war in 1914 may be described as the apostolic period of Socialism, when the movement developed an ideology and a set of values in sharp contrast to those which prevailed in the surrounding society. The Socialist parties had, for the most part, viewed the state as an instrument of the ruling class, had refused to participate in governments or to concern themselves with their 'own' national interests while the nations to which they belonged remained capitalist. This posture of 'non-commitment' had enabled them to advocate their principles and ideas while remaining uncontaminated by political power. With the outbreak of the war in western and central Europe there began the integration of the Socialist movement with the capitalist state, followed by the tremendous revolution in Russia which brought about a fundamental split in international Socialism.

In August 1914 the International embarked on a new phase in its development, a phase characterized by the national integration of Socialist parties in the West, while the Bolsheviks developed a new and autocratic brand of Communism in the East.

APPENDIX ONE

GENERAL RULES OF THE INTERNATIONAL WORKING MEN'S ASSOCIATION[1]

Considering,

That the emancipation of the working classes must be conquered by the working classes themselves; that the struggle for the emancipation of the working classes means not a struggle for class privileges and monopolies, but for equal rights and duties, and the abolition of all class rule;

That the economical subjection of the man of labour to the monopolizer of the means of labour, that is, the sources of life, lies at the bottom of servitude in all its forms, of all social misery, mental degradation, and political dependence;

That the economical emancipation of the working classes is therefore the great end to which every political movement ought to be subordinate as a means;

That all efforts aiming at that great end have hitherto failed from the want of solidarity between the manifold divisions of labour in each country, and from the absence of a fraternal bond of union between the working classes of different countries;

That the emancipation of labour is neither a local nor a national, but a social problem, embracing all countries in which modern society exists, and depending for its solution on the concurrence, practical and theoretical, of the most advanced countries;

That the present revival of the working classes in the most industrious countries of Europe, while it raises a new hope, gives solemn warning against a relapse into the old errors, and calls for the immediate combination of the still disconnected movements;

For these reasons—

The International Working Men's Association has been founded. It declares:

That all societies and individuals adhering to it will acknowledge truth, justice, and morality as the basis of their conduct towards each

1. These rules, drawn up by Marx, were, as 'Provisional Rules', approved by the General Council on 1 November 1864 and adopted at the Geneva Congress in September 1866.

other and towards all men, without regard to colour, creed, or nationality;

That it acknowledges *no rights without duties, no duties without rights*;

And in this spirit the following rules have been drawn up.

1. This Association is established to afford a central medium of communication and co-operation between Working Men's Societies existing in different countries and aiming at the same end; *viz.*, the protection, advancement, and complete emancipation of the working classes.

2. The name of the Society shall be 'The International Working Men's Association'.

3. There shall annually meet a General Working Men's Congress, consisting of delegates of the branches of the Association. The congress will have to proclaim the common aspirations of the working class, take the measures required for the successful working of the International Association, and appoint the General Council of the Society.

4. Each congress appoints the time and place of meeting for the next congress. The delegates assemble at the appointed time and place without any special invitation. The General Council may, in case of need, change the place, but has no power to postpone the time of meeting. The congress appoints the seat and elects the members of the General Council annually. The General Council thus elected shall have power to add to the number of its members.

On its annual meetings, the General Congress shall receive a public account of the annual transactions of the General Council. The latter may, in cases of emergency, convoke the General Congress before the regular yearly term.

5. The General Council shall consist of working men from the different countries represented in the International Association. It shall from its own members elect the officers necessary for the transaction of business, such as a treasurer, a general secretary, corresponding secretaries for the different countries, etc.

6. The General Council shall form an international agency between the different national and local groups of the Association, so that the working men in one country may be constantly informed of the movements of their class in every other country; that an inquiry into the social state of the different countries of Europe be made simultaneously, and under a common direction; that the questions of general interest mooted in one society be ventilated by all; and that when immediate practical steps should be needed—as, for instance, in case of international quarrels—the action of the associated societies be simultaneous and

uniform. Whenever it seems opportune, the General Council shall take the initiative of proposals to be laid before the different national or local societies. To facilitate the communications, the General Council shall publish periodical reports.

7. Since the success of the working men's movement in each country cannot be secured but by the power of union and combination, while, on the other hand, the usefulness of the International General Council must greatly depend on the circumstance whether it has to deal with a few national centres of working men's associations, or with a great number of small and disconnected local societies; the members of the International Association shall use their utmost efforts to combine the disconnected working men's societies of their respective countries into national bodies, represented by central national organs. It is self-understood, however, that the appliance of this rule will depend upon the peculiar laws of each country, and that, apart from legal obstacles, no independent local society shall be precluded from directly corresponding with the General Council.

7a. In its struggle against the collective power of the owning classes the proletariat can act as a class only by constituting itself a distinct political party, opposed to all the old parties formed by the owning classes.

This constitution of the proletariat into a political party is indispensable to ensure the triumph of the social Revolution and of its ultimate goal: the abolition of classes.

The coalition of the forces of the working class, already achieved by the economic struggle, must also serve, in the hands of this class, as a lever in its struggle against the political power of its exploiters.

As the lords of the land and of capital always make use of their political privileges to defend and perpetuate their economic monopolies and to enslave labour, the conquest of political power becomes the great duty of the proletariat.[1]

8. Every section has the right to appoint its own secretary corresponding with the General Council.

9. Everybody who acknowledges and defends the principles of the International Working Men's Association is eligible to become a member. Every branch is responsible for the integrity of the members it admits.

10. Each member of the International Association, on removing his domicile from one country to another, will receive the fraternal support of the Associated Working Men.

1. Article 7a, which is an abridged exposition of the resolution of the London Conference of 1871, was included in the General Rules by amendment adopted at the Hague Congress of the First International (September 1872).

11. While united in a perpetual bond of fraternal co-operation, the working men's societies joining the International Association will preserve their existent organizations intact.

12. The present rules may be revised by each congress, provided that two thirds of the delegates present are in favour of such revision.

13. Everything not provided for in the present rules will be supplied by special regulations, subject to the revision of every congress.

APPENDIX TWO

THE STUTTGART RESOLUTION ON MILITARISM AND THE INTERNATIONAL CONFLICTS

Resolution Adopted at the Seventh International Socialist Congress at Stuttgart, 18–24 August 1907

The Congress confirms the resolutions adopted by previous international congresses against militarism and imperialism and declares once more that the struggle against militarism cannot be separated from the Socialist class struggle in general.

Wars between capitalist states are, as a rule, the outcome of their competition on the world market, for each state seeks not only to secure its existing markets, but also to conquer new ones. In this, the subjugation of foreign peoples and countries plays a prominent role. These wars result, furthermore, from the incessant race for armaments by militarism, one of the chief instruments of *bourgeois* class rule and of the economic and political subjugation of the working class.

Wars are favoured by the national prejudices which are systematically cultivated among civilized peoples in the interest of the ruling classes, for the purpose of distracting the proletarian masses from their own class tasks as well as from their duties of international solidarity.

Wars, therefore, are part of the very nature of capitalism; they will cease only when the capitalist system is abolished or when the enormous sacrifices in men and money, required by the advance in military technique, and the indignation called forth by armaments, drive the peoples to abolish this sytem.

For this reason, the proletariat, which contributes most of the soldiers and makes most of the material sacrifices, is a natural opponent of war, which contradicts its highest goal—the creation of an economic order on a Socialist basis which will bring about the solidarity of all peoples.

The Congress, therefore, considers it as the duty of the working class and particularly of its representatives in the parliaments to combat the naval and military armaments with all their might, characterizing the class nature of *bourgeois* society and the motive for the maintenance of national antagonisms, and to refuse the means for these armaments. It is their duty to work for the education of the working-class youth in the spirit of the brotherhood of nations and of Socialism while developing their class consciousness.

The Congress sees in the democratic organization of the army, in the substitution of the militia for the standing army, an essential guarantee that offensive wars will be rendered impossible and the overcoming of national antagonisms facilitated.

The International is not able to determine in rigid forms the anti-militarist actions of the working class, which are naturally different in different countries and for different circumstances of time and place. But it is its duty to co-ordinate and increase to the utmost the efforts of the working class against war.

In fact, since the International Congress at Brussels, the proletariat has employed the most diverse forms of action with increasing emphasis and success in its indefatigable struggles against militarism by refusing the means for naval and military armaments, and by its efforts to democratize the military organization—all for the purpose of preventing the outbreak of wars or of putting a stop to them, as well as for utilizing the convulsions of society caused by the war for emancipation of the working class.

This was evidenced especially by the agreement between the British and French trade unions following the Fashoda affair for the maintenance of peace and for the restoration of friendly relations between Britain and France; by the procedure of the Social Democratic parties in the German and French Parliaments during the Morocco crisis; the demonstrations arranged by the French and German Socialists for the same purpose; the concerted action of the Socialists of Austria and Italy, who met in Trieste in order to prevent a conflict between the two countries; furthermore, by the energetic intervention of the Socialist workers of Sweden in order to prevent an attack upon Norway; finally, the heroic, self-sacrificing struggle of the Socialist workers and peasants of Russia and Poland in order to oppose the war unleashed by Tsarism, to put a stop to it, and to utilize the crisis of the country for the liberation of the working class.

All these efforts are evidence of the growing power of the proletariat and of its increasing ability to secure the maintenance of peace by resolute intervention. The action of the working class will be all the more successful, the more that its spirit is prepared by a corresponding action and the Labour parties of the various countries are spurred on and co-ordinated by the International.

The Congress is convinced that, under the pressure of the proletariat, by a serious use of arbitration in place of the miserable measures of the governments, the benefit of disarmament can be secured to all nations, making it possible to employ for cultural purposes the enormous expenditure of money and energy which are swallowed up by military armaments and wars.

If a war threatens to break out, it is the duty of the working classes and their parliamentary representatives in the countries involved, supported by the co-ordinating activity of the International Socialist Bureau, to exert every effort in order to prevent the outbreak of war by the means they consider most effective, which naturally vary according to the sharpening of the class struggle and the sharpening of the general political situation.

In case war should break out anyway, it is their duty to intervene in favour of its speedy termination, and with all their powers to utilize the economic and political crisis created by the war to rouse the masses and thereby to hasten the downfall of capitalist class rule.

APPENDIX THREE

LIST OF CONGRESSES AND CONFERENCES, 1864–1914

First International

1864 London (foundation meeting)
1865 London (conference)
1866 Geneva
1867 Lausanne
1868 Brussels
1869 Basle
1871 London (conference)
1872 The Hague
1873 Geneva
1876 Philadelphia (conference)

Anti-Authoritarian International

1873 Geneva
1874 Brussels
1876 Berne
1877 Verviers

World Socialist Congress

1877 Ghent
1881 Chur

Anarchist International

1881 London
1889 Paris (conference)
1893 Chicago (conference)
1896 Zurich (conference)
1907 Amsterdam

Second International

1889 Paris
1891 Brussels
1893 Zurich
1896 London
1900 Paris
1904 Amsterdam
1907 Stuttgart
1910 Copenhagen
1912 Basle (extraordinary congress)
1914 Brussels (extraordinary session of the Bureau)

APPENDIX FOUR

THE PROVISIONAL GENERAL COUNCIL OF THE FIRST INTERNATIONAL[1]

President: George Odger
Treasurer: George W. Wheeler
Corresponding Secretary for Germany: Karl Marx
Corresponding Secretary for Italy: Giuseppe P. Fontana
Corresponding Secretary for Poland: J. E. Holtorp
Corresponding Secretary for France: P.-V. Le Lubez
Corresponding Secretary for Switzerland: Hermann F. Jung
General Secretary: William R. Cremer

British Members of the General Council

William Worley	Pidgeon	Kethrick
John Bedford Leno	Benjamin Lucraft	Richardson
John Longmaid	John Weston	Merriman
E. Whitlock	William Dell	Vasbenter
Peter Fox	Shearman	W. Tremlett
Blackmore	John D. Nieass	John Robert Taylor
Robert Hartwell	Alexander Dick	George Potter
Henry Noble	James Carter	Grossmith
Robert Shaw	John Osborn	William Randal Cremer
Lake	E. Gray	Thomas Grant Facey
James Buckley	George William Wheeler	Charles Goddard
George Odger	William Stainsbury	Side
George Howell	M. Morgan	

French Members of the General Council

Jules Denoual	Leroux	Jean-Baptiste Bocquet
P.-V. Le Lubez	Henri Lefort	Alfred Talandier
G. Jourdain	Bordage	Eugène Dupont
Morrissot		

1. The members of the Provisional General Council of the First International were elected at the Foundation Meeting on 28 September 1864; the officers were elected at the first meeting of the General Council on 5 October 1864. Throughout the history of the First International there were changes in the membership of both groups through resignations and replacements. See *Founding of the First International, A Documentary Record* (London, 1939), edited by L. E. Mins.

German Members of the General Council

Johann Georg Eccarius	Karl Pfänder	Karl Marx
Wolff	George Lochner	Kaub
Friedrich Lessner	Otto Breidtschwerdt	Heinrich Bolleter

Italian Members of the General Council

Luigi Wolff	C. Setacci	Domenico Lama
Giuseppe P. Fontana	Aldrovandi	T. Solustri

Swiss Members of the General Council

G. Nusperly   Hermann Jung

Polish Members of the General Council

J. E. Holtorp   Rybczinski

Bibliography

THE FORERUNNERS

Advielle, Victoire, *Histoire Gracchus de Babeuf et du babouvisme* (Paris, 1884).

Aulard, A., *Politische Geschichte der Französischen Revolution* (Munich/Leipzig, 1924).

Bax, Belfort, *The Last Episode of the French Revolution* (London, 1911).

Beer, M., *Geschichte des Sozialismus in England* (Stuttgart, 1913); *A History of British Socialism* (rev. ed., London, 1940).

Bertrand, Louis, *Histoire de la démocratie et du socialisme en Belgique depuis 1830*, 2 vols. (Brussels, 1906–7).

Brailsford, H. N., *Shelley, Godwin and their Circle* (London, 1913).

Brettschneider, W., *Entwicklung und Bedeutung des deutschen Frühsozialismus* (Königsberg, 1936).

Brown, Anthony, *The French Revolution in English History* (London, 1918).

Brügel, Ludwig, *Geschichte der österreichischen Sozialdemokratie*, vol. I (Vienna, 1922).

Brugger Otto, *Die Wirksamkeit Weitlings 1841–1843* (Bern, 1932).

Buonarroti, Philippe-Michel, *Babeuf und die Verschwörung für die Gleichheit mit dem durch sie veranlaßten Prozeß und den Belegstücken* (Stuttgart, 1909).

Buonarroti's History of Babeuf's Conspiracy, translated and annotated by Bronterre O'Brian (London, 1836).

Burke, Edmund, *Reflections on the Revolution in France*.

Castlereagh, Lord, *Memoir and Correspondence*, vol. III (London, 1849).

Cole, G. D. H., *Chartist Portraits* (London, 1941).

A History of Socialist Thought, vols. I and II (London, 1953–4).

A Short History of the British Working Class Movement, vols. 1 and 2 (London, 1925–7).

Cunow, Heinrich, *Die Parteien der großen Französischen Revolution und ihre Presse* (Berlin, 1912).

Der Kommunistenprozeß zu Köln 1852 im Spiegel der zeitgenössischen Presse, edited by Karl Bittel (Berlin, 1955).

Diehl, Karl, *P.-J. Proudhon. Seine Lehre und sein Leben* (Jena, 1890).

Dolléans, E., *Histoire du mouvement ouvrier*, vol. I: *1830–71* (Paris, 1936).

Engels, Friedrich, *Condition of the Working Class in England in 1844.*
Zur Geschichte des Bundes der Kommunisten.
Garaudy, Roger, *Die französischen Quellen des wissenschaftlichen Sozialismus* (Berlin, 1954).
Geffroy, Gustave, *L'Enfermé—Auguste Blanqui* (Paris, 1897).
Gooch, G. P., *Political Thought in England from Bacon to Halifax* (London, 1914).
Hammond, J. L. and Barbara, *The Bleak Age* (London, 1934).
Hovell, Mark, *The Chartist Movement* (London, 1925).
Jakobiner und Sansculotten—Beiträge zur Geschichte der französischen Revolutionsregierung 1793–1794, edited by Walter Markov (Berlin, 1956).
Kaler, Emil, *Wilhelm Weitling. Seine Agitation und Lehre* (Hottingen-Zurich, 1887).
Laski, Harold J., *Communist Manifesto. Socialist Landmark* (London, 1948).
Lefebvre, Georges, *The French Revolution*, 2 vols. (London, 1962–5).
Lehning, Arthur, 'Buonarroti's Ideas on Communism and Dictatorship', 1962–5 *International Review of Social History*, vol. II.
Lessner, Friedrich, 'Vor und nach 1848. Erinnerungen eines alten Kommunisten', *Deutsche Worte* (1898).
Lichtenberger, André, *Le Socialisme et la révolution française* (Paris, 1899).
Louis, Paul, *Geschichte des Sozialismus in Frankreich* (Stuttgart, 1908).
Marr, W., *Das junge Deutschland in der Schweiz* (Leipzig, 1846).
Martin, Kingsley, *French Liberal Thought in the Eighteenth Century* (London, 1929).
The Triumph of Lord Palmerston (London, 1924).
Marx, Karl, *Enthüllungen über den Kommunistenprozeß zu Köln.*
Die Klassenkämpfe in Frankreich 1848–50.
Marx, Karl, and Engels, Friedrich, *The Communist Manifesto.*
Mathiez, Albert, *Die Französische Revolution*, 3 vols. (Zurich, 1950).
Metternichs nachgelassenen Papieren, Aus, edited by Richard Metternich-Winneburg and Alfons von Klinkowström, 9 vols. (Vienna, 1880–4).
Mignet, F. A., *History of the French Revolution* (London, 1846).
Müller-Lehning, A., 'The International Association, 1855–9', *International Review of Social History*, vol. III.
Namier, L. B., *1848: The Revolution of the Intellectuals* (London, 1964).
Nicolaevsky, Boris, 'Towards a History of the Communist League, 1847–50', *International Review of Social History*, vol. I.
Nicolaevsky, Boris, and Mänchen-Helfen, Otto, *Karl und Jenny Marx* (Berlin, 1933).
Obermann, Karl, *Zur Geschichte des Bundes der Kommunisten 1849–1852* (Berlin, 1955).
Paine, Thomas, *The Rights of Man.*
Parrington, Vernon Lewis, *Main Currents in American Thought*, 3 vols. (New York, 1927–50).
Pollard, A. F., *The German Federation, 1815–40*, vol. X of the *Cambridge Modern History* (Cambridge, 1907).
Postgate, Raymond, *Story of a Year: 1848* (London, 1955).
Rosenberg, A., *Demokratie und Sozialismus* (Amsterdam, 1938).
Rothstein, Theodor, *From Chartism to Labourism* (London, 1929).
Rousseau, Jean-Jacques, *The Social Contract.*
Salomon, Gottfried, *Proudhon und der Sozialismus* (Berlin, 1920).

Saville, John, *Ernest Jones, Chartist* (London, 1952).
Scheu, Andreas, *Umsturzkeime — Erlebnisse eines Kämpfers* (Vienna, 1923).
Schlüter, Hermann, *Die Chartisten-Bewegung* (New York, 1916).
Schoyen, A. R., *The Chartist Challenge, A Portrait of George Julian Harney* (London, 1958).
Sengier, Georges, *Babouvisme après Babeuf. Sociétés secrètes et conspirations communistes 1830–1848* (Paris, 1912).
Seton-Watson, R. W., *Britain in Europe, 1789–1914* (Cambridge, 1937).
Soboul, Albert, 'Klassen und Klassenkämpfe in the Französischen Revolution', *Jakobiner und Sansculotten*, edited by Walter Markov (Berlin, 1956).
Soltau, Roger, *French Political Thought in the Nineteenth Century* (London, 1931).
Spitzer, Alan B., *The Revolutionary Theories of Louis-Auguste Blanqui* (New York, 1957).
Stern, Alfred, *Geschichte Europas von 1815–71*, vol. I (Stuttgart, 1894).
Stewart, Neil, *Blanqui, a Biography* (London, 1939).
Tarle, E. W., *Germinal und Prairial* (Berlin, 1953).
Thompson, Eric, *Popular Sovereignty and the French Constituent Assembly 1789–91* (Manchester, 1952).
Tocqueville, Alexis de, *Recollections* (London, 1948).
Treitschke, H. von, *Deutsche Geschichte im 19. Jahrhundert*, vol. IV (Leipzig, 1897).
Voegt, Hedwig, *Die deutsche jakobinische Literatur und Publizistik 1789–1800* (Berlin, 1955).
Wallas, Graham, *The Life of Francis Place, 1771–1854* (London, 1937).
Wassermann, S., *Les Clubs de Barbès et de Blanqui en 1848* (Paris, 1913).
Webster, C. K., *The Foreign Policy of Castlereagh, 1815–22*, vol. III (London, 1925).
Weitling, Wilhelm, *Garantien der Gerechtigkeit und Freiheit.*
Garantien der Harmonie und Freiheit.
Die Menschheit, wie sie ist und wie sie sein sollte.
West, Julius, *A History of the Chartist Movement* (London, 1920).
Wittke, Carl, *The Utopian Communist, Wilhelm Weitling* (Louisiana, 1950).

THE FIRST INTERNATIONAL

Original Sources:

Minutes of the General Council of the First International in the archives of the International Institute of Social History, Amsterdam.
The George Howell Collection in the Bishopsgate Institute, London.
The Sorge Papers in New York Public Library.
The Hermann Schlüter Collection in the University of Wisconsin Libraries, Madison.
Minutes of the Congress: Geneva, 1866; Brussels, 1868; Basle, 1869. The Minutes of the Lausanne Congress in 1867 are untraceable. The Minutes of the Hague Congress in 1872 are in *The First International—Minutes of the Hague Congress of 1872 with related documents*, edited by Hans Gert (Madison, 1958).

Verhandlungen der Delegierten-Konferenz zu Philadelphia, 15. Juli 1867 (New York, 1876).

Documents of the First International, vol. I: *1864–6* (London, 1963); vol. II: *1866–9* (London, 1964).

Founding of the First International. A Documentary Record, edited by L. E. Mins (New York, 1937).

Karl Marx und die Gründung der I. Internationale. Dokumente und Materialien (Berlin, 1964).

Die I. Internationale in Deutschland (1864–1872). Dokumente und Materialien (Berlin, 1964).

Literature:

Adler, Victor, 'Peukerts Erinnerungen', *Der Kampf*, vol. VII.

Aranyossi, Magda, *Leo Frankel* (Berlin, 1957).

Auer, Ignaz, *Nach zehn Jahren* (Stuttgart, 1889).

Von Gotha bis Wyden (Berlin, 1901).

Bebel, August, *Aus meinem Leben*, 3 vols. (Stuttgart, 1910–14).

Bernstein, Samuel, *The Beginnings of Marxian Socialism in France* (New York, 1933).

Bertrand, Louis, *César de Paepe, sa vie, son oeuvre* (Brussels, 1909).

Histoire de la démocratie et du socialisme en Belgique, 2 vols. (Brussels, 1907).

Carr, E. H., *Michael Bakunin* (London, 1937).

Cole, G. D. H., *Marxism and Anarchism 1850–1890*, vol. II of *A History of Socialist Thought* (London, 1954).

Collins, Henry, 'The English Branches of the First International', *Essays in Labour History*, edited by Asa Briggs and John Saville (London, 1960).

Collins, Henry, and Abramsky, Chimen, *Karl Marx and the British Labour Movement: Years of the First International* (London, 1965).

Dutt, R. Palme, *The Internationale* (London, 1964).

Engels, Friedrich, *Friedrich Engels, Paul et Laura Lafargue. Correspondance*, vol. I: *1868–86* (Paris, 1956).

Études et documents sur la Première Internationale en Suisse, edited by Jacques Freymond (Geneva, 1964).

Foster, William Z., *History of the Three Internationals* (New York, 1951).

Freymond, J., *La Première Internationale, Recueil de Documents (1866–72)*, 2 vols. (Geneva, 1962).

Fribourg, E.-E., *L'Association internationale des travailleurs* (Paris, 1871).

Guillaume, James, *L'Internationale. Documents et souvenirs 1864–1878*, 4 vols. (Paris, 1905–10).

Hillquit, Morris, *History of Socialism in the United States* (New York and London, 1906).

Hirsch, Helmut, *Denker und Kämpfer* (Frankfurt, 1955).

Hochverratsprozeß wider Liebknecht, Bebel, Hepner (Berlin, 1894).

Hostetter, Richard, *The Italian Socialist Movement 1860–1880* (Princeton, 1958).

Howell, George, *Labour Movements and Labour Leaders* (London, 1902).

Huch, Ricarda, *Michael Bakunin und die Anarchie* (Berlin, 1922).

Humphrey, A. W., *Robert Applegarth* (London, 1913).

Jaeckh, Gustav, *Die Internationale* (Leipzig, 1904).
Jellinek, Frank, *The Paris Commune of 1871* (London, 1937).
Kautsky, Karl, *Sozialisten und Krieg* (Prague, 1937).
Kenafick, K. J., *Michael Bakunin und Karl Marx* (Melbourne, 1948).
King, Bolton, *Mazzini* (London, 1903).
Koechlin, Heinrich, *Die Pariser Kommune von 1871 im Bewußtsein ihrer Anhänger* (Basle, 1950).
Kropotkin, Peter, *Memoirs of a Revolutionist* (London, 1899).
Lissagaray, Prosper, *Geschichte der Kommune von 1871* (Stuttgart, 1894).
Lukin, N., 'Protokolle des Generalrats der Internationalen Arbeiter-Assoziation als Quelle für die Geschichte der Pariser Kommune', *Unter dem Banner des Marxismus*, vol. VI.
Mänchen-Helfen, Otto, and Nikolaewsky, Boris, *Karl und Jenny Marx* (Berlin, 1933).
Marx, Karl, *Die Inauguraladresse der Internationalen Arbeiter-Association.*
Die Klassenkämpfe in Frankreich 1848–1850.
Der Achtzehnte Brumaire des Louis Bonaparte.
Briefe an Kugelmann.
Marx-Engels Briefwechsel, vols. II, III and IV (Berlin, 1949–50).
Mason, E. S., *The Paris Commune* (New York, 1930).
Mayer, Gustav, *Friedrich Engels*, 2 vols. (Berlin, 1920, and The Hague, 1934).
Mehring, Franz, *Karl Marx. Geschichte seines Lebens* (Leipzig, 1918).
'Freiligrath und Marx in ihrem Briefwechsel', *Die Neue Zeit* vol. XXIX.
Geschichte der deutschen Sozialdemokratie, 2 vols. (Stuttgart, 1921).
Meyer, Rudolf, *Der Emanzipationskampf des vierten Standes*, 2 vols. (Berlin, 1874).
Michels, Robert, 'Proletariat und Bourgeoisie in der sozialistischen Bewegung Italiens', *Archiv für Sozialwissenschaft und Sozialpolitik*, vol. XXI.
Moses Hess Briefwechsel, edited by Edmund Silberer (The Hague, 1950).
Nettlau, Max, *Der Anarchismus von Proudhon zu Kropotkin* (Berlin, 1924).
Michael Bakunin, 2 vols. (London, 1896–8; privately printed by the author in an edition of fifty copies as a facsimile of his original handwritten MS. Copies are in the British Museum, London, and in the International Institute of Social History, Amsterdam).
'Zur Geschichte der spanischen Internationale und der Landesföderation (1868–89)', *Archiv für die Geschichte des Sozialismus und der Arbeiterbewegung*, vol. XIV.
'Londoner deutsche kommunistische Diskussionen 1845', *Archiv für die Geschichte des Sozialismus und der Arbeiterbewegung*, vol. X.
'Marxanalekten', *Archiv für die Geschichte des Sozialismus und der Arbeiterbewegung*, vol. III.
Peukert, Josef, *Erinnerungen eines Proletariers aus der revolutionären Arbeiterbewegung*, edited by Gustav Landauer (Berlin, 1913).
Postgate, R. W., *The Workers' International* (London, 1920).
Puech, Jules L., *Le Proudhonisme dans l'Association Internationale des Travailleurs* (Paris, 1907).
Rjazanov, D., 'Zur Geschichte der Ersten Internationale', *Marx-Engels Archiv*, vol. I.
'Die auswärtige Politik der alten Internationale und ihre Stellungnahme zum Krieg', *Die Neue Zeit*, vol. XXXIII.

Scheu, Heinrich, 'Erinnerungen', *Der Wiener Hochverratsprozess* (Vienna, 1923).
Schlüter, Hermann, *Die Internationale in Amerika* (Chicago, 1918).
Schröder, Wilhelm, *Geschichte der sozialdemokratischen Parteiorganisation in Deutschland* (Dresden, 1912).
Silone, Ignazio, *The Living Thoughts of Mazzini* (London, 1939).
Steiner, Herbert, 'Die Internationale Arbeiterassoziation und die österreichische Arbeiterbewegung', *Archiv für Sozialgeschichte*, vol. IV.
Die Arbeiterbewegung Oesterreichs 1867–1889 (Vienna, 1964).
Stekloff, Y. M., *History of the First International* (London, 1928).
Steklow, George, *Michael Bakunin* (Stuttgart, 1913).
Die Bakunistische Internationale nach dem Haager Kongreß 1872–1881 (Stuttgart, 1914).
Testut, Oscar, *L'Association internationale des travailleurs* (Lyon, 1870).
Valiani, Leo, *Storia del Movimento Socialista*, vol I: *L'Epoca della Prima Internazionale* (Florence).
Dalla Prima alla seconda Internazionale 1872–1889 (Milan, 1954).
Villetard, Edmond, *Histoire de l'Internationale* (Paris, 1872).
Wiener Hochverratsprozeß von 1870, with a 'Memoir' by Heinrich Scheu and an Introduction, 'Zur politischen und sozialen Geschichte 1848 bis 1870', by Karl Renner (Vienna, 1911).
Zirnheld, Jules, *Cinquante Années de syndicalisme chrétien* (Paris, 1937).
Zlocisti, Theodor, *Moses Hess, Der Vorkämpfer des Sozialismus und Zionismus* (Berlin, 1921).

THE SECOND INTERNATIONAL

Original Sources:

Minutes of the Congress: Paris, 1889; Brussels, 1891; Zurich, 1893; London 1896; Paris, 1900; Amsterdam, 1904; Stuttgart, 1907; Copenhagen, 1910; Basle, 1912.
Haupt, Georg, *La deuxième Internationale 1889–1914. Étude critique des sources. Essai bibliographique*, with an introduction by Ernest Labrousse (Paris, 1956).

Literature:

Adler, Victor, *Briefwechsel mit August Bebel und Karl Kautsky*, edited by Friedrich Adler (Vienna, 1954).
Allemane, Jean, *Mémoires d'un communard* (Paris, 1880).
Anders, Karl, *Die ersten hundert Jahre* (Hanover, 1963).
Aranyossi, Magda, *Leo Fraenkel* (Berlin, 1957).
Balabanoff, Angelica, *Erinnerungen und Erlebnisse* (Berlin, 1927).
Bang, Gustav, 'Ein Blick auf die Geschichte der dänischen Sozialdemokratie', *Die Neue Zeit*, vol. XVI.
Bauer, Otto, *Die Nationalitätenfrage und die Sozialdemokratie* (Vienna, 1907).
Der Balkankrieg und die deutsche Weltpolitik (Berlin, 1912).
Die österreichische Revolution (Vienna, 1923).

Bax, Belfort, *Reminiscences and Reflections of a mid and late Victorian* (London, 1918).
Bebel, August, *Aus meinem Leben*, 3 vols. (Stuttgart, 1907–11).
Briefwechsel mit Friedrich Engels, edited by Werner Blumenberg (The Hague, 1965).
Beer, Max, *Fifty Years of International Socialism* (London, 1935).
A History of British Socialism (London, 1919).
Bernstein, Eduard, *Aus den Jahren meines Exils* (Berlin, 1917).
Sozialdemokratische Lehrjahre (Berlin, 1928).
Die Voraussetzungen des Sozialismus und die Aufgaben der Sozialdemokratie (Stuttgart, 1904).
'Jean Jaurès', *Die Neue Zeit*, vol. XXXIII.
Bertolini, Angelo, *Die sozialistische Literatur in Italien* (Vienna and Leipzig, 1895).
Bertrand, Louis, *Histoire de la démocratie, et du socialisme en Belgique depuis 1830* (Brussels, 1906).
Borochow, Ber, *Sozialismus und Zionismus*, edited by Mendel Singer (Vienna, 1932).
Bourgin, George, 'Jules Guesde', *Archiv für die Geschichte des Sozialismus und der Arbeiterbewegung*, vol. XIV.
Braunthal, Julius, *Auf der Suche nach dem Millennium*, 2 vols. (Nuremberg, 1948); *In Search of the Millennium* (London, 1945).
Victor und Friedrich Adler. Zwei Generationen Arbeiterbewegung (Vienna, 1965).
Brouckère, Louis de, and Man, Hendrik de, 'Die Arbeiterbewegung in Belgien', *Die Neue Zeit*, vol. XIX.
Brügel, Ludwig, *Geschichte der österreichischen Sozialdemokratie*, 5 vols. (Vienna, 1922–5).
Bury, J. P., *France, 1814–1940* (London, 1954).
Champion, H. H., *The Great Dock Strike* (London, 1890).
Chausy, M., *Les Allemanists* (Paris, 1912).
Christiansen, Ernst, 'Die ideologische Entwicklung des demokratischen Sozialismus in Dänemark', *Sozialistische Weltstimmen*, edited by Julius Braunthal (Hanover, 1958).
Cole, G. D. H., *A Short History of the British Working Class Movement 1789–1925* (London, 1932).
The Second International 1889–1914, vol. III, book 2, of *A History of Socialist Thought* (London, 1956).
Commons, John R., *History of Labour in the United States*, 2 vols. (New York, 1921).
Delbrück, Hans, *Regierung und Volkswille* (Berlin, 1914).
Dolléans, Édouard, *Histoire du Mouvement Ouvrier*, 2 vols. (Paris, 1939).
Dommanget, M., *Histoire du premier mai* (Paris, 1953).
Egbert, Donald D., and Persons, Stow, *Socialism and American Life*, 2 vols. (Princeton, 1952).
Elster, Torolf, 'Die ideologische Entwicklung des demokratischen Sozialismus in Norwegen', *Sozialistische Weltstimmen* (Hanover, 1958).
Engels, Friedrich, 'Zur Kritik des sozialdemokratischen Programmentwurfes 1891', *Die Neue Zeit*, vol. XX.
Friedrich Engels' Briefwechsel mit Karl Kautsky, edited by Benedikt Kautsky (Vienna, 1955).

Frölich, Paul, *Rosa Luxemburg. Her Life and Work* (London, 1940).
Fusilier, Raymond, *Le Parti socialiste suédois, son organisation* (Paris, 1965).
Galenson, Walter, *Labor in Norway* (New York, 1951).
Scandinavian Labor Movement (Berkeley, 1952).
Gay, Peter, *Das Dilemma des demokratischen Sozialismus—Eduard Bernsteins Auseinandersetzung mit Marx* (Nuremberg, 1954); *The Dilemma of Democratic Socialism. Eduard Bernstein's Challenge to Marx* (New York, 1952).
Georgi, Elsbeth, *Theorie und Praxis des Generalstreiks in der modernen Arbeiterbewegung* (Jena, 1908).
Giovanoli, Fritz, *Die sozialdemokratische Partei der Schweiz—Entstehung, Entwicklung, Aktion* (Bern, 1948).
Gitermann, Valentin, *Geschichte Rußlands*, vol. III (Hamburg, 1949).
Glasier, John Bruce, *William Morris and the Early Days of the Socialist Movement* (London, 1921).
Gridazzi, Mario, *Die Entwicklung der sozialistischen Ideen in der Schweiz* (Zurich, 1935).
Grimm, Robert, *Geschichte der sozialistischen Ideen in der Schweiz* (Zurich, 1931).
Gualtieri, H. L., *The Labour Movement in Italy, 1848–1904* (New York, 1946).
Hardie, Keir, *From Pit to Parliament* (London, 1913).
Hardie's Speeches and Writings, 1885-1915, edited by Emrys Hughes (London, 1928).
Helms, Emil, *Die sozialdemokratische und gewerkschaftliche Bewegung in Dänemark* (1907).
Henriksson-Holenberg, G., 'Die Entwicklungsgeschichte der Arbeiterbewegung in Schweden', *Archiv für die Geschichte des Sozialismus und der Arbeiterbewegung*, vol. VI.
Herkner, Heinrich, *Die Arbeiterfrage* (Berlin, 1922).
Hillquit, Morris, *History of Socialism in the United States* (New York and London, 1906).
Humbert, S., *Les Possibilistes* (Paris, 1911).
Humphrey, A. W., *International Socialism and the War* (London, 1915).
Humphrey, Richard, *Georges Sorel. Prophet without Honor* (Cambridge, Mass., 1951).
Hyndman, H. M., *The Record of an Adventurous Life* (London, 1911).
Jackson, J. Hampden, *Jean Jaurès* (London, 1943; Frankfurt, 1959).
Jansen, R., *Georg von Vollmar. Eine politische Biographie* (Düsseldorf, 1958).
Jaurès, Jean, *Theorie und Praxis* (Berlin, 1902).
Joll, James, *The Anarchists* (London, 1965).
The Second International 1889–1914 (London, 1955).
Katayama, Sen, *The Labor Movement in Japan* (Chicago, 1948).
Kautsky, Karl, *Bernstein und das sozialdemokratische Programm* (Stuttgart, 1899).
Der politische Massenstreik (Berlin, 1914).
Der Weg zur Macht (Berlin, 1909).
Sozialismus und Kolonialpolitik (Berlin, 1907).
Sozialisten und Krieg (Prague, 1937).
Kuhn, Werner, *Hermann Greulich und Charles Fourier* (Zurich, 1949).
Laidler, Harry W., *Social-Economic Movements* (New York, 1948).
Socialism in the United States (New York, 1952).
Landauer, Carl, *European Socialism*, 2 vols. (Berkeley, 1959).

Lavisse, Ernest, *Histoire de la France contemporaine depuis la révolution justqu'à la paix de 1919*, vol. VII (Paris, 1921).
Lichtheim, George, *Marxism. An Historical and Critical Study* (London, 1961).
Lipinski, Richard, *Die Sozialdemokratie von ihren Anfängen bis zur Gegenwart*, 2 vols. (Berlin, 1928).
Longuet, Jean, *La Politique internationale du marxisme* (Paris, 1918).
Le Mouvement socialiste international, in J. Compère-Morel, *Encyclopédie socialiste* (Paris, 1912–13).
Lorwin, Lewis L., *Labor and Internationalism* (New York, 1929).
Lorwin, Val R., *The French Labor Movement* (Harvard, 1954).
Jules Guesde (Paris, 1929).
Ludwig, Emil, *Wilhelm der Zweite* (Berlin, 1926).
Luxemburg, Rosa, *Sozialreform oder Revolution?* (Leipzig, 1908).
Massenstreik, Partei und Gewerkschaften (Hamburg, 1906).
Malatesta, Errico, *His Life and Ideas*, compiled and edited by Vernon Richards (London, 1965).
Martow, J., and Dan, Theodore, *Geschichte der russischen Sozialdemokratie* (Berlin, 1926).
Mehring, Franz, *Geschichte der deutschen Sozialdemokratie*, 2 vols. (Stuttgart, 1921).
Messine, Jules, *Emile Vandervelde* (Hamburg, 1948).
Michels, Robert, *Sozialismus in Italien* (Munich, 1925).
Zur Soziologie des Parteiwesens in der modernen Demokratie (Leipzig, 1925).
Modern Socialism, edited and introduced by R. C. K. Ensor (London, 1904).
Miller, Susanne, *Das Problem der Freiheit im Sozialismus* (Frankfurt, 1964).
Naef, Eugen, *Zur Geschichte des französishen Syndikalismus* (Zurich, 1931).
Nettl, J. P., *Rosa Luxemburg*, 2 vols. (Oxford, 1966).
Nettlau, Max, *Errico Malatesta* (New York, 1922).
Nieuwenhuis, Domela, *Mein Abschied von der Kirche* (Berlin, 1891).
Noland, Aaron, *The Founding of the French Socialist Party* (Harvard, 1956).
Noske, Gustav, *Kolonialpolitik und Sozialdemokratie* (Stuttgart, 1914).
Orano, P., *Andrea Costa* (Rome, 1900).
Pease, Edward, *The History of the Fabian Society* (London, 1925).
Pease, Margaret, *Jean Jaurès* (London, 1917).
Pelling, Henry, *The Origins of the Labour Party 1880–1900* (London, 1954).
Pierson, Marc-Antoine, *Histoire du socialisme en Belgique* (Brussels, 1953).
Pirenne, H., *Histoire de Belgique*, vol. VII (Brussels, 1932).
Preuss, Hugo, *Das deutsche Volk und die Politik* (Jena, 1915).
Price, John, *The International Labour Movement* (London, 1945).
Rocker, R., *Johann Most. Das Leben eines Rebellen* (Berlin, 1924).
Roland-Holst, Henriette, *Generalstreik und Sozialdemokratie* (Dresden, 1906).
Rosenberg, Arthur, *Entstehung und Geschichte der Weimarer Republik* (Frankfurt, 1955).
Salomone, William, *Italian Democracy in the Making* (Philadelphia, 1945).
Schorske, Carl E., 'German Social Democracy 1905–17', *Harvard Historical Studies*, vol. LXV.
Severin, Frans, 'Die ideologische Entwicklung des Sozialismus in Schweden', *Sozialistische Weltstimmen* (Hanover, 1958).

Shaw, G. Bernard, *Early History of the Fabian Society* (London, 1892).
Fabianism and the Empire (London, 1900).

Soltau, Roger, *French Political Thought in the Nineteenth Century* (London, 1931).

Sorel, Georges, *Reflections on Violence*, with introduction by Edward A. Shils (Glencoe-Illinois, 1950).

Stewart, William, *J. Keir Hardie* (London, 1921).

Trotsky, L., *Die russische Revolution 1905* (Berlin, 1923).

Tschitchovsky, T., *The Socialist Movement in Bulgaria* (1931).

Ursin, N.R.af., and Wiik, Karl H., 'Die Arbeiterbewegung in Finnland', *Archiv für die Geschichte des Sozialismus und der Arbeiterbewegung*, vol. XII.

Valera, P., *Amilcar Cipriani* (Milan, 1920).

Valiani, Leo, 'Die ideologische Entwicklung des demokratischen Sozialismus in Italien', *Sozialistische Weltstimmen* (Hanover, 1958).

Vandervelde, Émile, *Le Parti ouvrier belge 1885–1925* (Brussels, 1925).
'Die innere Organisation der Belgischen Arbeiterpartei', *Die Neue Zeit*, vol. XVIII.
'Die belgischen Wahlrechtskämpfe 1902', *Sozialistische Monatshefte* (1902).
'Victor Adler und die Internationale', *Der Kampf*, vol. XXII.

Victor Adlers Aufsätze, Reden und Briefe, edited by Friedrich Adler and Gustav Pollatschek, 5 vols. (Vienna, 1922–5).

Voinea, Serban, 'Die Arbeiterbewegung in Rumänian', *Der Kampf*, vol. XVI.

Vollmar, Georg von, *Über die nächsten Aufgaben der deutschen Sozialdemokratie* (Munich, 1891).

Weinstein, Harold R., *Jean Jaurès. A Study of Patriotism in the French Socialist Movement* (New York, 1936).

Weltstimmen des Sozialismus, edited by Julius Braunthal (Berlin and Hanover, 1959).

Williams, Francis, *Fifty Years' March. The Rise of the Labour Party* (London, 1950).

Wirtz, J. Paul, *Der revolutionäre Syndikalismus in Frankreich* (Zurich, 1931).

Yearbook of the International Socialist Labour Movement 1956–1957, edited by Julius Braunthal (London, 1956).

Young, W. Hilton, *The Italian Left: A History of Political Socialism in Italy* (London, 1940).

Zechlin, Egmont, *Staatsstreichpläne Bismarcks und Wilhelms II, 1890–4* (Stuttgart, 1929).

Zévaès, Alexandre, *Le Socialisme en France depuis 1871* (Paris, 1908).
Le Socialisme en France depuis 1904 (Paris, 1935).
Histoire du socialisme et du communisme en France (Paris, 1947).
Jean Jaurès (Paris, 1951).

Indexes

NAME INDEX

SUBJECT INDEX